BUILDER of BRIDGES

BUILDER of BRIDGES

by R.K. Johnson

A biography of Dr. Bob Jones Sr.

BOB JONES UNIVERSITY PRESS, INC.
Greenville, South Carolina 29614

Builder of Bridges
The Biography of Dr. Bob Jones, Sr.
by R. K. Johnson

© 1982 Cover Photo and Design
   Bob Jones University Press, Inc.
   Greenville, SC 29614

© 1969 Sword of the Lord

All rights reassigned, 1982, to Bob Jones University Press, Inc.
ISBN 0-89084-157-8

Dedication

To the Jones family, whom I love and admire and with whom I have had the joy and privilege of working for the past thirty-seven years, I humbly dedicate this labor of love in appreciation for all they have done for me and for my family during all these blessed years. "Surely goodness and mercy have followed me all the days of my life . . ." (Psalm 23:6). The Lord has "dealt bountifully with me" (Psalm 13:6) in giving me "the heritage of those that fear His Name" (Psalm 61:5) and in casting my lines in such a "pleasant place" (Psalm 16:6).

Building the Bridge for Him

W. A. Dromgoole

An old man, traveling a lone highway,
Came at the evening cold and gray,
To a chasm vast and deep and wide.

The old man crossed in the twilight dim,
The sullen stream held no fears for him.
But he stopped when he reached the other side,
And built a bridge to span the tide.

"Old man," said a fellow pilgrim near,
"You are wasting your strength with building here;
Your journey will end with the ending day,
You never again will pass this way.

"You have crossed the chasm deep and wide.
Why build you a bridge at eventide?"
And the builder raised his old gray head:
"Good friend, on the path I have come," he said,
"There followed after me today
A youth whose feet will pass this way.

"This chasm, which has been as naught to me,
To that fair-haired boy may a pitfall be;
He, too, must cross in the twilight dim —
Good friend, I am building this bridge for him."

Dr. Jones frequently quoted this poem. He made bridges over chasms for thousands.

Foreword

For many years I have had a burning desire and an unexplainable urge to write a book on the life of Dr. Bob Jones, Sr., whom I loved and respected and under whose tutelage I learned much. Such a story cannot be told briefly; and certainly it cannot be told adequately, for Dr. Bob's ministry was long and varied, as well as fruitful and colorful. It was filled with a fragrance, a devotion, and a power that few men have known; and his influence reaches to the ends of the earth. Though beyond question his life defies adequate description in words, certain circumstances have seemed to indicate that I should attempt the task.

A number of years ago the late Dr. Homer Rodeheaver, long-time friend of Dr. Bob and a frequent visitor to the University, which he served for a number of years as a member of the Board of Trustees, was having breakfast with me in the University Dining Common. During the course of the meal, "Rody" (as he was affectionately called) commented on MIRACLE OF MIRACLES, a pamphlet containing a simple message I had given in chapel on the subject of God's blessings on Bob Jones University from my standpoint as business manager. Included in this message were some interesting facts about Dr. Bob which I had observed but which others might not have had the opportunity to notice.

To my utter amazement, Dr. Rodeheaver said, "Lefty, a book should be written about the life of Dr. Bob, and I feel that you are the one to write it."

I was speechless! It amazed me, first, that he should voice something which had been on my heart—the need of a book about our Founder—and, secondly, that he should suggest that I, who am not a literary man, should do the job. I told Dr. Rodeheaver that I agreed with him as to the need, but that I disagreed with his suggestion as to the one who should fulfill the need.

"You are the one to do it," he argued. "You have had a closer association with Dr. Bob through the years than has anyone outside his family. You have had an insight into both his spiritual life and his business dealings. You can almost read his thoughts. There is someone who could do a better job: Bob Jones, Jr., could do it the way it *ought* to be done. But Bob's modesty, as Dr. Bob's son, would never permit him to say some of the things that need to be said. You *can* say them, and you *should* say them. I definitely feel that you are the one. If you will attempt the job, I will help you."

This was the encouragement I needed. I would write the book. After all, I would have the able assistance of this outstanding man of God who had a good command of words and who had been in evangelistic work for a long time. He knew the work, he knew the field, and—more important—HE KNEW THE MAN! This gave me confidence.

Not long after this, however, the message came that the beloved singer had gone to be with the Lord, and I delayed starting the book. As I look back, I realize that God was in my decision. His all-seeing eyes—ever running to and fro throughout the whole earth, beholding the children of men, beholding both the evil and the good (II Chronicles 16:9; Proverbs 15:3)—saw the seed of compromise with apostasy being planted, saw the germination process already in progress, saw the resulting damage to the orchard, and saw the need for a prophetic voice to sound the warning. This voice I believe He provided in Dr. Bob. Though other voices have blended in the alarm and the note of each has been distinct, I believe that God chose Dr. Bob to spearhead the march against the compromise with apostasy. Had I written the book earlier, the closing chapter of his faithfulness, which needs to be set down to encourage and inspire others who may see darker hours than these in their service to God in this rapidly changing world, would not have been included.

Another incident which seemed to indicate delay was the fact that we received word that Dr. Melton Wright, an alumnus of Bob Jones University, was writing a history of his alma mater. It seemed logical to me to wait until Dr. Wright's book was published before attempting to write mine. Dr. Wright's book is a book *par excellence*. I cannot hope to compete with its quality of workmanship and style. But FORTRESS OF FAITH, according to its author, was written to present "a readable account of the highlights of the institution's development" and not to present "a detailed history of the University or a biography of . . . the founder . . . and president." FORTRESS OF FAITH includes many interesting aspects of the man Bob Jones and of the Evangelist Bob Jones, but there is still room for many volumes on the subject.

With these thoughts in mind, and after much prayer, I set about gathering materials for my project. I went deep into the archives; I read the files of his correspondence; I visited the places of his childhood and talked with friends out of his past; I made an exhaustive examination of files of his evangelistic work (Dr. Bob never kept files, but a secretary felt that they should be kept and she made scrapbooks);

I scanned newspapers of past years that gave detailed accounts of events as they happened; and I consulted with Mrs. Jones, Sr., beloved companion of this man, who was an eyewitness of his colorful career.

Dr. John R. Rice, well-known writer, publisher, evangelist, and staunch defender of the faith, advised me as to the format of the book. Dr. Rice was a close friend and ally of Dr. Bob and is my personal friend. Dr. Bob often referred to Brother John as "the outstanding evangelical of our day." From the depths of my heart, I thank Dr. Rice for his encouragement and cooperation.

Dr. John's first suggestion was that the book should be written in first person. "Do not be afraid to use the personal pronoun," he said. "You loved Dr. Bob, you love the school he founded, and you have been the servant of both. You have a story which should be told, and you are the one to tell it." I discussed the possibility of my doing the research and letting a professional writer put my notes into good form. He answered, "Lefty, a warm heart is better than a cold head." This was in no way a reflection upon professional writers. Dr. Rice was simply saying that the character, the warmth, and the glow that belong to a story about Dr. Bob could be better cast through the efforts of one who had been intimately associated with him. A professional writer who had not had intimate acquaintance with the man and with the many issues that confronted him would find it hard to give the facts the warmth of emotion that Dr. Bob's personality demands.

From the beginning of my service to Dr. Bob, I have looked upon my job as a sacred trust. I have felt that God was permitting me to help lift some of the heaviness of the burden which He placed upon the shoulders of this great man, although perhaps many times I have added to it. I thank the Lord for the privilege and inspiration of the more than thirty-seven years close association with Dr. Bob, with his son, and now with his grandson, who, under God, have labored to build and maintain a school that is different—a school that has put Christ first, has kept Christ first, and has never wavered in carrying out the purposes which the Lord put into Dr. Bob's heart when He led him to found this base of Christian testimony. Also, I thank the Lord for the opportunity to tell others about this man who never considered personal gain or cost, but who expended all his energies in service to his Lord and had as his supreme desire to honor God's Word and God's Son, and to contend earnestly for the faith.

I do not, however, seek merely to honor a man, as worthy a motive as that is in this case. I want to glorify the God Who, by His grace, love, and understanding, took a young lad and trained him to bless a world. God is interested in everything that pertains to His children, though some people have absolutely no conception of the fact. He wants to guide in every detail of our lives. God is no respecter of persons (Ephesians 6:9). He loves to do for all His children; and when we are willing to surrender to Him and be led by His Holy Spirit, He can mold our lives into something that will redound to His glory. Dr. Bob ventured on a life of absolute trust in God, and for more than seventy years God provided his every need and used him as a means of blessing to countless millions, not only through his ministry and his school but also through his many books, his syndicated articles in hundreds of newspapers, his messages over a hundred radio stations and through his religious films that are still being shown around the world. Dr. Bob stood as a beacon of light to warn of impending dangers facing our nation religiously and politically.

This great man was a link between two eras. At the age of thirteen he held his first brush arbor meeting, which meeting foreshadowed the sawdust trail, which in turn foreshadowed what some have labeled the "plush carpet on the sawdust trail." Dr. Bob reached the "top of the ladder" in his evangelistic career. Great parades welcomed him into towns, and streetcars had to be rerouted because of heavy traffic; and this in a day when news media and travel were limited as compared with our day. By divine appointment and guidance, I believe, this man added to his already busy schedule a college which he founded and which is described by discerning men of God as being "God's last large stronghold that is fighting aggressively, contending for the faith."

Dr. Bob was willing to make any sacrifice and pay any price to follow the One Who called him. He was so gentle of nature that children would leave their mothers' arms to get to him, and yet he was so strong of conviction as to be as explosive as a volcano. Dr. Bob loved God's Word and was aggressively loyal Thereto. He acted on the principle that not only the *message* of the Word is important but also the *method* by which the message is presented, and that to be delinquent in either aspect is to give aid to an antichrist and to be a partaker of his evil deeds (II John 9–11).

Dr. Bob never claimed to be perfect. Over and over he said to me, "I am not perfect. I have made every mistake that could be made. I am very human; and if it were not for the grace and goodness of God, I would be nothing." This attitude on his part added to his stature in my sight, for it has ever been characteristic of God's servants to feel this way. The Psalmist said, "Have mercy upon me, O Lord; for I am weak" (Psalm 6:2). "Cleanse thou me from secret faults" (Psalm 19:12). That great apostle Paul spoke of himself as the chief of sinners (I Timothy 1:15). Men of more modern times, on seeing evildoers, have had the attitude, "But for the grace of God, there go I." In spite of any shortcomings he may have had, Dr. Bob was in tune with God's program for this age; and I have seen God lead him through many rough places that would have stopped men of less courage and faith.

It is my prayer that, like Dr. Bob, we may have faith in God and trust His leadership even when the whole world seems to be sinking deeper into sin and when even some of the so-called spiritual leaders are falling into the error of compromise. To the saved, may the life of this unflinching servant of the Lord be a challenge to "go all out for God" and an encouragement to "keep on keeping on" in times of discouragement and seeming failures. To the unsaved, may it point the way to the One Who saves (Luke 19:10; John 3:16,17), Who keeps (II Timothy 1:12), and Who is able to present His own "faultless before the presence of His glory with exceeding joy" (Jude 24).

R. K. Johnson

Contents

PART V LAST DAYS

INDEX OF ILLUSTRATIONS

Introduction

Biographies generally follow patterns. The story of the successful financier is a variation of the "rags-to-riches" theme. The writer who deals with a famous artist, be he painter or singer, recounts a story of successes and failures laced with temperament and seasoned with scandal. The biographer of a politician attempts a "behind-the-scenes" account of events that made history and, according to his like or dislike of his subject, tries to make selfish ambition appear as high and noble statesmanship or presents genuine conviction as biased stubbornness.

Dr. Johnson's biography of my father is not cut by any of these patterns. My father, one of twelve children of a poor farmer, could have been a successful financier and died a wealthy man. It is certainly true he disproved the old saying, "Preachers are not good businessmen"; and he left behind him an institution whose assets at the time of his death were valued at more than thirty million dollars. He made money, but most of it he gave away or invested in this Christian institution.

Although he was an artist with words and few preachers have equalled him in his understanding of audience psychology and preaching techniques, he never used words solely for the sake of using them; and though a man of great heart and sensitive temperament, he was certainly never temperamental.

Though often urged to run for political office, my father felt his was a higher calling. He was, however, always fascinated by politics and never hesitated to deal with political issues or to campaign for a good man. His interest in the fields of politics and government was always motivated by his love for righteousness and truth. My father was too unique a personality to be forced into any mold; and his biographer faces a difficult task.

No man outside the family knew my father better or associated more closely with him than did the author of this book. A biography written by a close friend of the subject will have its weaknesses. But so does every biography—indeed every book. However, such a biography is far more accurate than that written by a completely "disinterested" author, if there can be such a thing—uninvolved with the man about whom he is writing. A man like Dr. Johnson, who for more than a third of a century was intimately associated with the man whose life story he tells, has an advantage over the most successful professional biographer who knows his subject only through a few brief interviews and a maze of papers, documents, and newspaper clippings, many of the latter of which are, of course, inaccurate. You do not re-create the presence and vivid personality of a man solely from research material. You may create a personality, interesting and colorful, but not entirely that of the subject. Biographies so researched are apt to be either a dry record of statistics, facts, and events or else a kind of "biographical novel." But because Dr. Johnson was close to my father and heard him discuss how he felt about causes, and people, and politics, and his family, and Bob Jones University, and his ministerial calling, he gives a pretty well-rounded picture of a most unusual man.

When friends would urge my father to write his autobiography, he would always say, "I do not want to do that; but I hope sometime to write my memoirs." Mother and I used to keep after him to get started; and time after time when we felt he was ready to begin, something would come up that he considered much more important; and the book was never written. Dr. Johnson, however, heard my father reminisce about his boyhood, his youth, and his experiences as an evangelist; and these reminiscences have become part of this biography.

Bob Jones (Jr.)

PART I
EARLY LIFE

Part I
Early Life

CHAPTER 1

Parents

Welsh-Irish Descent

In the mind of the average person there is probably no connection between Wales, North Ireland, and Southeast Alabama. There is a connection, however, and that connection has affected not only the United States but also other countries, for the influence of a Southeast Alabama descendant of a Welsh-Irish union in marriage has reached around the world. Perhaps many people who read this biography know little, if anything, about the state of Alabama; but I am sure that if you have known the subject of this biography, you are aware of the area which he affectionately termed "Southeast Alabama." This area includes such places as Dothan, Brannon Stand, Ozark, and others of which you will read as the story unfolds.

Of Rugged Stock

I have not taken time to find out too much about Dr. Bob's ancestors. Although he was a sentimental man, Dr. Bob was never one to magnify ancestry. Of those he heard boast of such matters, he would comment, "I have observed that the farther back they go in the family tree, the better they get." It was Dr. Bob's philosophy that it is not who your ancestors are but what you are that counts. "You cannot do anything about your ancestors," he often said, "but you can do something about who and what you are so that you can build the right kind of ancestry for future generations." That he surely did! I include enough of Dr. Bob's background to help better understand the man, his message, and his method of operation.

Many years ago some immigrants sought refuge in the country where men can worship God as they see fit and rear their families where they are free to work hard and make good. Among these immigrants were Dr. Bob's forebears. His great-grandfather came from Wales and settled in Charleston, South Carolina. The great-grandfather died, leaving three very attractive orphan children with the Atlantic Ocean between them and home. One of these children, Dr. Bob's grandfather, was adopted by a family in Georgia. (During the time that the grandfather was in Macon, Georgia, Alex Jones, Dr. Bob's father, was born.) Later the family moved to Macon County, Alabama; and still later the grandfather moved back to Charleston, South Carolina, where he died and was buried. These people had known bitter days in Wales, and they could fully appreciate our country, which, from its founding, had been dedicated as an asylum for the oppressed. They could endure punishment and could prosper by the hard lessons. They are the type that has made America great — honorable people with integrity and character, who have had to work for what they have and who have known the meaning of struggle.

"Peanut Jones"

Dr. Bob's father — William Alexander Jones, or Alex, as he was commonly called — was kind, brave, and godly. He was an "immersed" Methodist and a staunch Calvinist, though not as strong a Calvinist as his wife's family were. A tempestuous man by nature, Alex believed in meeting life "head on" and always "finishing the job." Perhaps this trait is the foundation of Dr. Bob's famous saying, *"Finish the job!"* Alex was a determined man, standing for his convictions with a stiff backbone, and had no respect for a coward. He was a man of integrity and was known as "a man whose word is as good as his bond." If anyone made a promise to Alex and failed to live up to it, Alex was ready to fight. He held lofty principles, and he instilled these principles into his children.

Alex had unusual ability as a farmer; and being a natural-born leader, he became an officer in the FARMER'S ALLIANCE, one of the strong organizations of his day. He foresaw the future of the peanut crop. His predictions about the lowly peanut caused people to refer to him laughingly as "Peanut Jones"; but his predictions came true in greater measure than even he had dreamed possible. Today that part of the country is noted for its peanuts, and the Peanut Festival is an annual event.

Georgia Creel

It is said that Dr. Bob inherited his Irish fighting spirit partly from the shepherds on his mother's side of the family. From all I have read, however, I would venture to say that Alex contributed no small part of this trait in his son! The Creels were strict Calvinists from North Ireland. Georgia Creel, Dr. Bob's mother, was a wonderful woman. She was a Primitive Baptist with deep devotion to her Lord. She believed that one is either "elected" or "not elected"; that is, one is destined for Heaven or for Hell before birth. So strong was she in this belief that even in the hour of her death she was still hoping that she was "one of the elect."

Georgia believed that one could not earn or pay for his salvation, that every minute detail of a life is fixed by Almighty God from before the foundation of the world, and that a man is immortal until God sees fit to take him. No doubt, her belief helped fix Dr. Bob's strong conviction that "*as long as a man is in the center of God's will, nothing can happen to take him from this world until God is through with him.*"

Georgia was patient, kind, understanding, tender, and loving; and everyone loved and admired her. A glance in her direction often called to mind the song, "When Irish Eyes Are Smiling," for Georgia had a smile and a good word for everyone. The soft, sweet voice of this young woman led someone to say, "She has the voice of a nightingale." Georgia was not a woman of formal education, but she had unusual spiritual discernment and such a high sense of honor that she could not stand for anyone to tell a lie or in any wise be dishonest. She would have nothing to do with dishonest persons. Georgia was a woman of industry, with a unique way of squeezing into every day an enormous amount of living. From all I have read and heard of her, I would say that Chapter 31 of Proverbs aptly describes this godly woman.

Wedding Bells

There is no time when a young couple is more radiant than when they pledge themselves to walk life's road together. Surely Alex Jones and Georgia Creel were not exceptions. When Alex was twenty-three and Georgia eighteen, they said their marriage vows in Southeast Alabama. They realized that "rough sledding" was ahead. Our country had been at war, and it was undergoing some of the hardest times it had ever known. Pressures from certain areas of the North had caused more bitterness and trouble than was necessary. However, from the very beginning of their married life, this couple dedicated themselves and their home to the Lord. They had no sooner settled themselves in a place of their own than they got down on their knees and thanked God for His blessings and goodness to them. Theirs was the attitude that with God's help they could "make the grade."

A Happy Family

Scripture tells us that "children are an heritage of the Lord" (Psalm 127:3); and when a young couple has married in Christ, they feel joyful over every child that comes to bless their home. The Lord blessed Georgia and Alex with twelve children — eight girls and four boys. First there was Jimmy; then followed Lou, Dolly, Georgia, Joda, Ella, Tom (who later became mayor of Slocomb, Alabama), Amanda, Ossie, and Exie. Bobby was number eleven. "Had they stopped with ten," he often said, "there would not have been a preacher in the family." The last child to come into this home was Richard. Because times were hard in that day, I am sure that Georgia and Alex would have taken issue with the theory "Cheaper by the Dozen."

With twelve children in a family, it could hardly be expected that all of them would agree *all* of the time. They had arguments as normal households do. They were, however, a closely knit group; and surely there was not a happier family in the whole state of Alabama.

My story, of course, is about the eleventh child, Bobby. Let us go back to early morn, October 30, 1883, on a farm in Skipperville, Alabama. A weary mother of ten children has given birth to her eleventh child. But every child—whether he is the only one, or one of many—has a special place in the heart and pulse of a Christian family, so Alex and Georgia Jones were happy and thankful to the Lord for their newest child. They welcomed this son as warmly as if he had been their first; and from the time that he was first placed in his mother's arms, this baby was dedicated to the service of the Lord.

CHAPTER 2

Robert Reynolds Davis

I suppose that most parents have difficulty in selecting a name for their children. Having exhausted a long list of names, Alex and Georgia were at a loss as to a good combination for this child, who was destined to be one of the great men of this era. The proud father decided to use a name that would honor one of his friends.

Thoughts of various friends passed through Alex's mind. Finally he thought of an old pal, Robert Reynolds, with whom he had fought side by side in the war and with whom he had shared many joys and sorrows. The thought of this friend brought back vivid memories of army days. It did not take much effort to think of his Confederate idol, Robert E. Lee, who had out-generaled the whole Union Army; of the various battles and the long, weary months of reverses the Confederates had known; of the bravery of the Confederates who in the face of thinning brigades had determined that they would fight to the bitter end, knowing full well the blood it would cost them; and of how tired of war the men became and how they languished for peace and longed for the day when they could go home to their families, and yet how they kept fighting and never once faltered in their purpose.

September, 1863, flashed before Alex; and his pulse quickened. He recalled the days he had spent around Chattanooga, Tennessee, and Chickamauga, Georgia, scene of some of the bloodiest battles of the entire war. The Confederates had won, but the victory had been costly. Both armies had suffered twenty-eight per cent casualties. Alex's Alabama regiment, with casualties of fifty-five per cent of their soldiers and fifty per cent of their officers, had been hit the hardest of all. Losses were so heavy that Chickamauga Creek was sadly termed "Sluggish River of Death." Alex thought of their beloved General Bragg who had strongly fortified Chattanooga—the prize, the key rail center and gateway to Georgia and the hub for rail lines to all parts of the Confederacy. Alex relived "The Battle Above the Clouds" on Lookout Mountain, when the

Confederate line extended from Lookout Mountain across Chattanooga Valley and along Missionary Ridge above Chattanooga to its northern end. Grief surged within him as he remembered the way the Confederates were flanked out of Chattanooga. But grief soon gave place to pride as he thought of the bravery of the men who would not let the General down, but took their stand along the banks of the Chickamauga Creek eleven miles below Chattanooga, determined to face the enemy even though it meant death. Thoughts of the tense moments in the trenches, with his buddy and all their company, faded as he remembered the result of that battle: Rosecrans, utterly defeated, was forced all the way back to Chattanooga. History states that if General Bragg had followed through and pursued his routed enemy, this hallowed Confederate victory might have been the turning point of the war. Rosecrans' defeat cost him the loss of the command of the army of the Cumberland to General Ulysses S. Grant, who, by this time, had been placed in supreme command in the West and had proceeded to Chattanooga, and who, with thirty-seven thousand fresh troops, was able to break the Confederate siege lines around Chattanooga in a series of battles that prepared the way for Sherman's sweep through the South.

September 18 stood out vividly in Alex's mind. The men had spent all day fording Chickamauga Creek and setting up the breastworks for the battle which was planned for the next day. As Alex's mind raced back, he became more excited. Step by step he relived that great battle. He could almost hear the sounds of the battle—the breathing of the men as they plunged at each other, the rattle of steel as bayonet struck against bayonet, and the groans of the wounded and dying men. He imagined that he could feel the bullet that had struck his right knee, could feel himself falling to the battlefield, and could hear his buddy at his side comforting him and giving all the help that he could. Yes, Alex decided, the new baby boy must bear the name of his brave friend in battle—Robert Reynolds.

President Davis of the Confederacy also stood high in the esteem of Alex Jones, and he decided to combine the names Davis and Robert Reynolds and call the baby Robert Reynolds Davis Jones. The Davis part, however, was soon dropped; and today many people have no idea that it was ever part of the name.

To Georgia Jones, this son was "Bobby." At college he was "Bob." Some of the boys liked to tease him by calling him "Railroad" Jones, a play on his initials R. R. He was called Robert by his early teachers; his beloved mother-in-law, Mrs. Estelle Stollenwerck; and his dear wife, Mary Gaston. For most people, however, he was simply, "Bob Jones."

Before I close this part of the story, I must tell you that Alex Jones always cherished his lame leg, souvenir of the war. His children insisted that he thought more of that lame leg than of them. Every time I pass through Chickamauga Park I am reminded that Dr. Bob's father was wounded there. Just to look at the markers and monuments somehow makes me feel close to Alex Jones.

CHAPTER 3

Jones' Family Life

Land of His Childhood

When Bobby was three months old, the family moved to Brannon Stand just outside Dothan, Alabama. Today Dothan is the county seat of Houston County, which is in the southeastern corner of the state. Formerly, Dothan was in the southern portion of another county — Henry County — when Abbeville, the present county seat of all that remains of Henry County, controlled the county affairs of the long portion of land from which Houston County emerged. Frank Stollenwerck — a cousin of Mrs. Bob Jones, Sr., a Bob Jones University Board member, and the University's attorney in Washington for a number of years — was the youngest man in the Legislature (about 1903) when this sixty-seventh county in Alabama, called Houston County, was created by the Legislature. The map of Alabama in Hammond's Library World Atlas shows an irregular prolongation of Houston County. Apparently this is the result of the widening of the Choctawhatchee River or a tributary protruding between Dale and Geneva Counties on the west. However that may be, this prolongation is a town of Wicksburg. Whether Wicksburg was formerly in Henry County, we do not know. One thing we do know is that Abbeville played a small part, at least, in the life of Dr. Bob, for he taught school there. Dothan, of course, has played a major role in his life. But we shall speak more of these places later.

"Train Up a Child"

Almost since the dawn of time, families have gathered around open fireplaces not only for warmth but also for companionship, to be drawn closer to each other and to their Lord as they have engaged in family devotions. Dr. Bob's childhood home had a large living room with a huge fireplace. Night after night the children gathered around the fireplace and listened to their father read Bible stories and tell them of God and of the great men that God had used. Alex would point out the strong characteristics that made these men useful vessels in God's hands. No matter how many guests might be present, nothing ever disturbed this family worship hour.

Dr. Bob said that when his father prayed, he seemed to be talking to an intimate Friend Who was nearby. First, the father would pray for each member of the family individually; and then he would ask God to bless their home that it might be a real Christian home. Dr. Bob often quoted the song "My Mother's Bible"; and as we listened, we felt that we were on hallowed ground—silent bystanders at the Jones' family altar.

Christian, but With Human Frailty

One should not conclude that this home had a Pharisaic atmosphere. One day a neighbor came over to try to sell Alex Jones forty acres of land that lay adjacent to the Jones property. Alex had only one hundred dollars savings. It was during the time of Grover Cleveland's administration, and times were at their worst. The neighbor told Alex that he needed the one hundred dollars more than he needed the land, and he begged Alex to trade. Alex, however, also needed the money; and he explained to his neighbor that he could not afford the land. The neighbor's son, a large, double-jointed fellow who was sitting in the wagon, said, "Pa, he is just trying to rob you." Nobody accused Alex Jones of lying, cheating, or stealing and got by with it. This was a day when men fought for their honor! Alex walked over to the wagon and asked the man to repeat what he had just said. Perhaps he had misunderstood the remark. The man repeated the same words. Quick as a flash, Alex pulled the man off the wagon and started whipping him; and it took Georgia and six of the children to separate the angry men. That night, still pouting because Georgia and the children had not let him "finish the job," Alex did not want to have family devotions. Georgia suggested that it would set the wrong example for the children if, because their father was angry, he failed to honor the Lord. Alex, good repenter that he was, soon had things right with the Lord and had devotions underway.

Earmarked for Blessing

It was during the time of Bible stories and memorizing of Bible verses that Alex and Georgia began to see something unusual in Bobby, and they felt the lad was set apart as having in his make-up something that the other children either did not have or had not as yet manifested.

These traits, they thought, if channeled in the right direction, would take him places; and fearfully and wonderingly they set themselves to do all they could to develop these.

The Jones' fireplace was more than a place for family devotions and instructions. It was also the place where the brothers and sisters had great fun. With almost a dozen children playing, joking, and yelling at each other, the parents could hardly hear themselves speak in the house; so each evening when the household chores were done, Georgia would stroll down to the barn to have a nice quiet talk with her husband while he finished his work. During this time the children delighted in boiling peanuts, popping corn, or baking sweet potatoes in the ashes of the fireplace.

One brother and one sister had died before Dr. Bob was born. The oldest boy, Jimmy, was buried in Dale County, Alabama; and Lou, who died one year after her marriage, was buried in the cemetery with her husband's family. The other eight children (Richard had not been born) adored their baby brother and, except for wise parents, would have spoiled him.

Home was the center of life for this family. Alex and Georgia nourished and nurtured their children tenderly in the Lord, drilling into them honesty and straightforwardness, teaching them never to tell a lie or misrepresent anything, and to respect their elders and not be impudent or disobedient to their teachers. Alex was gentle, but firm, and always positive. He understood how to reason with the boys when they got out of line and how to point out to them their errors. He was strict of discipline: if one erred in the least, that one was taken to the woodshed. Alex had no fear of causing his children to be maladjusted; he believed God's Word, which states: "He that spareth his rod hateth his son: but he that loveth him chasteneth him betimes" (Proverbs 13:24); "The rod and reproof give wisdom: but a child left to himself bringeth his mother to shame" (Proverbs 29:15). This father felt a personal responsibility to the Lord to produce children of integrity and character. He taught his children that to say "do" is more effective than to say "don't." With this background it is no wonder that Dr. Bob was always positive and was never a "don'ter." Two of his oft-quoted sayings deal with "don'ting." *"Some folks are so busy 'don'ting' that they don't have time to 'do.'" "A 'don't' religion is not enough. The way to keep from 'don'ting' is to 'do' so fast you don't have time to 'don't.'"*

Dr. Bob said that when he had done something wrong, his father would say, "Now, Son, look me in the eye." How hard that was! One day Bobby "fibbed" to his father. (In those days children did not use the word "lie.") That night Bobby could not sleep: he had a troubled conscience. Bright and early the next morning he went to his father and confessed. The wise father said, "I am glad you have told me the truth, Son, but I must punish you." We hope that Bobby did not mind too much the punishment; it taught him a good lesson that he has passed on to others: *"You cannot do wrong and get away with it!"*

From infancy all the Jones children were taught the value of a good name. They had it drilled into them that " a good name is rather to be chosen than great riches" (Proverbs 22:1). At the feet of their parents those children learned *"how to live, not merely how to make a living."* No doubt it was this type of home that our Lord had in mind when He said through the Wise Man, "Train up a child in the way he should go: and when he is old, he will not depart from it" (Proverbs 22:6).

No Luxuries

Bobby's childhood was not all sunshine. Far from it! As I have said, he was a child of those fearful and tragic days of reconstruction, soon after the War Between the States. It took years of hard work to get the land back into real productivity and develop markets, and Alex worked from early morning until late evening tilling the soil. Every farmer had to work hard and practice thrift. Times were so hard and money so scarce that it was almost impossible to hire the necessary help to run a large farm. It took perfect teamwork—the whole family pulling together—to prosper. The Jones children were taught to assume their part of the load. Certain responsibilities were given to each child with the idea that all honest work is honorable. This instilled in Dr. Bob another principle: *"For a Christian, life is not divided into the secular and the sacred. To him, all ground is holy ground, every bush a burning bush, and every place a temple of worship."* Alex was proud of the way his family helped him, and he always commended their efforts.

Being much younger than his brothers and sisters, Bobby could not do much to help at first; but he was given little chores, such as bringing in wood, raking leaves, sweeping the yard, and running errands for the others. As he grew older, Bobby took on heavier burdens, working from before sunup until after sundown—milking the cows, feeding the hogs, looking after the horses and mules, hoeing the corn and tomatoes, and doing other chores that are so common to a farm boy but so foreign to the boy of the city. By the time he was nine, Bobby could plow as straight a furrow as any other child in the neighborhood.

Dr. Bob drove yearling calves in his youth. "I'm sorry for a boy who never drove yearlings," he used to say. "I learned a lot about them. I got a little yearling and set him up to a little wagon—made my own wagon; it had wooden wheels. The yearling did not want to pull. He would lie down between the shafts, and I could not get him out. A fellow came along and said, 'I'll tell you how to operate — twist his tail.' I leaned over; and, brother, when I did that — you talk about cranking a car — that yearling was already in gear!"

On Bobby's fifth birthday the man for whom he had been named came for a visit. He gave Bobby five silver dollars. How rich the lad felt! He could not take in having so much money at one time.

Bobby would drive a horse and wagon into Dothan to sell vegetables. On one occasion Alex promised Bobby a quarter if he sold all the vegetables. Dr. Bob was always a "super" salesman, and he earned the quarter. On his way home Bobby kept admiring the coin and throwing it up into the air and catching it, as boys will do. All of a sudden, the quarter slipped through his fingers and fell through a crack in the floor of the wagon. Bobby searched diligently for his quarter, but he never found it. It had disappeared in the sand. Every time he passed that spot afterward, he mourned his "great loss."

Another key event of Bobby's vegetable-peddling days was a time when he *did not* make a sale. Naturally shy, Bobby always found it hard to walk up to a door, ring the bell, and ask a stranger to buy his vegetables. One day a lovely lady answered the doorbell and said to Bobby, "I wish I could help you; but I do not live here. I am visiting the lady of the house, and she is out for a while." Bobby thanked the woman and started walking back toward the wagon, trying his best to hide his disappointment. The woman must have noticed, for she called him back. Eagerly he retraced his steps. The woman patted his head and remarked, "I know that you are going to be a fine man when you grow up." This pleased Bobby very much, and this time he bounded from the porch with a song in his heart and with a determination in his mind that carried him through life. The kind-hearted woman never knew how much her act of kindness meant to a little boy who needed encouragement and who was never the same after that day. Though Dr. Bob never knew her name, he preached about her over and over again, saying that when he got to Heaven, he hoped to see her and thank her for her kind words. "Speaking kind words, of course, does not mean that she will be in Heaven," he always added, "but I wonder if she could have spoken so kindly if she had not been a Christian." God's Word tells us not to despise the day of small things. Even a cup of cold water given in His Name is sure to be a blessing.

One of the most exciting times of the year to young Bob was just before Christmas, when the weather got cold enough for people to kill hogs. "The smoking of the meat stimulated not only the people," Dr. Bob said, "but also every dog around. The dogs could be heard baying 'for miles.' "

Hardship No Foe to Success

Hardships are never foes to success. The hardships that Bobby endured groomed him for the great job that God had in store for him in future years. Nobody in the area in which the Joneses lived enjoyed even a hint of luxury. People did well to maintain the bare necessities of life. Cotton was selling for three cents a pound, and no one had any money. One Christmas Alex told his children that he was sorry but he was afraid that they would have no "Santa Claus" that year. The children hung their stockings anyway, hoping that Santa would surprise them. When the kiddies had been tucked into bed, Bobby overheard his father say to his mother, "Georgia, we must not disappoint them now. I will get up early in the morning and go into town and buy some candy and apples and other goodies to go in their stockings." By the time the children awoke the next morning, their stockings were bulging with "goodies." Their little prayers of the night before had been answered.

The low prices of the cotton affected the merchants as well as the farmers. Merchants found it hard to raise the money to restock their shelves. Someone "hit upon the idea" of offering customers a settlement of fifty cents on the dollar for their accounts. Alex Jones was insulted. "Do you mean to tell me that if I give you half of what I owe, you will accept it as full payment?" he asked. "Yes," the merchant replied. Straightening his proud, but tired, shoulders, Alex said, "That's an insult! I owe you 100 cents on the dollar, and I will pay you every cent I owe."

Dr. Bob used to say of these days of hardship:

> Times were hard. People were hungry. There was no money to buy clothes. It never occurred to us, however, that the Government should send us a monthly check or that we should have financial relief from any governmental source. We ate corn bread and molasses. We lived through the hard time. We may have been a little undernourished, but we built some character. I believe in charity and in certain kinds of relief; but it is mighty hard to help people and not hurt them. Men in America are suffering from a "leaning" complex.

Here is an example of how good a neighbor Alex was and the code of honor by which he lived. One time Alex recruited fifty children and friends to work the fields of another friend named Potts, who was ill and could not do the work himself. Bobby wondered why his father would go to such lengths to help this man. Later he heard the story from Mr. Potts himself.

It seems that when Alex was a small child, his father became ill. A man came to see the ailing father, and while there, he cursed the father.

Alex could not believe that anyone could be so mean. He vowed that when he got big, he would whip that man. Years went by. One day Alex got on his horse, rode forty miles to a logging camp, and asked for a certain man. Alex reminded the man of the incident of so many years before and informed him that he had "come to whip him." "If you whip me, you will be the first one to do it!" the man boasted. Without ceremony, Alex, who never weighed more than 135 pounds, jumped on the 200-pound lumberjack. Mr. Potts, nearby, grabbed an axe handle to keep the other lumbermen off; and Alex and the lumberjack fought for two hours. Finally Alex got the lumberjack down and pounded his head against a rock until the bigger man cried out for mercy. The two men got up and shook hands; and Alex got on his horse and rode home, feeling that he had accomplished a job that had needed for a long time to be done.

Alex never forgot the way Mr. Potts had befriended him that day at the lumber camp, and he felt that getting the neighbors together to help Mr. Potts in his time of need was the least he could do in return.

CHAPTER 4

Born to Preach

Bobby, in his play, often had "church." Invariably he would have children gathered around the yard or in the woods, listening to him preach. Later he found out that older people had hidden behind trees to listen to his "sermons." Bobby wanted the children to know that even though they were small, they could love God and could pray to Him. Sometimes in his enthusiasm and the excitement of the occasion, Bobby would make some little girl unhappy by baptizing her doll. If Bobby could not get the children to listen to his sermons, he would preach to trees and stumps, and as he grew older, he would preach to the old mule as he plowed the field. This lad was born to preach, and nothing could stop him! When he was only three, Bobby embarrassed his mother by standing on a bench in church and yelling, "I wanna peech," meaning he wanted to preach.

Groomed for God

Bobby's parents wanted to be sure that they did all they could to train him for the great calling they thought was his. Alex did not have much formal education, but he was well read, and God seemed to give him a preacher's mind. When he would read something interesting, he would mark it and have Bobby "learn it by heart," as the expression was. When company would drop in, Alex would ask the lad to recite these little poems. Bobby had much practice, for Alex loved company and often would invite the whole church to dinner. Sometimes there were as many as forty people as guests in this home. (The children had to eat on the third or fourth shift, and they were always fearful that the food would not last.) Soon after the meal was over, Bobby would be told to "speak his piece." The child began to dread to see visitors. He cringed at the thought of saying those pieces before people. However, because he had been taught early in life to be obedient, he suffered through the painful ordeal. Dr. Bob felt that this was an important phase in his training, a direct leading of the Holy Spirit in preparation for a public ministry that would reach around the world.

People were amazed that a mere lad could memorize such long pieces, and they would remark to the father, "A boy that young should not be doing these things. There is something different about Bobby." Alex's face would beam with pride; but fearing that Bobby might hear and might be spoiled by their compliments, the father would reply, "No, no, he just said a speech." Bobby did overhear the compliments, and could not understand their wanting to hear a mere lad say anything. One day Alex put his arm around Bobby's shoulder and said, "Bobby is capable and very talented." This embarrassed Bobby in the presence of his friends, and yet he felt proud to be able to please his father.

First Public Speech

According to a newspaper report,

> Bob's first public speech was made in defense of the Populist Party in 1895, when he was just twelve years of age. He had accompanied his father to Dothan on Saturday. The country folk from all around were in the town and political talk was running rife. Young Bob, an unlettered country lad, became imbued with the idea that was grasping the people at that time — populism.
>
> Along about 12 o'clock in the day, he mounted a dry goods box at the corner of Nix's Drug Store, and there made his first public speech. Such rare ability as a speaker did he exhibit that he held the crowd spellbound for twenty or thirty minutes. When he ceased, he received an ovation which outrivaled anything theretofore in Dothan.
>
> From that time forward Bob Jones was more or less before the public, but more in religious matters than in political. For several months he made speeches at the Sunday School of the Methodist Church at Brannon's Stand, and such knowledge of the Bible did he display that, at the age of twelve, he was made superintendent of the Sunday School over men who were old enough to be his grandfather.

According to another report, however, there was an earlier public speech than the one mentioned above. I refer to a report in 1949 by Mr. Oscar L. Newton in which the one hundred years' history of the Beulah Church is given. Page 13 of the minutes of this church gives this interesting story:

> From the minutes we learn that Mrs. Allen Barber was granted a letter from Beulah in 1891, and her going was a great loss. She joined Mt. Pleasant Church where she was an earnest, consecrated worker for half a century. Among other things, she sponsored a Children's Day at Mt. Pleasant and put on interesting programs. At the age of 10 we appeared on one of these, and the boy who followed afterward — also about 10 — was Bob

Jones, who really preached a sermon. He has been one of the most useful Christians of our day, and was the founder of Bob Jones College which is now located in South Carolina. . . .

It was not long until the lad was making talks at various meetings of THE FARMER'S ALLIANCE, at dinners, and at political gatherings. The Lord, even then, was thrusting Bobby before the public; and the seed of this early training germinated into the fruit of a useful life. As we view it in the light of the present day, we are aware that the seed was good, that it was well planted, and that it found root in rich soil.

Story of His Conversion

In the time of Bobby's youth, parents strongly emphasized and had their children memorize Exodus 20:8-11:

"Remember the sabbath day, to keep it holy. Six days shalt thou labour, and do all thy work: But the seventh day is the sabbath of the Lord thy God: in it thou shalt not do any work, thou, nor thy son, nor thy daughter, thy manservant, nor thy maidservant, nor thy cattle, nor thy stranger that is within thy gates: For in six days the Lord made heaven and earth, the sea, and all that in them is, and rested the seventh day: wherefore the Lord blessed the sabbath day, and hallowed it."

As you know, this is one of the Ten Commandments that God gave to His chosen people, Israel. We live in a different dispensation. We are not under Law; we are under Grace. Nevertheless, God must be pleased that men take a day to worship Him. Alex and Georgia Jones looked upon every day as a day that the Lord had given. That day belonged to Him and to His service. But Sunday was an especially holy day. On this particular day of the week, these godly parents would have their children up bright and early in order to get them to Sunday School and church *on time*. The Joneses belonged to a Methodist church and they were active in every phase of church work. They supported the church with their presence, their prayers, and their meager possessions.

Let me digress to mention another area in which Dr. Bob received from his father a philosophy that was dominant in his ministry: the principle of not supporting something merely because an organization sets it up and asks for cooperation. Christian support, he believed, is a personal matter between a man and his Maker. It is not to be entered into lightly, but is to be done in the fear of the Lord and in line with His Word. Alex kept his money for the Lord in a sock. When the church would ask for help, Alex would remove the money from the sock and would say, "I will contribute to this, but I would rather not contribute to that." Although Modernism and compromise were not so rampant in that day as in our day, there were certain things that Alex felt he could not conscientiously support, AND HE SAID SO! Dr. Bob, throughout his ministry, stood on the premise that *"it is never right to do wrong even to get a chance to do right."* A preacher should not support something that is wrong, he said, even to get a chance to preach.

Bobby looked forward to Sunday for many reasons. First of all, he loved church. Another reason for his enthusiastic attitude toward the day was that on Sunday afternoon after the dinner dishes had been washed and put away, Alex and Georgia would take Bobby and Richard, the youngest of their children, and make a sort of pilgrimage to the cemetery where two Jones daughters were buried. A person of deep sentiment, Bobby enjoyed the closeness of the family as they went to the burial place. The parents were careful to teach their children that only the bodies of the sisters were in those graves, and that their souls were in the presence of the Lord. "When Christ returns," they would say, "He will reunite the bodies and souls of our Christian dead, and all the family will be with Him throughout all Eternity." This little Sunday afternoon custom put across to Dr. Bob a lesson that enabled him to comfort the hearts of other people in the hour of their parting from a loved one.

Early in life Bobby saw his need of a Saviour. At the tender age of six, he felt a certain pull, a certain calling. However, people of that day thought that a child should be at least twelve years old before he could accept Jesus Christ as his Saviour. Bobby knew that within himself he was not good and that if he died, he would go to Hell. People were not afraid to speak of Hell to their children in those days.

One day Bobby heard an elderly country preacher tell of the men who took a friend up to the top of a house and let him down through the roof to the feet of Jesus (Mark 2:4). This young lad, who for five years had had a great yearning to get to Jesus, reasoned that if the sick man, by getting to Jesus, had been healed spiritually as well as physically, then he himself would be all right if he could just get to Jesus. When the preacher gave the altar call, Bobby was the first to go forward. Thus, at the age of eleven, in a country Methodist church south of Brannon Stand, under the ministry of a man who was eighty years of age, Bobby made his public confession of faith in the Lord Jesus Christ as his personal Saviour. Later that night God set aside the lad for His service and started him on a training program that would last more than seventy years and would take him to all parts of the earth to proclaim God's Word to countless millions.

Dr. Bob used to tell this story to illustrate his attitude about proclaiming the message of the Lord.

There was a little boy who had to stay in the hospital for a long time. He had a serious operation, and it looked as if he would never get well. Months went by, and one day the doctor came in and said, "My lad, you are going to get well. You are going to run and play and skip and have fun like other children. You are going to be well, my boy! What are you going to do when you get home and are well again?" The little boy answered, "Doc, I won't ever let them hear the last of you. When I get home, I'm going to tell them what a good doctor I had!" I made up my mind when Jesus saved me as a little fellow that I would never let people hear the last of my Doctor—the Lord Jesus Christ!

From the time when as a little country boy he turned over the reins of his life to his Lord, the best he knew how, until his death more than seven decades later, Dr. Bob tried never to take charge of the reins again. The Great Master Potter saw in this young dedicated life a useful vessel. He began to mold this life to His purpose, and the life that He molded was, in turn, a great help in shaping and molding other lives which were entrusted to his ministry. Dr. Bob served the Lord in spirit and in truth and with his whole heart. He was the epitome of the verse, "Not slothful in business; fervent in spirit; serving the Lord" (Romans 12:11).

CHAPTER 5

Boy Preacher

Bobby was a chubby little fellow. By the time he was thirteen years of age he weighed one hundred and fifty pounds. It was not by his size, however, but by his dynamic preaching that he caught the eye of the public. After his conversion he started preaching anywhere he could find someone to listen. He would walk miles down dusty roads, seeking a place to hold a service. Sometimes people would invite him to their homes to preach. They would go from neighbor to neighbor, saying, "The boy, Bob Jones, is going to preach in our home. Be sure to come, and bring someone with you!" At other times Bob would just stop at some house and request that the owners let him hold a meeting there, beginning that night. The people would eagerly round up fifteen or twenty neighbors, and Bob would see to it that they had a real meeting. At still other times the young preacher would stop at a house near a school and inquire the name of the school trustees. He would visit the trustees and talk them into letting him start a meeting the following Sunday in the schoolhouse. Even at the age of twelve, Bob Jones had quite a reputation as "the boy preacher," and people would flock to hear him.

Bob did not feel that he had many gifts, but he had a fervency and a slant that people liked. Although at first he knew very little Bible, God always gave him a message that was suited to the hearts of those who listened; and souls were saved. People were impressed with Bob's sincerity, and they trusted him. His first real meeting was in his home community at the old Mt. Olive Church at Brannon Stand. It was only a one-week meeting; but according to the newspaper, there were sixty conversions.

When Bob reached the age of thirteen, he talked his father into letting him build a brush arbor. (For some the term "brush arbor" may be unfamiliar. It was a shelter formed by putting brush on a rough lattice work which was supported by poles or trees.) Out of this brush arbor meeting came Bob's first little church of fifty-four members. He preached in this church for at least a year.

Bob held innumerable brush arbor meetings. His sister Ossie and her husband were converted at one of these brush arbors, and later the old Mount Olive Methodist Church was built on the same site.

In later years Dr. Bob said of these days:

The first two or three years I walked (not hitchhiked) and begged for any kind of place to preach. In one community I built a brush arbor and conducted a revival meeting for a week. We organized a church with fifty-four members. I did not receive one cent for my services, but I had good food, a place to sleep, peace of conscience, and the sweet assurance that I was doing God's will.

In the last forty years I have preached in large auditoriums in practically every city on the continent and in some cities in foreign lands. As I look back across those years, the sweetest and happiest memories I have are those that come to me from brush arbors, unceiled schoolhouses, and poorly-built country churches back in the rural districts. I can still see the families coming to the places of worship, some of them carrying kerosene lanterns and others carrying pine torches. I can see the dimly-lighted places of worship and can hear the old hymns of praise.

I have been more comfortable in cities and towns, but I was far more comfortable even in those rural communities than Jesus ever was. He Who was rich, for our sakes became poor, that we "through his poverty might be rich" (II Corinthians 8:9). He taught that life consists not in the abundance of things which a man possesses (Luke 12:15).

In the days of my early struggles I was rich in the things that make men happy. I had the love and appreciation and confidence of those who heard me preach. I had the joy that comes from seeing the Gospel transform human lives and make bad men into good men.

The ministry must be drudgery to a preacher who never sees sinners saved; but to see God work in the hearts of men is far more exciting than to see fortunes piled sky-high. Yes, it is big business preaching the Gospel.

One newspaper stated:

At fifteen Bob heard the call to service, and boy though he was, he laid his will on the altar of God, and gave himself to the work of the ministry, joining the Alabama Conference.

Actually, Bob was ordained before he was fifteen. He described his ordination as a time of much anxiety as he realized the responsibility that was facing him.

Dr. Bob learned early that "the door to success always swings on the hinges of opposition." The jealousy that hounded his successes and accomplishments started while he was still in his teens. The devil, ever on the alert

The Boy Preacher, Age 15

to stop God's man of the hour if he can, saw in this young preacher a man to fear; and he sought to hinder him even before he got started. Some of the folks in the area wanted to license the boy to preach. A highbrowed bishop opposed it, saying, "What are we doing, licensing boys around here? This boy is only a child. Have we come to the place of having to depend on *boys* to preach?" An old country preacher replied, "I know a good way to determine if the 'boy preacher' should be licensed." They asked Bob to leave the room, and then the old preacher suggested, "Why don't we let the Bishop preach a sermon, call Bob in and let him preach, and then let these folks be the judges to determine whether or not the boy should be licensed?" The highbrowed preacher pushed the point no further. Bob passed the examination and got his license.

In reflection, Dr. Bob said many times:

> I realize that I must have been rather dumb. In my early ministry it never seemed anything out of the ordinary that the public was following me and that the businessmen in the community would come to listen to a little country boy preach. The wonder is that the devil did not trap me. He tried to do it. I was pulled here and there and from house to house. People flocked to hear me preach. The buildings could not hold the crowds; people even stood outside and stuck their heads in the windows to listen. It is a wonder it did not spoil me. The devil could have trapped me so easily. But God in His infinite mercy did not let it affect me."

In every major experience in the life of this man, he was wonderfully preserved. God seemed to watch over him and push him along step by step. At the same time He kept him from the awful sin that has trapped many good runners in this race: overweening pride.

At sixteen Bob was called to the Headland Circuit of the Marianna district (now Dothan district) of the Alabama Conference of the Methodist Church. His residence was at Kinsey. As a "circuit rider" he ministered to five churches, including the little church that he had started. (The five churches together netted him the big salary of twenty-five dollars a month.) He did not wait until Sunday to preach; he would walk five miles to and from the homes of friends just to get a chance to preach at one place in the morning and another place at night. He had only one or two new sermons at a time, and he knew that there would be no problem if he preached the same one in two places. To his utter amazement, however, Bob found that many of the same people attended both meetings. They would listen to him in the morning, would "eat dinner on the ground," and then would hitch up their horses to their buggies or wagons and drive to the next service a few miles down the road. God always came to the rescue of His servant by putting the message in his heart and the words on his lips.

Because of his youth it was hard for Bob to take up his first charge as spiritual leader of a group of churches. It kept him busy, visiting the neighbors and inviting them to his meetings. But the Spirit of the Lord was on the young preacher, and souls were saved from the very beginning. Bob was energetic and boyishly exuberant, and he had a great sense of humor. He loved his work and never "counted hours" in getting the job done. God endowed him with a good practical mind that knew no bounds and that reached in all directions. It was not the profoundness of his message but the straightforward manner in which it was presented that touched the hearts of the people.

The first years on the circuit Bob received into the churches by profession of faith more than four hundred members. A certain newspaper stated:

> For two years he was appointed to a circuit. The great meetings held while on the circuit had attracted much attention to him and even while a beardless boy his services were in demand. The people saw in his work that of an evangelist rather than a pastor. His work was made plain to him and like Saul of Tarsus, he was obedient to the Heavenly vision, and he was fairly launched on his life's work.

The paper also stated:

> In 1912 Bob Jones went back to Headland and held a meeting in a tent erected for that purpose in the public square. People from 20 miles around came in wagons and buggies and camped on the grounds in order to hear the thrilling young minister who had been reared among them.

Lena Jones, Dr. Bob's sister-in-law, wrote him a letter in which she tells a humorous incident that makes a practical point. She said:

> My thoughts turn back to the old days in Headland. I remember how Bob entered into the joy of the various occasions exactly like the other boys; but when he entered the pulpit, one could feel the presence of God. I remember well the day you and Faye Whigham came for me to go practice a program at the church. My hat blew off, and you wanted to show Faye and me what a well-trained horse you had and how you could pick up the hat and not get out of the buggy, which you did; but in turning around, the wheels went into a ditch. I being perched very insecurely on Faye's lap, fell backward out of the buggy over the front wheel, grabbing the lines, leaving you nothing but your voice. You yelled a very commanding "WHOA!" and the horse stopped still. After disentangling myself from the lines and the lap-robe, we continued on to the church.

Since then I have often wondered how many sinners had been brought to an abrupt halt by that command "WHOA!" in your voice and turned to a better life.

Lena West of Headland, Alabama, a girl that Bob dated once or twice, wrote:

> Wish I was smart enough to write a book on what I have learned since I wore calico dresses down to my ankles at 16 years of age. We went to church together the first time you preached at Texasville. Even though you were just a boy, you had a large crowd. You took your text in 1st John.

Dr. Bob did not read books on theology when he was a boy. The only book that came near being a book of theology was an old battered book of sermon outlines. Both backs were off the book, and he never knew who the author was, but he memorized those outlines. Bob was eager to learn, and he had a teachable mind and spirit. Much of his learning came from his contacts with older preachers. He loved to listen to the debates of the Methodists, Baptists, and Presbyterians. "But they did not debate principles or fundamentals," he always reminded us. "They debated interpretation. These preachers did not know a great deal about theology. They were primitive preachers with rugged character. But they were real giants of God, and oh how they could preach!"

By the time he was sixteen, Bob was preaching all over Southeast Alabama; and people gladly followed the fiery preacher. According to the newspaper, "The people loved him so much he could not go down the street without being stopped by all the people who were glad to shake his hand and say, 'Bob, our Bob!'" When I mentioned this to Dr. Bob, he said, "Of course, I was not a great preacher, but I had sat at the feet of some great preachers, and I had made a study of these men. Many of these preachers lived in the country and had country churches. Many of them were not well educated, and they made mistakes in grammar; but they loved the Lord, and they could really preach. Some of the greatest sermons I ever heard were preached by these plain country men."

A Host of Friends

God's Word says that to have friends, a man must show himself friendly (Proverbs 18:24). Dr. Bob fulfilled his part of the demand, and God gave him many friends. There was always the right person at the right time to help in the work God had called him to do.

Some of the first people to help the young preacher were three lovely "old maids." These maiden ladies kept the little church in order, prayed for their "preacher," encouraged him, and had him in their home for meals. It was their delight to have "young Bob" in their home. They would see to it that he had his favorite pieces of chicken. When they served chicken pie, they would have the spot of his favorite pieces carefully marked. He often spoke of the lovely pies they would bake for their "favorite preacher boy," as they fondly called him. Dr. Bob was appreciative of even the smallest kindness. To him, *"when the flower of gratitude dies in a man, he is well-nigh hopeless."*

In the mid-1950's the founder of this world-famous school took time out to visit these wonderful friends who were then in their late eighties. They had a good time reminiscing about the old days; and yet it was somewhat sad, for they knew that this would probably be their last visit together on this earth. Dr. Bob described these women as "uneducated country women who wore black calico dresses which they made for themselves out of material that cost five cents a yard. They did their own farm work. They loved the Lord and the Gospel, and they will have front seats in Glory. I won't get anywhere near the front compared to those women."

Dr. Bob appreciated the interest and help of his friends, and he was never too busy to repay the debt by helping others. He lived by the motto, "Have you had a kindness shown? Pass it on!"

CHAPTER 6

Early Education and Training

Although Bobby's background was not one of wealth, there was culture and refinement. He had at his disposal the best resources available to fit a person for the work of the Lord. Alex and Georgia Jones wanted their children to have as much education as possible, but educational opportunities were limited. Children were needed on the farms; and school, of necessity, was in session only a few months at a time. Nevertheless, Alex and Georgia saw to it that their son was able to get all that the school in their community had to offer.

At the time of this writing, two schoolmates of Dr. Bob's are still living. One is Allen Smith. Dr. Smith says that he and Dr. Bob competed with each other to see who could get the best grades in spelling, reading, writing, and arithmetic. The other schoolmate is Minnie Floyd whom Dr. Bob described as a freckle-faced girl two years younger than himself who had "more pep and more 'get up and go' than any other girl in that part of the country." During one period of six months, Minnie and Bob were the only students in their school. The other children in the community were needed in the fields, and the Joneses and Floyds sent Bob and Minnie to school so that the school could get public funds to pay the salary of the teacher. Throughout many years Dr. Bob and Minnie enjoyed getting together to visit the old places where, as children, they walked dusty roads; stopped on creek banks to wash their tired, dusty feet; played marbles; and attended classes and programs.

To show how the Lord leads in the lives of those who are dedicated to His will, let me give this story to which Dr. Bob so often referred. Mr. J. C. Hammett, a man who was almost blind, came to visit their home. Mr. Hammett was the principal of the Kinsey High School in Kinsey, Alabama; but during the summer he sold books. Alex invited Mr. Hammett to spend the night; and as usual, Bobby had to "say his piece." Mr. Hammett had a literary mind, and later became editor of an Alabama paper. Impressed with Bobby's speaking ability, the principal inquired about the lad's schooling. Alex explained that his son attended a school a few miles *above* home for three months and then attended a school a few miles *below* home another three months. Mr. Hammett said, "Mr. Jones, it is necessary for me to be away from home a great deal of the time. I wonder if you would be willing to let your boy go with me to Kinsey, thirteen miles away, where they have school nine months of the year. It would help us—my wife and two children need someone to stay with them—and it would also help Bobby."

This was an answer to Alex Jones' prayers. He had felt that his boy had talent and that he would need as much education as possible. Thanking the Lord for this "open door" for his son, Alex immediately set about making arrangements to send Bobby to the nearby town.

On the appointed day Bobby said goodbye to his family and went away, the words of his wonderful mother ringing in his ears: "Be a good boy, Son." Bobby hated to leave home, and he bravely fought to hold back the tears. Later Dr. Bob said of this parting: "I didn't see how I could leave my mother. I didn't want to leave any of the family, but especially did I not like the idea of staying away from my mother. When I kissed everybody goodbye, I saved her kiss for the last. She handed me a shoe box and said to me, 'You are going away now, Son. I have put some food in this box so that if you get hungry and are too timid to eat at the boarding house, you can eat some of this in your room for a day or two until you get used to things. Be a good boy!'"

For a while Bobby was terribly homesick, often crying himself to sleep; but this did not interfere with his work. He was a real asset around the Hammett household. He waited tables for Mrs. Hammett and did everything he could to make her burdens lighter. He realized that if he were not faithful in small things, he could not be trusted with larger things. One of his mottoes was, "*Little is big, if God is in it.*" Throughout his life, he manifested the attitude that "*it is wonderful to march under God's orders—to be going the way God says to go.*" He often said in sermons:

I have tried to follow the policy that when I have a job to do, do that job, and do it to the best of my ability. I tell our students, "When you get into a room, clean up that room where God put you. Don't ask any questions. Just fix the room. When you get that room all fixed, God will open the door and put you into another room. When you get to the next room, fix it up—dust it, clean it, straighten it up. Don't leave any of it undone. When you get that job done, God may move you into a bigger room. This time you may be a little proud and stuck up that you have a 'big room' to work in. If you get stuck up, God may put you in a little attic. If He does, go up and profit by it; that is where you belong."

Day after day during my life I have been going from one room to another.

Some day, if the Lord tarries, I am going to be in a room somewhere. I am going to try to be busy, doing the job. After a while it will get a little dark. Something is the matter with the electricity, or maybe my eyes are not good. Things are not exactly right. Oh, the lights are going out, but yonder is a door. No, it is not a door; it is not like any other door. It is a gate—a gate of pearl. It is opening, and I am going to move into a Room He fixed for me, a Room He has been preparing and decorating for me for two thousand years. My Room is ready; all He has been doing is touching up the inside of it. Let us clean each room here the best way we can so that when we enter that final Room He has fixed for us, we will hear His "Well done, thou good and faithful servant."

I have never known God to use a lazy man. I have known Him to use crippled people, blind people, weak people, sick people, and people who were not too intelligent; but I have never known God Almighty to use a lazy man. The men God has used and will use are those men who hustle about doing the job at hand, knowing full well that it will accomplish that which pleases Him.

With few familiar faces about him at Kinsey, Bob turned to the Lord more than ever. His present plight was God's will for his life, and that was all that counted. Even as he attended high school, Bob was preaching every time and at every place he could. A former classmate of Dr. Bob's said in a letter to Bob Jones, Jr., that she and Dr. Bob and another couple attended a service at the M. E. Church. "The pastor did not show up," she said, "and Bob preached one of his first sermons there."

One day a family friend, Mr. Brown, made a trip to Kinsey and stopped to see if Bobby might like to ride home for the week end. Bobby was delighted! The week end passed much too quickly to suit him; and as he was sitting on the porch waiting for Mr. Brown to come by to take him back to Kinsey, Bobby reached up to kiss his mother. Her skin was hot and flushed. "Mother, are you all right?" he asked. "I'll be all right, Son," she answered. Mr. Brown drove up in the wagon; and tearfully, Bobby climbed up alongside the driver on the spring seat. Again he heard his mother say, "You are going away, Son; be a good boy."

As they drove away, Bobby kept looking back to wave to his parents.

CHAPTER 7

Death of His Mother and Father

Two weeks went by. Quite unexpectedly Bobby had an opportunity to go home and surprise his family. As he approached the house, Bobby saw his father coming to meet him, a sad look on his face. "I am glad to see you, Son," he said. "I was going to send for you tomorrow. Your mother is very sick." Bobby bounded up the steps and into the house. He knelt beside his mother's sickbed and kissed her fevered brow. "Have you been a good boy, Son?" she asked. With her tired, weak hand she stroked his hair. She knew that she would soon be going Home to be with the Lord; and in her low, gentle voice she said, "Son, you have always been a good boy. I want you to trust God and follow Him and let Him make something of you. I am going away. I want you to be a good boy and meet me in Heaven."

Soon Georgia Creel Jones had crossed into the Land where there is no suffering and pain and where she could get the rest her tired body needed. Dr. Bob never remembered seeing his mother look rested until she was in the coffin. Frail but faithful, she had always worked hard from early morning until late night. Georgia Jones was a real mother. She looked after her home and children as God meant them to be looked after. She was never ruffled and was always on time regardless of how many dishes had to be washed or how many children needed to be bathed and dressed. Dr. Bob said that there was never any complaint from her. Certainly no man has ever loved his mother or respected her memory more than Dr. Bob did. "Her children arise up, and call her blessed" (Proverbs 31:28) was practiced many times over by this faithful son.

One newspaper reported:

When only fourteen years old his mother was taken from him; and one of the most pathetic and beautiful things I have ever heard fall from the lips of any man is his story of that death bed scene. He tells how he knelt by her bed and pressed her hand against his face, that he may remember it there while it held warmth of life, how he looked at her, trying to fix in his mind her dear face, then how he missed her, how the world was a great blank wilderness, where he wandered about like one in a lonely dream for weeks and months, longing for the touch of her hand, the kiss of the mother's lips. As he tells it, your heart is fairly wrung with the anguish of that little barefoot boy.

Georgia Creel Jones was buried in the cemetery near their home, and it was a sad sight as father and son placed flowers on her grave and turned to leave. Bob hated to leave his father and go back to school after his mother's death, but that was the father's wish, and it was what the son knew was for the best. As father and son said their goodbyes, the father awkwardly but affectionately handed the boy a crudely wrapped package of food. "Here, Son," he said; "this is not the way your mother would have fixed it, but you may want something to eat in your room."

Dr. Bob often said:

When I went away this time, there was no mother to go with me to the gate and kiss me goodbye and say, "Be a good boy"; but I had the sweetest kiss I ever had. Mother threw me a kiss from Heaven. I seemed to hear a sweeter voice than I had ever heard. I heard it with the ears of my soul. It was Mother's voice mingled with the music that angels make on harps of gold saying, "You are going away now, Son. Be a good boy."

Dr. Bob sailed the seas and traveled around the world, preaching in most of its lands; yet he had the same simple faith and philosophy of life that he had when he kissed his dying mother goodbye and promised to meet her in Heaven. His tender memories of his mother were touching. Each time he visited the cemetery after her death—and this was often—he imagined that he could hear her ask, "Have you been a good boy, Son?" and then add, "Be a good boy, Son!" He always tried to obey that loving admonition.

"The next five years," according to a newspaper article, "were filled with keen perplexity and toil, labor and constant prayer in the struggle for an education; but God was with him and crowned his efforts with abundant success."

Bob visited his father as often as he could, and they enjoyed reminiscing about the past. Alex would remind Bob that he had been dedicated to the Lord before he was born. They would discuss the future, and Alex would thrill to hear Bob tell of his burning desire to serve his Lord in an acceptable way. This was the very thing God had had in mind when He had led Alex to train the lad by cutting out articles and having him "learn them by heart" and say them for visitors. These days of fellowship between father and son stood out in Dr. Bob's mind as days of great blessing.

There came a time when Bobby could no longer stay with the Hammetts, and he moved into a nearby boarding house which afforded "cheap accommodations" and where he had to do his own cooking. A grandson who heard Dr. Bob tell of this commented, "It is no wonder you were so thin in those days, Pop!" It was Bob's duty in the new place to get up early and make fires so that the other boarders could have a warm room when they got up. Dr. Bob did not mind doing this job; but he laughingly confessed, "I was young, and there was one lazy boy there who always slept late and would never help in any way. I would watch him as he slept and would think, 'Oh! if just once I could boot you out in the cold to see what you would do!' "

Orphaned at Seventeen

During Bob's seventeenth year he was called home because of the serious illness of his father. Although it was a time of sadness, the days with his father proved a wonderful experience for the young minister.

One day Alex seemed to be troubled all day. Finally he smiled and said, "It is all right now. At last I have got something off my chest. For many years I have carried a resentment in my heart because I have felt that I had not completed a job which at the time seemed necessary."

This is the incident to which Alex referred. A chief of police had shot two men. Though he had been justified in his actions, the policeman had to endure a trial by jury. Alex Jones, called as a character witness, did all he could to help the chief. But the chief misunderstood Alex's intentions; and later, under the influence of liquor, the chief walked up to Alex and said, "You almost sent me to the gallows." The policeman hit Alex in the face and knocked him down. Alex knew that the man perhaps was saying things which under ordinary circumstances he would never think of saying. But in that day, as I have said, men fought to defend their honor; and Alex was no exception. He wanted to whip the ungrateful police chief, and would have except that his friends intervened. Now in the hour of death, Alex had peace from the resentment that had troubled him so many years.

Dr. Bob lovingly watched over his father during that final illness. He would take his father in his arms and raise him up in bed so that he could breathe more easily. Alex would lie back in the arms of the son, and his face would be wreathed in smiles. God was blessing this good man with a glimpse into Glory before taking him there. One day the father began singing in his wonderfully clear voice, "Jesus, Saviour, pilot me over life's tempestuous sea"; and when he came to the words, "when at last

I near the shore, and the fearful breakers roar," he slipped quietly into his eternal Home.

Dr. Bob said of this experience:

> No one will ever know how lonely I felt as I watched the men lower my lovable dad into the ground. My mother was the saintliest saint I ever knew; but I owe much to my father. He had such an understanding heart! He kept me stirred up and on my toes. He kept pushing me along.

The young preacher, now an orphan, turned his heart to God and pushed harder than ever in performing God's will for his life.

CHAPTER 8

College Days

In the middle of December the year of his father's death, Bob entered old Southern University, later renamed Birmingham Southern, at Greensboro, Alabama. At that time two revivals were held each school year, and the president of the college would call mourners to the altar and get on his knees beside them and lead them to the Lord. This made a lasting impression on Dr. Bob and no doubt inspired him to have in his school an opening revival each semester and a Bible Conference each spring. Dr. Bob insisted that "education without God is no real education."

Teachers told students of Dr. Bob's day which subjects to take, and the students took them. Bob's studies included Latin, mathematics, and science. He often commented that he did not "set the woods on fire" as a student, and that may be true. However, he was popular not only with the students but also with the faculty. The professors saw in Bob an earnest student who loved the Lord and who wanted to train for His service. They realized that although he was not their most brilliant student, there was not a more hard-working or zealous student on campus. (How I would like to compare the final results of the lives of all who were trained at the same time that Dr. Bob was trained!) It was no effort for these teachers to give special attention to this "different" young man.

Bob tried to go as far and as fast as possible in college. At times things were rough. He was without money and this made his struggle for an education much more difficult, but he lived by the thought that *the test of your character is what it takes to stop you.* God would see him through. Had not God ordered this life for him, and had He not worked out all the details thus far? "Many times," Dr. Bob later admitted, "I was discouraged and blue, but not once did Jesus fail me. I borrowed what money I could not earn by preaching around the country or by doing extra jobs to meet the bills as they came due."

Because of these experiences Dr. Bob was able to encourage other young men to keep going in the face of "rough sledding." "Don't give up!" he would say. "Go all the way through. There is a way to do what you ought to do. Don't look for the easy road. In this day of bankruptcy of character, we need something. We need the grace of God, of course; but we also need driving power. It takes determination to do the job God has called you to do. *'Make stepping stones, not stumbling stones, out of your difficulties.'* "

Bob preached somewhere every week end, and with good results. Soon the pastors realized that wherever this young man preached on Sunday the crowds followed, leaving their own churches to get to hear this young man who could touch souls; and they started vying with each other to get him.

The demands of preaching became so heavy that Bob's studies began to suffer. While still an underclassman, he was holding big campaigns. He conducted week-end revivals when possible during the school session, and he accepted full-time meetings in the summer. His foremost thought was, "How can I win more lost souls to the Lord Jesus Christ?"

He held meetings in the state of Louisiana for three summers. People there were unusually kind and responsive to the young evangelist. They invited him to their homes for meals and served him gumbo, chicken pie, and everything else a Southern boy would like; and they also gave him substantial love offerings. He delighted his audience by saying, "You are the most wonderful people. You not only feed me, but you have given me so much money that I have had to stuff it in a pillowcase. Now I can go back to college, pay off my debts, and finish my education."

As he studied and increased in knowledge, he also grew in wisdom. A lover of nature, he learned to preach out in the woods. "My sermons have always been my own," he said, "for I had no source from which to get help. My illustrations came from life. Many times I went through the woods or along a dusty highway, preaching to the flowers." In every flower he could see a sermon, and in the song of every bird he could hear a message from the Lord. He could appreciate the spirit of the psalmist, who said, "The heavens declare the glory of God; and the firmament sheweth his handywork" (19:1). Dr. Bob could look up at the stars and talk to them and come away with a wonderful sermon. He realized that "the stars of the night, the golden hinges on the door of the morning, and the riches of the universe" belong to God's children, and that they belonged to him just as much as they belonged to any millionaire.

This man had the heart and soul of an artist. He could paint a picture in words that would deeply stir an audience. He could take an audience from one mood to another and could move them from laughter to tears within minutes. A cartoonist in Montgomery, Alabama, during

The Young Evangelist, Age 19

one of Dr. Bob's revivals graphicly portrayed Dr. Bob as an artist in words. He pictured him in an artist's smock and beret holding an artist's palette and brush, and standing in front of a canvas on which he was painting a picture of the devil. He was pointing out that the devil does not come to us as the creature pictured on the Red Devil Lye can but as an angel of light.

Although college athletics were not as much in vogue in that era as they are today, Bob loved sports, especially baseball; and he tried to participate in them as much as possible. During the 1964 World Series on television, Dr. Bob remarked to me that the players did not seem to have the pep, the spirit, or the enthusiasm that they had when he was in college. I asked him to tell me about his college days. He laughingly explained, "I was a little too fat to be a really good player; and because of small hands and feet, I was not very fast. However, I was fond of playing first base, and my fellow students thought that I was a good sport."

At college Bob received the "red carpet" treatment during fraternity rush week. Years later—on March 9, 1964—I was with Dr. Bob when he renewed acquaintance with a member of his old fraternity. They mentioned that in their day the first thing the "old" fraternity members did was to get all new members converted. This fact is also referred to in Dr. Bob's answer to a letter from his fraternity congratulating him on the wonderful success he had made in life. Dr. Bob thanked the group for their kindness in writing, and then he urged the members to keep their group spiritual and continue the type work the boys tried to do when he was a student.

Literary societies were the center of much of the student activities in Dr. Bob's college days. His field of achievement was speech and dramatics, an area in which he won many medals. Being a good speaker and a fast thinker, he became a popular debater. He would walk along the beautiful countryside or in the woods practicing his speeches. This served a twofold purpose: he got exercise while he was learning.

Bob had very few books to read. A converted lawyer, Philip Mauro, who had been an agnostic but who, after his conversion, became a scholarly student of the Bible, had written several books which came into Bob's hands while he was still a student in college. These books were helpful to him during his school days and also later in his ministry. The first book was *The World and Its God* (World system built on Paradise Lost), and the second was *Number of Man*. A volume of sermons by Dr. William Elbert Munsey stirred the young preacher's soul, stimulated his imagination, and made him a better preacher.

Throughout his ministry Dr. Bob was familiar with the names of the leading preachers in America. He contended that these men were greater than the average preacher of today—not meaning, of course, that all of them were as well educated or as good executives as the preachers of today, but that from the standpoint of great preaching they excelled the men in the average pulpit today.

Lower Peach Tree Circuit

In the summer of 1902 Bob left Greensboro and went to supply churches in Lower Peach Tree Circuit. He had a wonderful time and the people loved him. The Portis family took him into their home for several months. Years later Dr. Bob wrote to Miss Julia Portis:

> I can't realize that it has been fifty-three years since I was at Lower Peach Tree as an eighteen-year-old boy. It was the happiest experience of my life. You folks took me into your home, and you were good to me, and I have wonderful memories of those blessed days. . . . As I grow older I think more and more of the friends who were kind to me and encouraged me when I was a young fellow struggling to do the will of God. . . .
>
> I am enclosing a little booklet on evangelism. I gave this message in chapel and it has been put into the hands of more than forty thousand preachers. I am a sort of an old-time roughneck that goes ahead and builds on certain principles. I try to stay in my field. In the field where I have served for many years we are facing many perils. The line of demarcation between Bible-believing Christians and socialistic, liberalistic, modernistic religionists is being wiped out by a movement we call Neo-orthodoxy. We have contact with practically all the conservative constituency throughout America, and because of my background of experience, I hope I can be of some real service.

Miss Julia, eighty-eight years of age and partially blind, appreciated the books. She wrote:

> I can read just a little by using the strongest magnifying glass, and I am writing by faith because I cannot see. I am not writing you as a noted preacher but simply as an old friend. Anything pertaining to you or yours is of much interest to me. I remember so well the summer you were with us, and if I was the slightest help to you it is a source of gratification to me. I have watched your career and rejoiced in your success as a preacher and an educator—you have done wonderful work and may you live long to do much more. I recall helping you—sitting on the front porch writing your sermon on Peter—"Upon this rock I will found my Church and the gates of hell shall not prevail against it."

Mrs. F. E. Poole of Grove Hill, Alabama, sister to Julia Portis, wrote:

> I often think of the time when you were our pastor at Peach Tree and what wonderful sermons you preached. You were a great inspiration to all of us.

Mrs. Mittie E. Walters wrote:

Your picture and the article about you in "Christian Life" took me back to Marion, Alabama, Methodist Church when you were preaching at the age of eighteen and I was eight. Thanks for pointing me to a decision for Jesus.

Miss Gertrude Culverhouse, Selma, Alabama, wrote:

I suppose you have forgotten Adele and me by this time, but we will never forget you. . . . I may be poor, but I am rich in the Lord. . . . I have been reading out of a small Bible that you gave to Adele September 2, 1912. We have appreciated you down through the years.

Dr. Bob also heard from Dr. Tom Floyd, an outstanding physician from Abbeville, Alabama. Dr. Bob appreciated this letter from his old boyhood playmate. It brought to his mind fond memories of days when he and Tom had romped and played as all boys of that age do. One time while these two boys were wrestling, Bobby's arm was knocked out of socket. It "scared the boys to death!" But Tom kept yanking on the arm until finally he got it to fall into place. Dr. Bob always teased Tom about getting his practice in medicine on him.

CHAPTER 9

Popular Preacher

The characteristics so marked in later years began to manifest themselves as Bob turned more and more to evangelistic work. He was strong of character and had an impressive personality. His persuasive manner, generous heart, sincerity, and goodness won him many friends and were instrumental in the salvation of many souls. Young women of the day spoke of him as the "good-looking preacher boy," for he was handsome.

A Greenville friend, Mrs. S. S. Newell, a Bob Jones University Board member and wonderful and generous friend of the school, says: "While he was still a college student in old Southern College, Dr. Bob would hold meetings at different places on Sunday afternoons; and my sister would ride horseback for miles to play the organ in his services. Dr. Bob was only nineteen years of age, and he was a mighty handsome young man." Wherever Bob preached, the young people of the community planned picnics and "dinner on the ground" to get better acquainted with him.

From his youth Dr. Bob had the attitude: "Where He leads me, I will follow." Many of us have fond memories of his tapping a song book against his hand as he would have the congregation sing, "I'll go with Him, with Him, all the way." He would keep stressing the words until finally we would be singing only the last phrase: "all the way." God's gifts to this man did not include the ability to sing, but he was able to inspire others to sing "heartily, as to the Lord."

Young Bob soon began to receive invitations for city-wide revivals, the type that are rarely seen in this day of apostasy. Usually he would preach to the church people for about a week. He would get them straightened out and stirred up; then they would begin to witness, and souls would be saved. This young preacher realized early in his ministry that revival can come only as God's people turn back to Him, humbly pleading His mercy and begging His forgiveness. To him, this was a scriptural principle.

Dr. Bob was keenly alert to violations of scriptural principles. One time at the end of a little party in his back yard, he said, "Let's quote a verse of Scripture before we part." A guest who had been associated with his school from her youth attempted to quote II Chronicles 7:14. She said: "If my people, which are called by my name, shall humble themselves, and pray, and seek my face; then will I hear from heaven, and will forgive their sin, and will heal their land." Quick as a flash he said, with gentleness, "You omitted an important phrase. The verse reads, 'If my people, which are called by my name, shall humble themselves, and pray, and seek my face, *and turn from their wicked ways; then will I. . . .*'" A scriptural principle had been violated in the omission. Even in his years of failing memory from hardening of the arteries, Dr. Bob could not be "tricked" as to principle. A visitor said to him, "I have to make a talk on 'Jesus the Great Teacher.' How would you handle that subject, Dr. Bob?" He answered, "You have to be careful about a subject like that; it tends to 'play down' His deity."

Bob had many unusual experiences, some of which were very embarrassing. At the end of one service, a group of ladies were kneeling around the altar. All of a sudden a young girl of about seventeen, overjoyed with her conversion, reached over and kissed him on the cheek. This was most embarrassing to such a young preacher.

Bob had the ability to make his messages so plain that all people could understand them. Like Sam Jones, he had no patience with people who talked above the heads of the people. Sam used to say, "If you put the fodder on the hay rack, only the giraffe can reach it. Put it on the ground, and all the animals can feed on it. The giraffe's neck is long enough to reach down to the ground, but the short-necked animals cannot reach the food when it is up high."

Most of the preachers cooperated with Bob's efforts in behalf of the Lord's work. They thrilled at the young man's soundness of faith, purity of doctrine, ethical dealings, and obvious sincerity; and often they would become so interested in his messages that they would find themselves leaning forward in their seats as they listened. They would invite him into their homes, and soon he became known as "the preachers' preacher."

Then as now, however, trouble was always brewing. The Methodists were already "building a machine." Fearing any man they could not control, they decided to pass a rule that no Methodist layman or preacher could preach or hold a religious service within the boundary of a Methodist pastor's circuit *without* that pastor's permission. This move was designed to stop Sam Jones, Bob Jones, and others of their kind. Sam Jones defied the Methodist hierarchy, saying, "You are not going to back me up to a block and cut off my tail." Bob Jones took the same attitude. He would never allow anything or anybody to crowd God out of his life.

His supreme desire was to do God's bidding, to stay in close fellowship with God, and not to kowtow to some man-made hierarchy. Dr. Bob never sought to do *great* things; he merely performed to the best of his ability whatever job was at hand, and God honored his efforts.

Under the direction of Almighty God, Bob went higher and higher until in his twenties his fame reached around the entire nation. His name by this time was becoming a "byword" all around the country. The Baptists of the North began to call for him; and the word was passed around, "If you want a good meeting, get Bob Jones." He became noted not only for his fiery preaching but also for his flowery preaching. Older people said, "Young Bob can play marbles on the tails of the comets."

Though in those days preaching the Gospel meant hardship and sacrifice, men did not have to be coerced into the ministry. Instead, they had the attitude, "Woe is me if I preach not the Gospel."

Dr. Bob loved the older preachers who took such pains in teaching him things he should know. He enjoyed hearing those men of God discuss various other men of God who were being greatly used of the Lord. Especially did he enjoy hearing of "old Dr. Munsey" who could "preach the stars down" and who would pray all night before delivering one of his never-to-be-forgotten sermons, which sometimes caused entire congregations to rise to their feet in fascination under the spell of his preaching.

There was a Free Will Baptist named Dannily who took Bob around with him a great deal. Dr. Dannily was an effective preacher, and he made a deep impression on the younger preacher. Dr. Dan Barr also influenced young Bob. Dr. Barr was a man of prayer. People respected this man's prayers, for they knew that God heard and answered him. Dr. Bob used to tell an interesting story about Dr. Barr. Six young couples, on a hayride, made it up to go hear Dr. Barr preach "just for fun." At the time of the altar call these young couples were to flock to the front and pretend to be converted. Old Dr. Barr, sensing their insincerity, asked, "Why did you come to the altar?" "To be converted," they answered. Dr. Barr said, "I know that you did not come in the right spirit, and what you are doing is sacrilege. Now I am going to pray that God will either kill you right here or that He will save you." The young couples began to beg: "Please, Dr. Barr, don't pray that God will kill us. God will answer your prayer, and we are not ready to die." The result was that seven of the group were saved that night and the remaining five at a later date.

Bob respected his elders and sought their advice. He knew that there was no experience like that of the hoary-headed men who had been over the road. He knew the friendship of most of the giants of that day — Wilbur Chapman, R. A. Torrey, William Biederwolf, and Billy Sunday, to name a few. These men loved their younger colleague, and they did all they could to boost him. Of his association with these men, Dr. Bob said, "I would skim some cream from all these great men." He studied the works of great men such as John Calvin and Dr. C. I. Scofield.

During his early twenties Dr. Bob felt the need of some sound advice concerning an important decision. He knew just where to go. He boarded a train for Atlanta, Georgia, to see Dr. Robert Stewart MacArthur, a great man of God who was holding a meeting for another prince of a preacher, Dr. Len Broughton. Young Bob explained to Dr. MacArthur that he had been reared a Methodist but that his mother was a Baptist and had gotten him "in the creek." Since he was doing much of his preaching in Baptist churches, he wondered if he should join a Baptist church. Dr. MacArthur answered, "Bob, the Methodists need you. You know what is right. Your conscience is clear. I advise you to stay where you are." Bob followed the older man's advice, and soon he was preaching in big union campaigns all over the country.

As thickening clouds began to appear on the horizon, the young evangelist commented, "Christianity is facing real dangers." Then he advised, "If God's people, even though they are a minority group, would stay true to God's Word and do His will, they would be able to stand; and two could chase ten, and ten could chase a hundred, and a hundred could chase ten thousand."

CHAPTER 10

South's Beloved Evangelist

Dr. Bob had a particular love for the South. It was his birthplace; and in his younger days he had taught school in various towns, such as Blue Springs, Texasville, Abbeville, and Brannon Stand. The parents of his pupils respected him. They could see that he was stimulating their children in ways that they had never dreamed were possible. The young teacher's Christlike spirit and untiring devotion to his Master was apparent even in the classroom. He could not help preaching to the children, for he had done that since he was a lad. He told his pupils of God's great love, and he explained to them how they could be saved. He drilled into them the basic lessons he had learned years before, and he taught them to trust God for everything. When I asked him what subjects he taught, he laughingly replied, "The blue-back speller, reading, writing, and arithmetic."

Bob went through Alabama like a cyclone. He put thousands into the churches, closed saloons, and otherwise led people to "do right." He was opposed, of course. Personal attacks were leveled against him: he was misrepresented, misunderstood, and maligned. The liquor trust fought him on every corner. But the more the devil's forces fought him, the more the Lord seemed to bless him and the more Christian people rallied around him. Dr. Bob said that the way people lied about him, you would have thought that he was the dirtiest dog in the world. He commented:

> I thought that I could never face the world after all the lies had been told, and I was a little droopy in spirit. A politician—not much of a Christian, but a man of conviction—said to me, "Son, don't let 'em get you down. The hotter the battle, the more blood that is being shed, the greater the opposition, that is the time to put your thumbs in the armholes of your vest and walk out and bare your breast to the bullets. They tell me when you get scared of a bull dog, he can smell an odor from your body. If you're not scared, the bull dog says, 'There's a fellow that ain't scared.'"

The following incident points out one reason for the liquor crowd's hatred of Dr. Bob's ministry. Many towns depended upon dispensaries for their livelihood. In Dothan, Alabama, the town which Dr. Bob loved so well and which was only four miles from the place he was reared, Dr. Bob met with the city officials and asked why they, as Christians, would permit in their town a dispensary that would damn the souls of men. The officials said, "The law states that we can have one." "But the law does not say you *must* have one," he retorted. "You men are in the whiskey business whether you realize it or not; and you are responsible for, and guilty of many of these drunkards around town who go home and beat their good wives and innocent children." The group voted unanimously to close the dispensary, and an official sign was placed on the dispensary door, stating that the place was closed by the order of the city. The next morning when the owner came to open the doors of the dispensary and read the sign, he was overheard to say: "D . . . that man, Bob Jones! I knew he would ruin this town, doing something like this." The dispensary was never opened again.

Few men ever had incorporated in their personalities as many different qualities that would make a great evangelist as Dr. Bob had. He possessed strong conviction backed up by undaunted courage, keen imagination, dramatic ability, and obvious sincerity. In many a hard city in which other evangelists had failed, time after time Dr. Bob demonstrated what God can do through a courageous evangelist who uncompromisingly preaches the Gospel. Dr. Bob lived by the principle, "*Trust God as if it all depends upon Him, and work as if it all depends upon you.*"

From North to South, all over the nation, and around the world, this man whom Billy Sunday described as having "the wit of Sam Jones, the homely philosophy of George Stuart, the eloquence of Sam Small, and the spiritual fervency of Dwight L. Moody" continued to proclaim the unsearchable riches of Christ, never compromising and never wavering. Many times I heard Dr. Bob refer to Billy Sunday as "the greatest of the great" in the field of evangelism, and yet Billy Sunday is reported to have graciously said in Chicago that Bob Jones was the greatest evangelist of all time.

Dr. Bob developed a style all his own, and I doubt that the style of any man will ever be more picturesque or more effective. Cartoonists tried to depict him as a man of action. He had a distinct way of captivating his audience. At no time during his preaching could one's interest lag. He had a message for every heart; and his deep, penetrating eyes seemed to search out individually everyone in the room. The audience knew that they were being looked at, as well as preached to; and they heard him gladly, though often uncomfortably. It was difficult for one to pass over his shoulder to the person behind him the remarks of Bob Jones. They

South's Beloved Evangelist, Age 23

seemed custom-made for each individual. In every campaign he was recognized as a God-inspired preacher of the Word, whose love for his
fellowman was easily felt. He would close his messages with a Heavenly
benediction that would follow the people for days, even though they
were made to feel that they had been "weighed in the balances, and
found wanting" and that they must do something about the situation.

The name Bob Jones was always associated with sound business practices. By close supervision he was able to keep his evangelistic budget to
about one-third of that of other evangelists.

With all his achievements, however, there was something Dr. Bob
could not do: he could not whistle or sing. He told us of a time when as a
lad at school he tried to sing in the chorus. His "off-key" voice disrupted
so much that he was asked not to sing. This hurt him; but it proved a
blessing, for had he been a good singer, he might have tried to protect
his voice and throat. As it was, he hammered away with his voice, ever
faithful to the call of God. In those days of no "intercom" systems, a
preacher had to "bellow" to be heard in a large tabernacle which seated
ten thousand or more; and God used this man's voice in a great way to
reach the masses of people. In Glory there will be literally thousands and
thousands of souls that have been saved under his forceful preaching.

Dr. Bob said of his voice:

> The sorrow of my life is I can't sing. My vocal chords and my ear — I don't
> understand it — just don't work together. I want to sing. You know, I'd
> rather be a singer than anything I know. I said sometime not long ago: The
> thing you would do for Jesus if you could do it — He tells the recording angel
> to write it down that you have done it. It's not what you do; it's what you
> would do for Him that counts. You'd give Him a million dollars if you had
> it? All right; you haven't got it, but He knows what you'd do if you could.
> He knows I'd sing for Him if I could. So He's written me down up in Heaven
> as a singer, but I can't sing. I've got my plans all worked out. When I get to
> Heaven and thank Him for saving me and kiss my mother and put my arm
> around my father and greet my loved ones and say "good-morning" to my
> friends, I'm going to ask somebody to let me take over the music, and I'm
> going to ask the heavenly orchestra to set the pitch, and I'm going to dip my
> tongue in the melody of the sky, and I'm going to sing a song that Jesus
> Christ put in my heart when I was just a little country boy at the age of
> eleven. Nobody has ever sung that song.

No doubt, God has already allowed this song that was in Dr. Bob's
heart through the years to burst forth in swelling praise.

CHAPTER 11

Physical Difficulties

As a young man, Bob was not physically strong. He coughed constantly. In a bout with double pneumonia, it was thought that he could not live. He was malaria prone and had many other frailties which, humanly speaking, might have "downed" the average person.

Nevertheless, in spite of physical difficulties, Bob, by the time he was twenty-one, was having some of the greatest meetings of his career. He had an all-consuming passion for lost souls, and he would not let anything deter him from doing the work that he felt God had called him to do.

The results of his revivals were increasingly great. In a newspaper article under the headline "BOB JONES IN SELMA," it was stated:

Bob Jones in his evangelistic campaign is stirring Selma as Selma has never been stirred. Whether you want to accept this or not, it is the truth, and those who have heard this wonderful pulpit speaker—this man of God— must have been strongly impressed with the truth of his utterance. Not a man of large physique, not physically strong [Dr. Jones was not well. He had been told that he could not live more than ten years], with a voice seemingly weak with strain, yet more cutting than a two-edged sword, he unfolds the forgotten past and turns the light of truth into the very souls of men. Occupying a church with the greatest seating capacity of any church in the city, he is preaching to packed houses at every service. Sunday he conducted three of the most wonderful meetings Selma has ever known, and that too when it is recalled that men of no less power than Dwight L. Moody has been heard here. Several thousand people heard Mr. Jones Sunday at Church Street Church, and many were unable to get within the doors. Call it what you may, the man has a most wonderful influence and touches the hearts of men, moving them to acknowledge their own uncomfortable condition. The first week of his campaign has closed. It closed Sunday night with a great meeting when men and women looked through windows and hung to doorways . . . . Mr. Jones' coming here will be long remembered, and the work he is doing will stand as a monument to his name and the great cause he represents.

The young preacher's throat bothered him more and more. In his early twenties he went to consult one of the leading specialists of the South. The diagnosis was "tuberculosis of the throat"; and the case was considered hopeless. Bob was ordered to go West immediately.

What a blow! Already the young preacher had suffered great sorrow. He had chosen as his wife a young woman named Bernice Sheffield. Bernice possessed a keen mind and unusual ability. According to a newspaper article, she was an accomplished musician; and the two seemed the perfect team, she playing the piano for the services and Bob doing the preaching. However, for some reason—a reason known only to a wise Providence at the time—death, in the form of tuberculosis, claimed Bob's bride of only ten months. A tragedy? Humanly speaking, yes! Heartache? Definitely. A very deep heartache! But God never makes a mistake. In His Word is the assurance, "For we know that all things work together for good to them that love God, to them who are the called according to his purpose" (Romans 8:28). Bernice and Bob loved the Lord, were dedicated to His purpose, and bowed to His wisdom in taking her Home.

The all-wise, never-failing God knew that no heartache, however great it might be, would stop His messenger; indeed, it would put a note there that would increase his usefulness. Because of his own heartbreak he would be able to sympathize with others who sorrowed. Bob knew the comfort of God's Word and God's Holy Spirit. "Let not your heart be troubled" (John 14:1) and "Ye sorrow not, even as others which have no hope" (I Thessalonians 4:13) became more than mere words to him. Like the prophet Ezekiel, who was called upon to give up the desire of his eyes (Ezekiel 24:15–18), Bob humbly bowed in submission to the divine will. God had other plans for this young man, but this part of the story will be told in a later chapter.

In his effort to overcome his sorrow and in his eagerness to serve the Lord, Bob had overdone his strength. Now, according to medical authorities, death would shortly claim another victim. Friends spread the news that Bob Jones had gone West to die. But God intervened, and the young preacher began to mend and to grow stronger than ever.

While he was out West, Bob had an experience which I think the Lord permitted in order that His servant might warn others against a certain evil. I will give the experience in Dr. Bob's own words.

> I was in a certain city spending a few weeks resting up. I met a very brilliant woman . . . seventy-five years of age. She had a most beautiful home and the most magnificent private library I think I ever saw.
>
> One day as we were sitting together in the library, I asked, "Mrs. Adams, are you a Christian?"
> "No," she replied. "I have always been skeptical. But I have had a most interesting experience lately."

"Would you mind telling me what it was?" I asked.

"You won't tell on me?" she asked.

"Not in this town," I replied.

"Well, a few months ago I lost a fifteen-hundred-dollar brooch . . . given to me by my husband as a wedding present. I searched and searched and . . . even sought the aid of police and detectives. . . . I had just about given up hope of ever finding it when a friend told me of a certain Madam Blank."

"Who is she?" I inquired.

"She is a great medium . . . a plain, German woman who can hardly speak English. I went to her home and told her my story. She said she would try to help me. She leaned back in the chair and went into a trance and began to mumble something which I could not understand. After a while she said, 'I have located it for you. On a certain day a man was working at your home. He stole your brooch and sold it for a small amount to another man. This second man sold it to a pawnbroker. It has been in a half dozen different cities. It is now in the hands of a certain jeweler in blank town. This jeweler bought it from a traveling man and has broken it up and made three rings out of it. He still has the old setting.' I went to the place," Mrs. Adams said, "and hired a detective who went to the jeweler and found that the medium had given me the absolute truth. I have my brooch. What do you think of that, Mr. Jones?"

"It sounds wonderful," I answered, "but I don't know anything about it."

Several days later, without telling anybody of my plans, I called the medium over the phone and asked if I might come to one of her seances. I explained to her that I was a stranger in the city. That night I dropped into her home (At first I went out of curiosity; later I became fascinated). They had thirty-three or thirty-four, I think, in the circle. There was no cabinet. The room was not dark, but the lights were dim. Everybody joined hands, and somebody began to sing, "Nearer, my God, to Thee." The pale-faced, frail old German woman went into a trance. Notice, please—follow every detail. As we began to sing, the lady to my right said: "Do you know anything about this?"

I answered, "No."

She said, "I think it is lots of fun. Of course I don't believe in it."

I said, "I can't say that I do either."

By the time the woman to my right and I had finished our conversation, I looked at the medium. She was as pale as death. She fell to the floor with something like epilepsy or catalepsy. She foamed at the mouth and seemed to be choking. A man who was seated to the right of the medium (they called him "Doctor") began to shake the medium and say: "Let her go! Let her go!"

I inquired of a gentleman on my left what it meant.

He said, "You must not understand it."

I assured him that he was correct. . . .

"Every medium," he said, "has a guide. This woman's guide is an Indian spirit that left America before this country was ever settled by the white people. When Madam Blank goes into the trance, this Indian guide comes to her to reveal to her information from the other world. But sometimes a wicked spirit tries to get in ahead of her guide, and it produces this condition."

I will show you before I get through . . . that this was not a departed spirit of an Indian but a demon that choked the medium and threw her into that spell. This woman was what every genuine medium in the world is—a demon-possessed person.

After a while they got her back in the chair. Poor old woman! She was pale and haggard. They began to get communications. The lady who a few minutes before had said that she did not believe in the thing was told that there was a message for her. The medium said, "Somebody wishes to speak to you, Theresa," and she began to cry.

"Who is it?" the woman asked.

The medium said, "It is your sister; she wishes to thank you for taking care of her babies."

A moment later, when I thought there was no communication for me, as distinctly as if an electric spark had touched me I felt something touch me. I will never forget that sensation. The medium said, "Somebody wishes to speak to you. She is an aunt by the name of Anne."

"There must be a mistake," I said. "I never had an aunt by that name."

"Oh, yes, you did," said the medium, "and here is your mother. Her name is Georgia. Your mother says, 'I let Anne come first. She died years before the Civil War. You never knew her. I let her come first.'"

Then she called the roll of every dead relative I ever had. Some of them I had to look up (and it took me months to do that!). I sat there and wondered. There was something ghostly about it. I didn't find any Christian atmosphere there, but I kept going. I would sit in that room in the bright daylight, and this woman would go into a trance, and my dead loved ones were supposed to come and bring every kind of message.

One day when this woman was in a trance, my mother was supposed to be speaking through her. I said, "Mother, you say you are my mother?"

She said, "Yes, I am your mother."

I said, "I want to ask you something. You taught me that Jesus was God's Son, that He died on the cross to save me, and that if I would trust Him, He would save me. Why haven't you said something to me about Jesus? You claim to be in the spirit realm. Isn't He up there somewhere?"

Just then the old hag, under the demoniacal spell, cried, "Ha, ha, ha!" She said, "You have such a wrong idea, Son, about Jesus. You world folks don't understand. Jesus was just a great medium like Madam So-and-So through whom I am speaking. Moses and Elias were His guides. I am just as high in the spiritual realm as He is. He is no higher than anybody else. You have the wrong idea."

I said, "Wait a minute. You say you are my mother."

"Yes."

"Well, if you taught me the wrong thing about Jesus, what about your standard of morals? You taught me that some things were right and some things were wrong. Have you changed your opinion?"

She said, "Well, Son, to tell you the truth, I think your standard of morals is too high. Of course, you can't understand my saying that."

I said, "That isn't my mother. There is somebody impersonating my mother." That somebody was a demon.

When that old lady threw back her head and laughed, and the voice went on to say, "You poor, benighted, earth-bound creature; Jesus was no more than a medium," that gave me the answer I was looking for. I knew the whole thing was of the devil, because my mother would never have spoken those words.

I left that place, never to return. I went to my room, got my Bible, and stayed on my knees for three hours. I looked up Scriptures to get the true answers. I saw from God's Word that this was a demon-possessed woman. Even though I had played the fool in going there, I felt that I had learned something from it that might help others. I read in my Bible about the devil entering the garden and tempting Eve to pursue knowledge — to be like God. As I read on, it became clear to me how the demon systems work in pagan lands and also in the various cults. I read that every spirit that confesses not that Christ is of God, is of the devil (I John 4:3). I was impressed that the basic fundamental truth is "Jesus Christ — God in the flesh"; and this great truth is denied by the devil and every off-brand religion. I realized as I studied God's Word there on my knees that I had consulted a familiar spirit, and that if I had not been converted and a strong Christian, the devil might have gotten me off beam. That woman had power, but it was not from God. It was the power of demons. The devil knows my mother's name was Georgia. The devil knows I had an Aunt named Anne. Most mediums are fakes, but I dealt with a genuine medium.

How do I know Spiritism is of the devil? Because it is so absolutely devilish. There is not one good thing to be said about it. It is destructive physically, mentally, and morally. It makes physical wrecks of men. It sends some of them to insane asylums.

The manner in which young Bob had this issue clarified for himself is important. It is to be noted that he had *no vision* in which the Lord bodily appeared and taught him; the Holy Spirit taught him *from the Word of God.* On his knees in prayer, Bible in hand, the question was settled. God's Word gives the sure promise that "if any man will do his will, he shall know of the doctrine" (John 7:17). Dr. Bob had both the desire to know and the will to do God's will, and God kept His promise and taught the young man and the doctrine. We are not to believe *every* spirit; we are to try the spirits to see whether they are of God (I John 4:1).

In this day of constant warfare waged by evil spirits, we need to be able to discern these spirits and not come under their power. THIS WE CAN DO ONLY THROUGH THE WORD OF GOD!

Spiritism, according to a pamphlet I read, has as "its central aim to communicate with the dead. It denies the fall of man, the evil of sin, the need of blood redemption, the Deity of our Lord Whom the Spiritists describe as 'a Jewish religious enthusiast who came to an untimely death.' It declares there is no hell, no resurrection, and no judgment; ad infinitum." In Dr. Bob's day, there was not much information available on such subjects; but he clung to the Lord, and the Lord showed him the right way.

Miraculously Healed

God graciously restored Bob to health; and he left San Antonio, Texas, where all of this had happened, and headed back to Southeast Alabama. When he was re-examined by the same specialist who had sent him West to die, the specialist declared, "It is a miracle." God was not through with His servant. There were many things he must do for the Cause.

Mary Gaston, Life Partner

Sometime after Bob's return from the West, he held a meeting in the small town of Uniontown, Alabama. As usual, the meeting was wonderful. There is a phase of this meeting that has made history and has been a part of the success of Bob Jones University. A young lady in Uniontown was to figure largely in the future work of this young evangelist. Her name? Mary Gaston Stollenwerck.

Mary Gaston's family were people of culture and social distinction. Her grandfather had died, leaving his wife a beautiful old Southern plantation and four hundred and fifty slaves to be looked after. (A picture of this home appears in ANTE-BELLUM MANSIONS OF ALABAMA, by Hammond, pp. 144, 145. It is listed as the Welch Home. The cover plate of the book may be the same home.) The grandmother loved these "darkies," as they were called in that day; and she was kind to them. She trained them according to Christian principles and educated them to the best of her ability. After the war she was heard to remark, "One of the happiest days of my life was when 'The Emancipation Proclamation' was issued, freeing the slaves. I felt that I was the one who was being freed—freed from a very great responsibility. A heavy burden rolled from my shoulders. Although I had made every effort to make Christians out of all who were dependent on me, there was always the gnawing fear that some of them might die and go to Hell, and I would be responsible."

Estelle Siddons Stollenwerck, Mary Gaston's mother, was one of those Southern ladies of whom you read. A cousin of the family, Dr. Frank Stollenwerck, told me of his first visit to the family. He spoke of how lovely and charming "Tellie" (Estelle) was. He said, "Many men had been very much enamored of her loveliness and beauty. My father, in his younger days, was one of them." Mrs. Stollenwerck was small of stature, but oh so brilliant and so striking of character! A lady of the old school, she was full of grace and charm; and she radiated culture. She was kindness personified. Estelle and Eugene, her handsome husband, were considered by many people as "the most attractive couple in the whole state of Alabama."

Eugene Stollenwerck was a tall, impressive looking man. Those who knew him well, described him as "standing out in any group of men like a race horse amongst scrubs." When death claimed this young father, his wife, dear saint of God that she was, accepted her responsibility and reared her children as she felt the Lord would have her to rear them.

Mary Gaston was a child who never knew the meaning of the word "fear." When she was only seven years of age — and this will sound incredible to those who know her now — she engaged in a tussle with some neighbor boys. It seems that these boys were always "into something," and often they took advantage of one of Mary Gaston's brothers, who was much younger and smaller than they. On one occasion of their "picking on" her brother, this young lady decided to do something about the situation. Did she run to her mother for help? She did not! She waded into those boys with all the vigor of her seven years; by the time she had finished, they were begging for mercy. Biting into the leg of one of the bullies, she held on for dear life. The boys were much better after that, especially around the Stollenwerck home; and for sometime after this incident, Mary Gaston was known as (pardon the expression!) the "little hellcat" of the community.

Mrs. Stollenwerck painstakingly taught Mary Gaston that life consists of more than merely washing dishes and keeping a house neat and clean, as important as these things are. From babyhood this young lady was taught and trained — perfectly groomed — for the exalted position that God had for her in life. Mary Gaston had dedicated herself to the Lord at an early age, and she wanted His will in her life. Like other popular young girls, she was invited to numerous parties; and the young men in the community saw to it that she was "escorted"! At one of these parties a boy friend remarked: "Just wait until that Bob Jones comes here for a revival; he will get you straightened out." Mary Gaston laughingly retorted, "He won't bother me any. You will see." Later she was to "eat those words."

When young Evangelist Jones arrived in Uniontown, it did not take him long to notice the "belle of Uniontown." Needless to say, she became quite interested in his campaign; and under his strong, straight preaching, she was converted. Little did she dream that she would play a most important part in the future work of this young man.

It was during choir practice that the young couple met. Dr. Bob used to say, "Even to this day I can see Mary Gaston sitting there on the arm of the pulpit chair. She had all the culture and refinement that I lacked."

I guess it must have been "love at first sight," for he lost no time in making a real friendship out of an introduction; and soon it was courtship instead of friendship. It was characteristic of Dr. Bob to get what he set out to get, and even Mrs. Jones admits that he was an ardent suitor.

Dr. Bob did not immediately sweep all Mary Gaston's family off their feet. There was at least one "dissenter" in this romance: Uncle Gaston, her guardian. A quiet and dignified Methodist, Uncle Gaston was unfavorably impressed by what he considered young Bob's super-activity in preaching and in courting. He quietly disapproved the match, and yet the more the uncle saw of the young preacher—and Bob saw to it that this was often—the better he liked and respected the young man.

Once while Mary Gaston was visiting an aunt, Mrs. Aimeé Battey, of Rome, Georgia, she received a long distance call from her "beau." The aunt heard her say, "Bob, you must not come here to see me. What will these people in Rome think?" Bob did not seem to mind what they thought, for he said, "I will be there. I am on my way." AND HE ARRIVED! Aunt Aimeé, sensing what was developing, concluded, "There will be a marriage soon."

Bob was keenly aware that in his type of work it was most important that he have the right kind of wife. He had made this a matter of earnest prayer, for he did not want to marry out of God's will. Had he looked the whole world over many times, he could never have found a more suitable person to be his companion than this lovely girl. Mrs. Jones has been a wonderful wife, an excellent mother, an inspiring spiritual leader, and a genial hostess to preside over the various affairs connected with his work.

Word spread that Mary Gaston and the young evangelist were getting serious, but this did not daunt the spirits of some of her boy friends. At least one "hopeful" insisted that "as long as there is life, there is hope"; and not until she was actually married did he "throw in the sponge."

On June 17, 1908, about a year and a half after their first meeting, Bob Jones and Mary Gaston Stollenwerck said their marriage vows. She looked lovely in her wedding finery, touched off by white carnations; and surely no groom was ever more handsome and dashing than this young preacher, who also wore a carnation in the lapel of his coat! Mrs. Jones often commented, "There has never been a husband who was more thoughtful than Robert. He is the best husband and father God ever made."

Mrs. Jones has many virtues, but one of the most outstanding has been her sympathy and understanding with regard to her husband's work. Realizing that his love for the Lord and his service in the Lord's Cause must be first, she was content to be "second fiddle" to his work. He had to be away from home much of the time, but he always contacted her daily by phone or by mail.

Little did these two dream when they started out, how far God would take them on the road to fame. Mary Gaston's whole-hearted support of the work of her companion was a real help and encouragement to him, and he gave her a great deal of credit for his success. Reading of his evangelistic days and his educational endeavors, one can see the important part she has had in his work.

A Son Is Born

Bob Jones, Jr., arrived on October 19, 1911. To some degree, at least, Mary Gaston had to be both mother and father to the boy. But as he grew older, Bob, Jr., and his mother accompanied Dr. Bob on some of the evangelistic trips. It was excellent training for Bob to hear his father preach, to meet people, and to have the spiritual stimulation of the "sawdust trail."

Mrs. Jones was well-received in Dr. Bob's meetings, and numerous newspaper articles referred to the part she played in the work. I quote from a paper in Anniston, Alabama:

The earnest work of Mrs. Bob Jones has been an important factor in the success of the campaign. It has been a real privilege to have Mrs. Jones in Anniston, for she does not often accompany her husband on his evangelistic tours because she doesn't like to interrupt the school work of her eight-year-old son, Bob, Jr. She cannot often be persuaded to take part in the larger services of his meetings, although well equipped for such services, and very active in church work in Montgomery. However, Mrs. Jones accepted two invitations to speak to Anniston women, speaking once at a mass meeting at Parker Memorial and on last Sunday afternoon to the girls of Anniston. Before her marriage Mrs. Jones was lovely Mary Gaston Stollenwerck of Uniontown—a member of one of Alabama's prominent families. She is unusually pretty and possesses a charming personality. Every morning during the three weeks series of services, Mrs. Jones has led a morning prayer meeting at some of the homes, giving most delightful and instructive Bible lessons.

"My wife has thoroughly enjoyed meeting the Anniston women in the cottage prayer meetings," Mr. Jones told me, "and we have both been most happy over the splendid results of these sweet hours of prayer. One woman told me that the women in her neighborhood had decided to continue the cottage prayer meetings, holding them on one afternoon of each week after the close of the meeting. These prayer meetings are continued in nearly every place we visit, and always prove a blessing to all who take part."

Mrs. Jones was honored at many charming social functions, besides numbers of lovely luncheons given in her honor. She was special guest of honor at a dinner party given at the officers quarters at Camp McClelland by Captain Meeker on Saturday evening. . . .

PART II
EVANGELISTIC DAYS

Part II
Evangelistic Days

Introduction

The more I have read of Dr. Bob's meetings, the more I have come to realize that regardless of how much men try to "blow up" meetings today to make them look big, they fade into insignificance when compared with the meetings of Dr. Bob and other evangelists during the horse-and-buggy days.

Neither time nor space will permit my telling about all the great meetings which Dr. Bob held around the country. In many cities page after page of the local papers was given over to his work in their midst. I have selected only a few meetings to point out the immediate and the long-lasting results of this man's efforts in the Cause of Christ. Dr. Bob's work needs no embellishment. The newspaper accounts from which I quote set forth clearly and in detail the man, the message, and the methods which accomplished great things for God. Many towns dated their history from this man's meetings. People would say, "This happened *before* Bob Jones' meeting" or "This happened *after* Bob Jones' meeting." Because of the mighty impact of his ministry, many dispensaries, saloons, and gambling houses were closed. He left towns much better, and moral and spiritual people were never dissatisfied.

Dr. Bob's method of dealing with people and issues was as important as the message itself. Although modernism was not rampant in those days, as it has been in our day, it was prevalent enough to cause Dr. Bob and others to band themselves in an all-out effort against it. It was Dr. Bob's policy not to knowingly allow any modernist to help sponsor his meetings. He said, "It is all right to preach *to* the modernists in the audience, but it is wrong to have them on the platform as sponsoring pastors and call them 'Brother' and give them Christian recognition."

There were a number of reasons for Dr. Bob's attitude. First of all, giving Christian recognition to such men violates a direct command of the Lord (II John 9–11). To disobey this divine injunction is to give aid to the enemy. Also, a question of ethics is involved. When a pastor is on the sponsoring committee, his church deserves some of the converts of the meeting. If the pastor is not "sound," it would be like turning lambs to the wolves to put new converts into his church. By no stretch of the imagination, then, could it be right to compromise with men who do not abide in the doctrines of Christ.

Before his thirtieth birthday Dr. Bob had preached in twenty-five states, making a name for himself wherever he went. Large towns sparred with each other to get him first, and he soon became known as "The Billy Sunday of the South."

CHAPTER 1

Atlanta, Georgia, 1911

Under the headline "BOB JONES STIRS AND BLESSES ATLANTA, GEORGIA," William D. Upshaw, who later became a congressman, wrote:

Is "Bob" Jones any relation to Sam Jones? That is almost the unvarying question of throngs who have been hearing and hearing about "Bob" Jones, the "flaming evangel" of orthodox Christianity, who has been conducting great revival meetings in Atlanta for two weeks under the auspices of the First Methodist Church, of which Dr. S. P. Wiggins is the beloved and successful pastor.

"Bob" Jones "any kin" to Sam? Not a "speck"—that anybody knows of. But he will conduct the meetings at the Sam Jones Tabernacle at Cartersville the first week in August. He is just named Jones—Bob Jones—that's all—an honored member of the four royal families—the Smiths and Joneses, the Browns and the Johnsons—and beginning much earlier in life and possessing a rare order of consecrated genius, he bids fair to be reckoned in the Sam Jones class as a hero of Christendom and a benefactor of mankind.

Mr. Upshaw explained further about Dr. Bob:

He is a Methodist preacher—a sort of "Hardshell Methodist," like Whitefield was, who preaches salvation by grace and the miracle of regeneration with apostolic power.

Two notable services which especially impressed the city were the meeting for "Women Only" at the Forsyth theater the afternoon, Sunday, June 2, and the mammoth gathering of "Men Only" at the great city Auditorium on last Sunday afternoon.

Concerning the evangelist's fearless and faithful strictures of the faults and failings, fancies and follies of aimless self-seeking women the people are talking yet, while the spirit of his never-to-be-forgotten message on "The Secret Sins of Men" can be only imagined from the following paragraph:

"The man who is deceiving his wife," he declared, "is not the meanest man in Atlanta, bad as he is. But the worst type I have seen since my arrival is the church member who keeps a long way from questionable neighbor-hoods and spends much of his time in a front pew of a church, while at the same time he is taking the blood money that is paid as rent."

And by the time the young "tribune of Truth" got through proving the partnership in sin of all who abet it or share in its shame and its profits he had a good many "respectable" men feeling like "a yellow dog under a wagon!"

Magnifying the cardinal doctrines of sin and salvation, the Book and the Blood that great crowd of men went away from that Auditorium seeing Christ on Calvary as their only escape from their defiling sins.

BOB JONES, I think we can truthfully say, of the little brown-eyed baby, born near Dothan, Alabama, twenty-eight years ago, as the prophet said of Solomon, "The Lord loved him."

Perhaps for a time he did not seem especially favored, born in an humble home, reared in comparative poverty, yet the eye of God was on him, the hand of God was leading still.

He came a short time after this a guest into my home, and through his genial, lovable, sweet spirited, appreciative nature proved himself an ideal guest. He impressed me, as one man who had made a brilliant success of life, and yet bore absolutely no warning stain of egotism.

His successes then as now are all God's victories, just the power of the in-finite working through an humble human instrument. He told of his great meetings in such a way as to make you forget it was the great evangelist him-self talking to you, you almost believed he was telling of the achievements of another.

I heard Sam Jones say once that every man of every profession, and partic-ularly of the ministry—yes Mr. Jones said, "Particularly the ministry"—were possessed of a little jealous devil that, by virtue of Adam, belongs to Bob Jones, [but it] looked into his sweet boyish face, listened to his un-stinted praise of his brothers in the ministry and the evangelistic work, and slunk away forever.

Absolutely orthodox, this young evangelist is sane and sound. His heart is as broad as humanity, and every denomination is dear to him if it repre-sents his risen Lord. He believes in a thorough work of grace in the heart, nothing superficial satisfies him. His methods are the methods of fifty years ago, he preaches repentance and the power of the blood of Jesus Christ to cleanse and keep us clean, and he has the old-fashioned "mourners' bench," where penitents come to be led to a saving knowledge of Jesus Christ. His sermons are short and to the point, not a dull moment from the time he takes his text until he closes. His keen eyes flash, his face changes with every varying mood and his nervous, restless body is in constant motion.

.   .   .   .   .   .

Wherever Bob Jones has touched a town or city in all these years of his public work, a harvest of souls has been the result, without exception. Ala-bama has felt the effect of his work throughout her entire borders. Three years ago while they were waging the prohibition fight, he canceled his evangelistic engagements, and stumped the state, for God and the right, making a friend of every man, woman and child who touched his life.

In Texas he has held wonderful meetings in Galveston, Fort Worth, Dallas and other points. In California, Missouri, he had some of the greatest victories of his life. From there he went to New York city to the Church of the Strangers, and God was with him in power, and blessed him signally. . . . From New York he came back to his own sunny Southland, and in Griffin and Rome, of our own loved Georgia, he has held meetings that meant hundreds, even thousands of souls for the kingdom of God. And out of these meetings have come ministers, missionaries, and consecrated laymen by the score.

Let us give him our sympathy, our love and our prayers, as he goes up and down over our land working for the Master. . . .

CHAPTER 2

New York Campaign, 1916

One New York writer wrote of this meeting:

> The Reverend Robert Jones was a "licensed" preacher at fifteen. Today, at thirty, he commands audiences so vast that in many towns there is no building large enough to hold the crowds. . . . He is staying in the apartment of his friend, Supreme Court Justice Ransom, on West 106 Street. With Mr. Jones is his lovely young wife and the small Bob, Jr.

> The Joneses hail from Southern Alabama and have a country home near Montgomery. The Reverend "Bob" stands a full inch over six feet. His shoulders would arrest the attention of every one. His head is shapely and fine-featured. His eyes are hazel, and his voice is vibrant. This voice of Jones' must be one of his strongest weapons. It entereth not only your ears but your very spirit, and is free of oratorical bellowings. It fits a small room or fills a coliseum. "Bob" Jones is the successor, though no relative, of Sam Jones, one of the best-known and dearly beloved evangelists the country has seen. "Bob" Jones carries on the same work in the South, and uses the same "sensational" and forcefully picturesque methods.

This New York meeting proved to be one of his greatest meetings up to that time, and even today there are people who remember the man and the messages he preached. Dr. Bob had the first page of the NEW YORK WORLD for more than a week. He was interviewed by two of the most brilliant writers in American Newspaper World. It is interesting to see the large headlines that appeared in some of the papers. One headline read: "NEW YORK WOMEN ON ROAD TO RUIN—LURE MEN TO TREAD IT WITH THEM, SAYS REV. BOB JONES." Another stated, "TANGO AND BATHING SUITS SHOW PREACHER BOB JONES A NEW FIELD FOR HELLFIRE." Again, "COCKTAILS, DANCING AND CIGARETTES ARE MILESTONES ON WOMEN'S PRIMROSE PATH, DECLARES EVANGELIST, WHO THINKS THEIR CLOTHES ARE MORE IMMODEST THAN EVE'S FIG-LEAVES."

In one sermon Dr. Bob told the audience:

I said two years ago the only difference I could see between New York and Hell was that New York was completely surrounded by water. But there is plenty of sin in other places. I believe the war, as well as women, is responsible for the outcropping of the bestial in men's natures. Since the war we have more prize fights and cock fights in the country.

What women need is more home life. They are so idle today. That is why many of them fill up their time with drinking, smoking and wearing immodest clothes. I believe that women are still better than men, but they must stop traveling in the wrong direction.

"SIR PROPHET, HERE IS A JOB FOR YOU—TO SAVE NEW YORK" flashed another headline; and in the article this question was discussed:

Could a great prophet save New York? Evangelist "Bob" Jones, who is holding nightly tent meetings in West 124 Street, near Morningside Drive, believes such a one could. Mr. Jones' opinion was expressed afterward, in company with a reporter for THE WORLD; the editor of the New York WORLD sent his special reporter to take Dr. Bob around to what was then supposed to be the underworld of New York City.

In later years Dr. Bob remarked, "The Underworld in that day and time was not worse than the upperworld now." A reporter gave this account of a trip about New York which he and Dr. Bob made:

Dr. Bob made a tour of tango tea emporiums, lobster palaces and cabaret restaurants where New York's very latest in rollicking wickedness was set out for his view. The caustic-tongued young Southerner, who has been a preacher fifteen years, proposes a simple, yet Herculean task for his prophet. "Let him make character fashionable again. . . . That would bring about a return to old-fashioned standards of morals and conduct. Character and the modern dancing craze, with its concomitant evils, are incompatible." And he blames the women! Modern women, who claim sponsorship for all reform propaganda, he says, are at fault, more than men. The thirty-year-old evangelist, who doesn't care whose toes he happens to step on in his war against what he thinks is wrong with our present mode of life, doesn't even stop at "modern" women. "Women's suffrage," he said, "is going to bring about a few immediate reforms, but its ultimate effect will be laxity and license. The 'new freedom' has already wrought a great difference in girls and women—a difference too apparent to one who travels about, as I do, watching the world's conduct, and more apparent here in New York than elsewhere."

After an afternoon and evening of taxicabbing from one dancing place to another; after seeing some seven thousand New Yorkers at their favorite pastime; after visiting resorts underground, places at the street level and roofgardens, Mr. Jones was quite clear as to what ails New York. "Your city is dancing on the brink of Hell." Dr. Jones took the position that the parents were at fault, and he was amazed at their laxity in permitting these young boys and girls to go to such places as he saw that afternoon and evening. Dr. Jones goes on to say, "I found all the resources of your great city, all that money and art and skill can do, have been done to accomplish a harmonious, blended atmosphere of harmless gayety. Soft light, rich color, sensuous music, highly seasoned foods, stimulating drinks, and an air of good-natured, broad-minded tolerance have been combined to create that terribly misleading atmosphere of these places. If that word tolerance would only be eliminated from our language; if men would call looseness by its name; if women would recognize that, as never before, they are devoting themselves to the low art of sex appeal, your hundreds of tango teas, cabaret restaurants and dance halls would go out of business overnight.

"I suppose the people will call me a crank for saying all this. But they called Jesus a crank and they accused the apostles of being drunkards, and the Old Testament prophets were known as the pessimists of their time. New York wouldn't stop this side of Hell and damnation if someone didn't come here and shout a plain warning now and then. Not that the sermon is all for New Yorkers. I saw hard-shelled Baptists and shouting Methodists and persons of all sorts in those places who, I am sure, were not New Yorkers. There were plenty of them who would have made just as much noise hollering for the Lord in my tent as they did applauding and shouting in the dance halls. Back home hundreds of them, thousands I suppose, wouldn't dare do what they do here in New York, nor would they permit their children such indulgences.

"The older, downward paths were ugly and steep and hideous, but New York has constructed for itself a broad, sloping highway into Hell, built of a mosaic of drinks and dancing, and it is tangoing to the bottom just as fast and furiously as it can. Certainly the New Yorker is an artist at making vice simple, easy and attractively disguised. I'd like to see a million mothers and fathers in this town suddenly awaken to what is happening and drag their sons and daughters away from these shameless places. A good spanking would bring home to a lot of these youngsters how far they have one-stepped from the paths of maidenly modesty and youthful cleanliness. . . .

"Drink and dance; dance and drink. That's their merry round to the devil. I had rather have a young daughter of mine drink arsenic than cocktails. Any doctor and any man of the world knows that a cocktail pierces a woman's armour as nothing else can. The dance gives her the thirst, the drink robs her of her senses; and the tango tea has been carried out to its logical result. I'm a Southerner, born and bred, and my respect for real women is second to none, but I am bound to say the fault of this modern wickedness lies with the women, and it is upon the woman that the wrath of God is going to be visited. They wanted to peep over the fence and see how the men galloped about at liberty. They peeped, then they climbed to the top rail and learned to look unblinkingly at what they saw. Then they began vaulting over, and now they're leaping the barriers in droves. Social reforms they do advocate, but they have insisted upon paying the price of association on equal terms with men. Men welcomed them, of course. The grinning devil in all of us was quick to see his advantage. And that left man without anything to look up to except his God; and, alas, looking up to God is no longer a popular pastime."

An interesting editorial was written about the evangelist and the meeting; but because much of what was said appears in other articles, I shall not repeat. The editor referred to Dr. Bob as "one of the best known evangelists in the country" who had "conducted revival services in twenty-five states," and "in great demand as a preacher at summer Bible Conferences."

CHAPTER 3

Crawfordsville, Indiana, 1915

Crawfordsville was the home of General Lew Wallace, famous author of the novel *Ben Hur*. It was built on the banks of the beautiful Wabash River, was an agricultural center, and was known as the Athens of the Midwest. Wabash College was at its best in those days.

For a long time many evangelists—including Billy Sunday—avoided Indiana. It was considered a hard state for revivals. But Dr. Bob waded in and had wonderful success. Although the newspapers were quite lavish in their praise of the meetings, the best advertising was from the people on the streets. They would stop friends and say to them, "Have you heard Bob Jones? You must hear him; he is wonderful." One newspaper man was impressed with Dr. Bob's pungent and pithy sayings. "Why don't we call his statements JONES THUNDERBOLTS?" he suggested. Another man who was active in the campaign commented:

> This man Jones has made the headlines of the CRAWFORDSVILLE JOURNAL since he started the campaign. Never saw anything like these revival meetings. Business has really boomed since he came to town. All of Crawfordsville has turned out to hear him. Theatres are closed down; parades are being held in the streets for him. This revival business sounds like a pretty good thing. Come on, step on it! What are the THUNDERBOLTS to add for today?

Dr. Bob gave the people of Crawfordsville some of the straightest preaching they had ever heard. He said to them:

> Popularity is what got some of you church members off the track. No man gets into trouble unless he crosses the purpose of God. The freest man that walks the streets of Crawfordsville is the man that walks in fellowship with God. There is only one way out of sin and ruin and that is God's Way!

One newspaper headline—"WOMEN'S THOUGHTS HAVE GONE FROM THEIR HEADS TO THEIR FEET!"—enraged fashionable women. They said, "Fashions! Women can't do anything! Why doesn't he stick to preaching and quit meddling?" The good people of the town rallied to his defense, saying:

> We can't see that he is picking on anything that he shouldn't pick on. It is high time we got back to some old-fashioned notions about women and their place. Modest, sweet, keep the home fires burning. There's nothing worse than a bad woman! Her influence is extensive.

THE CRAWFORDSVILLE JOURNAL, Saturday, March 27, 1915, had these headlines: "SINS OF SCARLET CAN'T BE HID FROM EYES OF THE WORLD, SAYS EVANGELIST JONES." Feelings became intense, interest great, and Dr. Bob announced that he would preach his sermon "The Modern Women." (This sermon became noted as his sermon to Women Only.) The newspaper stated:

> It was a representative audience of Crawfordsville women and nearly every type and every grade of society was represented. The evangelist did not spare the knife and it was keen as a razor.

> Over 4,000 women gathered from the city and surrounding rural district heard an earnest opening invocation by the evangelist who thanked Almighty God for all good women in the world and their influence on the lives of men, and he prayed, too, for women with the stain of sin upon them.

> "Don't take offense at anything I may say when I hit you," said the evangelist, "for if you do, you are the one I am after. Somebody has said, 'The hand that rocks the cradle is the hand that rules the world.' If unholy hands rock the cradle, what else can you expect but an unholy world? Godless mothers mean a godless world."

Merchants closed their stores during the hours of the services. Later, they commented that after the Bob Jones' meeting bills were "easier to collect," for people had been "changed" during the meeting. Preachers reported that it was easier to get the people to attend church. The citizenry of Crawfordsville had never seen anything like this revival meeting; and they gladly took to the streets, telling about the wonderful results.

No matter how much people talked or how much coverage the newspapers gave, Dr. Bob never took anything for granted. He operated on the principle, *"Figure on the worst, and hope for the best."* The second week of a revival might show a let-down in attendance, he figured. To safeguard against this, he invited certain groups as special guests. Certain nights were set aside for particular groups or delegations, such as policemen, firemen, various fraternal organizations, delegations from the different churches, laboring men, boy scouts and girl scouts, YMCA and YWCA.

Dr. Bob was always popular with young people. It was a part of his ministry to speak at the high schools and colleges of the town in which he was holding a meeting. In many cities he helped the Christian people safeguard the youth of their town by fighting the liquor trusts. Having heard many sad stories of wrecked homes and suffering children, he became a valiant crusader against traffic in drink; and he gained the reputation of being one of the greatest fighters for prohibition in this country.

"MEMBERS LOCAL CLERGY DECLARE JONES A SUCCESS" was a headline in the CRAWFORDSVILLE JOURNAL. "Platform Methods Are Heartily Endorsed," was the subheadline. The Rev. R. E. Moss, pastor of the First Christian Church, said:

> Like the prophet Amos, he speaks forth a message red hot with stern rebuke of sin. He hates sin with all his intense nature. He is a Gatling gun with fast and furious fire, giving no one time or chance to dodge. He aims, shoots, and hits his mark. He is direct, simple, clear and full of force. I think the secret of his power and success is that he loves God and His Son Jesus Christ and wants his fellow man to see and enjoy the beauty of holiness.

The Rev. B. E. Antrobus, pastor of First Baptist Church, said:

> When off the job he is genial, approachable, and even childlike, possessing a rich fund of southern humor. On the job he is alert, fiery and fierce in the punishment of sin; witty, sarcastic, sometimes eloquent, but never weak. When he enters the building where he is to speak, he perceptibly stiffens with a fighting energy that manifests itself chiefly in his eyes.

Rev. N. P. France, pastor of the United Brethren Church, said in part:

> I heartily endorse his methods. Bob Jones always gives straight-from-the-shoulder talks and these practical messages won many prominent businessmen. A Bluffton pastor recently wrote, "The work still abides." Bob Jones is a man who has the courage to speak his convictions.

"Bob Jones has my most hearty endorsement," said Rev. C. B. Stanforth, pastor of Trinity M. E. Church. Pastor Stanforth also said:

> He exalts the word of God; he preaches the truth; he makes sin look sinful; he makes people feel the need of salvation; he makes church members feel the responsibility of their profession; he is using methods that God has blessed elsewhere. . . . I believe much and lasting good will be done in the Bob Jones meeting.

Rev. S. K. Piercy, First Presbyterian Church, stated:

The big thing about Bob Jones is his genuineness. He has been gripped by the great realities of God and life. He knows the world, its wickedness, its woe, and its wants; he knows also his Master, His righteousness, His grace, His love. Sure of his Christ, he is both strongly and sweetly sure of His saving message unto every man who will surrender. Hence comes Jones's courage and conviction and earnestness and eloquence and power.

The following is the quotation from Rev. Blaine E. Kirkpatrick, pastor of the First M. E. Church:

I regard Bob Jones as a prophet with a message from God to our city. His absolute genuineness and sincerity are beyond question. His ability as an evangelist is of the first order. . . . Like Sunday, Jones is cast in an intense mould, and is burning his life out in the fiery earnestness of his efforts to lead men and women to Jesus Christ. Like Sunday, he knows men and is an expert in creating the conditions for a genuine revival. Like Sunday, he gets results. He leaves behind him a trail of happy homes, regenerated lives, and transformed communities. . . . The actual results are at least as great as, if not greater than, Sunday's, when Sunday was working in cities of this size. But fortunately, Jones is a college man, and is free from much of the narrowness and intolerance which sometimes cause a difference of opinion in regard to Sunday's work. Bob Jones is not a copy of Billy Sunday. He is himself; but if his health can stand the strain, he will some day be as well known and accomplish as great results. . . . He deserves the unqualified endorsement and support of all who love the Lord Jesus Christ and are anxious for a revival of pure and undefiled religion.

Under headlines "BOB JONES SOUNDS WARNING IN EARS OF FOND PARENTS," a paragraph headed "No Trace of Fatigue" points out Dr. Bob's physical endurance:

Evangelist Jones throughout the night service threw himself into the soul-saving work with unusual vim. He showed not a trace of the exertions of the evening before. Those who have watched the man night after night marvel at his strength, his vitality, his courage — even when fields seem barren. His strength apparently exhausted at the close of the sermon, seemed to come to him renewed and freshened when the time arrived for the invitation. A new sparkle flashed to his eyes. His cheeks flushed with color. His voice, always big and strong, rose far above the voices of the choir. "Come on, boys, and . . . do it tonight, while you have the chance; come on and accept God tonight," he cried, with outstretched arms, and when a big fellow from the brickmakers' delegation came forward the evangelist's "Bless God for this man," could be heard far above anything else. . . .

In a regular column SAWDUST TRAIL, many quotations and interesting sidelights were mentioned. I quote from that column:

A Crawfordsville paper hanger and a carpenter met on the street the other day. "Pretty good season for our work," suggested the carpenter. "Fine," said the paper hanger, "only there can't be nothin' done till Bob Jones gets out of town. You can't find a woman at home long enough to get the measurements of her dining room."

Councilman Henry Schenck's latest observation: "I'm a frank man . . . and I like frankness in other people. I never beat about the bush in my life. That's why I like Bob Jones. If a fellow's got anything to say, I want him to spit it out. Jones certainly does that."

"This is a 'tabernacle' and not a 'taber-nickel,'" remarked Evangelist Jones, in urging his audience to average a contribution of fifty cents apiece, the other night.

Mr. Charles A. Casad, a wonderful newspaper man, described Dr. Bob thus:

Strenuous young man is Bob Jones, with great future. He's in *WHO'S WHO IN AMERICA* and in the hearts of men and women. He is no matinee idol but an every day man's man.

CHAPTER 4

Gloversville and Johnstown, New York, 1916

Mrs. Jones has told me about the wonderful results of this meeting; and from the coverage given by the press, I would say that it was outstanding. It seems that much of the paper for the entire time was given over to this campaign.

THE MORNING HERALD, Thursday, April 13, 1916, had large headlines: "BOB JONES LAUNCHES SAVAGE ATTACK AGAINST SALOONS AND LIQUOR TRAFFIC." Subheadings, also in very large letters, said: "Picturesque Description of the Saloonkeeper's Home Builded of Human Hearts and Filled With Music Ground by the Hand of Devil From Hell's Awful Organ." Charles A. Casad, Special Staff Reporter of the MORNING HERALD, explained:

> In a ringing discourse that bit and stung and fairly blistered where it hit, Evangelist Bob Jones, in the presence of an audience of between 3,000 and 4,000, last night launched into a savage attack on the saloon, and declared that the liquor traffic, lack of discipline in the home and a fading reverence for the Bible, are wrecking the American home.
>
> Dealing with the topic, "Some Problems of Home," Jones bitterly arraigned the saloonkeeper. His vehement assault was hurled forth with all the passion at his command and with the fearlessness of one who knows the ruin wrought by rum and isn't afraid to voice his views about it. The sermon was a blow at what people call "personal liberty," the evangelist declaring: "You say you have a right to do as you please? Yes, you have a right to do as you please and go to hell and be damned in eternity if you can do it singly and alone, but you can't do it."
>
> SALOONKEEPERS' HOMES BUILT OF HUMAN HEARTS. Jones declared that there "never was a baser lie hatched in hell," than that a man has a right to take a drink of whiskey if it pleases him to do so. After one fiery denunciation which stilled the audience into a dead silence, he burst forth with this picture of the home of a saloonkeeper: "He builds his home out of human hearts and uses life-blood for mortar. The plastering on his walls is made from the lining of human stomachs. In his shop of hell he hardens human brains out of which to make tile for his bathroom. The carpets on

his floors are the linings clipped from the coffins of the dead and woven into fabrics of blood. His window curtains are widows' weeds, colored by a demon brush, dipped into liquid fire. His home is lighted by the smile of a baby and the luster of a mother's eye, stolen by his own hands from his neighbors' homes. The flowers about the place are roses of beauty plucked from the cheeks of the innocent. His pleasure fountains are tears of woe distilled in the house of despair. The music by which he dances is the wail of the widow and the cry of the orphan ground by the hand of the devil from hell's awful organ, and every demon keeps step to the music."

GLOVERSVILLE HOMES BUILT OUT OF WHISKEY BUSINESS. Breathlessly the audience listened, too intent on the scathing, dramatic arraignment to applaud. Fairly hissing his words Jones went on:

"You have got saloon men in Gloversville who have built their homes out of the whiskey business and every time they step into their bathrooms they walk on the tiles built of human brains. I'd rather live in a cabin in a desolate swamp, than in a palace built of money out of the tears wrung from the orphans of this country. I'd become a 'highway robber' before I'd go into the liquor traffic and damn human lives."

It has been said that "one picture is worth a thousand words." The Morning Herald, Friday, April 14, 1916, carried a large cartoon that was a sermon in itself. Headed "GLOVERSVILLE, YOU'VE GOT TO HAVE A BATH" it shows Dr. Bob standing over a large bathtub. In his hand is a big scrub-brush with which he is scrubbing the people of Gloversville. The front page has half-inch letters stating: "BOB JONES GRABS GLOVERSVILLE SATAN BY THE NECK AND BREAKS ITS BACK." The subheading states: "Biggest Crowd of Week Hears Southern Evangelist Arraign Glove City Folks for Their Foibles and Dissipations and Alleged Low Grade of Morals." This article (also by Charles A. Casad, Special Staff Reporter) states:

An audience that packed the big Gospel Temple from stage to entrance, estimated anywhere from 4,000 to 5,000 people, listened to the story of "The Sins of Gloversville," from the lips of Evangelist Bob Jones last night, and after it had been pilloried and bruised and kicked until it was sore, went home and pinched itself to find out if it were really awake.

The evangelist's vicious arraignment of Glove City Folks, their foibles and dissipations, their shortcomings and their general low-grade of morals, so alleged, brought forth all the flaming verbal pyrotechnics for which Jones is famous. With supreme oratorical strength the evangelist grabbed the Gloversville satan by the neck, broke its back, strangled it and flung it into the discard. The whiskey traffic, Sabbath desecration, card playing among the "four hundred" and the modern dances, were shining marks for his bitter attacks. He rapped every evil and reprehensible thing that came within his vision. Modern dance steps like the tango, the hesitating waltz and about everything the Vernon Castles have sprung on society — the product of their artistic legs — came in for a share of the evangelist's rapid-fire ammunition.

Flaunts City's Sins in the Faces of its People. Jones prayed earnestly for strength to address the people, asking for divine guidance in presenting conditions and asked to be guided in speaking nothing but a great truth. He flung himself into his task with startling fury and warmed up to a white-heat as he went on. He flaunted the city's sins in the faces of its people. He worked himself up to a frenzy of passion until his strength was spent. His collar wilted. His eyes flashed as he denounced what he termed the evil and the vicious. He jumped on the city administration with both feet. He charged that a city official who did not enforce the law was either a thief or a perjurer. With it all was a wonderful exhibition of oratory.

Flings Wide Challenge to Disprove His Charges. The evangelist dared anybody to disprove the charges he made. "You young upstarts down there," he shouted. "You who have been going around this town sneering at Bob Jones and telling that I came here for graft—I fling this challenge into your faces: You look up my record and if you find one single thing against it, I'll give you every cent that we get in this town by what you call graft. Somebody said to me, 'Be careful, ain't you afraid you will go too far?' They said that to me once in a town and said I had better leave. Do you know what I told them? I said, 'I have a little son at home, and I'd rather that boy be left an orphan than ever have it said to him that his daddy ever left a city before he was ready.' I didn't go and I'm here tonight. Somebody said you might drum me out of town. You just remember that we church folks have got the drum."

THE MORNING HERALD, Saturday, April 15, 1916 carried the headlines: "BOB JONES DELIVERS BLUNT, FORCEFUL SERMON TO CHURCHMEN AT TABERNACLE." There was a large picture of Dr. Bob with his fist clinched and his arm raised. The caption reads, "Characteristic Pose of Bob Jones Declaring 'I've Got Lots More Respect for the Devil Than I Have for Some Church Members:'" Subheadings state: "Evangelist Rebukes Sham, Humbuggery and Dishonesty in the Church and Demands More Honesty in Business, Cleaner Politics and More Prayer in the Homes." Other headlines include:

"STIRRING EXAMPLE OF SOUL-SCORCHING ORATORY IN SERMON ON JUDGMENT DAY."

"BOB JONES CALLS ON GOSPEL HUSTLERS TO GO OUT AND BRING IN THE SINNERS."

"BOB JONES PAINTS VIVID WORD-PICTURE OF THE FIRES OF SIN THAT BURN THE SOUL."

"THE SOUTHERN EVANGELIST HOLDS GREAT AUDIENCE IN GRIP OF HIS MASTERLY ELOQUENCE AND BRINGS CROWD OF SLIDING SAINTS AND FLOUNDERING SINNERS DOWN THE TRAIL."

On the first altar call 330 people hit the "Sawdust Trail." Large headlines continued day after day throughout the entire meeting, but space will not permit use of all of them. Dr. Bob challenged the women to watch their influence. Headlines "BOB JONES MAKES SCATHING

SEE AND HEAR BOB JONES.

LOREN G. JONES
MUSICAL DIRECTOR.

The Bob Jones
Fighting
Face—

AN
USHER.

ATTACK ON BAD INFLUENCES EXERTED BY WOMEN," were subheaded, "In Words That Burned and Scorched to the Very Soul, Evangelist Vividly Compares the Women Who Take Men to Heaven with Those Who Drag Them Down to Depths of Hell." The article was accompanied by a full-length picture of Dr. Bob leaning forward. The caption was: "Bob Jones in Characteristic Pose Declaring: 'The Best Thing Out of Heaven is a Good Woman and the Worst Thing Out of Hell is a Mean One.'"

Dr. Bob did something in this campaign that he vowed never to do again, because it almost killed him.

I announced I would visit every shut-in and sick person in that town if they'd give me the names and addresses. A wealthy woman turned her chauffeur and her car over to me, and I started out. I didn't know that in a town the size of Gloversville, New York, there could be so many cripples and shut-ins. I went from home to home. I could write a volume about it. I never had such a blessing in my life.

I went into one home, and I saw a woman who was blind and kept her own house; and it was as nice as some houses I've seen that were kept by people with good eyes. Everything was so nice. I said, "Aren't you afraid you'll get burned when you cook your meals?" She said, "No, I'll tell you how it is, Brother Jones. The little children are so kind to me. They come in and make my fire. Some of them come in and watch me cook. You know, I'm a good cook." I said, "Well, everything looks nice." She said, "That's what they tell me." Then she led me over to the window and showed me a little box of flowers. I can see her now. Oh, her face was so lighted, and I was standing there crying as I thought about it. I said, "Don't you love flowers?" She said, "Oh, yes!" I kept talking to her, and finally I asked, "Why don't you go to the old women's home?" She answered, "I suppose I'll have to go when I get old, but my husband and I lived here many years, and I just don't want to give it up." I asked, "Don't you get lonely?" She answered, "In a way, I do. But Jesus is with me. I've learned to read a little with my fingers, you know, and I've got a Bible, and I've learned to read some of these verses from it." In my heart I said, "O Jesus, how good You've been to me!" This woman was alone. What an example of patience and grace!

I went to see a woman who had been bedridden for over sixty years. I'll never forget her as long as I live. I got down on my knees by her bed. She took my hand and cried. She told me how good Jesus had been to her and how she had been praying for me. She said, "I want you to pray for me." I said, "I'll try, but you had better pray for me." And I began to pray for myself and thanked God that I had met her.

There was a man in Gloversville named Alvah H. Rogers. He was an usher during the meeting, and he became very much interested in Dr. Bob and his ministry in their midst. Through Dr. Bob's faithful preaching, this man and his wife were drawn much closer to their Lord; and for many years they followed the work of this evangelist. They watched

the growth and development of the school he founded, and they decided to help the work by leaving the school in their wills. Upon the death of her husband, Mrs. Rogers notified Dr. Bob of their intention.

Dr. Bob answered Mrs. Rogers' letter on January, 1959:

I just want to tell you how much we appreciate your interest in Bob Jones University. I want you to know that under our by-laws and charter, it is mandatory that this school be carried on as it has been or it must be closed and the property sold and the money used for the direct spread of the Gospel to the ends of the earth.

I thank God for my son, Bob, Jr., who was just a very little boy when we were in Gloversville years ago. The Lord is using him, and he is just as uncompromising (or even more so) than I am.

The Lord has been so good to us. Our missionaries have gone to the ends of the earth. We have hundreds on many foreign fields. We have scattered over this country literally hundreds of preachers and school teachers and Christians in various other walks of life, and they are standing true.

I hope you will pray for us; and any money that you may leave the school will be spent carefully and prayerfully along the line of my own ministry for sixty-two years. . . .

In less than six months after the last will was made, Mrs. Rogers was called Home. The attorney who looked after the Rogers' affairs was a good Christian man. He and his wife had visited Bob Jones College and they knew first hand of the good work we were seeking to do. This attorney wrote us that Mrs. Rogers had left a substantial estate "estimated to have a gross value moderately above two hundred thousand dollars," but that benefits were not to accrue to the University until the death of Mrs. Rogers' son, Louis Schmitt, who was sixty-two years of age. The son was not well at the time of his mother's death, and he never really regained his health. Two years later we were notified of his death and told that we would soon receive the "approximately two hundred thousand dollars."

Dr. Bob appreciated this vote of confidence from the Lord with regard to the work here. He wrote attorney John D. Wood in Gloversville and said:

I just cannot tell you how this touches my heart. When I was in Gloversville, New York, years ago, I did not know the Lord was going to lead me to found a school; but He did. Through the years we have been clipping coupons from the old evangelistic days, and these coupons have helped us carry on this school.

When I get to Heaven, I am going to thank Mr. and Mrs. Rogers personally. I am thanking you now, and I am also thanking the Lord from the depth of my heart for all His wonderful blessings.

This is one of many incidents that I could cite with regard to God's providential care of Bob Jones University throughout the years. We have never sought money from rich people or from large foundations. We have no one in the field raising money. Dr. Bob always felt that the Lord wanted us to look to Him for our help. God has laid it on the hearts of certain saints from time to time to help us in big amounts; but most of our money has come from Christian men and women from all parts of the world — a dollar here, five dollars there, ten, or maybe twenty-five to a hundred and sometimes five hundred or a thousand. During the thirty-eight years I have had the privilege of being business manager of our school, I have never seen the barrel empty. God has supplied our every need.

One of Dr. Bob's best known remarks in the early days of the school was that "Bob Jones University has not been built with the gifts of millionaires, but with money from the corners of handkerchiefs which have been untied with the horny hands of women who manicured their fingernails on the washboards."

Dr. Bob proved God's promise: "But seek ye first the kingdom of God, and his righteousness; and all these things shall be added unto you" (Matthew 6:33).

I think that you will find this short article interesting:

The MORNING HERALD is carrying the news of the Bob Jones Tabernacle campaign to remote corners of the earth. Subscriptions have been received for persons living in England, Colombia, South America, and Hawaii. Papers are also being mailed daily to nearly every state in the union, to Canada, Alaska and Mexico. Many Gloversville people have sent in subscriptions for relatives in distant states and countries.

And how about this?

Evangelist Bob Jones invaded theatrical realms yesterday afternoon when he held a short service in the Darling theatre for the benefit of the stage folks attached to the different playhouses. . . . The service, held at 1 o'clock, was attended by a considerable number of actors, vaudeville performers and stage employees. Jones held the service at the invitation of some of the players who said they were interested but could not attend the Tabernacle.

The theatre folks sat in groups in the dimly lighted auditorium. Jones had the stage to himself. Mrs. Bob Jones sat in the audience. The evangelist wore a brown business suit and with a little stage paint might have easily passed for a matinee idol of the Dustan Farnum or Robert Hilliard type. Devoid of the artistic effects of the "make-up" box his face was rather pallid in the garish stagelight. The evangelist was genial and the audience forgave him for some of his hard raps at the theatre. He gave one of the short sermons on "What is a Christian?"

A group of girls from the "Fashion Revue of 1916" sat well down in front.

The stage paint was absent, the trailing silken finery they wear in the show was lacking. . . . The melody of "Jesus Included Me" sounded oddly when Choir-chief Jones led it . . . and the audience sang. Here and there a soprano voice, sweet and clear, rose above the rest. . . .

The evangelist did not try to stir up the emotions of the audience but preached a practical little sermon. . . . To make use of a Tabernacle expression, seven in the audience "hit the saw-dust trail." Of course, there was no "trail" of saw-dust—they just held up their hands and indicated that they wanted to accept Christ as a saviour. Six of them were women.

In 1966 ROAMIN' ROUND, Etaoin Shrdlu, reported:

Gloversville was in the midst of a spiritual revival to win converts to Christ during the Easter season 50 years ago.

Rev. Bob Jones, Southern evangelist, arrived in the Glove City the afternoon of April 8, 1916, to conduct a 6-week revival.

Crowds lined city streets to get a glimpse of the evangelist as his car proceeded along the route of a parade-of-cars to the Tabernacle on Temple Street, according to the MORNING HERALD issue of the next day.

Bells of 12 churches cooperating in the revival rung out a welcome to Rev. Jones.

Attendance totaled 175,700 for the services conducted during the revival, and there were 1,780 converts to Christ, the MORNING HERALD reported.

CHAPTER 5

Quincy, Illinois, 1916

A release from Quincy will give a sort of resumé of the life of the evangelist and of the meeting.

Face to face with Bob Jones, the stirring Southern evangelist, one is confronted by an athlete in stature. He weighs 202 pounds and stands 6 feet, one inch. He is brawn and muscle and life and vitality. His towering height, long legs and long reach, give him the appearance of a big fellow who is every inch a man.

Bob Jones, born and reared in Southeastern Alabama, might be termed a "self-made" man, since he has been fighting the battle for bread and the Gospel since he was fourteen years old. It is said of him that considering his age he has spoken to more men about their souls and swayed more hearts to Christ than any other man in America. He has had evangelistic campaigns in 25 states. His work in soul-winning has frequently taken him into New York City where his earnest, emphatic personality has readily taken hold of men's hearts.

. . . . . .

Bob Jones wields a quiet influence in Southeast Alabama where he was born. One of his remarkable experiences in Christian work was at Dothan, Alabama, his native town, when he went back there to conduct a campaign in 1908. On the ninth day of the meeting the city officials, several of whom had been converted, called a meeting of the City Council and closed the dispensary; and since that time, the town has been without intoxicating liquor. When a lad, Bob Jones sold vegetables in the streets of Dothan. Ten years afterward, he sat in his room across from the auditorium and watched thousands of people crowding in to hear him speak.

The evangelist's home is at Montgomery, Alabama, where he is popular and highly esteemed by the citizens. He says that the greatest single service he has ever conducted was in Montgomery, where an audience of several thousand men gathered to hear his noted sermon on "The Sins of Men." In the midst of the service, the whole audience stood up, fired with enthusiasm, and when he appealed to men to live right, two thousand started with a rush to the stage to shake hands with him.

Jones, as his intimates say of him, sticks to the old-time uncompromising Gospel with the blood of Calvary held up as the only remedy for sin. He cannot be classed among the type of sensational evangelists, although he has a way of hitting hard from the shoulder, and he does not grope about for polished expressions in telling people of their sins. His short, crisp epigrams are telling and original and to the point. Mr. Jones admits that he is much of a "man's man," and a majority of his converts are men. It is the men he is after, and it is said that he gets them. His attractive personality, strong, cleancut features, and deep manly voice, seem to catch the fancy of his audiences and holds them spellbound. While he says many things that cut and sting, his language is never coarse. He indulges very little in the slang of the street.

The evangelist has a charming wife who is thoroughly in sympathy with his work and a little boy of four years, Bob, Jr. The acquaintance which led to his marriage to a beautiful Southern girl took place while Jones was conducting a revival at Uniontown, Alabama. The young woman, who afterward became Mrs. Bob Jones, was a member of an Alabama family of social distinction. She became interested in the campaign, was converted by the evangelist, and at once became his ardent co-worker.

Mr. Jones has been singularly successful in his evangelistic work since he has been conducting his campaigns on the larger plan. In the last two years he has made thousands of converts in the Middle West. Last year his work took him as far West as Joplin, Missouri, and as far East as Gloversville, New York, closing the year in New York City.

Life Threatened

Mrs. Jones relates the following incident:

I will never forget the Quincy meeting. While we were there, my husband's life was threatened. I can remember it as if it were yesterday. We had set up housekeeping, and our colored maid, Emma, was with us to help with the care of our small son. One afternoon we heard a knock on the front door. Emma answered the knock and ushered three men into the parlor. As soon as they were seated, the men said, "We hate to be the bearers of bad news, but you need to know something that we have just heard. Dr. Bob has preached hard in his effort to clean up the town, and he has stepped on the toes of the bootleggers and the liquor trust. They have declared that they will kill him sometime during the evening service. They will turn out the lights. Then during the commotion, Bob will be killed."

Naturally this worried my husband. But that night he was at the Tabernacle earlier than usual. He could not wait to get the service under way. He knew that he had to put over his message as never before. Shortly after he began his sermon he said, "I understand that some of you men have come here tonight to kill me. You are not fools; you know that you cannot get away with it. Even if you get me out of the way, another evangelist will come in tomorrow to carry on the work that I have started. I came here to straighten out the bad elements and to help clean up this town."

Dr. Bob's straightforwardness and his dynamic preaching soon had the crowd in such good humor that no one dared to leave his seat. This servant of the Lord had not sold out. He had not run. When the altar call was given, God touched the hearts of the people, and many were saved. This service was one of the greatest of the entire campaign.

CHAPTER 6

Zanesville, Ohio, 1917

Dr. Bob was never a man to think of self and what he could get out of something. Several times during his evangelistic days big towns would try to get him to cancel a meeting in a small town so that they might have him first. But he never sold out! God honored his willingness to go wherever he felt the Lord wanted him.

A committee from a certain large town wrote Dr. Bob and offered "the largest offering you have ever had and will see to it that you have the biggest meeting you have ever held if you will come here on a certain date." (This is not the only time such an incident occurred.) Dr. Bob declined the invitation because he had already accepted a meeting in the small town of Zanesville, Ohio. This little town of 22,000 could not plan on anything very big; but because Dr. Bob followed God's leadership and did not compromise or sell out, the Zanesville meeting turned out to be one of his greatest meetings. There were 3,284 converts; 2,200 joined churches on Easter Sunday alone. One-inch headlines on the front page of the paper stated: "BOB JONES CAMPAIGN CLOSES WITH 3,284 CONVERTS." Another headline gave "JONES CAMPAIGN IN A NUTSHELL." The following facts were given:

Started February 18; Ended April 1. Number of addresses by Bob Jones, 102. Total people addressed, 266,000. Participating churches, 17. Expense fund of campaign, $5,500. Signers of convert cards, 3,284. Free-will offerings to Mr. Jones, $6,000.00. Attendance closing day, 18,000.

During the time of this meeting, a man went into a saloon and said, "Give me a drink of whiskey. I'm shot to pieces. I've got one dime; give me all you can give me for it." He tried to drink the liquor but his hands shook so that he could hardly hold the glass. The bartender said: "Why don't you go up to Bob Jones' tabernacle — Bob Jones' mint where he's holding that meeting! Why don't you go up there and get religion? Bob

Jones will take your dime! They're running it for money; go on up there and give it!" The man took the glass of liquor and threw it in the bartender's face. Then he said: "My wife is an invalid—dying because I'm a drunkard. But when you talk about religion, you're talking about something my mother had. I'm no good; I'm a miserable, dirty, drunken bum—I know it—and ruined—gave you my last dime this morning because I couldn't help myself. But before I get out of this place, I'm going to do one thing decent. I'm going to beat the devil out of you!" He climbed over the bar, took that hog-jowled bartender, dragged him out from behind the bar, and beat the fire out of him!

When Dr. Bob heard of the incident, he remarked, "That's a man after my own heart!" He sent for the bum and said to him, "Buddy, I sympathize with weak men. I could have been a drunkard; anybody could be a drunkard. You just went off on the wrong foot. But there's something in you. I want you to get right." The drunkard was converted. Later, the converted man said to Dr. Bob, "I could make you some money. If you will let me have a picture of you, I will make some postcard photos and sell them to the six thousand people who come to the tabernacle at night. Then I can get a doctor for my wife and get her to the hospital." Dr. Bob explained that he had never had his picture "peddled around." But the man argued, "These are exceptional circumstances." Finally, Dr. Bob agreed to the proposition, and the man had thousands of pictures made. Outside the tabernacle each evening the converted drunkard gave his testimony and sold the postcards. The five or six thousand dollars he cleared made it possible for him to get his wife into a hospital. "That guy had a weakness," Dr. Bob said, "but there was something in his character—a memory of his mother—something in that poor, drunken, wrecked life—something still left in the depths of him! There was something about his mother's religion that was sacred to him."

At the end of the meeting the newspaper headlines read, "JONES PARTY GOES FROM HERE TO GRAND RAPIDS, MICHIGAN" and "EVANGELIST AND PARTY BID FAREWELL TO CITY AFTER SIX-WEEKS' WORK." One article stated:

> While Zanesville ministers are enthusiastically endorsing the Jones meetings as successful beyond their expectations, the evangelist himself is thoroughly pleased with his campaign here, and late last night proclaimed it far ahead of any meeting he ever conducted in the North, and everything considered, the best meeting he ever had. Bob Jones and every member of his party were cheered to the echo during the closing service Sunday evening when Reverend K. B. Alexander read a resolution endorsing the work of each member. Bob Jones gave a few suggestions for continuing the work now under way and retired from the platform amid a volley of cheers."

Another article thanked the TIMES RECORDER for its work in the revival and stated, in part:

> Reverend H. E. Porter, pastor of the Brighton Presbyterian Church, president of the Zanesville Ministerial Association, and Chairman of the Ministerial committee in charge of the Bob Jones evangelistic campaign which came to a close Sunday night, commented, "The revival was the greatest thing that ever happened in Zanesville. . . . The evangelist spoke to about 7,000 people each day, and your paper bore his message to many times that number. I thank you, and the ministers associated with the revival have thanked you in resolutions they adopted." Reverend Mr. Porter said of the evangelist Jones: "I regard him as, next to Billy Sunday, the greatest man now engaged in evangelistic work. He is a man of wonderful power. He not only preaches, but he lives his religion."

"LAST SERVICE BY BOB JONES IS SORROWFUL" was subheaded on the front page by "Many Eyes Dimmed by Tears When Evangelist Said Goodbye." The article went on to say:

> Bob Jones' evangelistic campaign is now a thing of the past, but Sunday, the closing day, will ever remain afresh in happy memory to the church folks of Zanesville. No such demonstration was ever before held here, no religious effort was ever so richly productive of fruit and no party of workers was ever so enthusiastically received as was the Jones party during their six-weeks' sojourn here. Sunday services from the moment the doors were thrown open in the morning until the last door was locked at night, were revelations. Bob preached three eloquent sermons.

Still another article explained:

> Thousands took a stand for Christ, and thousands of others reconsecrated themselves to His work. And the influence of the meetings will not stop there. It will reach out in all directions through these people to other thousands. In short, the Bob Jones evangelistic meetings will mark a renaissance of religion in Zanesville.

> The TIMES RECORDER is highly gratified that it has been able to be a factor to a certain extent in the success of the revival. Through its own staff, which has always been able to meet the demands of any emergency, the TIMES RECORDER conscientiously directed its best efforts toward disseminating the news of the meetings throughout Southeastern Ohio. . . .

> The TIMES RECORDER has been commended again and again for these efforts. Our position before, during and since the meetings, has been that they constituted a great news item, and we sought to treat them accordingly.

The last headlines said: "S'LONG, BOB!" Then the reporter added:

> The train's called! It's time to say Good Bye, Bob! You came a stranger

among strangers, and you leave a friend among friends. We wish you well, Bob, in your next campaign—and the next—and the next!

You're taking the blessings of thousands and thousands with you, Bob, Ol' Man—and you've earned 'em. Good Bye.

And Mrs. Bob, and others of the team, s'long! The old town'll miss you mightily, folks! The tabernacle is just an empty shell . . . but it's filled with pleasant memories. . . .

In the early '60's a friend brought a couple to visit Bob Jones University. These visitors had the noon meal with my family in the Dining Common. During the meal they spoke of Dr. Bob's Zanesville meeting. They had remembered the campaign and the results all these years, and they said that the people of Zanesville still talk about the meeting. It was thrilling to find that the wife was one of the converts of that meeting.

On March 13, 1960, *forty-three years after the campaign,* there appeared in the Sunday issue of the TIMES RECORDER, a large write up, citing many interesting events of this great meeting. The article covered five columns with bold headlines saying, "TABERNACLE CONSTRUCTED HERE IN 1917 FOR REVIVAL MEETINGS." The story was written by Norris F. Schneider under the caption, "Bob Jones Served as Evangelist."

Evangelist Bob Jones in the spring of 1917 persuaded hundreds of converts to walk down the sawdust trail to the altar in his tabernacle on the old Hook-Aston Mill site north of the White Chevrolet Company, now the home of the Commercial Motor Freight truck terminal. Dr. Jones, Founder and now president of the Board of Bob Jones University at Greenville, S. C., says that he considers the Zanesville campaign "one of his best revival meetings."

. . . . . .

Chairman C. H. Denny of the building committee announced on January 22 that work would be started on construction of a tabernacle 120 feet wide and 178 feet long with seats for 5,000 people. The board walls and roof were covered with heavy paper to insure warmth and to keep out rain. Sixteen coal burners heated the structure and it was lighted by electricity.

An apartment on the main floor of the Montana apartments on South Sixth street was rented for Evangelist Jones, his wife, his five-year-old son and his housekeeper. Twenty carpenters were employed to build the tabernacle. January 31 was Ministers' Day. "Togged in overalls, rubber boots and slouch hats," fourteen ministers jumped into one of the hardest day's work they have done in a long time.

Workers of the seventeen participating Zanesville churches made rapid progress in preparing for the services. Because the evangelist could not stand babies crying while he spoke, the authorities named a revival Supervisor of babies to keep children in a nursery on West Main Street. Dr. Bob loves babies and adores children . . . but Dr. Bob has always felt that babies in a service tended to distract the people from the message of the Lord. C. M. Mock enlisted 600 singers to occupy the stage on the west end of the tabernacle. E. H. Perry was in charge of 50 ushers. Two cinder walks were laid from West Main Street and lighted with electric bulbs. A ton and a quarter of coal per day was burned in the 16 stoves to take the frost out of the ground and warm the building. Total cost of the structure was $4,700.00.

Three hundred men, women, and children attended a sawdust party at the completed tabernacle on the night of February 15. They scattered sawdust and shavings on the floor and decorated the building with flags and bunting. Bob Jones arrived in Zanesville on Saturday, February 17. Three services opened the campaign on Sunday. At 10 a. m. Sunday school pupils marched to the tabernacle for a meeting. Rev. Jones addressed crowds at 2:30 and 7:30 p. m. at the rate of 175 words a minute.

The TIMES RECORDER quoted some of Bob Jones' "rifle shots" of the first day as follows:

"You have got to put away sin. This campaign is going to run a knife through some of you." "Many a woman has an old man around with only a heartbeat between him and hell." "Some women give more attention to their hair than they do to their souls."

Jones announced that the expenses would be about $5,000.00. Nearly $1,000.00 was offered the first day.

The evangelist refused to tolerate distractions. He demanded that women remove their hats while he preached. "If you must cough," he said, "stop up your mouth with a handkerchief; that way you will annoy only about 12 or 15."

The TIMES RECORDER reporter said:

There had been a grand chorus from a tickle to a giant whoop until he told 'em the tabernacle was no place for coughing.

Monday night Bob had a "test meeting" to see whether the preparations were successful. In spite of bad weather about 2,500 heard Jones preach on "Prayer." Trainmaster Earl Painter placed extra street cars in service to Putnam, Linden avenue and the Terrace.

On Thursday, February 22, Bob addressed a capacity audience of 5,000 on "The Sins of Zanesville." He said: "You've got low church standards. Your prayer meetings are deserted. You pay starvation wages and you grind the life out of your workers while you get rich and choke the spiritual life out of them. You chase the silver dollar to Hell and jump in after it. Your merchants are afraid of saying anything against the saloon for fear of losing a dollar."

In emphasizing these statements, Bob pounded the altar so hard he broke it. The custodian replaced the broken top with a thicker board and a pad.

There were noon shop meetings, meetings with the high school students, and women's meetings.

When the revival ended on April 1, more than 3,000 had surrendered. A crowd of converts and ministers gathered at the B. and O. depot to bid goodbye to Bob Jones. All agreed to carry on his work. J. T. Miller treasured the New Testament bearing scratches and dents from Jones' emphatic pounding on the pulpit.

CHAPTER 7

Grand Rapids, Michigan, 1917

Grand Rapids, Michigan, started a selling campaign by running several articles on the proposed meeting:

GRAND RAPIDS IS AFTER BOB JONES FOR APRIL REVIVAL

He may come here next April to give Grand Rapids some dynamic evangelism.

"BETTER THAN I AM" IS BILLY SUNDAY'S ESTIMATE

Declared to be second only to that of Billy Sunday. Indeed, Billy Sunday when here recently, endorsed "Bob" Jones in such enthusiastic terms as to convince the Grand Rapids Ministerial conference that no mistake could be made in securing "Bob" Jones for a big, soul-saving campaign.

Groups were sent to visit other Bob Jones' meetings to persuade him to come to Grand Rapids as soon as possible.

MINISTERIAL COMMITTEE LEAVES FOR QUINCY, ILLINOIS, TO CONFER WITH EVANGELIST

Last night at midnight, a committee of five clergymen left Grand Rapids on their way to Quincy, Illinois, where Jones has been holding a revival. E. J. Sharpe, Religious Secretary of the YMCA, left here Wednesday morning, as the advance agent of the committee. Mr. Sharpe's purpose in going ahead of the committee was to confer with the business and professional men, bankers and manufacturers of Quincy about the results of the revival just closing in that city. When the committee arrives, they will have the benefit of reliable opinions regarding the effectiveness of the "Bob Jones evangelism," and be prepared to meet the evangelist.

Who is "Bob" Jones? He is a typical Southerner of the explosive sort, whose explosions have saved souls.

His personality is said to be magnetic—appealing, where appeals are needed, and convincing to the doubters. That is why "Bob" Jones is a successful evangelist. And that is why he is wanted in Grand Rapids.

It was later reported of Dr. Bob:

"GOES BIG" IN QUINCY

If anything should be required to convince Grand Rapids that "Bob Jones is the right man to bring here, the spiritual upheaval in Quincy, Illinois, leaves little, if anything, lacking that is convincing.

Quincy, it is declared, had a reputation for wickedness. "Bob" Jones invaded the town, and the result of his revival is declared to have wrought wonders in bringing men to see the errors of their ways—and hundreds of conversions have been obtained. "Bob" Jones struck Quincy like a bombshell, and immediately the city became inflamed with religious enthusiasm.

SIX WEEKS' REVIVAL CLOSED IN ZANESVILLE, OHIO

From the beginning until the close, the large tabernacle did not accommodate the throngs, and it was necessary to use the nearby churches for the overflow. It was the greatest religious demonstration Southern Ohio has ever witnessed. During the revival, the evangelist brought about the conversion of almost 4,000 persons. . . . A men's League of one hundred members, organized, will look after the cleaning up of Zanesville, and there is no doubt in the minds of the people but that the city will be voted dry at the fall election. One man is declared to have said that after the "Bob" Jones campaign his beer receipts fell off fifty per cent. Attendance during the day reached 20,000, and the churches will receive at least 3,500 new members.

Finally, it was reported:

THE GRAND RAPIDS MINISTERIAL CONFERENCE HAS BEEN INFORMED OF THE SPLENDID ACCOMPLISHMENTS OF JONES IN QUINCY

Fortified by the endorsement of Billy Sunday, a committee has been dispatched to secure Jones for Grand Rapids, if possible.

The committee is expected to return to Grand Rapids Saturday afternoon, and should their report be favorable, preparations will at once be made to give Grand Rapids the greatest evangelistic revival in its history.

This prophecy was fulfilled beyond everyone's fondest dreams. There was a great parade to welcome Dr. Bob, and a reporter wrote:

The evangelist arrived on Saturday and was tendered a cordial reception. Probably one thousand people, largely representing the church element of Grand Rapids, crowded into the waiting rooms and train sheds to extend the glad hand to Bob and his family. Among those on hand to extend a welcome were the Reverend J. C. Willets, Chairman of the local evangelistic committee; Dr. Oliver W. Van Osdel, Vice-Chairman; E. J. Sharpe, Secretary; and G. L. Daane, Treasurer.

The civic side of the city was represented by Mayor Tilma, Chief of Police Carroll, and other members of the city's official family. Mel Trotter, the noted Rescue Mission worker, his round, genial face wreathed in smiles, threw his arms about the evangelist the instant he alighted from the pullman. "Bob, old Bob, I'm glad to see you," exclaimed Trotter, and he meant it. A moment later, when he presented Bob to Sam Slater of the City Detective Department, he slapped both of them on the back as he remarked: "Here's Bob Jones, and he's our kind of a fellow," which was one of the highest compliments Trotter could pay the evangelist. Automobiles were in waiting for the party and prominent citizens of Grand Rapids, and headed by the East End Improvement Association Brass Band, which combined hymns with patriotic airs, the procession marched to the tabernacle, where several hundred people took part in a short welcome service, presided over by Mayor Tilma. More than ten thousand crowded the sidewalks during the parade, cheering the evangelist, who quietly raised his hat.

"This tabernacle," said the Mayor, "has been dedicated to the services of the Most High. Sometime, I realize, this earthly tabernacle will be pulled down, but I hope that other tabernacles will be builded here by the Lord God Almighty, through His servant, that will stand through time and eternity. I feel that what is done here in the next weeks will be lasting."

He then officially extended the city's welcome to the evangelist and presented him to the audience, which gave him a great ovation.

Bob smilingly said the mayor had really preached a good sermon. "I want to say that if the mayor would preach that kind of stuff throughout this city, he would have a revival that would reach all Michigan." The evangelist said that the great problem in Gospel work today is to convict men and women of sin. He said he had seen more real conviction in Zanesville, Ohio, in six weeks than he had seen in ten years.

"I am going to tell you Grand Rapids folks what I am not here to do," he continued. "I am not going to tell your pastors how to run their churches . . . , your merchants how to run their stores, nor your doctors how to practice medicine, but I'm going to show you men and women how to find God. I'm going to do and say things you won't like, but I know we all stand together on the fundamentals of the Bible.

"Just as we are mobilizing our forces in this country for a great war, I want you Christian people to come together as never before. This is a time when Christian people need to get on their knees before God. We bow our faces in the presence of the Stars and Stripes, but bless God there is another flag, THE BANNER OF THE CROSS, and we don't want any deserters."

The first headlines of the meeting read: "MONTGOMERY EVANGELIST IS HEARD BY OVER 15,000 PEOPLE IN OPENING SERVICE." The next day large headlines stated:

30,000 HEAR BOB JONES IN GRAND RAPIDS

The tabernacle built for the revival was too small, and 3,000 were turned away the first day. When Bob gave his first call for converts on Sunday, 568 marched down the sawdust trail, a large majority of whom had never made a profession of faith.

Under headlines, such as "CHRISTIANITY IN SOAP AND RAGS, SAYS BOB" and "JONES SLAMS BOLT AT SHAM CHURCH GOERS," excerpts of the sermons were given. Dr. Bob said that "most Christians are like matches—they strike only on their own box." He went on to defend revival meetings: "They are good for what ails you. A good revival will build up a church, no matter what its condition; a good revival will build up politics; a good revival can correct the crookedness in a city; a good revival can build up business. If we could have the right kind of revival, we could solve every problem."

Following the second Sunday of the meeting, large headlines said, "CROSS DODGING IS POPULAR SIN, SAYS BOB JONES" and "HUNDREDS HIT TRAIL AT CALL OF EVANGELIST." The report stated:

A total of 538 came forward. In three forceful sermons during the day, the big, hard-hitting preacher drove home a message and a summons that could not be resisted by the hundreds who responded to give their hearts to God. There was a wave of exultation throughout the tabernacle; some wept, others shouted for joy; women led their husbands down the trail, while some men led their wives to answer the call. Mothers, with tears streaming down their faces, took their sons and daughters down the trail; children gave themselves willingly and hundreds made new resolutions of faith.

So great was this revival that Grand Rapids closed the schools early in order that the children might attend special sessions for them at 3:00 p. m. City officials, businessmen, school officials, and teachers streamed into the tabernacle to hear this wonderful preacher. On Sunday they had a Sunday School parade in which more than 2,500 marched, carrying banners and flags and big placards, and keeping step behind the large brass band. There was much enthusiasm, and 10,000 were packed into the tabernacle.

One sermon that caused much comment had as its theme "the poor, miserable, sleeping, snoring, sluggardly sinners, of whom there are thousands in Grand Rapids." Reporters wrote:

The rain beat down upon the roof so hard the evangelist had to get louder and louder, but it did not dampen the ardor of the evangelist. In fact he put on more steam and added more ginger to his verbal opinion of those who nap at the spiritual switch.

At the end of the week, this article appeared:

The sawdust trail has been crowded every night with those turned to Bob's way of thinking by his forceful control of the English language and his happy faculty of expressing truths in a peculiarly effective manner. Last night he spoke on the subject

"AWAKENING IS COMING"

Bob said that there are thousands of sinners sleeping right now on the brink of Hell, and if they are not careful they are going to turn over and tumble in. "And then," the evangelist shouted, "they will wake up!" He then lit into the preachers who preached nothing but "lay me down to sleep sermons." "Sleeping man, wake up! That's my job. To awaken you and then to get you up. When a preacher preaches a sermon to you and it makes you comfortable, he's not a good preacher. A sermon ought to be like a surgical operation. No one should enjoy it, save the doctors and nurses. The man undergoing the operation won't enjoy it. His family and friends won't like it, but the good that is accomplished is the reward. If I haven't made you flinch, I am a poor preacher.

"One way to get along with the devil is to let him alone. If you back him into a corner and then begin to punch him and stick forks into him, you are going to have your hands full. You are going to find a devil incarnate. My business here is to make him uncomfortable, to make him flinch. Sinners, wake up before it is too late!

"The prodigal saw himself and God Almighty will never take the chains off you 'til you look up in His face and tell Him you are a lost sinner. Crying is not religion — if it is, my baby used to get religion about 12:00 every night. If crying is a religion, I know an old drunkard in Alabama that will have a front seat in Heaven. Folks think they are good because they can cry. Women go to funerals and weddings and cry, and why a woman should cry at a wedding I don't understand. Some of the meanest women who ever lived have been crying women. I have known some men to literally sob themselves to Hell. You can weep your way to the bottomless pit. No, it's all right to cry, and I thank God I have been able to shed some tears to bear my sorrows. I'm sorry for the man who can't cry, but there is no Christianity in tears.

"The prodigal said, 'I'm going home!' and when you see sin like that boy did, you'll go home. You say, 'Well, but the father of the prodigal was waiting to welcome him.' Yes, that's true, and God the Father is waiting to extend the same welcome to you."

At the close of this meeting, large headlines stated, "CHURCHES HAVE BEEN TAKEN OUT OF RUT BY BOB JONES' CAMPAIGN, SAYS REV. WILLETS," and in a box was the following:

DO REVIVALS PAY?

Over 5,000 converts were made during Bob Jones evangelistic campaign which closed Sunday. They cover the entire range of social condition. Hundreds have already become affiliated with churches. . . . Hundreds of others expressed no denominational preference. The Rev. John C. Willets of the First M. E. Church said of the revival: "Mr. Jones worked against tremendous odds in a community that is surfeited with an easy-going religious life and lack of positive religious experience. No community can pass through a series of revival meetings of six weeks' duration with a sane and fruitful presentation of the Gospel and not be greatly benefited."

Mr. Willets went on to tell of a meeting in Aurora, Illinois, where Dr. Jones preached, where one of the most notorious saloonkeepers of the city heard one of his sermons, "hit the trail," went back and closed up his saloon, and now occupies a pew in one of the churches. Mr. Willets ended by saying, "I know that revivals pay."

Grand Rapids Echoes

THE GRAND RAPIDS HERALD, October 3, 1937, had this headline: "WORLD NEEDS A RETURN TO GOD, ASSERTS BOB JONES, BACK IN G. R. AFTER TWENTY YRS." The article said, in part:

Twenty years ago Grand Rapids had a revival with capital letters – in the spring, just after the United States had entered the World war, and emotion, religious and patriotic, ran high. Hundreds of people jammed a specially erected tabernacle down on the Island night after night, and for six weeks the crowds continued and the nightly processions to the altar.

The revivalist was Bob Jones, a thirty-three-year-old southern evangelist, who'd already been preaching then more than half of his lifetime. . . .

What the country needs today, he holds, is just one thing, "a return to God."

Ethics and educational philosophy, he says, have gone astray following the satanic principle of "do as you please" instead of the Christian discipline of self-denial. Lawlessness at home and communism abroad, he thinks, both stem from this educational error.

CHAPTER 8

Columbus, Ohio, 1919

It took many months for this city to find a time that would fit into Dr. Bob's busy schedule. Finally they agreed upon the month of July. The fame of the evangelist preceded him, and he was received with open arms. By the time the meeting was really underway, the people had fallen in love with this man of God. Although they had not been accustomed to his type of straight preaching, they respected him for it. One of the earliest newspaper reports of the services stated:

ANOTHER COLUMBUS DISTINCTION

Bob Jones says that Columbus is the coldest, most unresponsive place he has yet struck this season. He has been to quite a number of cities in recent months and has opportunity to compare the state of religious fervor in various places, and so he is in position to pass expert testimony on this particular matter.

Mobile, Alabama, by the way, seemed to catch the fancy of the Bob Jones party. They came to Columbus from Mobile and must have had a wonderful experience in the Alabama seaport city.

Mr. Jones made a plea in his sermon Sunday night for a more thorough cooperation on the part of the church people. As a matter of fact, he is having very large audiences — some of them tremendous audiences, and the responses seem to the writer above the average of Columbus revival meetings.

Columbus people were enthralled with a sermon that Dr. Bob preached on "Daniel in the Lions' Den." The newspaper said:

Bob Jones supplied some further details (hitherto unpublished) Sunday evening relative to the experiences of Daniel in the lions' den. Of course, his elaboration of the occurrence was fanciful, but such a framework could well be constructed from the short, simple, and direct account of the occurrence that comes down to us.

The old lion, according to the evangelist, was pretty hungry. When he saw Daniel coming in, the situation looked distinctly promising to him. But a change came over the spirit of his dreams, and he did not proceed to sup.

"What's the matter? Ain't you going to eat me?" Daniel asked the lion, according to Mr. Jones' somewhat more detailed description of the incident. "I thought I was hungry," said the lion, "but I have lost my appetite."

"Daniel turned around," said Mr. Jones, "and there was an angel by his side to guard him. The angel said: 'Daniel, you have been on a strain and are tired; why don't you lie down and take a nap?' Daniel said that he didn't see a pillow. 'Lie down, old lion,' the angel said, and the lion lay down. 'Stretch out,' said the angel, and Daniel lay down, with the lion's neck for a cushion, and dreamed of golden streets, and the angels playing on golden harps in the Heavenly city."

The papers reported a fine response and went on to say, "By the way, Mr. Jones must feel better after last night's service—he certainly had the response there. The audience was in a sympathetic mood." The article gave a synopsis of Dr. Bob's life, stating that he was thirty-four years of age and that "he looks like a certain lumber manufacturer in Jacksonville and a certain hotel clerk in Atlanta. He has a face like one and a voice like the other. The lumberman is, as the boys would say, a cutter; and the hotel clerk is the nicest, politest man you ever saw and in his friendly, agreeable way can sell you a $3.00 room when you vowed privately beforehand that you wouldn't take anything over $1.50."

"OLD-TIME METHODISM VOICED IN BIG TENT"

were the next day's headlines. Subheadings read, "The Church Was Born in Revival, and Evangelist Jones Stirs the Revival Spirit."

Reverend Jones, familiarly known as "Bob," one of the most popular evangelists of the country, is holding services during the present week in the Big Tent. This is in line with the avowed purpose of the Centennial celebration to represent all the manifold activities of Methodism for the past century. Of these, evangelism plays no small part.

Methodism was born in a revival. It was when John Wesley's heart was "strangely warmed" that the great modern evangel began; and all along, it has been the glory of Methodism to keep the heart fires burning.

In an interesting interview, Mr. Jones said that there was never a time when, in his judgment, a revival was more needed than now. Most preachers feel this need, and the people are responding to conviction as never before. This, he said, was due to the great missionary spirit that is sweeping over the country.

On the last day of Dr. Jones' stay in Columbus, the papers carried a large picture of him with an accompanying brief synopsis of his past history. The following special statement was made by the official committee that had invited Dr. Bob:

COMMITTEE EXPRESSES HIGH APPRECIATION OF ALABAMA EVANGELIST

The committee . . . desires to give public testimony to its very high appreciation of the service which has been rendered by Reverend Bob Jones. He has preached night after night for two weeks with great effectiveness *without any charge* whatever for his services [italics mine — R.K.J.]. The committee believes that in this expression it fully voices the sentiments of those who have been worshiping from night to night under the Big Tent. He will carry with him the best wishes and the prayers of thousands of hearers who have been profited by his message.

This article was signed by every member of the committee and dated July 14, 1919.

Dr. Bob's desire was to serve his Master in every way that he could, with no thought of personal gain. The world will never know the many sacrifices he made in his effort to help promote the Cause of the Lord. Many times he gave his services without remuneration, paying not only his own expenses but also the expenses of his entire organization.

CHAPTER 9

Winona Lake, Indiana, 1920

Before World War I, Dr. Bob was the President of the Association of Evangelists, meeting annually at Winona Lake. They had a membership of more than a thousand. He and Dr. W. E. Biederwolf—considered to be the most intellectual of all the evangelists—introduced a resolution to back "to the hilt" the eternal essentials of the Faith. Dr. Biederwolf made the motion; and Dr. Bob, president, with the help of the others, put into effect in those early years a resolution that they would not knowingly go out under the sponsorship of modernists. The resolution was passed without a dissenting vote.

Sunday, August 29, 1920, was one of the greatest of all days for the Winona Conference. Outstanding men of that day gathered for a meeting that made history. Among the men were William Jennings Bryan, Billy Sunday, and W. E. Biederwolf. Madame Schumann Heink had come from New York to sing *without charge*. Professor E. O. Excell of Chicago led the choir of six hundred voices, which included one hundred and fifty of the leading evangelistic singers. What an occasion!

William Jennings Bryan, president-elect, made the main talk of the morning and was delighted to be able to assist his young friend Bob Jones in his service in the afternoon. Bob was at his best, and God blessed the service.

CHAPTER 10

Abbeville and Ozark, Alabama, 1908

Two outstanding experiences that thrilled the evangelist's heart and soul occurred in Southeast Alabama, the territory of his birth and childhood. That these experiences followed each other adds to their interest. They would not be repeated in a lifetime.

The people of Abbeville loved this man who had got his start in their midst. As beloved teacher in their small town, he had helped many people; now they would cooperate with him in a meeting that would bring honor to the Lord.

One night during the invitation, a man came forward and was converted. Dr. Bob did not recognize him, but was overjoyed to find that he was the man for whom he had been named—his father's buddy in battle, Robert Reynolds.

In Ozark another unique experience! During the altar call one evening, a blind man came forward. After his conversion, he arose from his knees at the altar, his face beaming, and began to question Dr. Bob.

"What is your whole name?" the man asked.

"Robert Reynolds Jones," was the answer.

"When were you born?" the blind man asked further.

"October 30, 1883," replied the evangelist, a somewhat puzzled expression on his face.

"That is exactly right," the man remarked; "I had someone to look it up this morning. My name is Dr. Dick Reynolds. I am the doctor who brought you into the world."

That night Dr. Bob knelt beside his bed and gave special thanks for being allowed to lead these two men to the Lord. Dr. Reynolds had attended Dr. Bob at his physical birth; Dr. Bob attended Dr. Reynolds at his new birth—his spiritual birth.

CHAPTER 11

Steubenville, Ohio, 1921

Several years ago a certain man who is well-known in denominational circles in the South visited Bob Jones University. During a conversation I had with him and his wife, the wife said, "We wanted to visit your wonderful school. We have heard so much about it. Our interest in your Founder dates back to a revival meeting he held in Steubenville, Ohio, in 1921. I was saved in that meeting." It thrilled my heart to hear her tell how much that meeting had done for the town. She said that even after all these years the older people still talk about the meeting Bob Jones held there.

This was not the first time I had heard of the Steubenville meeting. Many times through the years I had heard similar remarks; and as I have read some of the newspaper accounts of this meeting, I have been able to understand why people still speak of it and why many "old timers" say that in this modern day we do not know what the word "revival" really means.

Before the Steubenville meeting began, an article appeared in the newspaper with regard to the feelings of various pastors toward the meeting. Under the caption "WHAT JONES CAMPAIGN MEANS TO STEUBENVILLE," comments of eleven preachers were given.

A large picture of Dr. and Mrs. Jones was captioned "Evangelist Bob Jones, accompanied by his wife and their son, Bob, Jr., are scheduled to arrive in the city this evening from their home in Alabama. Arrangements have been made to give them a royal reception."

And what a reception it was! There was a parade of several thousand people. Mrs. Jones never felt comfortable in the parades. She would crouch down in the car, but Dr. Bob would respond as he knew the people wanted him to do.

"THOUSANDS FLOCK TO BIG 'SHED' FOR REVIVAL OPENING" read the opening headlines of newspaper reports of the big meeting. Other early headlines spoke of an "OVERFLOW CROWD SUN-

DAY NIGHT." It must have been thrilling to read in the newspaper that at one of the first meetings "100 PROFESSED THEIR FAITH AFTER SERMON."

From all accounts this was one of Dr. Bob's greatest meetings in the North. It seems that the newspapers did very little headline reporting of anything for five weeks but of this man and the great meeting he conducted. Many articles quoted every line of his sermon. Dr. Bob appreciated the efforts of the press and he took occasion at a Sunday night service to express his appreciation. "There is no power more wonderful than that of the press in making a campaign a success," he said.

One reporter said:

In his sermon Sunday evening, Bob Jones suggested that citizens of the city in attendance at the tabernacle subscribe for the newspapers during the period of the campaign for absent friends who may be benefited by reading the reports of the sermons preached. He stated that at the end of a campaign in Joplin, Missouri, he received a letter from a deaf and dumb man who had followed the series of services through the press. . . . "I am deaf and dumb, but have read the reports of the meetings in the paper and have learned enough Gospel to give my heart to Jesus Christ. I cannot hear or speak, but I have found peace, and I want to be enrolled as one of the converts of the campaign."

Another reporter wrote:

"Here is a motto for every one of you during these meetings. Make it yours by consecration now," said Bob Jones Sunday morning. "'I am only one, but I am one; I cannot do much, but I can do something; what I can do, I ought to do; and what I ought to do, by the grace of God, I will do.' Let every person take the counsel of Gypsy Smith: go home and with a piece of chalk, draw a circle about yourself, and then pray, 'O God, begin in MY RING.'"

From every paper daily headlines flashed the subject of the forthcoming sermon as well as reporting, almost verbatim, the previous sermon. Typical headlines follow:

"HOMECOMING OF SINNERS MARKED SUNDAY MEETINGS was subheaded, "Wonderful Day for God, Says Evangelist Bob Jones At Close of Evening Service — Evangelist Brings Powerful Message on Sin, Judgment, and Hope of Jesus."

"NO MIDDLE GROUND, SAYS EVANGELIST — ACCEPT OR REJECT."

"STARVING SOULS HEAR BOB'S PLEA." The subheading: "Many With Hungry Hearts Go Forward and Accept Christ As the Bread of Life At Tabernacle Meeting — Bob Jones Preaches on 'Food for the Hungry' — Big Delegations."

"REVIVAL KNOCKERS FLAYED—EVANGELIST GOES AFTER OPPONENTS IN LIVELY FASHION." Subheadlines: "Bob Declares There Must Be Something Good About Revival When Gamblers, Crooked Politicians, Sabbath-Breakers, and Their Ilk Are Opposed to Them—Evangelist Speeds Up and Hands Out Some Hot Ones." "WOMEN PACK 'SHED' TO HEAR BOB JONES ARRAIGN THEIR SEX." Subheadlines: "Tabernacle Jammed to the Doors Friday Night. Evangelist Delivers Famous Sermon 'The Modern Woman' and Wins Hundreds to Standard of Christ."

"BOB JONES SCORCHES SIN AND SINNERS." "Evangelist Cuts Loose on Dancing and Card-Playing and Denounces Other Outstanding Sins of the Age—People Must Choose Between Jesus Christ and Hell, 'Bob' Declares." "4000 Persons Accept His Program At Close of Scorching Sermon."

"PRODIGAL SON WAS SUBJECT AT BIG SHED." "Bob Jones' Application of Old Text Impressed Great Congregation—Delegations of Masons, Woodmen, Royal Neighbors, and Boy Scouts in Attendance—Interest in Meetings Grows Constantly."

On Washington's birthday Dr. Bob had a special meeting for fathers and sons. The headlines stated: "WASHINGTON'S BIRTHDAY AT TABERNACLE—DELEGATIONS ATTENDED—CHRIST'S CRUCIFIXION WAS SUBJECT OF SERMON BY EVANGELIST." The next day large headlines stated: "FIVE THOUSAND MEN HEAR BOB JONES AT TABERNACLE SUNDAY." Subheadings were: "Evangelist Delivers Powerful Discourse on Sins of Men. Great Numbers Came Out for Christ At the Close of the Sermon. Tabernacle Was Crowded Again At Night Meeting."

Another day large headlines reported in block letters: "BOB JONES WINS HIGH SCHOOL STUDENTS," and in one-inch subheadlines, Several Hundred Hit Trail—Pupils of Steubenville and Mingo High Put Punch Into Revival Meeting With School Songs and Cheers—Hundreds of Young People Take New Stand for God."

Other headlines were:

"MANY HIT SAWDUST TRAIL";

"SCORES OF PROFESSING CHRISTIANS ANSWER CALL, MAKING PUBLIC CONFESSION, AND SEEKING RE-CONSECRATION AT CLOSE OF THRILLING AFTERNOON SERVICE";

"HUNDREDS ENLIST FOR PERSONAL WORK";

"AN IRRESISTIBLE APPEAL MADE BY THE EVANGELIST LEADS MANY TO SALVATION AT SUNDAY EVENING SERVICE";

"GREAT THRONG PARTICIPATES IN SERVICE, OVERFLOW MEETING BEING NECESSARY."

Dr. Bob met with businessmen, with the Chamber of Commerce, with all the city clubs, and with high schools and colleges of the area. Schools and colleges dismissed classes so that the students could go to hear this great man preach, and "BIG DELEGATIONS FROM NEIGHBORING TOWNS" came to "HEAR 'BOB.'"

At a Chamber of Commerce Forum, which Dr. Bob addressed, the chairman said:

> There is one thing about Bob Jones which impresses the people who hear him. . . . That is his earnestness and the fact that he never for a minute forgets his work and the object of his visit in Steubenville. He can keep people in gales of laughter, then strike them silent with a pointed epigram. He can talk in the softly modulated effective tones that he uses when he makes a particularly earnest appeal; he can hit straight from the shoulder with his earnest denunciations; but he never forgets what he is here for. It might really be said what he is living for. He is here to save souls, and he never forgets it.

This Chamber of Commerce chairman expressed in words the same thought that a cartoonist expressed in a picture in the Montgomery Advertiser (BOB JONES IN REPOSE, page 84).

There were big parades of thousands of people, sponsored by various groups of the city on different days. Of one parade it was said, "THOUSAND OR MORE MARCH TO THE SHED AND HEAR MASTERFUL SERMON FROM EVANGELIST 'BOB' JONES." Of another parade it was reported that in spite of inclement weather, "MORE THAN 4,000 PEOPLE PARTICIPATED IN A SUNDAY SCHOOL PARADE."

A pastor who was helping with the meeting wrote a letter on the subject—

WHY I REJOICE IN THE REVIVAL AT THE TABERNACLE

> We have now finished our first week of meetings . . . so that we are no longer talking about hopes and expectations but about realities. Already it has more than fulfilled my hopes, and I rejoice in it and consecrate myself to it for the following reasons:
>
> 1. Because it is a movement manifestly of God's Spirit and fulfills the desire of the ministers of our city which He put into their hearts for such an awakening.
>
> 2. Because of the man who preaches and those who compose his party. Bob Jones is a man filled with the Spirit of God and given to His service.

3. Because the Gospel that is preached is true to the Bible, the only kind of religion that will meet the needs of this chaotic world.

4. Because these meetings are a proclamation to the entire city that the Protestant churches "are" (not "shall be") all one in Christ Jesus.

5. Because the combined evening weekday attendance in one week is as great as the combined attendance of all our prayer meetings for six months, and one Sunday night's attendance is twice as large as the combined Sunday night attendance of the churches of our city. Also the attendance at the morning prayer meetings in a week is far larger than the combined attendance of any prayer meeting night.

6. Because wayward church members are being brought back to an open and public worship of Almighty God, so long neglected. Lukewarm church members are being refreshed and developed spiritually — this includes me.

7. Because precious souls that never would be saved by our sitting snug in our church homes are going to be redeemed to all eternity because we are obeying God's command: "Go out into the highways and hedges and compel them to come in."

Beloved, these are my reasons; and for these same reasons I urge each one of you to dedicate yourself, your money, your service to these meetings, that Christ may be glorified in them and in you. George W. Arms.

About midway of the meeting, these large headlines heralded interesting facts: "HALFWAY POST IN BOB JONES REVIVAL PASSED LAST NIGHT. MEMBERS OF FRATERNAL BODIES HIT THE TRAIL IN GREAT NUMBERS FOLLOWING EVANGELIST'S SERMON ON 'THE PRODIGAL SON.'"

Toward the close of the meeting, according to large headlines, "BOB JONES DEEPLY IMPRESSED GREAT GATHERING OF PATRIOTIC ORGANIZATIONS WITH SERMON ON 'FOR BY GRACE ARE YE SAVED THROUGH FAITH.'" "GREAT NUMBERS CAME FORWARD TO SEEK SALVATION."

Also featured in the meeting were the Sunday schools. "HUNDREDS CAME FORWARD AND ACKNOWLEDGED CHRIST AND HUNDREDS MORE WERE PLAINLY UNDER CONVICTION."

An article that merits inclusion in its entirety, I think, is one that was written by a man named Tom Blodgett. It is cleverly worded and, as you will see, ends with a "commercial" for the man's business. People who write commercial advertising for television and radio could certainly learn a lesson from this man's witty report.

BOB JONES MEETING A FAILURE

I have attended nearly all the Bob Jones meetings at the big tabernacle, and while I must admit that the evangelist seems to be an honest, earnest man, yet as a critic that pays for the privilege of finding fault, I am compelled to say that Jones in many respects is a failure.

When I work hard all day and go to the meeting at night, I want to rest and enjoy myself, but I have failed thus far to find any rest and quietude of mind at the Jones meetings.

About the time I get settled down in my seat and listen to the wonderful songs, then Jones gets up and takes a text and begins getting under my hide. By the time he gets to second base, I am wide awake and staring myself in the face and trying to dodge some of the thunder bolts.

When he puts a spitball of truth over, I begin to grin and think how well that fits a fellow across the aisle that I know, and while the smile is still warm on my facial map, he sends another in-shoot over that hits me right in the ribs, and I forget all about the shortcomings of the man across the aisle.

Under Bob Jones' preaching, a man in the church has either got to "fish or cut bait."

I am sure glad that I am not a public official for Bob said and proved that any public officer who does not enforce the law is either a thief or a perjurer. If he admits he cannot enforce the law, he is a thief for taking the public's money for something he cannot do; if he can and doesn't enforce the law, he is a perjurer for he took an oath to enforce the law; so there is no chance for an official to take a nap in Bob's meeting that is loafing on the job.

Bob Jones can burn the naked truth in to the marrow of a man's bones second to no evangelist in America; and from the standpoint of easy recreation and taking a pious nap, his meetings are a failure.

If a man really wants to know the truth and has the backbone to line up with Bob's yardstick, the meetings are a huge success.

When I am not at the meetings I am still helping folks buy and sell houses and farms and trying to help folks find a home in which they will be happy if Bob's rules of living are lived up to.

Bob came to my office and got off the elevator on the fifth floor of Citizens Bank Building, the way you come when you want to buy a home. The phone company still sends me a statement every month for the use of phone 2616 on which you can call me at any time.

The papers also reported each day "Bob Jones Sidelights," " 'Bob' Jones Shrapnel," and "Headlights on Jones' Sermon." I quote a few of these pithy sayings to give you an idea of this type of reporting.

"If labor and capital would accept Jesus, all the problems of the nation would be solved in 24 hours."

"The democracy that rejects Jesus Christ, the Son of God, seals its doom."

"What you do for Jesus, God will do for you. If you spurn Jesus, God will spurn you."

"God loves all, but God cannot save any man who rejects Jesus Christ."

"Bob Jones is not an issue in this campaign. Jesus is the issue and you must accept or reject Him."

"This old world will never know any peace or real joy until it accepts Christ."

"You say you can't be happy leading a Christian life. You're a fool. You can't be happy unless you are a Christian."

"The man who rebels against the Stars and Stripes should be shot, and the man who rebels against the Kingdom of God and rejects Jesus will go to eternal death."

At the close of this meeting, the Steubenville Ministerial Association sent out a letter dated February 24, 1921, to the various ministerial associations around the country, giving their opinions of Bob Jones and the results of his meetings.

Brethren:

Greetings! We the members of the Ministerial Association of Steubenville, Ohio, feel that we owe to our ministerial brethren in the different sections of this and other states to inform them of the great spiritual awakening which has come to us and to our churches during the evangelistic campaign now being held in our city.

The large tabernacle erected near the business center of the city was filled to its capacity from the opening service of the campaign, and many evenings was too small to accommodate the crowd that thronged to the services.

For this unusual religious interest which has brought hundreds into the kingdom and has quickened the spiritual life of all the members of our church we are indebted to the blessing of God on the services of Evangelist Bob Jones of Montgomery, Alabama, and his party of consecrated and capable helpers.

We felt for some time the need of a great evangelistic movement, but realizing this was a most difficult field and knowing that only strong leadership could bring about the desired result, since Mr. Sunday had been here in a great campaign a few years ago, we carefully looked over the field for a man to lead us. After a thorough investigation of the work of Evangelist Bob Jones in other cities, we extended to him an invitation and his work has far exceeded our expectation.

These are the things about Mr. Jones and his work that have impressed us most: his exaltation of Jesus Christ; his continued relationship with Him from childhood; his invitation demanding a definite decision for Christ; his Bible expositions in the afternoons; his ability to draw and hold by his messages large audiences without resorting to clap-trap methods; his clean financial plans; his frankness, approachableness and his fidelity at all times and all ways to the pastors.

Here are some of the results of the meeting: Hundreds have been converted and thousands of church people have been renewed in their spiritual life. Mr. Jones makes no effort to "count numbers" but our churches have already had a large ingathering and there are many others to be received. The hands of the pastors have been strengthened, the leadership of the churches enlarged, and Jesus Christ means more to our people than ever before.

This is sent out by us because of our interest in the cause of clean evangelism. Mr. Jones has not asked for a testimonial. However, we voluntarily commend him to any city where there is a desire for a constructive, spiritual and clean evangelistic campaign. We will appreciate your reading this to your Ministerial Association.

This letter was signed by all the co-operating pastors — seventeen men.

As I typed the account of this meeting, I could not help making a contrast in my own mind of the difference from many of our modern campaigns which, instead of leaving the towns better off and strengthening the churches and building up the leadership of the fundamental, Bible-believing preachers, leave the churches weak and anemic. This shows how far afield we have gone from the type of revivals that Dr. Bob and others had in the days of real revival.

CHAPTER 12

Montgomery, Alabama, 1921

I have checked this meeting from several different angles. Dr. Bob has told me much about it from time to time; I have read newspaper accounts of the meeting; I have talked with Alabamians who knew of the meeting; and I have discussed it with Mrs. Jones, Sr., who was an eyewitness. Mrs. Jones says that this was the biggest meeting he ever held in the United States. "Robert was especially eager to conduct this meeting," she says. "As you know, Montgomery is the capital of the state, and also our old hometown. My husband would not take a cent for his services, but he consented to let the people take special offerings for worthy charitable causes. The people appreciated this attitude; and to show their appreciation, they insisted on giving me a beautiful Sterling tea service. I have treasured this gift all these years, but I well remember how very much it embarrassed my husband. You know that he never wanted anything for himself. Money never meant a great deal to him except as he could use it for the good of the Cause."

One day when Congressman George Grant and I were visiting Dr. Bob, I asked Dr. Bob to tell us about the Montgomery meeting. The Congressman, being from Alabama, already knew about the meeting, but he enjoyed hearing Dr. Bob's version of it. In substance, this is the account as Dr. Bob told it:

One of the greatest meetings I ever held was in my old town of Montgomery. In one day they built a large tabernacle that would seat thousands of people; and we packed it out every night. Mayor Gunter and his staff sat on the platform many nights. Senator Lister Hill of Alabama was one of the converts of that meeting. After the service a friend said to me, "Bob, get to Lister as fast as you can; and he will join the Methodist Church." Lister's mother had been Catholic and some of his friends were afraid that he would join the Catholic Church. Senator Hill joined the Court Street Methodist Church in Montgomery [It is interesting that on the same Sunday that Senator Hill united with the Court Street Church, a little nine-year-old boy also joined it. The lad's name? Bob Jones, Jr., son of evangel-ist—R.K.J.]

I held several wonderful meetings in Montgomery. Perhaps the greatest single service I ever conducted was there in my early twenties when I gave my address on the "SINS OF MEN." In this service something unusual happened that in all my years of experience I never saw before nor since. It was Sunday afternoon in special service for men only. While I was still preaching, an old atheist came running down the aisle to be saved; and all the men—and there were about three thousand of them—arose from their seats and surged forward en masse.

The paper reporting this incident, stated:

At the close over two thousand men started with so great a rush to the front to shake hands with him that he was forced to rush back to the platform and appeal to the men not to create a panic but to respond to the proposition to live right by holding up their hands.

Monday morning's headlines (May 23, 1921) stated: "GREAT THRONG HEARS FIRST MESSAGE BY REV. BOB JONES." Sub-headings explained: "More Than Five Thousand Held Spellbound By Eloquence of Splendid Evangelist: Hundreds Turned Away at Each Service Sunday: Sermons Not Sensational."

Tuesday morning headlines flashed: "BOB JONES ADDRESSES BIG AUDIENCE IN THIRD SERMON." Subheadings: "Immense Tabernacle Overflows for Meeting Monday Night—Evangelist Declares Violators of Law Oppose Revival; Meetings Will Be Held Tuesday Afternoon and Tuesday Night."

There was a cartoon of an old man with the caption: "Squire Jabez Melton of Beat 18, Henry County." The old man is saying, "Me an' Bob Jones will prob'bly hit it off purty well t'gether. I allus had a weakness for him anyhow, as him an' me were born an' raised in th' same country an' larned how t' make men good. He b'lieves Heaven is a better uplifter than the legislatur'. He d'pends on th' decalogue more'n he does statutes t' git folks straightened out. That's my ticket."

Wednesday headlines were: "INTEREST GROWS IN GREAT REVIVAL BOB JONES IS CONDUCTING." Subheadings: "Throngs Gather Three Times a Day to Hear Great Evangelist."

OUTSTANDING SINS OF AGE GIVEN HARD BLOW BY BOB JONES

Later headlines (Friday, May 27) carried this statement:

Mundane extravaganza and present day reckless proclivities received a hefty blow from Bob Jones in his sermon Thursday night on the theme,

"The Outstanding Sins of the Age." He flayed various forms of evil and warned that the time has come when a line must be drawn between the world and the church for the preservation of Christianity.

Dr. Bob always loved people regardless of their nationality, their color, or their creed. This is manifest in some remarks he made early in this meeting—remarks that were broadcast far and wide. I refer to a sermon in which he took occasion to explain God's Word with reference to the Jews, God's own chosen people. Through the years Dr. Bob talked about, promoted, and helped the Jews when he could do so. I am glad to include this portion of his sermon because I have heard a recent remark to the effect that Dr. Bob Jones did not like the Jews. Anyone who knew him knows that this is not true. Read his remarks about them as reported in the paper:

AN EXPRESSION OF REGARD

There is something heart-warming about it when someone comes right out in the open and speaks a good word for the Jew. They do not often receive a public declaration of appreciation such as Bob Jones voiced the other day, though a trifle florid.

Mr. Jones spoke of the Jews as the greatest people on earth, all things considered. He foresaw a future for the race, and regarded hopefully the beginnings of the movement back to Palestine, "the country to which God has given them a deed."

This tribute is in contrast to the vicious anti-Jewish propaganda that springs up occasionally, and to the rather cynical, half good-natured tolerance frequently manifested in the pulpit, in publications, in conversations, and on the stage.

People who are sufficiently fair minded to recognize the virtues of their fellow citizens and neighbors, irrespective of race or religion, are not guilty of this.

Throughout the campaign the MONTGOMERY JOURNAL and the MONT-GOMERY ADVERTISER cooperated in promoting the meetings. Each paper had large-spread cartoons depicting various phases of Bob Jones' life. These cartoons cleverly portray the spirit of the man, the spirit of the messages, and the spirit of the age. The JOURNAL pictured the devil, life-size, with large captions: REFORMED——AGAIN. The next, equally as large, was a picture of Bob Jones straddling the entire United States and having in his hand a large baseball bat. Dr. Bob hits the ball into space. Hanging on to the ball is the devil, who is yelling, "Ouch! 'What a Wallop that Guy's Got!'"

The ADVERTISER'S answer to the JOURNAL'S cartoons were whole page spreads of all kinds of cartoons that depicted the evils of the day and how Dr. Bob, in one way or the other, was overcoming them. A typical cartoon shows hundreds of people working like bees in a hive. The workers are busy in the construction of the large tabernacle for the Bob Jones meeting. In the background is a schoolhouse, with the caption "School Dismissed." Under the picture of the tabernacle, that has been built in record time, are these captions: "THEY ARE BUILDING A TRAINING CAMP." "THIS PLACE IS BOOKED SOLID—FOR THE FIGHT WITH THE DEVIL." At the bottom of the page there is a large coffin. Towering over the coffin, hammer in hand, is Bob Jones. Dr. Bob is pressing down the lid of the coffin, the devil, peeping out, is saying, "He sure does wield a wicked hammer."

On June 10, 1921, the ADVERTISER printed another page of cartoons entitled, "ALONG THE BELT LINE." The way Bob stormed about the platform, it was difficult for him to keep his pants up or his shirttail in. In fact, he wore both belt and suspenders as precautionary measures against an "accident." One of the cartoons shows Dr. Bob leaning over, pounding his fist, and accidentally "snapping" a big chain that is being used as suspenders. One man is saying to another, "They don't make harness strong enough to hold him—that's why he wears a belt." The next statement is, "Stuart May, who is an authority on things pertaining to the belt line, said a mouthful about Bob Jones' reasons for not wearing suspenders." The next picture shows Bob Jones with many arms swinging in every direction. One pair of arms is holding his belt and his pants. The next picture shows the devil running. Chasing him is Bob Jones, still holding on to his belt and pants. Just as the evangelist gets to the devil, the devil plunges over the cliff into the water, and says, "I'm going home and stay there 'til the chase is over with." The cartoonist captioned this interesting picture with the words, "There is no doubt about Bob being able to hold his own."

The next page tells all about booze in the form of home-brew and depicts Bob Jones cleaning up the town. Dr. Bob is pictured as a magician who is pulling out of the hat a rabbit which has on its side, TABERNACLE. In the next picture the devil is in the background holding some plans captioned TABERNACLE PLANS. The devil is looking at a large man to whom he is saying, "You doublecrossed me." The man is replying, "Yes, I know it is Friday the 13th—but Leon McCord subsidized me—so you keep on getting behind me Satan."

The next set of pictures describes the evangelist waking up the city. The city's potential strength is represented as a giant prize fighter sleeping in his corner of the ring. In the fighter's gloved hand is a bottle with the label: PROCRASTINATION CORN. Depicting the city fallen, a man is down in the mud with only the bottoms of his feet and one arm visible. Written across the soles of his feet are the words, "Welcome to our City" and "Our Fallen Civic Sign." In his hand there is a bent-up sign saying, "Your Opportunity." Also in the picture is a little man carrying a suitcase to signify that he is a visitor to the city. "Bring your own lodging" is the caption. Another man from the city is at a Tourist Camp. This man has outstretched hands and is saying, "And you can hang your clothes on a hickory limb."

To me, the greatest cartoon of all is "BOB JONES IN REPOSE." Dr. Bob is in the pulpit, preaching his heart out and treading wheels that are in constant propulsion. Underneath the platform on which he stands, wheels are grinding away. Written across the big wheel are these words: "RIGHT FROM THE HEART." Various sins, such as Jazz, "Corn," Cards, Dice, and Corrupt Politics are being ground into bits and are falling below the platform. Alongside and somewhat below the platform is a large picture of the devil, who is pushing a wheelbarrow of rubbish and saying, "It Wouldn't Be Near So Rough if He Only Kept Union Hours." No words could ever describe in a better way than this the true spirit of this man, for even in his repose, the wheels of God's purpose for his life were always grinding, grinding, g r i n d i n g. With this man, in whatever capacity he served, it was TWENTY-FOUR HOURS A DAY FOR GOD.

Obviously I cannot mention all the cartoons. I shall skip several pages and end with the June 12, 1921, Sunday edition of the MONTGOMERY ADVERTISER. The large one-inch headlines at the top of the page state: "ANOTHER BIG CROWD HEARS BOB." In the cartoon section many pictures portray the life of the people and what Bob Jones was doing about it. The caption at the top of the page was in big block letters: "K I C K S." It shows Bob Jones kicking out the devil. Dr. Bob is wearing large spiked shoes and is leaning over the pulpit rail and kicking high with both feet as he preaches. In desperation, the devil is backing to the platform a mule which has written all over it the different vices of the day, such as Jazz, Gambling, Dancing, Styles, Movies, Golf, and Baseball. The devil is saying to the mule, "Don't Use Your Head — Use Your Heels — Now Back Up."

A writer tells this story about Dr. Bob's message to men:

FIVE THOUSAND MEN HEAR SUNDAY AFTERNOON SERMON

The greatest meeting that Bob has ever held, by his own admission, was in Montgomery, at which meeting he delivered his famous lecture, "Sins of Men." Evangelist Jones . . . described and expressed his opinion about a wide range of masculine sins in a sermon delivered to men only.

Mr. Jones discussed the sins of men very fully and comprehensively, and without any mincing of language or mitigation of offenses. Some five thousand men heard the sermon, applauding at times. . . . Among all the sins mentioned by the evangelist, none was more severely denounced than that of infidelity in the married man. "Don't tell me that there is no such thing as a lake of brimstone," he said, after expressing his contempt for this sin in language which no man could misunderstand. "IF God never made a hell for anything else, he would have made one for this class of men."

Another writer wrote of this episode:

At a certain juncture of the meeting the men which filled the Auditorium jumped to their feet with one accord, waved their hats and hands and cheered time after time. They sat down only to rise again and repeat their cheers for the young evangelist.

"THE WOMAN IN THE CASE" was another sermon that stirred much excitement. With the subheading, "There Is Nothing on Earth As Good As a Good Woman, But There Is No Fall So Tragic As That When a Woman Falls," the article explained:

"The woman crook is more devilish and venturesome than the man," declares evangelist. A warning against succumbing to female wiles when detrimental to the influence of Christianity, was sounded by Bob Jones in his sermon . . . "The Woman in The Case." He cited several historical instances of men who according to the evangelist are today in Hell because they preferred their woman to their God, the biblical character who furnished the text of the sermon being among these unfortunates. In this sermon the evangelist also took a rap at "highbrow" sinners, and ministers of the same type.

The MONTGOMERY ADVERTISER, Wednesday morning, June 1, 1921, stated: "SQUARE POLITICS URGED BY JONES IN SERMON TUESDAY." Subheadings: "City, State and County Officials Attend Revival Meeting in Body; Hundreds from Surrounding Sections." The article stated:

Bob Jones spoke strongly against political expediency in his sermon at the tabernacle. He referred to the trait of "selling out," and declared that a man who adopts such a course in politics is doomed to ultimate ruin. His hearers were told very plainly that they must "play square" or eventually be replaced by some man who does.

In addition to the officials present, there were hundreds of persons in delegations from towns around Montgomery: Sellers and LaPine. . . , Wetumpka, Greenville, Lowndesboro, Luverne, Mt. Carmel, Ramer, Mt.Meiga, Cecil, Pike Road, Pine Level Tuskegee, Haynesville, Abbeville and Prattville.

"JONES TAKES ISSUE WITH MAYOR PRECEDING SERMON" caught the eye of the public, who also read, "Evangelist Discusses Meeting Held With City Commissioners at City Hall Friday Morning; Declares It is Mayor's Duty to See That All Laws Are Enforced in City."

Dr. Bob set about trying to "straighten out" conditions, and headlines were strong: "CHURCHES WOULD WELCOME A VOTE ON RESIGNATION." Subheadings, all in block: "EVANGELIST JONES READS STRONG REPLY TO GREAT AUDIENCE STATING POSITION ON ACTION OF MAYOR GUNTER AND COMMISSIONER HARDAWAY—PAPER IS ENDORSED BY CONGREGATION AT TABERNACLE." "TO REQUEST SUNDAY CLOSING WITHOUT CALL OF ELECTION" was subheaded, "Bob Jones Announces That More Than Thirty-five Hundred Names Urging Closing Signed to Cards."

Mrs. Jones says that Dr. Bob got the city officials to close theaters and other such things on Sundays. The MONTGOMERY JOURNAL, Saturday, June 18, 1921, confirms her statement. "SUNDAY LAWS WILL BE STRICTLY OBSERVED." "STATE, CITY AND COUNTY TO AID IN ENFORCEMENT." "Governor Calls Mayor and Sheriff in Conference and Gets Promise of Help."

> Governor Kilby called the conference which lasted until nearly noon. Cooperation of the State, County and City forces toward law enforcement in Montgomery was said to be assured at a prolonged conference between Governor Kilby, Mayor W. A. Gunter, Jr., and Sheriff John L. Socgin at the executive offices at the Capitol Saturday morning. As a result of this decision it is expected renewed vigor will be focused on the enforcement of laws in the city.

I found the following excerpt particularly interesting, for it gives insight into this evangelist's thorough and earnest methods:

> The evangelist appeared on the platform in his shirt sleeves with a half dozen or more law books piled high in a chair on the platform. "Mayor Gunter told me," said the preacher, "that it was no more his business to enforce the law in Montgomery than it was mine or any other citizen. I am going to show you by law that he is dead wrong.
>
> "And by the way, let me say in passing, that I do not draw forty-five hundred dollars a year, paid by the people of Montgomery, for enforcing the laws of the city of Montgomery."

The headlines in the MONTGOMERY JOURNAL, Sunday, June 12, 1921, were "GREAT REVIVAL HERE STARTS ON ITS FINAL WEEK." Subheading: "Interest Continues Unabated in Evangelistic Campaign of Rev. Bob Jones." Following are excerpts from the article:

Sunday marks the entrance of the Bob Jones revival on the last lap of its four weeks program in the capital city and from all points of view indications forecast even greater interest and attendance than has characterized the three weeks gone by.

Enormous throngs have wended their way to the tabernacle since the meeting has been in progress and especially large attendance has been accorded the night services at which thousands have flooded the sawdust trails to express acceptance of Christ. Evangelist Jones has delivered forceful and soul-stirring messages throughout the revival and the spirit of the campaign has stamped a strong imprint from the length and breadth of Montgomery.

The MONTGOMERY JOURNAL outlined day by day every program and everything that Bob Jones was doing in that final week. One writer expressed the opinion that "a man can scarcely hear Bob without being moved to a better life."

The following article by a newspaper writer who had interviewed many of the great men of that day is written in such a delightful manner that I cannot refrain from including it. It is by Mr. C. E. Johnson and appeared in the MONTGOMERY JOURNAL on June 7, 1921.

I have always believed in Bob Jones since seeing, knowing and hearing him many years ago. He is a great big-hearted brother to the human race; he just loves everybody but the sinners more than anybody else. It is my opinion that he would go far out of his way by foot without coat, shirt, or shoes to help somebody in trouble if need be.

That's my idea of the man. Some fellow asked me how I liked the meeting. I just told him that up to date I would not take a cool ten thousand dollars for it. "But how do you like the preaching?" he asked further. "If I had been doing it myself and could have done it, I would not have changed a word of it."

"But it is a fright the way he antics about on the pulpit," said a woman to me, "and they tell me he turned up a pitcher and drank from it three times during his sermon. He cannot preach that way." For all I know that is just the latest style of preaching and I always accept the new styles without much argument. If a man wants to drink ice water from a pitcher while he is preaching, I have no quarrel about it, especially while he is handing out stuff as hot as Bob Jones deals it. He's got to have ice water and plenty of it. Only thing I would suggest is more of it.

I wouldn't make serious argument about the coat question either. If the "Old Boy" has things as warm around his premises as I feel sure he has, it won't be very long after some of us are dead before our coats, shirts, shoes, socks and under-clothings will be consumed in raging flames and the parching skin will be all that is left to tell the tale.

I just love to go to the tabernacle because you have to hurry and argue a little about getting a place to sit while there. No begging of men and women to come to church necessary. They are just glad to get into the tabernacle and if somebody gets up and leaves, two or three others are there to get in the place.

"If he would preach on baptism I would go to hear him," said a woman in speaking of Bob Jones' preaching. He preaches about the baptism of fire from Heaven and a holy enthusiasm for the redemption of lost and perishing souls. He doesn't argue doctrinal differences.

I have been writing newspaper stories a long time, won't say how many years. I wrote up Theodore Roosevelt once on his tour through Alabama and the South. I have been on the stage several times with William Jennings Bryan to 'get notes.' I have followed Richmond Hobson, second highest paid orator in America, from stump to stump and have slept in the same room with him to write stories about him. I have listened at the feet of Woodrow Wilson to "cover" his speeches. I have heard Bishop Warren A. Candler, Bishop H. C. Morrison, Len G. Broughton, George Stuart and others who dipped their tongues in fountains of eloquence and who delved into the great deep wells of knowledge, to "get the dope" and write newspaper stories about them. I have sailed through the blue of Heaven at a height of six thousand feet above the ground just to tell folks about it when I came down. I have traversed the peaks of the hills and the waters of the deep in order to write and gather inspiration for news stories. I have sat in legislatures and convention halls about press tables and heard giants in debate rage and rave and roar and fly at each others' throats in verbal combat. But I have always managed to keep cool and gather the data as a newspaper man and be able to write the story afterwards. I have never been tempted to quit writing and just listen until I heard the great Bob Jones.

As you can see from these articles, Dr. Bob was known as an energetic man. Many people kept asking, "How is Bob able to preach so hard and do so much and yet never seem to run out of enthusiasm or energy? What he does would kill the average fellow!" One of the reasons for his energy and success was the fact that he was able to relax. He was a sound sleeper. He could sleep any time and any place he might have the opportunity. He made it a practice to take a brief rest after lunch. In a big campaign, such as this Montgomery campaign, he would return to his hotel after the noon meal and would take a complete rest. He never had time to exercise by playing golf, or any other sport; but no one ever expended more energy than he did in the pulpit as he preached. That is the reason so many newspaper writers and cartoonists pictured him in such an active manner. A physician once remarked to Dr. Bob, "I heard you preach last night, and you incorporated in your delivery every rule of motion I lay down for physical culture."

A writer signing himself "Trip Notes" in the BUTLER COUNTY NEWS, Georgiana, Alabama, had this to say about his visit to hear Dr. Bob:

Sunday morning, "Trip Notes" and family boarded the car for Greenville and from there to Montgomery to hear Bob Jones at the 11 o'clock service on "Ye Are the Light of the World." The tabernacle was filled and multitudes looking on and listening from outside. We mean listening. Not any street car or automobile disturbances.

When Bob Jones begins to preach, he pulls off his coat and asks his audience to do likewise. The marvel is how can he put every ounce of energy he has in his sermon and then in a few hours is back again and again for weeks at a time and sometimes for months. And then between sermons waiting on the Mayor and the Governor and a host of others. He is the easiest man to listen to we ever heard.

He is not still a moment and gives the most pathetic illustrations we ever heard. At times, his voice is husky, but his voice was very clear Sunday night and doubtless 20,000 could hear him distinctly. He is only thirty-seven years old and has been preaching since he was fifteen. The Sunday night sermon was the last one of the four weeks. Bob Jones said there were 12,000 there and if he agreed two years later to hold another meeting there the tabernacle would have to be twice as large. All of this great multitude of people and the meeting running four weeks and three times on the last day and not a sleepy eye. It was wonderful. The key to Bob Jones' success is his passion for lost souls. He said, "There are people here tonight that if they don't accept Jesus as their Saviour now, they will never do it, and they will be somewhere in eternity as long as God lives." There must have been thousands redeemed during this campaign. Dr. Stakeley, pastor of the First Baptist Church, said he had been in the world famed Moody and Sankey revivals and many others but the greatest was the Bob Jones Revival.

The local ministers commended the work of this evangelist:

Montgomery ministers of the local Ministerial Association, headed by Rev. Peerce N. McDonald, president of the association, are unanimous in their endorsement of the work of Rev. Bob Jones here. The following letter has been prepared to be sent to the various ministerial associations over the country. . . .

"The members of the Ministerial Association of Montgomery, Alabama, desire through this medium to inform the Ministerial Associations of other cities of the great spiritual awakening that has come to our city in the united Evangelistic Campaign conducted by Rev. Bob Jones and his consecrated and capable workers, which is now coming to a close.

"A large tabernacle was erected near the business center with a seating capacity of more than five thousand. This building was crowded to capacity every night and many times there were hundreds standing around the outside of the tabernacle. This tabernacle was built in one day by volunteer labor from the various churches and the entire expenses of the campaign were raised during the first two weeks of the meeting.

"As you know the State Capital is located here and Montgomery like most capital cities, is ordinarily very conservative, but as a whole this city stood solidly behind the movement from the very start and thousands of men and women have given their lives to Jesus Christ under the powerful preaching and influence of Mr. Jones. There have been many additions to the various churches throughout the city, and many more are to be received. Churches have received a spiritual awakening such as has never been known in our city.

"This is the home of Rev. Bob Jones, he having lived here for the past fourteen years. No one can know or appreciate him better than his fellow citizens. The fact that this is his home city naturally would make it difficult for him to put on a great revival. We confidently believe that the Rev. Mr. Jones is the best loved man in the city of Montgomery today.

"Here are some of the things that impress us most: His exaltation of Jesus Christ; his continued fellowship with Him from childhood; his clear-cut invitation for people to accept Jesus Christ as their personal Saviour; his ability to draw and hold large audiences; his earnest eloquence and passion for lost souls. His financial methods are clean. His fidelity at all times to the co-operating pastors has been greatly appreciated by us.

"Mr. Jones has not asked for testimonials but we are so very grateful for the splendid work accomplished in our city that we feel it our duty to let the ministers of other cities know the joy that is ours. . . ."

Approximately twenty churches and pastors signed as cooperating pastors.

The Montgomery Evangelistic Club also wrote an endorsement. I quote an excerpt:

We want you to know that the Business Men's Evangelistic Club has always stood for just the things you promulgate, and we wish to pledge ourselves further to stand by to the best of our ability the splendid work which the Lord is doing through you in our City.

We have fully resolved that if it comes to a decision between our Lord and our very best friend, we will not forsake our Master.

The following account in a newspaper article shows Dr. Bob's fearlessness and the love and respect that the people of the area had for him. A young man under the influence of alcohol had killed his wife and was in prison, awaiting death by electrocution. Dr. Bob had been asked to visit this young man and to be with him to the last. The request had come from the boy's father, from the prison chaplain, and from the boy himself. Dr. Bob's tender heart stirred him to go to the rescue of this sorrowful family, but Mrs. Jones says that experience almost killed her husband; for two weeks he was so sick he could not eat or sleep very well. He told Mrs. Jones that never again could he endure such an ordeal. "There was never a sweeter person than this young man," Mrs. Jones said. "He did not mean to harm anyone. It shows the evil and tragic effects of alcohol."

The Montgomery headlines read: "THOUSANDS ATTEND FU-NERAL SERVICES FOR VIRGIL MURPHY."—"Impressive Cere-monies Conducted by Rev. Bob Jones for Electrocuted Slayer of Young Wife." "NOTED REVIVALIST CHARGES TRAGEDY TO BOOTLEG-GERS." "Minister Calls Upon Illicit Dealers in Liquor to 'Come and View Your Victim.'"

The funeral was held in Pinckard, Alabama. The paper reported:

There were between nine and ten thousand people—the largest crowd that has ever assembled in this section of the state on any occasion, attended the impressive funeral services here today for the late Virgil Murphy who was executed from the electric chair at Kilby prison Saturday morning for the murder of his wife. The ceremonies which began at 10 o'clock were held in the large open space in front of the school house here. Rev. Bob Jones, widely known evangelist, delivered the impressive funeral sermon in which he denounced the rum-running and rum-selling element in the most scathing terms, and called upon any bootleggers who might be within the sound of his voice to come forward and view the remains of their victim. Murphy, in a dying statement, declared that whiskey was the cause of his tragic fate.

Draped with an American flag in tribute to the honorable service of the deceased in the armed military forces of the nation overseas during the World War, the casket containing Murphy's remains was placed directly in front of the speaker's stand. On the platform with the officiating min-isters sat Murphy's aged father and mother, and his two little sons. By actual count, 5,253 persons passing in line, viewed the remains.

The Rev. M. S. Brassell of Montgomery, chaplain of state prisons in Ala-bama, opened the services with a brief and earnest statement. He said at the request of Virgil Murphy, the deceased, he and Rev. Bob Jones were there to bring a message of warning against the traffic in illicit liquor. "I was with him almost daily for three months," he said, "and I have come to tell you that Virgil Murphy died like a Christian soldier, singing the old song, 'Just As I Am Without One Plea But That Thy Blood Was Shed for Me.'" At the minister's request, the assembled thousands then joined with him in singing this great hymn. The remarks of Rev. Brassell and the hymn were followed by prayer by Rev. E. P. Smith of Auburn, director of the edu-cational work in the state prisons.

Then Rev. Bob Jones began his sermon, which was declared by many to be one of the most forceful and impressive of his career. He began by say-ing that Virgil Murphy was a Christian man and that he had never been a bad man. He was a man as good as the average but that he was a victim of the bootlegging evil which he declared was directly responsible for sending him to his death. The evangelist called upon all present to spread Murphy's message of warning against bootleg whiskey. The minister paid high tribute to W. L. Lee, Dothan lawyer, and counsel for Murphy, and told of his final appeal to the governor for a reprieve for Murphy just a few hours before the execution, stating that tears welled from the governor's eyes when he shook his head in refusal.

CHARGES TRAGEDY TO BOOTLEGGERS

The Rev. Jones called on the bootlegging element to come forward when the casket of the dead was opened and look upon their victim. He declared he had in his possession the names of the men who sold Murphy the liquor that caused him to kill his wife on the tragic day of the murder, and stating that Murphy's blood was on their hands, called on them to come forward and view their handiwork. He also called upon officers of the law to come and see what bootleg liquor had done. All officers of the law, he declared, must do their duty in stopping the running and sale of liquor in order that the boys now growing up may be saved.

The minister further called upon all mothers and fathers to establish family altars in their homes for their children and themselves, and urged all who believe in saving men from the fate of Virgil Murphy, to help enforce the law. He requested all those who would help to rid that section of the country of the bootlegging element to raise their hands, and every hand was raised. He then called upon all who would accept Christ as their Saviour and fight for His Cause to raise their hands. Fully 5,000 hands were raised by men and women who gave the minister their promise to lead better lives. Among those making professions of faith and promising to lead a better life was Murphy's father.

Ex-Service Men in Charge—all funeral arrangements were made and carried out by upward of 300 World War veterans present, who took charge of this part of the last rites. When the remains of the deceased were laid to rest in the little burying ground near Pinckard, a last salute of three volleys was fired over the grave by a squad picked from among the ex-servicemen present and after that a bugle sounded the notes of "Taps."

Rev. Brassell, who is an overseas veteran of the World War, said upon his return to Montgomery, Sunday evening, that the funeral of Virgil Murphy was the most impressive and the most touching that he has ever witnessed.

Murphy, who was tried, convicted, and sentenced to death in Houston County for the murder of his wife, maintained to the last that at the time of the tragedy he was crazed with drink and had no recollection of what he did.

First Honorary Degree

Following the close of this meeting, Dr. Bob went to New Concord, Ohio, to be honored by Muskingum College. The account of this honor is from a newspaper in Pittsburgh, Pennsylvania, under date of June 17, 1921. Headed "MUSKINGUM COLLEGE TO HONOR BOB JONES," this article stated:

> Muskingum College . . . will confer the degree of Doctor of Divinity upon the Rev. Bob Jones of Montgomery, Alabama. The ceremony of conferring the degree of D. D. upon the Rev. Jones will take place August 12, in the college auditorium, during the Bible Conference. . . . The beautiful and impressive ceremonial was to have taken place during the college commencement exercises last week, but as it is a rule of the College Board that

the candidate be present to receive the degree and the hood, the date was changed, as Mr. Jones is holding a great Evangelistic campaign in his home town and found it impossible to be present during commencement.

Dr. Bob felt honored to receive this first of many honorary degrees. Dr. J. Knox Montgomery, Muskingum President, had many wonderful comments to make about the evangelist and also predicted great things for his future. In reply, Dr. Bob said, "I am not much for titles. I am just plain Bob Jones, but for this degree I am grateful because you stand for the uplift of mankind and the glory of our Lord, the purest and the best." Then Dr. Bob spoke to the faculty, students, and guests about "the curse of the day" — the false teaching found in so many universities and colleges in the land that is wrecking the lives of young people.

Aftereffects of Montgomery

One year after the great campaign in Montgomery, there was a great issue in the State capital. The bootleggers, thugs, underworld, and some would-be do-gooders made strong attacks against Dr. Bob because of the fine work he had done.

In defense of Dr. Bob, the JOURNAL printed a message from Dr. W. B. Crumpton to the good people of Montgomery. I think you will enjoy the JOURNAL's article about and including Dr. Crumpton's message.

It is a protest as well as a message, and it is most timely, and coming from one of his pure life and Christian character, should cause people to pause, ponder and consider.

It is hardly necessary to say that this man of God to whom Dr. Crumpton so feelingly refers, is none other than the Rev. Dr. Bob Jones, whom the Protestant ministers and churches more than a year ago invited to hold a meeting here, and who accepted their invitation, and for four weeks he addressed thousands, hundreds confessing and joining different churches, and other hundreds were brought back from a backslidden state to their allegiance to Jesus Christ.

There are those who would make Dr. Bob Jones an issue in the Montgomery campaign; at least the public is led to this conclusion, as Dr. Crumpton so well puts it.

WHAT ARE THE ISSUES IN THIS CAMPAIGN?

"I write to ask: Is Bob Jones an issue in the Montgomery Campaign? One would think so from the expressions, too vile to be repeated, coming from some men in the city. The Protestant pastors and churches more than a year ago invited Dr. Jones, a well-known citizen, to hold a meeting here. At great inconvenience to himself, it being his vacation time, without a cent of remuneration, he accepted their invitation and for four weeks he addressed thousands in his characteristic way. Hundreds confessed and joined the churches, and other hundreds were brought back from a back-slidden state to their allegiance to Jesus Christ. The whole city felt the great moral uplift. Like all faithful ministers of Christ, like the prophets of old, he denounced sin in every place. While his manner seemed severe and often his language harsh, his appeal to the sinner was couched in tenderest terms. That meeting will go down in history as the most uplifting religious awakening in the history of the city.

"Jesus, on one occasion, when the Jews were about to stone Him, said: 'Many good works have I showed you from my Father; for which of these works do ye stone me?' We might ask of those who are denouncing Bob Jones: 'For which of the good works he has done do you abuse him?'

"Just as we are now studying in the Sunday Schools how Jeremiah, the faithful prophet, told the people of Judah of their sins and warned them what was coming on them. He was arrested and confined in a dark dungeon and his life threatened. He told them the truth and all his predictions came true. A kindred passage in the New Testament tells of the imprisonment of John the Baptist, because he denounced the sin of Herod the king. His faithfulness cost him his head. We do not live in the days when preachers may be thrown into prison; but men hate the denunciation of their sins as they did in olden times, and do all they dare do to injure the man who denounces their sins.

"Dr. Jones did not denounce sin because he hated the sinner. Like Jeremiah, he and all faithful preachers love the people—all of them—none so far gone in sin they would not befriend him and win back to right living. God has said it, and all history has proved it: 'Righteousness exalteth a nation but sin is a reproach to any people.'

"The king of Judah hated God, His Book and His minister. When the Book, so tediously prepared, every word written by hand, was handed him, he took his penknife, cut it into shreds and burned it. Jeremiah's God lives and His Book lives. Voltaire made the prediction that in one hundred years nobody would believe the Bible. The century has long passed, and the printing presses find it difficult to supply the ever-increasing demand for God's Book. Men with their penknives and all the methods of destruction their wicked hearts can devise, are trying to destroy the Book; but their efforts will prove vain.

"I am writing this in the interest of no candidate, or set of candidates, but solely because I have thought for months some one should write something of the sort as a protest against the foul-mouthed sayings of wicked men against one of God's most useful servants.

"Maybe I am better situated to write than anybody else, as I have few responsibilities, few days and the experiences of a long life. Unless the parties whom I write 'God has given over to reprobate minds, because they do not like to retain Him in their minds,' I shall hope these words will not be in vain."—Signed W. B. Crumpton, Montgomery, Alabama, June 10, 1922.

The impression made on the city of Montgomery is shown not only in the article in the 125th anniversary edition of the MONTGOMERY ADVERTISER which states that Dr. Bob's meeting there was the greatest historical religious event of the City in 125 years but also in an editorial in the Sunday issue of the paper on September 7, 1958, by J. Fred Thornton, Associate Editor of the MONTGOMERY ADVERTISER. I quote from this editorial:

CRUSADING FERVOR: RING VS. REFORMERS

An echo of the time Montgomery got religion on a bigger scale and with greater zeal than ever before or since comes to mind at this time.

A couple of weeks ago, I mentioned the old fights between the Gunter Ring and the reformers. I pointed out that the ring sometimes won by margins of 3 to 2 and 2 to 1, and that once, when the Rev. Bob Jones got the crusading Christians all keyed, it was close.

. . . BOB JONES TO THE RESCUE—The 1922 Election was preceded by a mighty revival, in May and June of 1921. The post war situation had Montgomery fathers and mothers upset, not without cause. It has ever been the habit of waning old codgers to view with alarm, sometimes tinged with envy, the doings of unimpaired youth. But in 1921 they had more than that to worry about. The women had just been unshackled and were kicking up their heels. Fiery lads, back from the wars, went on celebrating the Armistice indefinitely. Youth of both sexes were drinking defiantly, a nose-thumbing gesture at the reformers; the new wine of freedom spiked with bootleg liquor proved a potent breaker. The uses of the automobile as an accessory to sin were being discovered and exploited. When we remember that in those days a woman who smoked a cigaret was looked upon as almost or quite a fallen woman, it is no wonder that old heads were apprehensive.

In front of the state capitol, at the corner of Dexter and Bainbridge . . . a vast wooden tabernacle was built in a single day. Business and professional men turned out with hammer and saw. The Rev. Bob Jones, renowned evangelist, filled the pulpit. The opening service drew an overflow congregation of 6,000, exceeding the seating capacity by 1,000. On the platform were nearly all the Protestant ministers of Montgomery, including one Episcopal rector. Governor Thomas E. Kilby was also there.

I was assigned by the ADVERTISER to cover the revival, which lasted four weeks. Never have I seen a man hold such mastery over his hearers as did Bob Jones. When he summoned sinners to come forward, hundreds, young and old, men and women, hit the sawdust trail. Some sobbing forth their repentance. Let me say right here that I did not view all this as one sitting in the seat of the scornful; as between an excess of religious fervor and cold fish complacency, my preference is for the former.

THEIR ALL WAS NOT ENOUGH. The campaign took a political turn when the chief of the state prohibition enforcement unit, fanatical Conrad W. Austin, spoke by invitation. He savagely assailed the local political ring. Then the Rev. Jones led a delegation to city hall to demand the closing of movies and swimming pools on Sunday.

I have always thought the reformers would have done better if the election had come right on the heels of the revival, instead of a year later. But a vast amount of zeal and fervor carried over, as Methodist and Baptist shock troops, and others, hurled themselves upon the ring, grimly entrenched and waiting.

On the eve of the election, the Rev. Jones came back and delivered a series of addresses on "moral conditions in Montgomery." He must have found them deplorable, for thumbing through the files I came across a big advertisement saying that Judge Leon McCord would speak the night before election day and answer "the vicious and unfounded assaults of Bob Jones."

NAPOLEON WITHOUT WATERLOO. Mayor Gunter was invincible when running himself, a Napoleon who never knew a Waterloo. Sometimes, though rarely, a lieutenant lost. Bob Phelps, elected sheriff on the Gunter ticket in 1922, broke with the mayor and in 1926 performed the extraordinary feat of being elected county tax collector with Gunter against him. . . .

INTRUSION RESENTED. Montgomery's spirit of independence was never better manifested than in the 1927 mayor's race. The newly installed governor of the state, Bibb Graves, was a Montgomery man, identified with the reform crowd locally. Gunter opposed him for governor, and Graves sought to repay Gunter in like coin; both Graves and the attorney-general, Charlie McCall, took the stump against Gunter, and the Rev. Jones fought him, too. But the unterrified voters of Montgomery rejected their pleas.

In my previous piece I alluded to the happy reconciliation that took place later. Men came to see that all the good men were not on one side, nor all the undesirables on the other. Whatever the faults of the reformers, it took courage for a man to stand up against the machine in those days; on the other hand, Gunter clearly gave Montgomery what a majority of its citizens preferred. I am not sure, but I think that even Bob Jones and Gunter finally buried the hatchet; I know Graves and Gunter did.

I talked with Dr. Bob and Mrs. Jones many times about these days and some of the "bloody" battles they fought. Mrs. Jones says that regardless of how hard her husband fought, all the men he opposed knew that he would be honest and fair in his dealings with them. Some of the men said: "Even though we fear Bob Jones, we must respect him for his convictions." Many of these men would later come and shake Dr. Bob's hand and apologize for the things they had said or done and assure him that they respected him and wanted to be his friend.

CHAPTER 13

St. Petersburg, Florida, 1921

Judging from the newspaper accounts of this meeting, it must have been one of the biggest things the city had experienced. There were pages and pages of notes and articles about the evangelist and about his meeting.

"THE BOB JONES REVIVAL MEETINGS BEGAN TODAY," said one paper. Then it explained:

> The fame of the evangelist has preceded him and it is certain that crowds will fill the large tabernacle at each service.
>
> The mammoth choir, composed of many of the best singers in the city, will add much to the interest of the meetings and their effectiveness for music has a universal language which appeals to and is understood and appreciated by all.
>
> It is hoped that these meetings may bring to St. Petersburg a great spiritual awakening and result in great good to the community.

Other headlines on the front page stated "BOB JONES REVIVAL OPENS IN GOSPEL SHED SEATING 5,000." Under this, in large caption, was the heading: "ARMY OF MEN MARCH TO REVIVAL." The article went on to say:

> Every man who is in sympathy with the cause of Christ and desires to be a better man is invited by Bob Jones to report in Williams Park at 7:15 o'clock tonight and march to the tabernacle. The men this evening will be the special guests of the revivalist and his assistants. An entire section will be reserved for them."

"TRAMP OF MARCHING MEN HEARD AGAIN IN STREETS" headlined this article:

> St. Petersburg streets resounded to the tramp of marching men last night for the first time since the World War and not since the Armistice has this

city seen so large a number of men in line as there were in the column that left Williams Park and marched, shoulder to shoulder, to the Bob Jones Tabernacle on First Street, North. There were some 800 men who formed the great church army of the Sunshine City and they marched as soldiers though they carried no flags, had no arms and did not wear uniforms. But the sight of this army as they marched down Central Avenue was very impressive and also imposing. These marching men gave notice to the world that St. Petersburg churches are not made up of women and children. These men told the people of the city that they are proud to march under the banner of the Lord and are ready to fight for the church, if need be. . . .

Dr. Bob went to St. Petersburg with the determination that he would preach his heart out in an effort to bring Christ and righteousness to the town. People responded in a marvelous way. They were enthusiastic about the meeting and they appreciated the evangelist and his workers. Besides cooperating in the meeting, the people had beach dinners and all types of clean entertainment to show their appreciation for this man and his efforts in their behalf.

The battle waged heavy, for the devil knew that he was up against a hard time. Headlines said: "BOB JONES BEGINS BATTLE WITH DEVIL IN THIS CITY." Subheadings in big print stated: "1,500 Men and Women Pledge Themselves to Help Jones Fight." The article said:

Bob Jones, leader of the army that is to fight against the devil in St. Petersburg, yesterday morning enlisted 1,500 men and women to stand with him in the battle front. Most of them are veterans, church folks who have been working for the Cause of Christ for years, but a few are recruits, new to the duties that they have undertaken.

Every day the meeting gained momentum. Crowds began gathering long before the appointed hour, and all roads seemed to lead to the tabernacle. Policemen gave full cooperation and handled the traffic well.

Parents were thankful for the results that Dr. Bob was having with the boys and girls of the St. Petersburg high school. Young people by the hundreds flocked to the front of the big tabernacle in response to the appeal to declare publicly that they would adopt the evangelist's motto in life, which is *"DO RIGHT."* It is interesting that up to the end of Dr. Bob's ministry he was still quoting this motto.

The expenses of the meeting were raised the first week, and Dr. Bob, true to form in always thinking of the other person, conceived the idea that after they had raised the $5,000 budget, the rest of the money should be donated to the Florida Children's Home in Jacksonville.

One night the people flocked to the front. The next day the paper stated:

BOB JONES PREACHED HELL AND DAMNATION WEDNESDAY NIGHT—and got better response to his plea for converts than he did the night he pictured the beauties and joys of a Christian life. It seems easier to scare them than to lead men into the fold.

Early in the campaign a tropical storm hit the town and caused much excitement. Dr. Bob used this as a springboard for a message. Headlines stated:

NEED RELIGIOUS EXCITEMENT—DECLARED EVANGELIST JONES

St. Petersburg needs to get as much excited over religion as it gets over the prospects of a storm hitting the city. The people of this city are much more excited about the prospects of their homes being blown down than they have ever been over the fate of their souls. There is not any danger of too much religious excitement in this country today. The church has been subnormal so long that it does not know what the normal is.

Newspaper men were always in the meetings, and one of the papers always reported in full each sermon. One day the headlines blared forth: "ORDERS ALL OUT OF CHOIR WHO REFUSE TO QUIT DANCE." In large letters the subheadlines said: "Evangelist Says He Does Not Want Them—Young People Also Held up to Scorn for Declining to Quit." The article said:

All men and women who decline to give a promise they will quit dancing are ordered out of the choir at the Bob Jones tabernacle by the evangelist, who declared that he does not want them again to sing on the platform at his meetings. He told them to sit with the sinners from this time on.

Mr. Jones held up to the scorn of the congregation 18 young folks, members of the young people's societies of the local church, for refusing to give their promise to quit dancing. . . . Then he directed the attention of the people to these girls and young men and branded them as sinners who endorsed the wickedness inspired by the devil.

The sharp arrow of this message pierced the hearts of the women because the next day the headlines said: "WOMEN WANT DANCE HALLS CLOSED HERE." The article had this to say:

A group of women who have been stirred by the preaching of Bob Jones in the big tabernacle, last night asked Mayor Frank F. Pulver to close his public dance halls in this city. By request the mayor met the women in the tabernacle at 7 o'clock before the evening service began and before Mr. Jones reached the building. Mr. Jones did not know of the meeting until it was over.

In every big revival, Dr. Bob preached on the cardinal sins of men.
The EVENING INDEPENDENT headlined the sermon this way:

FOUR CARDINAL SINS OF MEN BITTERLY SCORED
BY JONES

In a sermon to men only yesterday afternoon Bob Jones used plain language in scoring roundly the four cardinal sins of men. He declared in the
opening that there is a devil who is actively at work at all times. The evangelist's sermon was in part as follows:

"The devil works in an intelligent manner. He always tries hardest to get
hold of the man with the most influence. You need not be uneasy that your
son will be made a drunkard by the drunkard in the ditch. There isn't a
boy in this town that wants to be like that man. Here is what I mean; you
need not be uneasy about your daughter being ruined by the direct—you
notice I say direct—influence of that old prostitute yonder in her earthly
hell, that poor, wrecked, ruined, disgraced, fallen creature. There is not a
girl in this town that would wish to be like her. But you watch out for the
butterfly of your community that sips from life's sweetest flowers and yet
engages in the impure. One crooked, impenitent shadowed society woman
can do more to damn girlhood of a town by direct influence than all the
prostitutes of America. You know the devil wants you to keep a form of
respectability; he wants you to be decent and wants you to act the gentleman."

The paper said further:

SUCCESSFUL MEETINGS HELD DESPITE HEAVY RAINS
HERE

In spite of the heavy rains that fell all afternoon and evening, two successful meetings were held at the Bob Jones tabernacle, a fine meeting for
women and also a wonderful meeting later for men. There were over 1,500
men who responded to the talk and they wanted to go out to build Christian homes and to be better men.

Different groups gathered to hear this great preacher. One night
approximately 3,750 persons from the Woodmen of the World, the
Maccabees, the Woodmen Circle, the League of Women Voters, and the
Parent-Teachers Association, and delegates from the Gulfport schools
were special guests. Many souls were saved.

Observe this interesting report:

CROWD CHEERS AND APPLAUDS JONES' ATTACK

He had vigorously assailed card playing, dancing, divorce and bootlegging.
And he also claimed that women used profanity. Evangelist Bob Jones did
not mince words in discussing his subject, "Outstanding Sins of America,"

and the audience cheered, applauded and laughed as he drove home some point or told a humorous story.

On account of bad weather the crowd was smaller than at any previous meeting, but the evangelist kept the undivided attention of those present. . . .

Dancing, bootlegging, profanity, Sabbath-breaking, divorce, card playing, and evolution came in for a vigorous attack from the evangelist. Some of the points made . . . were:

"There are many frizzly headed high school girls who can give your boys lessons in cursing." "There are more women swearing today than ever before." "There is no danger of a Blue Sunday, but you are about to have a Red Sunday." "The bootlegger spits on the Stars and Stripes and tramples the Constitution under his feet." "If I were prosecuting attorney, I would prosecute these poker-playing women." "There was a time when a bad woman was kicked out of society, but now you elect her president of your club." "Folks are pleasure-wild in this country." "The most cruel theory the world ever saw is the materialist theory of evolution."

"We have enough people here tonight to run the devil out of St. Petersburg."

Evangelist Jones kept his audience in a good humor. He announced that tonight he hoped every one would bring in $1.00 to help defray expenses. "If you cannot afford it, you will be as welcome as the flowers in May, anyway." He stated that he hoped to secure half the expenses this week, but to his amazement by the end of the week he had collected practically all the money for the expenses.

"JONES PLANS PREACH HELL FROM NOW ON" were big headlines on one day's paper. Some of the newspapers claimed that he did actually preach the hell out of their city. One message is still talked about after all these years. The headlines ran: "CITY WARNED NOT TO PLACE MONEY FIRST." Subheadlines said: "Bob Jones Urges St. Petersburg Not to Sell Out to the Devil." In this particular meeting testimony was given by many in the audience who wanted to tell about God's goodness to them, how much the meeting had meant to them, and how they thanked God for sending such a man as Bob Jones to their city.

Another subheadline in the article said: "Women Lead in Number of Converts for the First Time at the Revival in This City." Then it was explained:

St. Petersburg was warned by Bob Jones at the tabernacle meeting last night that if it places money and business above God it will be cursed. His subject was "THE MAN WHO SOLD OUT," and he declared that a city can sell out just as well as an individual. He declared that if St. Petersburg opens the town wide to attract tourists it will not stand and he thanked God that no tourist has ever come to this city because it was wide open. The first cry when any reform is proposed, he said, is that it will hurt business and too often the public sells out to business. Dr. Bob said, "I have never seen a city in which there is so much general prosperity and so little poverty as in St. Petersburg." He is right.

The meeting last night was unusual in several respects. The evangelist preached to Christians mainly, hurling denunciation on the church folks who sell out for money, position, society leadership or business. But the appeal reached more unconverted than it touched the church members and the people who went forward in response to a double invitation were nearly all men and women who had never made public profession of faith in Christ.

At the close of the service, Bob Jones turned it into an experience meeting, something he said he had not done in ten years at an evening gathering. Scores of men and women gave their testimony as to what the revival has meant to them. . . . One of the first to stand and give testimony was a Jew who has embraced Christianity at the revival. One girl stood and declared she would never dance again and an elderly woman said: "Thank God, I never danced in my life and do not have to quit." Men, women and children gave testimony, declaring they intend to put God first.

One writer reported this story which Dr. Jones had related:

"One night after I had concluded a service in El Paso, Texas, I was invited to address a gathering of men. I did not know what the meeting was but nevertheless, I felt urged to go. There were 500 men packed into a room that was supposed to hold 200. I found out that they were members of the Ku Klux Klan, and among them I found ministers and many of the outstanding consecrated Christian laymen of the city. The lodge was not in session. They had adjourned and were waiting for me to talk to them. They told me that the minutes of their order would show that the entire organization had gone on record against anybody taking the law into their own hands, that they worked through constituted authority and worked in no other way. I talked to those men in that lodge room about Jesus Christ and urged them to be true to Him in everything. I pleaded with those men that night to accept Jesus Christ as their Saviour. My plea there met with as much approval as it had in the tabernacle in any of my services."

Dr. Bob knew that throughout America at that time the Ku Klux Klan included many outstanding Christian men of the community, that these men went to prayer meeting, and that they were official members of the various churches. There were exceptions, of course; but in every place he had found that many of the most spiritual men belonged to this organization.

It was not possible for Dr. Bob to attend all the special meetings and the various clubs to which he was invited day after day. I will quote from one message which he gave to the Kiwanians, because Dr. Bob himself was an honorary Kiwanian for many years. His subject was "HOW TO SUCCEED."

He emphasized the need of co-operation, pep, enthusiasm, tact, continuity and love of God as the essentials to accomplishment in achieving things worthwhile. He said: "I never knew a successful man who did not accomplish greater things if he had 'love of God' as one of the controlling elements of his life."

Another day Dr. Bob addressed the Rotary Club, and this summary was given:

Bob Jones never said a truer thing than when he told the Rotarians that success is not accumulating money or gaining power or fame or popularity. Too many people think one or all of these things are the acme of success.

After Dr. Bob had been in the city for awhile, the headlines read: "PRAISE GIVEN TO THIS CITY BY EVANGELIST." Dr. Bob praised the city and the good work they were doing. He said, "I have been in this city long enough to get the fever . . . the 'St. Petersburg fever!' Continuing, he said:

"I like your city and the energy and accomplishment that the citizens are producing. If the business men of St. Petersburg were as much interested in God, as they are in their particular businesses, St. Petersburg would be crowned with success."

He thanked the newspapers for their splendid cooperation and complimented various projects of the city.

Through the papers it was announced: "VAUDEVILLE CLOSES FOR JONES REVIVAL." The manager was quoted as having said: "When I heard that Bob Jones revival meeting would be here for five weeks, I wired a cancellation of all Keith shows until December 1." Many other questionable or competing places were closed also.

Because the tabernacle held only 5,000 people, sometimes it was necessary to have two services in order to accommodate all the people. The headlines stated, "9,000 IN BIG TABERNACLE AT TWO MEETINGS." By the end of the first week, people were being turned away in droves. Under the headlines of "SECOND WEEK FOR REVIVAL," was written:

Evangelist Bob Jones is facing a strenuous program for the second week . . . . He spoke the first night of the second week on "What is a Christian?" On that night he not only had a great many high school children but there was a delegation of realtors that had come to a state convention and they all turned out to hear Bob Jones.

Dr. Bob always scored success in preaching to women. On November

8, big headlines stated: "FIRST STEP TO GOD TAKEN BY SCORES OF WOMEN HERE." According to the newspaper article,

> Scores of women not members of any church and who had never before taken a public stand for God last night responded to the appeal by Bob Jones to join the forces of Christ and promised to put Him first in their lives. Of the hundreds of women who flocked to the platform when the evangelist asked for a decision, nearly 200 had never before professed their faith in the Christian religion.

After an unusually successful service the headlines said, "JONES URGES HOME PRAYER." Subheadlines announced, "Evangelist Talks to Large Crowd at Shed on the American Home." This article followed:

> Failure of some children to become Christians is due to the way they are trained at home by their parents, Evangelist Bob Jones charged Thursday night in his sermon on The American Home.

> The big shed was crowded and the evangelist was cheered time and time again as he appealed to the mothers and fathers to be more careful in training their children.

> During his sermon the evangelist took a shot at "personal liberty." "The only folks you hear talking about personal liberty are those who want a drink," he said. "I am tired of that expression. They want light wines and beer, but they are not going to get it." Then there was great applause.

> "There are men in this house tonight who have built their homes out of money stolen from widows and orphans"—and again there was loud applause.

> "It is just as much the duty of a girl to help her mother at home as it is for her to go to the B.Y.P.U. or Christian Endeavor Society," the evangelist declared getting back to his subject.

Dr. Bob went on to tell the men that they had a duty to help around the house.

> "If I could I would pass a law to compel every man to keep house for a week each year," he said. He also attacked the loafer saying—"God save this country from a bunch of good-for-nothing loafers. It is a crime to be idle. Some women raise their daughters to parade the streets. God will hold you to account if you permit your daughter and son to grow up as loafers."

> "There is too much damnable immodesty in this country," he said. "When the sun is shining, they ought to walk on the shady side of the street."

> He also urged his hearers to be kind to the children and not to always be saying, don't, don't. He said that some children had never heard their fathers pray and that the present method of raising children is too soft.

> He then went on to urge family prayers. "There are mothers and fathers here who do not know where their twelve-year-old children are tonight."

He called attention to the necessity of family prayer and urged all to have prayer in their homes.

On Friday, November 17, 1922, under the headlines of "FALSE FAITHS . . ." and subheadlines of "Evangelist to Preach on Devil's Part in Newer Religions," it was reported:

> "The Devil and False Religions" will be the subject of the last week-day sermon by Bob Jones, evangelist, at the tabernacle tonight. Touching briefly upon this chosen subject at Thursday night's meeting, Jones intimated that his talk would be directed against some of the teachings of Pastor Russell, Spiritualists, Christian Scientists, ethical doctrine propagandist and the Roman Church.
>
> Circus goers, card players, dancers, all who preferred pleasures to preparing for the second coming of Christ, were attacked . . . in a little modernized version of the story of Noah and the flood.

As a result of this meeting, the church men formed a new organization: "The Protestant Christian Council of St. Petersburg." One of the main purposes of the organization was to close all dance halls in St. Petersburg.

Dr. Bob made a strong attack on the evils of the city. One headline said, "DR. JONES URGES ST. PETERSBURG TO BUILD ON CHRISTIANITY." Another said, "JONES ATTACKS THE LIQUOR BUNCH." Dr. Bob was quoted as saying that the liquor people were trying to take over the soldier boys and trying to bribe them by offering them bonuses to be received in taxes from the sale of light wines and beer. "The devil never takes such attacks lightly," he warned. Some repercussions were felt.

People were delighted with Dr. Bob's sermon in defense of revivals. The next day there were big headlines in bold letters: JONES DEFENDS REVIVALS IN SERMON LAST EVENING.

> On the subject of revivals Bob Jones last night preached the following: "Some folks say that the day of revivals is over. Well, if that is true, then not only Christianity but all the world is doomed. If there was not a Democratic revival every four years, the party would have been dead years ago; if the Republicans did not have a revival every four years, it too would die. If the same shouting could be brought about in revivals that results from political revivals, the echo could be heard around the world. When a political revival breaks out, speakers appear everywhere and folks are swept off their feet. In the midst of all these revivals, however, some eternal decisions are made. When Uncle Sam went into this last great war, he put on the greatest revival of patriotism ever known in America. If a revival of patriotism is necessary, a revival of Christianity is just as imperative.
>
> "The growth of the Christian church has been due to revivals. One wave has followed another, and each has contributed its part to the growth of the Kingdom of God on earth."

CHAPTER 14

Hartford City, Indiana, 1915

Dr. Bob felt strangely led of the Lord to accept an invitation to this small town of only 7,000 population, even though larger cities were clamoring for him at the time. And what a meeting it turned out to be! The people in the area said that there had never been anything like it. According to the newspapers, "Not less than 100 people came forward each service on a clear-cut call and accepted Christ as their Saviour." Before the meeting the town had a total of 1,500 church memberships. After the meeting, the churches had almost 4,000 members—an increase of 150 per cent.

Just imagine—a small town of 7,000 taking in more than 2,400 new church members! On the last Sunday of the meeting, 1,600 joined the churches. In this number were several saloonkeepers who had just been converted. Two churches were in the process of being built, and the preachers exclaimed: "Our churches even though unfinished are already too small." One church tore out the sides and enlarged, and the other tore out the end and added onto the church in order to take care of the great influx.

Sunday movies were just coming into vogue at that time, and they were closed. Another issue was liquor. (This was a great issue in all Dr. Bob's campaigns!) The paper stated:

> Mr. Jones makes an uncompromising fight on the liquor traffic. Hartford City, Indiana, a manufacturing city with a large foreign element, voted dry and put out of business 16 saloons within two months after Mr. Jones had closed his campaign there. The city had been controlled by the wet element since 1842. It is said that the deep spiritual effect his campaigns leave on a city is immeasurable.

An editorial about the meeting was headed "ALABAMA EVANGELIST HOLDS WONDERFUL REVIVAL IN INDIANA." It stated in part:

> The greatest religious campaign ever held in Hartford City is the way the papers are speaking of the revival just closed by the Reverend 'Bob' Jones

at Hartford City, Indiana, in which he succeeded in winning over 2,000 people to the church. The Indiana papers declared that no such meeting had ever before been held in that section in a city of similar size as the revival just brought to a close.

The Hartford City TIMES-GAZETTE reported:

The close of the tabernacle meeting Sunday evening came at the end of a memorable service. With a choir singing "God Be With You 'Til We Meet Again," and the 4,000 people in the building giving the Evangelist the Chautauqua salute, the biggest series of gatherings at Hartford City or any other town its size in Indiana has ever known came to a close. There was a great meeting at the tabernacle Sunday evening but the other services Sunday were also momentous ones. The building was crowded to the doors Sunday evening. It was literally packed, and hundreds were unable to get a seat. It is estimated that over 1,000 were turned away.

That seats were at a premium is evident in this paragraph from the same article:

When the men's meeting closed Sunday afternoon, many men remained in the building, and there were many women waiting to get inside. A number of the women carried baskets of food and ate their suppers in the tabernacle. At 5:00 the big building was almost full, and at 6:00 there were few seats left. It had been announced that the service would begin as soon as the building was packed, and the promise was kept. At 6:30, an hour earlier than customary, the services were started. There was not an inch of standing room unoccupied, and boys who didn't object to a little speculation on the Sabbath had little difficulty in disposing of choice seats at a nickel a sitting. After one of the most interesting and impressive sermons that 'Bob' Jones delivered during his stay at Hartford City, 158 converts came forward Sunday evening. The invitation was not prolonged, and had the evangelist cared to hold on, the evening service might have been continued for hours. After four weeks' work, however, everyone was worn out, and the services were reluctantly brought to a close.

Bobby Jones' Meetin'

Old Blackford now is mighty proud —
For in her midst reposes
A power for good that's brave and strong
And sweet as fragrant roses.
The curious, idle, good and bad —
Montpelier, Roll and Eaton —
But most of all is Hartford folks
Made good at Jones' meetin's.

The churches now have cleared their skirts
And dare approach a brother,

Peace, love, and harmony prevail,
  Each works to win another.
Our high school's made a wondrous change,
  Our ball team may get beaten,
But all will sail triumphant on
  Since Bobby Jones' meetin'.

Men have their views, seem firm and strong,
  But hearing Bob they fail,
And though impossible it seemed,
  They finally "hit the trail."
The liquor forces great and small
  All surely now feel beaten,
For men have by the hundreds changed
  Since Bobby Jones' meetin'.

'Tis great to see the children come,
  The lassie and the laddie,
It melts our hearts when mother starts,
  And next we see is daddy.
But oh! it's greater yet to see
  Old folks so worn and beaten
Catch glimpses of the heavenly rest
  At Bobby Jones' meetin'.

We are so happy over it,
  This glorious new relation,
We want to pass the cup of joy
  Along to all creation.
'Twill be a better place to live
  At Hartford, Roll or Eaton—
All owing in the years to come
  To Bobby Jones' meetin'.

Lo! politics and all its tricks,
  Are for a time forgotten,
And in the future let us hope
  Will never be as rotten.
No matter what our party tiffs,
  Or how our party's beaten,
The county now united stands,
  For Bobby Jones' meetin'.

                    —Mrs. Charles Ritter
                    Hartford City, Ind.

CHAPTER 15

McKeesport, Pennsylvania, 1927

More than mere coincidence, I believe, is an incident connected with the McKeesport meeting. How else could it be explained that Dr. Bob, who, like other evangelists, had to set up his meetings in advance — sometimes years ahead — should have accepted January, 1927, for the date of this meeting? Why is the timing so significant? It was the year that Bob Jones College was founded in Panama City, Florida, and also the year that Dr. Bob met Mr. J. S. Mack who did so very much for the school in a financial way. I believe that God arranged all the events surrounding the meeting of these two men and that He put in them a kindred spirit for each other and for the work of this Christian school. The history of Bob Jones University is replete with similar happenings which to the unspiritual may seem coincidental, but which to the spiritual bespeak divine prearrangement.

Day after day big headlines appeared in the McKeesport papers, and many times there was word-for-word coverage of the sermons. One outstanding sermon was headlined: "HOPE OF THE WORLD IS IN GOODNESS OF ITS WOMEN, SAYS BOB JONES." Under another headline — "HIGHLIGHTS IN BOB JONES TALK TO WOMEN ONLY" — the reporter quoted pithy sayings from the sermon. I quote from an article which was written about his sermon on "PRAYER."

Evangelist Jones took no particular page of Scripture for his text, but in his talk frequent references were made to those Biblical inscriptions which referred to prayer.

"The greatest need of our life today is prayer," declared the minister in launching off into his sermon. "There is not a problem in our lives that we could not solve if we resorted to prayer to Almighty God.

"Don't you think for one moment that you can put God into bankruptcy. You say to yourself that you are wealthy, that you are rich, that you have a dollar whenever you need it. Let me ask you who gave you that dollar, and you come back and say, 'I worked for it.' That's all right, but where did the dollar come from? You say from the mint. Good. Where did the mint get the mineral? Why, from the bosom of nature, and there you have the wealth of God, and He has given you the opportunity to get that wealth of His. He has all kinds of resources.

"There are plenty of boys walking the streets today who could be used as preachers in their own way through prayer. They have the ability, and they have the power, but it will take your prayers and my prayers to make them heed the Divine commandment to go out among men.

"Don't you know that we do God's work in such a slipshod way? There is no substitute for prayer. Up here in the North you have revivals in the winter when you freeze to death. Down South they have revivals in the summer when they sweat to death. You need a revival in your own heart all the year round. I believe in good choirs . . . good preachers, in evangelists, and in revivals; but what good are any of these if the spirit of prayer is not there?

"Prayer is one job that anyone can do in any place at any time. No one can stop me nor can anyone stop you if you want to pray. Prayer is the biggest job any Christian man or woman can do at any time, any place, anywhere. When a man or woman prays, he has a part in every Christian work in every part of the earth.

"How many of you offer a daily prayer for your pastor? If you want power in your pulpit, it is up to you to put power in your pastor. It is not right to let your pastor do the whole job. Peter and John always did something for someone else before they prayed to God to help them. Folks who go to the place of prayer are the people who make the crippled walk. There are lots of crippled people in McKeesport and everywhere else. They have been crippled since they have been born.

"My hat's off to the man or the woman, white or black, rich or poor, high or low, who tries to lead a man to prayer.

"Your mother and father taught you how to pray. You say you can't pray in public. I won't want you to make a show of yourself. Listen! You may fool your neighbor, but you can't fool God. He will open the door for you if you will knock, if it takes the angel band of Heaven to assist Him. It is up to you to let Him know that you are there knocking, waiting for Him to open the door to let you in."

The paper stated that the people were so interested in promoting the meeting that even the yellow and green cabs carried big signs advertising the Bob Jones meetings. People attended in great masses, and hundreds were turned away.

Now for

John Sephus Mack

One night the building was packed and jammed. Looking up from the pulpit, Dr. Bob saw a man walking down the aisle. He had trouble finding a seat. Dr. Bob got up, walked down the aisle, extended his hand in greeting, and invited the man to come up to the platform and sit with the preachers. The man was J. S. Mack. But let us hear Mr. Mack's version of the story:

> That night as I sat behind Dr. Jones on the platform looking around, I heard him saying something. At first I thought he was practicing his sermon for the evening. I leaned over and was startled to hear him say, "O Jesus, help me; help me to get hold of this crowd tonight. Speak through me and use me as never before." I was a Psalm-singing Presbyterian, and was used to praying to God the Father. Dr. Jones was talking directly to Jesus. I was intrigued with this man who had an audience with the Lord and in whom there was no "sham." I made up my mind that if God prospered me, I would help Dr. Bob if he ever needed help.

It was by divine appointment, I believe, that these men met and by divine appointment that they formed a working team—one a giant in God's business, promoting His Cause to the ends of the earth; the other a genius in making money, which he used to help in that promotion.

Mr. Mack was the Chairman of the Board and also President of the G. C. Murphy 5 and 10 cent Stores located through the Northeast. The following incident points out the type of businessman Mr. Mack was. He went to the bank to borrow money to buy the G. C. Murphy Stores that had gone bankrupt during the depression. He asked for one million dollars. The banker thought he was crazy. He could not believe that at the height of the depression any man would dare to come in and ask for a loan of such a staggering amount. "Do you know what to do with a million dollars?" the banker asked. Mr. Mack laughed and said, "I know what *not* to do with that much money." The answer pleased the banker and he said, "It is just as important to know what not to do as it is to know what to do. You may have the money." More about Mr. Mack and his generosity to Bob Jones College will be told in EDUCATIONAL ENDEAVORS, Part III of this book.

A reporter wrote of the evangelistic campaign in McKeesport (abridged here):

> Last week, after he had appeared once or twice, many opinions were passed upon Bob Jones. With one accord they all pronounced him a success in evangelistic circles, and bright predictions of results in McKeesport were made. These opinions however complimentary in themselves, said nothing of Bob Jones as a man.
>
> It is hard to describe Bob Jones. He is a "he-man" and he employs "he-man" tactics in both his evangelical and private life. He sees one path and he follows it, but is always ready to stop and do any favors within his power.
>
> He tells the truth and makes you like it. Oftentimes he says things which

strike home, and sometimes cause you to wince, but still you like it. Why? you ask. A reason is hard to find, unless you want to take comfort in the thought that "there is one man who doesn't give a hang whether you like him—he is going to tell you what he thinks of you."

A good example of the character of the evangelist was set out in a meeting last week. The tabernacle was pretty well filled and the sermon had begun, when a little fellow around eight years old walked across the front of the building and before the evangelist . . . plainly seeking someone whom he had lost. An usher not wishing to have the congregation disturbed asked the boy to sit with him. He did, but it was not many seconds until it could be seen that his body was being shaken by heavy sobs.

The boy made no sound, but his grief was noticed by the evangelist, who immediately stopped his sermon. . . . "What is it son?" he asked in a voice that could not be heard farther back than the fifth row. "Have lost my daddy," sobbed the youngster.

"What's your name son?"

The name was given, and Bob Jones paged the child's parents, and restored him to them in a seat away back in the middle section of the tabernacle, after which he went calmly on with his sermon, just as though nothing had happened.

He means what he says in his meetings. After yesterday's sessions, two reporters asked for permission to use the number of converts. . . . He had previously announced that they would not be published, but the reporters thought that he would not hold out on the press. Closing his lips in a manner that left no room for argument, he said, "We do not care to publish that."

There you are! The only way to describe Bob Jones is that he is a "he-man," a "he-man" who means what he says with no "maybes" about it.

One of the converts of this meeting was a "FORMER UNDERWORLD WIT." He had lived by his wits since 1918. He was what we might call "a con man." This man, a graduate of one of the best universities in the country, was from an environment of culture and spoke several languages. He had traveled in most of the civilized countries of the world. Here is his own story:

All of these assets I have combined and used to become one of the worst crooks in the world. I came to McKeesport last Sunday to practice my vices, but was not going to begin operations until Monday. I dropped in to a corner drug store and asked if any theaters were open. I was told that there would be no entertainment of any kind open till after midnight. The druggist said that almost the whole city would be at the Bob Jones tabernacle. I cannot bear to be alone for one minute. . . . I had a good Christian mother, and memories of her would almost break me down when I was alone. . . . Sunday night . . . merely to get my mind off myself, I went to the tabernacle. I sat on the end of one of the seats near the rear so that I could get up and leave unnoticed at any time I became bored. I believe Mr. Jones was inspired by God that night to hit at me. God used that sermon to touch my heart. . . . I did not sleep a bit that night. I read the Bible and tried to pray all night. Next morning I resolved to go to work, and believing God would find a way for me to earn and pay back the money I have stolen from people, I set out—for the first time in years—in search of honest employment. I went to several preachers and told them of my sins, and by 10 o'clock Monday morning, I had the peace of God in my heart. He took away that awful sin and gave me new desires.

CHAPTER 16

Andalusia, Alabama, 1927

From McKeesport, Pennsylvania, Dr. Bob headed South to begin a lecture tour all over the country on "The Perils of America." In February of 1927, he gave this lecture in Andalusia, Alabama. This excerpt from the newspaper will give an idea of the meeting and the message.

DR. BOB JONES NEW LECTURE HEARD HERE. . .

The honorable J. Morgan Presswood introduces noted divine. Lecture was replete with scathing denunciation of those who are striking at the foundations of our national life. Large audiences greeted speaker and listened intently to stirring zeal that is always manifest when he confronts an audience. . . .

"I want to talk to you about some of the perils that confront America," said he. "I am not a pessimist and neither am I an optimist. I would rather be a pessimist than an optimist. A pessimist will see the facts and probably enlarge upon them, but the optimist is so blind by the light of his consuming optimism that he cannot see the facts as they are presented by a view of the real situation.

"America is the greatest country in the world. I love America. I know more about America than I know about any other country. I have traveled some in many foreign countries but great as America is, there are certain perils. . . and I want hurriedly to call our attention to some of them.

"First, the peril of the city. America has accomplished in a few years what it took other nations centuries to accomplish. She has already concentrated a majority of the population in the cities. New York is not a Christian city, and the majority of her population is not even American. I sat ten days in the Democratic national convention in New York, and I felt that I was in Hell during that time. There I witnessed the yelling and the cheering by the mob for Alcohol Smith. These men did not know what they were saying except to say what the ward heelers told them to say. I went to Boston, and there around the monument of Paul Revere is the Italian settlement whose people do not even speak our language but who shout the praises of Mussolini. Chicago has twenty-seven per cent of the population foreign born. I want to tell you that one of the leading divines of the Methodist church told me that there were more Methodists in New York fifty years ago than there are today. And the same would probably apply to all other Protestant denominations. I believe Birmingham is the best city in America of the smaller sized cities. . .but I want to tell you people that the Christians in the cities are fighting with their backs to the wall. The enemies of Christianity are seeking to break down the very bulwarks of Christian civilization. You say, 'How does the city affect us who live in the rural sections?' I want to tell you that 'as goes the city, so will go the country.' " Dr. Bob went on to tell the various other perils that confront us.

"Second, we are facing the perils of thoughtlessness. Third, there is the peril of extreme wealth and poverty. Fourth, the peril of unrest. Fifth, the peril of uncertainty. Sixth, the peril of lawlessness. Seventh, the peril of a nation without a Sabbath. Eighth, the peril of sensuality.

"Now in conclusion, what shall we do? We must Christianize the inevitables. What are the inevitables? First, there is labor and the labor unions. They are essential, and they are with us and a part of us. We must Christianize them. England has Christian labor, and that is what saved England in her labor crisis. Second, we must recognize the fact that in this country we are going to accumulate wealth. You can scarcely engage in any kind of business or manufacturing endeavor without accumulating wealth. We must Christianize the men who control the wealth of our country. Third, we are going to educate. We must Christianize education, and here I want to say that I have no objection to your teaching my boy evolution as a theory, but you have no right to teach it as a material fact. Bryan believed in teaching evolution as a theory."

Back to His Hometown—Montgomery

From Andalusia, Dr. Bob went to Montgomery, where the headlines stated:

BOB JONES SPEAKS TO PACKED HOUSE. . .

The editor of the ADVOCATE spent Tuesday night in Montgomery en route to the Dothan Methodist conference. When he stepped from the train, he learned that Bob Jones, the distinguished evangelist, was to deliver his famous lecture on THE PERILS OF AMERICA that night. He said, "In company with other brethren, I went to hear him. When we reached the Grand Theatre, we found it packed. We started to the galleries which were already packed to the limit. Finally, we wedged our way into a great crowd standing around the wall and for two hours we stood and listened to this matchless pulpit orator. Round after round of applause, thunderous applause, greeted the evangelist as he preached the truth. In graphic way, he pictured the sins of Americans today and earnestly urged his hearers to stand by the Bible and evangelical Christianity.

"In closing, he told us about his new school, Bob Jones College at College Point near Panama City, Florida, which he said would be the bulwark of Christianity. That he would keep it evangelical, Christian, and orthodox. He told us the school would open the next September. He asked his hearers to remember the school in prayer."

CHAPTER 17

Anniston, Alabama, 1920

This campaign was heralded by the newspapers as "A wonderful success." I will refer to one article and one editorial that appeared during the meeting and to a short article that appeared during a later meeting in the same town.

First, the article:

ANNISTON'S GREAT RELIGIOUS CAMPAIGN
CLOSES THIS WEEK

One of the greatest religious campaigns ever waged in Anniston will close with the last of the series of services to be held at the Lyric Sunday evening.

The campaign has been conducted by the renowned evangelist, Reverend Bob Jones, who came to Anniston under the auspices of the Methodist and Baptist churches. The members of the Church of Christ and all other denominations have co-operated and worked for the wonderful success of the campaign.

"The beautiful spirit of unity and good will that exist in Anniston between the various denominations has been a wonderful inspiration to me," said Mr. Jones during an interview with him last week. "The members of all your churches have entered heart and soul into all phases of the meeting, all united in sweet bonds of fellowship and loving interest for the greatest Cause that faces humanity. I am a union man. I love to hold union services. I am a Methodist but have a mighty tender place in my heart for the Baptists, because my mother was a Baptist. I have never been in a town that I enjoyed or admired more than Anniston. It is so very progressive, and an ideal place for a home."

Dr. Bob was very much impressed with the young people and said: "You certainly have a fine crowd of school girls and boys in Anniston. I have deeply appreciated the loyalty and attendance at the services of the 'Noble Institute' girls, the 'Presbyterian College' boys and the high school girls and boys, and have enjoyed talking in all the schools."

One night following a special dinner in honor of the Joneses, Dr. Bob spoke to a large number of soldiers who were stationed in Anniston. . . .Mr. Jones is an enthusiastic patriot, and in his talks frequently pays beautiful tributes to the American soldier boys who fought so valiantly in the World War. . . . During these trying days of reconstruction when the world is perplexed and unrest and discord on every hand, religion is needed more than ever before, and only through Christ can men find peace and rest. He alone is the solution of every problem, and the answer to all perplexities.

Now, the editorial:

GREATEST THING IN AMERICA: THAT "OLD-TIME RELIGION"

America just now is passing through one of the most critical periods in the history of the nation. Our social, economic and financial equilibrium is upset, and the whole fabric of our civilization is more or less awry.

There is under way a great political campaign. Two seats in the Senate of the United States are to be filled. The men that we shall select to fill these seats will play a big part in the shaping of the future history of the country. They will decide questions of morality, of statecraft, and economic import.

The gentlemen who set out for selfish purposes to murder the League of Nations have been successful. They have almost murdered the great man whose altruistic mind and heart conceived the beneficent covenant of international law.

The nation that set the world on fire and precipitated a struggle at arms that minimized all other human conflicts by comparison is on the verge of civil war. The black hand of Bolshevism is reaching out to claim new victims, and to stifle the uplifted voice of civilization.

All of these issues and others are to be considered in connection with the political campaign now in progress in Alabama. Yet, if any one of the men who are asking for the suffrage of the people of this state were to come to Anniston to present his claims, he would be fortunate if he drew an audience of five hundred persons.

The people of Alabama are not very much concerned over political issues, and there has been so much talk in so many different directions concerning all the issues outlined above that we have assumed a somewhat fatalistic attitude toward them all. . . .

There is one thing, however, of which the American people never tire. They are eternally and everlastingly interested in the "OLD-TIME RELIGION," and the enormous crowds that are going every morning, afternoon and evening to hear Bob Jones at the Lyric Theatre give eloquent testimony to this fact. They may grow weary of things materially, but the appeal of the spiritual is ever-present.

This fact is reassuring for as the faith of this people is founded on the Rock of Ages, the safety of this nation is secure. It was there that it was born, it was from that source that it gained its strength, and it was from the lighthouse there that its ideals were shed forth to wayfaring men of all other nationalities.

The Declaration of Independence and the Constitution of the United States were created in an atmosphere of prayer, and as long as we continue to look to the great Statesmen of the Souls of men for guidance in our everyday life, the future of this republic shall be secure.

It is inspiring to be among the great crowds that come out every evening to the interdenominational revival. It was particularly enjoyable to be there yesterday evening and hear the great sermon that was preached to the boys and girls of our schools; for they were being educated in the greatest thing in America, in the world — the "OLD-TIME RELIGION."

* * *

Later, Dr. Bob returned to Anniston to speak three days in a two-week inter-denominational evangelistic conference, which was held at the Moore Avenue Baptist Church. While there he was interviewed by Jane Marxer, who wrote, in part:

"U. S. LOSES ITS SENSE OF SIN," DR. JONES SAYS

"I think that America has more church members, less spirituality, and more immorality in supposedly decent circles than ever in the history of the country," he said. "We have lost our sense of sin.

"What this country needs is about twelve months of Hell-fire-damnation preaching, to let people know that sin is sin.

"There is in America today no dominant prophetic voice," he said, giving Billy Sunday as an example of one who possessed a prophetic voice, a voice of warning of the spiritual dangers that confront us.

CHAPTER 18

Miscellaneous Incidents

The life of a fiery evangelist is not a bed of roses, and neither is it dull. There are countless stories to prove this, but I can mention only a few. The first few incidents to which I will refer are in Dr. Bob's own words.

I remember when I started in the ministry. I had five sermons, had to preach twice a day, and stayed five days. There was a man in that community who was said to be the smartest man in the country; some said he was an infidel, others said he was an agnostic, and others said he was an atheist. I did not know what some of the words meant, but I knew he was a sinner and needed God.

I said to the pastor, "I am going over to see the old colonel." The pastor said, "He will insult you in his home. He has insulted three or four preachers."

I said, "He needs God, doesn't he?"

He said, "Yes, but you cannot handle him; he is the smartest man in this country. You had better let him alone; he will eat you alive."

I said, "All right."

But that night I thought of the old man in sin, and I was troubled. Yes, I was impulsive — but did you ever think how God can take the impulsive spirit in a young Christian and use it? Did you ever think how it is that some men succeed in evangelistic work when young and when old they cannot? It is because they lose the impulsive spirit. God wants a man to be venturesome.

The next morning I hitched the horse to the buggy, and I drove up one red hill and down another. After a while I came to the old home, a magnificent Southern home. I got out and hitched the horse. I was so scared that my legs shook. I went up the front walk with my knees hitting together. I went into the house scared to death. Inside the door there sat the handsomest man I ever saw. He had long grey hair, and he looked to me like a giant, physically and mentally.

I said, "This is the colonel?"

He said, "Who are you?"

I said, "My name is Jones, sir."

He said, "What Jones is this?"

I said, "I am Bob Jones who is holding meetings over here."

He said, "I am glad to see you, Brother Jones. I have been thinking about sending word for you to come to see me. They will tell you that I am a skeptic, an atheist, and agnostic. I have been a sort of doubter all my life, but I have felt wretched the last day or two. I read the Bible all day yesterday. I know I have got to go before long, and if there is anything in Christianity, I want it. Talk to me like I was a little child; take that Bible and tell me what I must do to be saved."

I said, "God bless you! I came here for that business."

I read the Bible and prayed with him, and after a while he got up with the light of Heaven on his face; and he said, "I see it now."

*   *   *

Years ago out on a speaking tour in North Alabama I closed the week on a Friday night. I was tired. I had been speaking three times a day for several weeks. After I went to my room from the auditorium where I had addressed a large crowd, I got in bed and remembered that next day I was to rest. I decided to go to Birmingham, have my car gone over, go to a hotel, and shut myself up for the entire day.

Next morning when I got up it was pouring rain. I asked the Lord to let me get to Birmingham without any trouble. I had to travel over a dirt road. There was mud and clay. I had faith to believe the Lord would hear my prayer and I would reach Birmingham in safety and without delay. I got into the car and started. I went down the country road about ten miles and my car slipped into a ditch. I tried to get out of the ditch, but I could not do it.

I said to myself, "This is funny. I prayed with faith. I cannot understand why this happened. God said if I would ask in faith, He would hear my prayer."

But it wasn't any use in arguing; I was in the ditch. I got out in the pouring rain, walked up the road about fifty yards to a simple little country home. I went on the front porch and knocked at the door.

Somebody said, "Come in."

Inside I found a man with a lot of children around him. The man was trying to dress a little fellow.

"I'm in the mud," I said, "and I thought you wouldn't mind getting a mule and pulling me out."

The man looked up at me and I noticed that tears were running down his cheeks. "I'll help you as soon as I get the children dressed," he said. "I am not much good at dressing children. I have never had this to do. I buried their mother yesterday."

My heart went out to that father. There is nothing so pathetic as a man trying to nurse little children. He just does not have that mother touch. I told him I would help him. I took a little girl in my lap. She was about two years old. Her little stockings were ragged, but I got them on her. Her little shoes were worn. I put them on.

After we got the children dressed, I asked the father, "Are you a Christian?"

He said, "No, but my wife was. She prayed for me and talked to me a lot of times. I ought to be a Christian. I have these children to raise."

I put my arm around that father and said to him, "Well, we'll stop here and settle that."

I had prayer with him and led him to Jesus. Then we got the car out of the mud and I said to myself, "I know why God stopped me. He wanted me to help Him put over His program. That wife's prayer reached over the battlements of Heaven and pushed my car off the road at just the right place."

It is worth getting in the ditch to help God with His program. It is worth going to jail as Paul had to do. It is worth suffering and torment. It is worth dying for.

* * *

I was in a meeting in one of the best-known churches in the South. On the second night of the meeting, someone in the choir said, "I see the leading soprano of the city on the front row in the balcony."

I said, "Why don't you get her in the choir?" The choir member replied, "Oh! she wouldn't ruin her voice with simple Gospel singing. She is a 'classical' musician. She sings only on special occasions."

Everywhere I go, I find a few people like that. They always have something they think is too good for the Lord Jesus Christ. What they have is not too good for the Rotarians or Kiwanians or the P.T.A. or the rest of the folks, but it is too good for our Lord. I wonder who these people think Jesus is. He has heard some pretty good music. He heard the morning stars sing together, and up in Heaven the angels dip their tongues in the melody of the sky and cover their faces as they sing, "Holy, Holy, Holy."

After the service we asked all who wished to do so to remain for the after-service, and we told the rest of the crowd they could go. The choir member said, "I note that the leading soprano is staying." I said, "That is fine. Maybe she will get converted." After a few words of exhortation, we gave the invitation, and down all the aisles a number of unsaved people came to the front. I noticed that the leading soprano in the balcony was slowly moving out into the aisle, and I could not tell whether she was leaving the building or trying to find a stairway to come down to the front with the other penitents. She was on her way to the front! There are no high-brows and no low-brows at the foot of the cross. Here all get on a common level. The cultured, classical, educated, refined musician gets on the same level with the bummiest of the bums. A great many were saved in that after-service.

When the fat soprano got up off her knees, she took her big fat hand and wiped the tears from her eyes, and said, "I found the Lord! I am saved!" I replied, "That is fine. How about singing a solo tomorrow night?" She answered, "I will be in the choir from now on; and if you would like me to sing a solo, I will be glad to do it."

The next night she was in the choir. She really could sing. I could hear her soprano voice, even when the choir was singing. Just before I preached, the director of music said, "We will have a solo by Miss So-and-so." It was the leading soprano, and now she was going to sing for the first time for the Lord Jesus Christ. Up until this time, she had been singing for herself. She walked out to the front, and I could tell by the way she was holding her song book that something had happened to her. She did not have the usual strut that is characteristic of even good singers when they sing for themselves. She was so natural and so much at ease. She sang my favorite song — that wonderful old hymn:

> *I was once far away from the Saviour,*
> *And as vile as a sinner could be.*
> *And I wondered if Christ the Redeemer*
> *Could save a poor sinner like me.*

She had hardly started the second stanza until I noticed that people were crying. Everywhere they were wiping their tears away. Someone whispered to me, "This is the first time anybody ever cried under her singing."

It makes a difference when singers sing for the Lord Jesus Christ. There never has been an unconverted prima donna that ever sang that could not have sung more sweetly if she had been a Christian. There is not one legitimate thing a man can do that he cannot do better when he is a genuinely born-again, consecrated Christian.

* * *

One day Dr. Bob was describing various means the devil uses to break up a meeting — especially when God is working and souls are being saved — and he told this story:

In a certain meeting there was a boy who was a half-wit and who continually disturbed the meeting. If I asked for testimonies, this boy would be the first to testify. When I asked for prayers, he was the first to pray. He could do neither very well.

Finally I took the boy aside and said, "Buddy, you and I are doing all the testifying and praying. Let's make the others do some of it. Tonight when I call for testimonies and prayers, you just sit there."

The boy felt proud to be a party to putting over something on the others. When people would start to pray, he would lift his head and give me a knowing wink all the way across the room. The battle was won, and the devil was defeated.

* * *

Dr. Bob was noted for his energy in the pulpit. He was never still — feet or arms. Because of this he had to use "suspenders" to keep his shirt tucked in. The suspenders were attached to his sox. In one campaign he preached so hard that these suspenders came loose and started

A painting of Mrs. Bob Jones, Sr.

dragging. People began to laugh, and Dr. Bob realized that something unusual was happening. The more they laughed, the more concerned he became. Finally, he looked down and, to his chagrin, saw that with every step he took, his suspenders trailed behind. It did not "faze" him, however. He simply removed the suspenders, laid them on the pulpit, laughed with the crowd, and went on preaching as if nothing had happened.

* * *

A group of bootleggers became quite upset with Dr. Bob for his outspoken manner in dealing with the liquor issue in their town, and they conspired to "beat him up." Their plan was frustrated, however, when Congressman Stegal, who had somehow heard of the plan, came out and linked his arm in Dr. Bob's and walked with him to the station. Dr. Bob did not know of the danger until it was told to him sometime later.

* * *

One time when Dr. Bob had been lambasting the bootleggers and racketeers, a man became upset and accused Dr. Bob of telling a lie. Dr. Bob's Irish blood boiled.

"You had better be careful," he warned the man; "I might forget that I am a preacher."

Johnny McCloud, a loyal friend, was standing nearby; and he came hobbling up on crutches, pulling from his pocket one of the biggest knives Dr. Bob had ever seen, and said, "Bob, I'm not a preacher. Let me at him. I'll cut his throat."

Johnny might have done it, too, had not Dr. Bob and some other men stopped him.

* * *

A newspaperman wrote of Dr. Bob:

In speaking Mr. Jones has a forceful, non-assuming delivery which never fails to command attention. There is a peculiar twang to his voice which distinguishes it from all others. His manner is one of intense earnestness with unusual persuasiveness.

One peculiar feature about his meeting is that during every one of them some man pays back some money to some one from whom he had stolen it. At one meeting, a man who had formerly been a street car conductor in Jacksonville, Florida, sent the company $600 in cash in payment for sums he had taken from them in fares 5 cents at a time.

* * *

The meeting Dr. Bob held in Cambridge, Ohio, was one of the greatest in that part of the country up to that time. He described it as a "very high-grade meeting."

Mrs. Jones recalls that Cambridge was a very friendly place and people were always inviting them out to dinner. It was in Cambridge that she first saw women smoking cigarettes. Also, this place was noted for its Roquefort cheese. On their "days off," they used to go into the French section and get some of the delicious Roquefort. Dr. Bob ate so much one day that it made him sick, and he never liked Roquefort again.

* * *

In a certain large campaign in which Mrs. Jones was singing in the choir, this humorous incident occurred. Many souls were saved one night, and among them were two little boys. For some strange reason, during prayer Mrs. Jones opened her eyes just in time to see one little boy pull the hair of another little boy who had red hair. The redhead motioned for the first little boy to let him alone. The first little boy ignored the sign. Finally, the little redhead slowly rose, drew back his arm, and let go with a real wallop to his "friend." Then he sank back to his knees and continued praying. Dr. Bob said of the little redhead: "That boy will amount to something, for he can pray and fight at the same time."

* * *

Speaking of the Mansfield, Ohio, campaign, Mrs. Jones says:

I remember that meeting so well. It was held in a large tabernacle. A well-known attorney — a judge — was converted, and the meeting broke with wonderful results.

A few weeks before this meeting I had had a tonsillectomy and had almost hemorrhaged to death. I was pale as death and was not at all well during the meeting, so I could not take as active a part as I usually did. Because of my weakened condition, we took our "colored mammy" — Emma Hunt — with us and rented an apartment. We needed Emma to help with Bob, who was only four at the time.

We loved Emma. She was a wonderful asset to the family, and she took excellent care of Bob while his father and I were busy about the work of the Lord. When because of illness Emma had to leave us, we felt a great loss.

Emma had been reared by a white family by the name of Hunt. The Hunts had taken her when she was seven years of age. They cared for Emma during her last illness, and the last request Emma made was that Dr. Bob preach her funeral. As she lay dying in the hospital — it was owned by the Hunt family — she said, "I wish I could hear Dr. Bob preach once more. I wish he could be here to pray for me." The surgeons and nurses prayed with her the best they could, and then she repeated the prayer that Dr. Bob had taught her many years before. Emma was laid to rest in the Hunt family plot in the white cemetery, and her pallbearers were surgeons, internes, and orderlies from the hospital.

Dr. Bob always loved the Negro. He had a special section reserved for them in all his big campaigns, and he never failed to acknowledge their presence. Often he would have them sing some of their Spirituals, as only they can.

* * *

Having heard much about the Fort Deposit, Alabama, meeting, I inquired of THE LOWNDES SIGNAL, local newspaper, and Mrs. Leila M. Buchanan, who had witnessed the episode I want to mention and who had written about the incident years later. This is the story as I understand it.

On the last night of the revival, Dr. Bob, in his closing prayer, prayed, "Lord, what is it going to take to really wake up this town? If necessary, send a cyclone or a tornado." People scoffed at the idea saying, "It is impossible for this town to have a tornado; we are surrounded by mountains." Within three weeks, however, during a big dance in the Fort Deposit Armory, a tornado struck, and off came the roof of the building, and down on their knees went the people inside, begging God to save them.

Mrs. Buchanan said to me in a letter:

I am very familiar with all references, both to Dr. Jones' revival and the cyclone. His revival was in the early Spring of 1908 and of course made a tremendous impact on the little town. We Methodists sponsored the revival but the Baptists and the Church of Christ were loyal, both in attendance and financial assistance.

This revival wasn't very long after he lost his first wife so we were sympathetic both as to his emotions and his ardent plea for us to come to Christ. He preached like John the Baptist. A small faction on City Council was influencing our little town for whiskey revenue, all of which had us torn asunder. Mr. Jones prayed that somehow, someway, God would reveal Himself and our better forces would prevail. The evil would be removed. Well, very soon, in fact April 26th, we had a cyclone which did much damage to the town, especially in the business area, and one man was killed.

The young people were having a dance—the Auburn Band was playing for it. Lightning struck the Armory (or Dance Hall) . . . . Many who weren't in sympathy with the revival said, "Bob Jones caused God to send the cyclone." My own opinion (I was sixteen at the time) and that of most Christians was that it was absurd—since really no material harm came to the unsympathetic faction. Any disaster makes us stop and think—and we frequently see God's hand in these experiences and profit by them. Bob Jones' revival changed my life—(though I had planned to go to the dance, but the cyclone came early). Our young people who danced didn't drink or leave the Dance Hall—we were all very sedate and tame compared with the dancing of today. No smoking there, never familiarity of any kind was indulged in.

In a summary of Dr. Bob's life—you would be derelict not to mention the profound influence he had on the lives of two-thirds of the people in Fort Deposit—a little town of about 2,500.

His son married one of our lovely girls, Fannie May Holmes, the daughter of my dearest Sunday School teacher, Mrs. J. E. Holmes.

* * *

Dr. Otis R. Holmes, brother of Fannie May Jones, wife of Dr. Bob Jones, Jr., writes about the tornado at Fort Deposit:

My mother told me that after the first tornado (or cyclone) which struck on Friday night, another hit the area on Sunday afternoon. She told me that a man knocked at the front door. He asked to stand on the porch until the approaching storm passed. As she stood at the door, insisting that he come inside, the house across the street suddenly disintegrated. The man darted through the door before a second invitation needed to be given. The tornado lifted and missed doing any harm to our home.

The writer's mother has told him of the meeting that Dr. Bob held in the City Auditorium of Lynchburg, Virginia, in 1916.

The crowds were so large that the street cars had to be re-routed. Dr. Bob held wonderful Bible Study classes in the afternoon, thus giving the people a love for and an understanding of the Word.

Dr. Bob preached so hard! After ten days of his "straight" preaching, the meeting broke, and the people flocked forward. You could feel the whole atmosphere change. The preachers as well as the people got right. Dr. Bob preached to the Sunday School superintendents and teachers, the preachers on the platform and in the audience, the professional and business men and women — he did not leave out anyone.

Dr. Bob held another successful campaign in Lynchburg. It was in a large tent in a field across from the City Park. Both my mother and my sister took an active part in the choir. They report:

Dr. Bob was worried about Modernism, and he preached a great deal against it. "This country is in a terrible fix," he said. "We are suffering from a bankruptcy of character. America started out right. We started with God. But we are a backslidden nation. The young people of America are in a terrible fix. If nine-tenths of the books on how to raise children were turned into paddles to beat the devil out of the younger generation, they might do some good. There is an organized effort to destroy 'the sabbath,' and there is a wave of lawlessness that will damn the country. People are profane."

The crowds overflowed the tent each service, with hundreds sitting around outside listening and straining to hear every word. The people had never heard a man preach harder and with more conviction and sincerity. I have followed Dr. Bob's work down through the years with a great deal of interest. Little did I realize when I first fell in love with the Jones family back in 1916, when Bob, Jr., was only five years old, that my baby boy would some day be associated with Dr. Bob and the great organization God would lead

him to found. I shall never cease to thank the Lord for this great man and
for his great school.

*   *   *

Many newspaper writers commented on Dr. Bob's voice and his magnetic appeal. In addition to comments in preceding articles, I should like
to add this:

> One of Bob Jones' greatest assets is his voice. He talks directly to the indi-
> vidual with such a sincerity that it goes directly to your very soul.

An outstanding businessman said:

> I would write a check for $100,000 if I had the voice of Bob Jones.

Another said:

> When you give yourself completely to God, as Bob Jones had done, it makes
> all the difference in the world. No one can ever question Bob's dedication to
> God's Cause.

Still another remarked:

> Isn't it wonderful to have lived such a wonderful, dedicated life that every
> one has been able to see such a God-filled life that runs over to bless souls?

> We have heard Billy Sunday and we have listened to some mighty fine evan-
> gelists. Of those we have heard, however, none can sell religion to an audi-
> ence like Bob Jones. We use the word "sell" because Dr. Bob is definitely a
> born salesman.

*   *   *

Dr. Bob could never be stopped from performing his duty as he saw it.
He often quoted General Robert E. Lee's statement — "The noblest word
in the English language is 'duty.' " Dr. Bob never held back. If he promised to be at a certain place at a certain time, HE WAS THERE! Mrs.
Jones refers to an incident, about which I had read in an old newspaper
clipping:

> Dr. Bob was to have a meeting in a certain town in West Virginia. They had
> one of the worst floods that part of the country had ever seen. Houses,
> cattle, and trees came floating down the raging river. Dr. Bob traveled as
> far as he could by train, and then he asked the neighbors in the vicinity if
> anyone had a boat. One man had a boat, but he said that it was too dangerous
> to attempt using it. Others tried to discourage my husband, but to no avail.
> Dr. Bob felt that the Lord wanted him to get to this meeting. He offered the

owner of the boat twice the regular fee if he would try to get the boat through and get him to the meeting. They made it, but the boatman said that he had never had such a job rowing 'up current,' dodging things as they floated toward the boat.

When they reached the town, they found it deserted and half submerged in water. The man guided the boat through the hotel doors and right up to the desk. My husband actually registered while still standing in the boat. The man behind the desk was standing on a big box, and he just could not believe that my husband had attempted such a trip.

We never had a dull moment. My husband never let any grass grow under his feet. If a job needed to be done, he could not rest until that job was done. Nothing was unimportant to him. He made much of little. To him, everything was an opportunity.

* * *

This article was taken from an Atlanta paper:

BOB JONES TO USE TABERNACLE

Rev. Bob Jones, of Montgomery, has been elected as the successor of Rev. Sam P. Jones, to conduct the great annual revival in the SAM JONES TABERNACLE at Cartersville, Georgia. The selection came Sunday at the Tabernacle at the close of a successful revival. At this meeting there were 7,000 persons present. The revival had been conducted by Bob Jones and in spirit and fervor, it was like one of the old Sam Jones revivals.

The Sam Jones Tabernacle has been erected in Cartersville, Georgia, at considerable expense for the holding of a great annual revival by Sam Jones. At the death of the great evangelist, the revivals grew less and less in size. Until this summer for five years no revival had been held in the Tabernacle. It was feared by the people of Cartersville that the Tabernacle would never be used again for its original purpose. After the enthusiasm and power of Bob Jones had been shown in a revival of eleven days, Mrs. Sam P. Jones suggested Sunday, at the closing service, that the crowd present vote on restoring the custom of an annual revival and that they select the successor of Rev. Sam P. Jones. The congregation of 7,000 persons voted unanimously for the selection of Bob Jones to conduct the annual revival.

In THE ATLANTA CONSTITUTION, Paul Jones, a son of Rev. Sam F. Jones, said of Bob Jones:

He much resembles my father in manner of preaching, though he is younger than my father, and the people could not help but be attracted by the power of his strong sermons. I am glad that he is chosen to succeed my father in this annual meeting and believe that he is the best living evangelist in the South.

* * *

In TIME, February 22, 1937, a reporter wrote:

One of Manhattan's most oddly located churches is Calvary Baptist, a stronghold of pure Fundamentalism in West 57th Street within denouncing distance of bars, smart shops, noisy apartment hotels, racy night clubs. . . . Calvary is seldom without a guest evangelist who fills its auditorium not with the demimonde from nearby streets but with Manhattanites in no need of evangelization. Last week when the newspapers were still carrying dispatches from Tennessee where a nine-year-old girl had become a bride (TIME, Feb. 8, 15), news hawks turned up at Calvary to hear a visiting Tennessee preacher, Rev. Dr. Robert Jones. He said Tennessee had set no age limit for marriages because "we just took it for granted that everybody had sense enough not to marry so young. . . . We have fifty colleges and universities in Tennessee, and there isn't a more cultured state in the Union."

One of Tennessee's fifty colleges is the most informally-named in the U.S. and according to its founder, the only one in the world where Greek and Hebrew are required subjects for students majoring in Religion — Bob Jones College. . . . Alabama-born Bob Jones, a tall, husky Methodist who held his first service at thirteen and was licensed to preach at fifteen, founded his institution a decade ago in northern Florida, planning it as a college for preserving the Bible and the "old-time decencies" and still appealing to young people. He began with 132 students, confounded pedagogs who thought he was setting up a Fundamentalist camp-meeting by soon proving that his freshman class averaged eight points better than those in other Florida institutions. . . . Today he has four hundred students, thirty-five teachers, among whom is many a Ph.D. . . . "We don't hire any teacher who believes in Evolution. We tell students about Darwin, Huxley and Spencer, but we also tell them that evolution isn't science, it's guess-work."

*   *   *

I wish that I might give this incident exactly as the one involved printed it in a newspaper. Unfortunately, I have "lost sight" of that particular paper and must depend upon my memory for the story. This is the gist of it:

A certain noteworthy news reporter was addicted to drink and could not hold a job for very long at a time. This reporter was in a certain town during one of Dr. Bob's campaigns there. Newsmen were lamenting the fact that they had no reporter who was qualified to cover the Bob Jones' meeting as it deserved to be covered. The alcoholic reporter knew that he could do the job, and he volunteered to go talk with Dr. Bob.

Upon hearing that the man was an alcoholic, Dr. Bob said to him, "I am going to try to get you converted." AND HE DID! The man was gloriously converted, overcame his drinking problem, and then started traveling with Dr. Bob as a special news reporter of his meetings.

One day this reporter was riding on a train toward St. Louis or Kansas

City or some other place near those cities (I do not recall the exact town) where Dr. Bob was to hold a meeting. He tells this story of a battle he fought on the train:

As I sat on the train, John Barleycorn came and took a seat on one side of me, and Satan sat down on the other. The thirst for "drink" became so intense that I felt I must do something about it. I had not had this sort of experience for a long time. I decided to go to the Club Car and get "just one drink." That would satisfy this thirst I had; and by the time I would reach my destination, Bob Jones would never know the difference.

In the Club Car, there were no hard drinks available. But this was not the end of my temptation. I had another temptation that was much stronger. Back at my seat, I had the same visitors — John Barleycorn and Satan. This time they had the suggestion that I get off the train at a certain town near the place I was to meet Dr. Bob, go into a saloon located near the station, get a drink, go to the hotel and "sleep it off," and then board a later train for my meeting with Dr. Bob. After all, I was not due there until the next day.

The temptation overpowered me, and I got off the train, as planned, and headed for the saloon. For some reason, however, I decided to walk past the saloon, and then turn and go back to it. Just after I had passed the door of the saloon, I felt a hand on my shoulder. Turning to see whose hand it could be, I stared into the eyes of **BOB JONES**. Not only was I relieved that I had not gone into the saloon; I was thankful to the Lord that again Bob Jones had been a human instrument to save me from this damning evil.

Never again did I have this battle to fight.

God's Word promises that He will not suffer us to be tempted above that we are able, but with every temptation will make a way of escape. It is interesting that Dr. Bob was at the right place at the right time to help this man when he needed help.

* * *

PART III
EDUCATIONAL ENDEAVORS

Part III
Educational Endeavors

CHAPTER 1

Bob Jones College in Florida

As he had traveled about in the post-war period of World War I, Dr. Bob had observed that the mood of life was changing. Clocks were being set to conform to the world, and the whole world seemed to be slipping. Young people seemed to be running wild. Compromise was rearing its ugly head in politics, in religion, and in education. Even supposedly Christian schools were beginning to let down the bars and admit into their ranks teachers who were not true to God's Word and who began to sow seeds of doubt in the minds of unsuspecting students. What a far cry, Dr. Bob thought, from the first Christian school in America that had been founded in order to give students an opportunity to study Greek and Hebrew so that they might better understand God's Word!

One day Dr. Bob and his beloved Mary Gaston were driving through Florida. They stopped at a drugstore in the town of Kissimmee for some sandwiches. While Dr. Bob was waiting for his order, his mind, as usual, was hitting on all cylinders. Suddenly there came into sharp focus something that had been plaguing his subconscious for some time. It was almost as if someone had adjusted the lens on a movie projector to make a clearer picture. He could hardly wait to get outside and talk it over with Mary Gaston.

Finally, bounding out of the drug store, Dr. Bob said to his wife, "Mary Gaston, I am going to build a school."

We can hardly wonder that she asked, "Robert, are you crazy?"

But even as she asked the question Mary Gaston could see written all over her husband's face the determination that was so characteristic of him. She had lived with this man long enough to discern when he was joking and when he was in earnest. This was one of the "dead-earnest" times. Although she did all she could to discourage the venture — she was afraid the devil might be trying to sidetrack her husband from a job to which he had been divinely called to the saving of countless souls — eventually she came to realize that this was God's plan whereby in years

A Sketch of Bob Jones College in Florida

to come, through the medium of an evangelistic educational institution, Dr. Bob was to achieve something he could never have achieved as an evangelist alone. With all his great contributions to this world—and without question they are many—I believe that history will prove that Dr. Bob reached his zenith in developing this divine vision.

There were a number of orthodox, independent religious schools, of course, that were doing a good work in their special fields; but Dr. Bob realized that something was lacking. They "were not exactly 'clicking' as they should," he said later. "A school was needed to supply the missing element." Dr. Bob would have preferred that someone else build the school, but after many hours of prayer, heart-searching, self-examination, and earnest consideration, he made a decision in line with another of his principles: *"The measure of your responsibilities is the measure of your opportunities."* God was opening the door and he dared not fail to enter it. He must build a school that would provide a sound educational background and yet would have "definite religious and cultural emphases." When people thought of this school, they must "think of the Bible and of the fundamentals that are accepted by all orthodox, Bible-believing Christians, and not of some particular doctrine."

Setting the Wheels in Motion

Always a man of action and with definite assurance of the Lord's leading, Dr. Bob quickly set into motion the wheels that would start the operation of his great dream. First he headed for Panama City, Florida, fifty miles from his old home place, to search out a site. Next he set about contacting influential men.

One of the men he approached was Governor-elect *Bibb Graves* of Alabama, who was one of the best friends Dr. Bob ever had. Mr. Graves loved Dr. Bob, and he was able to be of much assistance during the formative years of the school. The MONTGOMERY ADVERTISER in its 125th-year special edition, Sunday, September 27, 1953, said editorially:

> If asked to name the most remarkable public figure I have known since I started in 1916, I would without hesitation pick Governor Bibb Graves.

Governor Graves spoke at the groundbreaking ceremonies of the new college, he spoke at the first Commencement of the school and attended succeeding Commencements, he was one of the first members of the Board of Trustees, and he served as Vice-Chairman of the Board for a number of years. In appreciation for this service, the Joneses named one of the men's dormitories in Greenville, South Carolina, "BIBB GRAVES."

R. L. McKenzie, an outstanding real estate man in Florida, worked closely with Dr. Bob in Florida, in Tennessee, and in South Carolina, until the time of Mr. McKenzie's death.

Certainly we could not overlook the part that *Mrs. McKenzie* and her sister, *Miss Mary E. Dixon,* played in the landscaping and other work. The Dixon-McKenzie Dining Common bears the names of these lovely friends.

Location of the School

Dr. Bob established his unique school at a location just 85 miles due south of Dothan, Alabama; 150 miles east of Pensacola, Florida; 250 miles west of Jacksonville, Florida; 2 miles from Lynn Haven, Florida; and 7 miles out of Panama City on the beautiful St. Andrews Bay. From the very first, Dr. and Mrs. Jones had fallen in love with this charming spot. No place in America, they thought, could boast of a more beautiful or pleasant place in which to live and build a school. The semi-tropical climate would attract the Northern students, and the beautiful St. Andrews Bay would draw people from everywhere. They chose as the name for the campus site "College Point, Florida."

Educational Standards

Dr. Bob knew his limitations in setting up the educational standards. Although he had served in the extension department of Moody Bible Institute and had attended the good, old-time, denominational Southern University, where he had studied Greek, Latin, mathematics, and all the other subjects that were routine in most colleges, he had not kept up with the development of modern standardization. The fact that he was aware of his limitations in this field probably prevented his making costly errors in the setting up of his curricula.

Here again we observe two of Dr. Bob's outstanding principles: *"You can borrow brain, but you cannot borrow character"* and *"Always go to the right source for advice. I would not ask a man on Broadway in New York who says 'opossum' how to catch 'possums.' I would ask a fellow from the country who owns a 'cur dog' and who says 'possum.' "*

Dr. Bob began to look around for the right people from whom to borrow the brain to set up the high educational standards which he desired. He arranged a conference with several of the most progressive and up-to-date educational authorities he knew. He explained to them the purposes which he had in mind, and then he asked their help in standardizing academic work that would keep within the framework of those purposes. "I want the academic standards to be accurate enough to 'pass muster' in any institution anywhere in America," he said. That seemed easy enough. But when he explained that incorporated in the curriculum must be all the fine arts without additional cost above the regular academic tuition, the men gasped. This was unheard of. But Dr. Bob insisted, and they did it. I will say of these experts that they did such a good job in standardizing the academic work of the school that within a few weeks after its formal opening, Bob Jones College was fully accredited by Florida State University.

Greatest Boom of All Time

The whole country—particularly Florida—was undergoing one of the greatest booms this country could ever experience. Everything seemed to be "bursting at the seams." Dr. Bob took advantage of the situation, and with his shrewd business acumen he was able to work out a deal with the Minor C. Keith Corporation, a company which at that time was developing the northern part of Florida. Calling into play his practical slant, his good common sense, his sound business approach, his perceptive mind, and his basic understanding of the problems of the day, Dr. Bob was able to chart a course that took him far beyond his fondest hopes and dreams. Mrs. Jones states that they never fully realized all that was taking place; if she had, she would have kept a diary.

Selling Lots

Not willing to follow the usual plan of soliciting funds by asking people for outright gifts, Dr. Bob conceived the idea of working with the Minor C. Keith Corporation on a percentage basis. The plan was to sell lots from a 2500-acre tract of land, and 25% of the proceeds would go to the building fund of the proposed school. The people would get valuable land for their money, and at the same time they would be helping to build a much-needed Christian school. This method of investment was well received by county and state. The Chamber of Commerce promoted the cause, and preachers, bankers, merchants, and other people of the area gave full cooperation.

The Minor C. Keith Corporation also had a development company called The College Point Development Company. I quote from a letter that was written by the vice-president of this company:

Dear Sir: Your name has been referred to me by Mr. Fred Phillips, Secretary of the Chamber of Commerce, and I take great pleasure in writing you since you are desirous of locating in this section.

I have only recently come to St. Andrews Bay. . . . I have traveled all over America and Europe, and I can truthfully say that this is the best all-year-round climate. . . .

In the second place, I find they have splendid schools. . . .

In the third place, the moral and spiritual conditions here are better than the average town.

. . . . . .

One of the greatest projects is now being started here through the efforts of Rev. Bob Jones of Montgomery, Alabama. He is building . . . an inter-denominational, orthodox Christian college. The money necessary for this project is being derived from the sale of real estate which is a very unique idea. . . .

These lots are being put on the market in units of 350 each and the development is being completed one unit at a time. The sale of this property began about February 1, and already the first unit is sold out. . . . Bob Jones begins his home next week.

The lots range in price from $1,000 for a 50 × 150 foot lot to $2,000 for a 50 × 300 foot lot on the water front. These prices include all improvements such as paved streets, sidewalks, electric lights, and water connections. And . . . 25% goes to the college trustees for the building of the college.

If you are looking for a home site, I would advise you by all means to investigate College Point. . . .

Dr. Bob always took pains to explain in detail whatever he was trying to sell to the public. On June 3, 1926, he wrote to several friends. Among these friends was Mr. Travis Smith, Slocomb, Alabama:

Dear Friend: Next Tuesday morning at 9:00 in my office we are going to have a special conference with all the representatives of Panama City and Southeast Alabama.

We are perfecting a big organization leading up to a big drive the fifth of July.

I want you to come down here and get here by 9:00 Tuesday morning, June 8, and be at this sales meeting.

Bring one or two persons you think we can sell if possible. . . .

Now, by all means, if you want to work for us, meet us here for this important conference next Tuesday morning. . . .

Remember, we will be looking for you next Tuesday. Come before that time if possible but be sure to come Tuesday.

This letter suggests another principle that Dr. Bob always sought to instill in his boys and girls: *"Remember, a quitter never wins, and a winner never quits."*

The College Point Development Corporation sent out a catchy announcement about the August sale:

Dear Sir: Thursday, August 12, put this date down where you will not forget.

Get out your car next Thursday, fill it with gas and plenty of oil, and start for Panama City, Florida.

Get an early start. Get up before breakfast next Thursday, and don't stop until you drive up to Bob Jones College office in Panama City.

Bob Jones himself will be in town that day and will have an important announcement to make which you must know about.

Here is some good news: we are beginning at once clearing of the land for the College and our plans are really running ahead of time.

The Great Sale

On July 5, 1926, people from the North, from southeast Alabama, and from all parts of Florida poured into College Point to attend "the great sale." Excitement was high. People were delighted to be able to buy good land at a reasonable price and at the same time take part in the building of a Christian school.

Ground-Breaking

The ground-breaking ceremony was held on December 1, 1926, at 2:00 P.M. The local newspaper reported it under headlines of "BIG DAY AT COLLEGE POINT—Hundreds Attend Event at College Point Wednesday." In the article it was stated:

Rev. Jones again spoke briefly, stating that all papers were now in his hands which had any bearing on the land, and that the Minor C. Keith Co., Inc., had given to them the four hundred seventy acres of land to be used for the college purposes, and he held the deed in his hand as he spoke the words. . . .

Bob Jones introduced the speaker of the hour, Governor-elect Bibb Graves of Alabama, who spoke in clear Christian terms on the question of Christian education. . . . Suffice it to say that no public man in Alabama or in the South is looming larger in Christian schools than Gov. Graves. On this occasion his voice rang out among the pine trees with the ideals of the great Orthodox College. He turned prophet and pictured to his great audience the gathering of thousands from the North, from the South, from the East, from the West to the center of learning magnetized by the power of Jesus Christ and to point with the convictions of the campus needle to the foundations of our Christian faith. He swept his audience with his eloquence, and then charmed their very souls with his ideals of true citizenship.

Being a personal friend of Rev. Jones for a great many years, Mr. Graves spoke from his own personal view of the nearness they have felt all along and of the many talks that naturally have been exchanged regarding this movement ever since the time the idea was first born in the mind of Dr. Jones. "The idea seemed," he went on to say, "at first that it just couldn't be done." But little by little things have begun to shape themselves and more and more he was given to believe that there might be a possibility that some day a long way off something might come of this wonderful dream.

"So earnest has this friend and brother been," continued Mr. Graves, "that it seemed nothing could dampen his belief that some day he would live to see, God helping him, a monument arise consecrated to the Christian movement, dedicated to Jesus Christ."

Why the Name "Bob Jones College"

Two months before school opened, Dr. Bob sent out a release to many of the papers telling why the college was named Bob Jones College and why it was located outside Panama City, Florida. I quote an excerpt from this release:

I was averse to calling our school the Bob Jones College. My friends overcame my aversion with the argument that the school would be called by that name because of my connection with it and to attempt to give it any other name would confuse the people.

Dr. Bob Underwrites Expenses

The full responsibility of raising the money for salaries and other expenses rested upon Dr. Bob's shoulders. Before the school opened, he decided to underwrite personally $20,000 a year over and above the income of the school to help with these expenses. He also took out a $500,000 life insurance policy payable to the school in case something happened to him.

The Board of Trustees met to discuss Dr. Bob's salary. He had been getting the largest income of all the evangelists, with the possible exception of Billy Sunday. The Board felt that since Dr. Bob was using his position, his prestige, and his money for the benefit of others by trying to build this great center of learning, and since he was giving up so much and was putting into the work everything he had accumulated, they should give him the best salary possible. He refused a salary, but agreed to a small drawing account—an account that never paid his expenses for any given month. Instead of taking money out of the school's treasury, Dr. Bob always poured his money into it to keep the operating expenses up to date. The contacts that Dr. Bob made as he went about in his evangelistic work are paying us great dividends even today, for most of our donations and bequests have come from contacts which he made.

Administrators and Faculty

It is said that an institution is the shadow of a man. Dr. Bob put his whole being into his calling from God, and he wanted the same kind of dedication on the part of his faculty and staff. He did not want to "man" his school with people who were just looking for jobs; he wanted people who were willing to pay any price, to make any sacrifice to serve the Lord. He prayed that God would give him wisdom in selecting the right ones to work with him. Even enemies of God, he observed, put cause above self. With fanatical zeal they directed their energies toward the cause they represented. God's servants, Dr. Bob felt, should not do less.

Dr. Bob had no selfish axe to grind. He wanted to pay his teachers the largest salaries of any teachers anywhere. But soon he realized that in this plan there was inherent danger: it attracted applications from people who were not spiritual. Finally, he decided to set up a spiritual program, and then let those who loved the Lord and were willing to put service above self gravitate to it.

Dr. Bob was an able administrator. His boundless energy and ardent zeal made it difficult to keep up with him. Hours never counted with this man. Well do I remember the many evening hours he spent in the office, figuring out the problems of paying bills and "staying ahead of the game." His individualistic approach to every problem showed up in everything he did. He figured things from different angles, seeking and praying for the right solution. This strategy kept him and his school from entangling alliances and from getting his business "in a jam."

Although Dr. Bob had many virtues, patience, as his wife expresses it, was not one of them. He had just the right measure of impatience to keep all about him on their toes. Understandably, his impatience was more noticeable during times of construction and deadlines.

It was characteristic of Dr. Bob to always figure the cost several times, and to this cautiousness can be attributed much of the school's success. Efficiency and economy were key words in his organization. He would not tolerate waste of any kind. He "pounded into us" the idea that we must never get careless with God's money and that we must never presume upon God's goodness.

Dr. Bob was a realist. He wanted and demanded all the facts, whether they were good or bad. Some people accused him of being hard to get along with. This was an unjust criticism. He knew what he wanted, when he wanted it, and how he wanted it done. But he never took unfair advantage of anyone. He would give a man the shirt off his back, but no one could take it from him.

I worked closely with this man. I knew him. To me, he was fair, ethical, and thoroughly Christian in all his dealings. He was wonderful to work under and to work with. I am convinced that no man was ever more unselfish than he; and the same characteristics that some people questioned and criticized inspired intense loyalty on the part of those who were perceptive of the vision as it was put there of God. Dr. Bob allowed his co-workers to develop their own initiative and maintain their own individuality. In such a wonderful Christian atmosphere, with such love and understanding, and with conditions "made to order," how could employees help giving their best?

First Faculty and Staff

When Bob Jones College officially opened its doors, Dr. Bob, Sr., was President; W. E. Patterson, Dean and Head of the Education Department; Dr. Hall, History; W. F. Monk, just out of the Legislature, Mathematics; Mrs. Ellen W. Laudenslager, Romance Languages; Miss Katie Nell Holmes, English; Mr. R. S. Gentry, Science; Mr. P. W. Lott, Bible. The head of every department had at least an M. A. degree.

Dr. Floyd Collins, a well-educated and cultured gentleman, was a wonderful asset to the school during the formative years in Florida. Dr. Bob described Dr. Collins as "the most cultured man I ever saw." I believe that God sent Dr. Collins to Dr. Bob at the right time to help set up the high standards that were needed.

The lovely Mrs. Estelle Siddons Stollenwerck, mother of Mrs. Jones, Sr., also had a large share in setting the pattern of culture in Bob Jones College. Because Dr. Bob knew that he would have to be away from home much of the time in evangelistic campaigns, he invited Mrs. Stollenwerck to make her home with them. Mrs. Stollenwerck exerted great influence on the lives of the students. Dr. Bob leaned upon Mrs. Stollenwerck's wisdom, cherished her love, and was indebted to her for financial assistance to Bob Jones College at critical times.

Miss Eunice Hutto of Ariton, Alabama, who had a good background in the field of education and mathematics and who loved the Lord and seemed to catch a glimpse of the vision that Dr. Bob had in mind, stayed with the school until we moved to Greenville. She served in such positions as Principal of the Academy, Dean of the College, and Instructor in Math.

The Writing of the College Creed

Dr. Bob wanted to set up a creed to which all Christians — regardless of denomination — could subscribe, a creed which would include all the fundamentals of the faith. But not even Dr. Bob himself seemed to come up with exactly what he wanted. One day an Atlanta evangelist friend, Sam Small, and Dr. Bob were together. Dr. Bob said to Mr. Small, "George Stuart told me that you are the smartest man and the best writer he has ever seen. I need a creed for my school; will you please help me write it?" Mr. Small took from his pocket a large envelope on which he wrote:

The general nature and object of the corporation shall be to conduct an institution of learning for the general education of youth in the essentials of culture and in the arts and sciences; giving special emphasis to the Christian religion and the ethics revealed in the Holy Scriptures; combatting all atheistic, agnostic, pagan and so-called scientific adulterations of the gospel; unqualifiedly affirming and teaching the inspiration of the Bible (both Old and New Testaments); the creation of man, by the direct act of God; the incarnation and virgin birth of our Lord and Saviour Jesus Christ; His identification as the Son of God; His vicarious atonement for the sins of mankind by the shedding of His blood on the cross; the resurrection of His body from the tomb; His power to save men from sin; the new birth through the regeneration by the Holy Spirit and the gift of eternal life by the grace of God. This charter shall never be amended, altered or changed, as to the provisions hereinbefore set forth.

Incorporated in these words were all the fundamental truths of the Bible, and it was so simple that anyone could understand it. Dr. Bob said, "I have traveled all over the world, and this creed is acceptable to all conservative fundamental Protestant beliefs." Later, Dr. Bob said, "God was with us in the writing of this creed. If I had not been an evangelist and had not known the Bible as I did, I might have let something slip into the creed that would have given us trouble. I had all types of pressure to include certain pet doctrines of certain denominations; but Sam Small, bless his heart, knew exactly what to put into it."

Many people feared that Dr. Bob was getting his eye off the goal of evangelism when he founded Bob Jones College. Little did they realize that he was actually creating the fundamental base for future evangelism — that his school would produce more outstanding evangelists than many other schools combined, that his "preacher boys" would hold true conservative bases in all parts of the world, and that his school would be due more credit than the world could ever realize for its strong stand that would help stem the incoming tide of liberalism that would become prevalent on every hand.

Three weeks after "the grand opening," Dr. Bob left for a big evangelistic campaign in Bellingham, Washington; and he continued to hold as many evangelistic campaigns as any other evangelist. Dr. Bob always did the work of three or four ordinary men. He kept many of us who were much younger, "hopping" to keep up with him.

How Did Dr. Bob Learn?

Someone asked Dr. Bob how he knew about running a Christian school. He answered, "I learned a good deal from observing my good friend, the late Dr. James M. Gray, of the Moody Bible Institute." Some of Dr. Bob's best training, of course, came from his evangelistic work. He had been able to keep his budget the lowest of all the evangelists, and not in his entire ministry had he left a financial deficit on a town.

Dr. Bob said that he learned much from Governor Graves. He even studied law in Governor Graves' library. But as I have done my research, I have observed that the reverse is also true: Governor Graves learned a great deal from Dr. Bob. Not only did Dr. Bob help get Governor Graves elected; he also helped the Governor set up his legislature.

Dr. Bob's philosophy was that education is more than a mere training of the mind—it involves the heart, the soul, and every aspect of life. He knew from God's Word that wisdom comes from God and that "knowledge puffeth up," but that the right kind of knowledge, used in the right way, can be powerful. He sought, therefore, to drill into the students a philosophy of life that would make them strong and courageous Christian leaders in a degenerate age. He challenged them to scale all obstacles with a satisfaction and pride that they were doing God's will. He inoculated the students, so to speak, with the idea that *"it is a sin to do less than your best"* and *"it is no disgrace to fail, but it is a sin to do less than your best to keep from failing."* Although he opened each school year with a revival, he did not want the students to think that they had come for just a revival meeting; he wanted them to realize that they would have to study and work hard.

Chapel

Dr. H. C. Morrison, president of Asbury College, Wilmore, Kentucky, advised Dr. Bob, "No school will die spiritually if you keep your chapel platform hot." Dr. Bob generated inspiration at chapel; and he attributed much of the success of the school to the fact that he brought in as chapel speakers and Bible Conference speakers great men of God who would help him drill into his students the fundamental truths of God's Word. To this day, the chapel hour is one of the most important phases of students' training. Dr. Bob had observed that many Christian colleges had let down first in their chapel programs, and then on their chapel-attendance requirements, which had been costly to those schools from a spiritual standpoint. Determined to avoid this pitfall, he took great pains during chapel to grind the truths of God's Word into his students and to apply Scripture to the building of character and backbone. His theme was "line upon line, and precept upon precept." He emphasized using whatever gifts—great or small—that God had given to defend His Cause. "David did not match the giant with the armor, the sling, or the stones," he said; "David went forth in the Name of the Lord."

Dr. Bob did not exclude the social graces from the students' training. I can still hear him say, "You are never really educated until you can get in and out of a lady's parlor with ease." The practical side of life was of major importance to Dr. Bob. He "hammered" into his boys and girls, *"True success is finding God's will for your life and doing it. Being faithful is being successful."* It was his philosophy that Christians should always excel. Everything else being equal, he said, they should be better doctors, better lawyers, better singers, better speakers, better businessmen, and better athletes. He warned that the things of this world will profit little, that it is the spiritual that counts. He cautioned:

> Even scholarship can be used wrongly. Remember this: the world always majors in the minor. Godliness is the main thing; so be sure to give God His rightful place. "Seek ye first the kingdom of God, and his righteousness; and all these things shall be added unto you" (Matthew 6:33).

Someone asked Dr. Bob what he liked best about his work in education. He replied, "It is the finished product we turn out." From the beginning Dr. Bob's heart was thrilled when at each Commencement many strong, courageous, Christian leaders were sent out to serve in every phase of life. He declared that he would rather clip this type of coupon than those from million-dollar bonds.

Keen Sense of Humor

Dr. Bob had a keen sense of humor that kept a twinkle in his eye and kept him young and active. Without this sense of humor, he could never have stood the strain of those formative years; and from the first, God used Dr. Bob's sense of humor to win students to his heart.

One girl recalls her first day at Bob Jones College and how homesick she was. Dr. Bob came up and started teasing her about the boys. "Do you know how you can tell whether or not a girl loves the boys?" he asked. "Prick her finger, and if it bleeds, she loves the boys." This was a little thing, but it helped the girl forget her homesickness. Dr. Bob was sympathetic to people who were homesick. He said that there was something wrong if a student did not feel some homesickness, but he deplored a student's giving in to the feeling and going home. Having known the feeling himself, he certainly was in a position to know that it could be conquered.

Strict Disciplinarian

Dr. Bob could be as firm as was necessary in order to keep things straight. One day he walked into the social hall and reprimanded some students about a record they were playing. Removing the record from the record player, he broke it across his knee. Then he went to chapel and preached a "straight" message to the students with regard to maintaining high Christian standards. Whatever the ordeal, Dr. Bob had the character to handle it. He had to "ship" seventeen students the first year. That took courage and faith as well as character, because the student body was very small. He had promised God that he would run the school right and keep the spiritual first, or he would not run it at all; and he constantly drilled into us the fact that "if we ever ease up on that type of preaching and emphasis, we are gone."

Dr. Bob had no respect for those who acted "pious" and would not study or work hard. He often used the story of two "Stone Cutters" to drill into students the proper regard for their work. The attitude of one cutter was that "I am working for $1.50 per day!" The attitude of the other was that "I am building a Cathedral." Dr. Bob told the students that not all of them could be big chandeliers in the parlor, but that by being faithful, they could be the little back hall lights that might light men who might fall in the darkness.

Amazingly enough, instead of resenting the discipline and high standards, the students gladly accepted them, and there developed devotion and loyalty to their leader and their school. This attitude on the part of the student body was known all around. The seventeen students who had to be "shipped" the first year tried to stir up trouble in the town. Some of the businessmen of Panama City listened to the stories and began to criticize the school. The student body protested the unfavorable criticism of the rules of the College, saying that it was a reflection upon their loyalty to the school. They said further that unless the criticism ceased immediately, the student body would refuse to patronize these businesses. This attitude deepened the admiration and respect of friends in that area for Bob Jones College.

First Graduates

It is interesting that from the first classes came several presidents of schools, outstanding evangelists, preachers, businessmen and women, and school officials, and missionaries who have made enviable records. Among these are Dr. Bob Jones, Jr., chairman and president of Bob Jones University, author, actor, and one of the outstanding exponents of orthodoxy of our day; his wife, Fannie May Holmes Jones, dietitian, home economics teacher; Mrs. Frances Porter Yielding, who holds a responsible position in Birmingham, Alabama; Dr. Monroe Parker, author, evangelist, pastor, and past president of Pillsbury College; Dr. Henry Grube, author, pastor, and president of a Christian Day School in Mobile, Alabama; Dr. Clifford Lewis, author, evangelist, and past president of a Bible college in Kansas City, Missouri; and Ruth Mahan Stewart, missionary and wife of Scottish Evangelist James A. Stewart.

1929 Crash

God had given Dr. Bob long years of experience and contacts around the world; and when he started his school, Dr. Bob reached out and "cashed in" on these contacts. He trusted bankers, lawyers, businessmen, and others to help safeguard his school. He soon realized, however, that many businessmen never stop to take into consideration the uncertainty of riches. His policy was to *figure on the worst, and hope for the best.*" When certain men in Florida kept talking about their "wonderful assets in sunshine," Dr. Bob answered, "Gentlemen, if something happened to this country, you could not spend your type of asset." They assured him that nothing could happen. Later, Dr. Bob remarked that he had never seen anything as crazy as people in Florida before the crash. They were wild and reckless, and he knew that it was time for this nation to wake up before it was too late. Dr. Bob sensed that the men were "boring with an auger" that was too big, and that what they were doing could burst the balloon that had been getting bigger and bigger, for nothing had ever been bigger than the Florida Boom.

As dark clouds began to gather on the horizon, Dr. Bob became greatly concerned. He had borrowed the brain to get started, he was trusting the best businessmen to keep him out of trouble and danger, and yet he could feel an impending doom. But the darker things looked, the more he turned to the Lord and trusted Him.

Expressing his feelings about the morning of "Black Thursday" when the bubble finally burst, Dr. Bob said:

> I had watched the balloon get bigger and bigger and I knew that something was going to happen. I was plenty sick and worried. Big businessmen and leaders of that day kept saying, "There is no danger, nothing is going to happen." I sought the very best advice; nevertheless, I was still uneasy. When the balloon burst, it was too late; the crash was upon everyone before they knew what had hit them. Everyone was wiped out and completely broke. Because everybody was so upset and broke, I got scared, and it gave me a complex that has followed me down to this day.

The whole world felt the blow of the catastrophe, but Florida was probably hit harder than any other section of the country. There were haggard faces at every turn. Everything seemed paralyzed. Businesses had to close because the banks were closed. Many men who did not have strong faith in God saw no way out except, as they thought, to "end it all." Every day the newspaper reported that many people could take it no longer and had committed suicide.

Dr. Bob's sympathetic heart and his years of ministry of helping others drew a number of bewildered people to him. He did his best to encourage these friends, but he, too, was caught in this squeeze. When the banks closed, Bob Jones College had over one-half million dollars in assets wiped out.

This Florida crash was the most critical test Dr. Bob had had. It was a time to practice what he had preached. Although he never claimed to have the kind of faith that some people seem to have, he had a great deal more faith than he admitted. To me, he had the perfect combination: *"Work as if it all depended upon you, and trust God as if it all depended upon Him, and everything will work out all right."* Not once did his faith waver, and yet no man ever lived under a more terrific strain than he did. Dr. Bob had "learned the ropes" the hard way, and he knew them well. His was an indomitable spirit that could not be stopped by circumstances. In fact, it was hard to discourage him. When the depression came, instead of giving up as many others were doing, he was more determined than ever to keep fighting. God had led him up to this point, and God would see him through.

Had the crash not come, every one who had helped Dr. Bob in any way would have got all their money back fourfold, for we had more than enough assets on our books to pay out. But the crash did come, and people such as those of the Minor C. Keith Corporation who had promised to take care of everything were ruined, thus leaving Bob Jones College to struggle.

It was during the turmoil following the crash that God permitted me to join Dr. Bob and his school. I felt then, and I feel even more so now, that God was good to bless me in casting my lines in such a pleasant place. I have felt God's presence and His leadership in our institution, and time after time I have seen Him do the impossible. I have seen Him intervene to keep us from making mistakes; I have seen Him overrule some mistakes we unwittingly made; I have seen Him open doors that we could not open; and I have seen Him supply our every need. The story of this school is the story of a miracle. There has never been a school more blessed of God.

Aftermath of the Crash

The crash taught Dr. Bob a good lesson: he stopped trusting men for advice and began to use the "good old horse sense" that God had given him. He saw that adversity would do for us something that prosperity never could do; for it seemed that the harder the times and the less he seemed to be able to do for his employees, the more they were willing to "tighten their belts," so to speak, and "do without" in order to help him. Everyone at the school had observed the sacrifices which Dr. Bob and Mrs. Jones had made, and they were more than glad to "follow suit."

Dr. Bob called the faculty together and said to them: "We are broke, and we cannot continue to pay the large salaries that we have been paying. We will give you a place to live and something to eat for all members of the family, plus a little cash." I still remember the answer of Mr. Mountain, one of our music faculty. "Let me see if I understand you correctly, Dr. Bob. Did you say that you would give us a place to live, plus the food we eat, plus some cash? I have never been any better off than that. I will take it."

Unrest in Educational Circles

There was quite a bit of educational unrest in the country. There was strong feeling on the part of certain educators against educational standardization. A movement to get Dr. Bob to head up a fight against the modern standardization was plotted, but he would have nothing to do with it. He wanted to work *with* the educational leaders, not *against* them; and the educational leaders appreciated his position. Just before we were ready to move our school from Florida, a letter came from the office of the State Superintendent of Education, stating that the Secretary of the Committee on Accrediting Relations of the University of Florida had written him about the good work that Bob Jones College was doing, that they appreciated the progress the school had made, and that our work was approved by the University of Florida. A similar statement, he said, was on its way from Florida State College for Women stating that Bob Jones College was placed on the 1933 list of institutions approved for purposes of Teacher Certification.

God Uses Crash to Force Move

The depression was a stepping stone to proper connections in another state. Dr. Bob realized that God had used Florida as a training ground for the school, and that now He was leading us to a new location. The first question to be considered was the place of the new location. Bob, Jr., on a preaching mission, traveling between Knoxville and Chattanooga, Tennessee, saw a school boarded up in Cleveland, Tennessee. When he told his father about it, Dr. Bob remarked, "That is the old school that was run by Dr. Sullins Stuart. It is quite interesting that he told me that someday I would live in Cleveland."

Word spread fast that Bob Jones was thinking of moving his school, and numerous invitations came to Dr. Bob. He called a special Board meeting and wrote Governor Bibb Graves:

Be sure, by all means, to make your plans to be here for the Board meeting Friday night. I am depending upon your brain and your advice on the human side. I had a long distance phone call from Cleveland, Tennessee, today. They say that they are enthusiastic and that their proposition will be wired to us Wednesday morning. The situation as it looks now will narrow down to Cleveland, Tennessee, and Anniston, Alabama.

People in Anniston, Alabama, loved the Joneses and would have been happy to have had them locate in Anniston. There was a school in Anniston that the friends wanted Dr. Bob to take over, and they were willing to raise $25,000.00 for the project. The state of Georgia also invited us to locate in their midst. But Dr. Bob felt that God was leading us to Tennessee; so at its special meeting, the Board voted to move the school to that state.

Dr. Bob hated to leave Florida, but it seemed necessary. We needed to enlarge the school, which up to this point had limited its enrollment to three hundred. Furthermore, Dr. Bob knew that if he stayed in Florida and held the work to just two years' training, he could not work out the educational experiment he felt he must carry on. The only students he had kept beyond two years were those who were interested in some definite Christian work. In Tennessee we would have a more central location, which would make it easier for students to get there by train, bus, plane, and car; moreover, the State Department of Education and the State University promised their full cooperation.

Dr. Bob contacted the Chamber of Commerce of Cleveland, Tennessee, telling them of the Board's decision to accept their invitation; and it pleased the group very much. They were thankful for the opportunity to re-open old Centenary College, the Methodist girls' school that had been closed many times and this time had been closed for seven years. The fact that the depression was still on and money was hard to come by did not daunt the spirit of this happy group; they envisioned what the move of Bob Jones College to Cleveland would mean to the economy of their community. They pledged themselves to raise $10,000 to "un-crate," to remodel, and to put the school in condition for our arrival in Cleveland on June 1, 1933. The town officials, the Chamber of Commerce, and individual men enthusiastically supported the project; and some of them even donated their time to supervising the work in order to meet the deadline of our arrival.

Funds for Moving

We did not have the money to make the move. Dr. Bob had sacrificed everything—even cashing out his life insurance—to keep us going. But again, he acted on two of his principles—*"Go as far as you can on the right road"* and *"Man's extremity is God's opportunity."* Trusting God to work out the problem, he thanked Him for the enthusiastic and loyal friends who always came to our rescue.

A saintly little lady by the name of Grace W. Haight, a faculty member whom we loved dearly and for whom one of our dormitories is named, brought $3,000 to Dr. Bob and said:

> I have been waiting to see just how God would lead you in this matter, and I did not want any of my money to influence you in any way. Now that the decision is made, I want you to use this money to help with the moving expenses to the new location in Cleveland.

Having been left money by her father, Dr. Haight had served as a self-paid missionary to China for a while. She had also taught on a mission boat on the Nile. But she became disturbed by the encroaching modernism in the camp of the denomination which she served, and she returned to the States to work on a denominational paper in Memphis, Tennessee, to try to fight the modernism. When it became apparent that they were fighting a losing battle, the paper closed; and Dr. Haight felt led to further her education ideals at Bob Jones College in Florida.

From the first day she walked onto the campus, Dr. Haight was an outstanding, unique character; and any time Dr. Bob needed financial help for the school, she seemed to sense it and was standing by to slip him a little extra money. She refused to accept a penny for her services throughout the years of her service with us. She said that she was thankful to God for the privilege of being in such a wonderful atmosphere, and she felt that she was the one who should pay.

Dr. Haight's services to our school were invaluable. With the training she had received in working with Dr. R. A. Meek on the Southern Methodist paper, she was able to help set up and co-edit a paper with Dr. Bob. Her background in missions and her love for the great old hymns fitted her for her position as teacher of Missions and Hymnology, which post she occupied until she reached the age of eighty-eight. When because of her impaired hearing and weakened physical condition it was suggested that she give up certain phases of her work, she was crushed; but we assured her that her work on THE FELLOWSHIP NEWS was a worthy contribution to the Lord's Cause here.

Many times during our first years in Cleveland, Dr. Haight paid some students to help her try to beautify the campus. But Dr. Haight's greatest asset to the school was not her money or her service, even though both were wonderful and were greatly appreciated. Dr. Bob said many times, "I would rather have Dr. Haight's prayers than the prayers of anyone I know." She continued praying for us and working on the weekly paper until the time of her death.

At the age of ninety-one, Dr. Haight entered Bob Jones University Hospital with a broken hip. She was a blessing and benediction to the doctors and nurses who waited on her. They were touched by the large callouses on her knees that indicated years of constant prayers. Dr. Haight pasted maps of the various mission fields onto cardboard pieces; and at prayer time, she spread the maps on her bed and knelt and prayed for missions around the world. This woman loved the Lord. She had the faith of a child, and she talked with Him constantly. Her death on September 22, 1955, just one month prior to her ninety-second birthday, was a great loss to all who knew and loved her.

Mr. Raymond T. Crane of New York also played a part in the move to Cleveland. This man had been a long-time friend of Dr. Bob, and he concurred that this decision to move was of the Lord. To help with moving expenses, Mr. Crane made a donation of $3,000, which, with Dr. Haight's $3,000, helped to finance the project.

Goodbye, Florida

To leave Florida was especially hard on Dr. Bob and Mrs. Jones. They had a lovely home on the edge of St. Andrews Bay, and naturally they hated to leave it. Dr. Bob wrote a local friend:

> I just want to tell you how much we love you and how sorry we are that we had to hurt you folks by doing what we thought was our duty. I know, though, that you love the Lord and that you enter into the fellowship of this thing with us. I believe that you know that we have done what we believe the Holy Spirit led us to do. I am confident that if the Lord tarries we will all live to see that the action taken was directed of God. We are going to miss you folks when we get to Cleveland. We will miss you more than you can possibly miss us.

The last Commencement in Florida was the most successful of all. Bay County friends flocked in; and many notable figures, along with our Board members from all over the country, came to bid farewell to the many friends we had made there. It is wonderful to be able to report that many of those Florida friends are still living, and that they are good friends even to this writing. We thank the Lord for their love and loyal support.

CHAPTER 2

Bob Jones College, Cleveland, Tennessee

What a glorious day it was when we arrived in Cleveland, Tennessee, June 1, 1933, and looked on the one big building which had been known as "Old Main" through the years! And how busy we became in getting ready for the fall opening, just three months away! Our Founder plunged headlong into the business of building. He was always a good "trader." One day a lumberman came to the office to sell us timber for the first new building. This man asked fifteen dollars a thousand board feet. Dr. Bob, not knowing the value of lumber at the time, exclaimed, "Fifteen dollars a thousand!" The man quickly responded, "Maybe I can do it for twelve." With that, we bought the lumber with which to build a classroom building.

Since there was only the one big building, it had to be used for many purposes. "Old Main" was a three-story, T-shaped building with two circular stairways leading up from the main lobby to the second floor. There were other stairways, of course, that led to the second and to the third stories. We built a partition across the upstairs halls and gave the girls one end of the building and the boys the other. This setup lasted for a year or two, until we could build new dormitories. On the first floor of "Old Main," the south end, we had our offices and library; at the north end we had our chapel; and on the east side was our dining hall.

How proud we were to be re-located! And how unforgettable the days of preparation! Mr. Walter Lee, a former faculty member who joined the faculty the same year that I came to school, was reminiscing on a recent visit to the campus and said:

I remember how hard we worked during that summer of 1933. It was during the depression when we had just moved from Florida. We, along with others, had no money or anything else. Everybody was begging to work for just anything. First-class carpenters were getting twenty-five cents an hour, and that was big money. I worked for fifteen dollars a week plus the living for my family, and that summer was one of the happiest I have ever known. I worked from early morning till late evening, getting out eighty-five letters a day. I saved one dollar a week for thirteen weeks and offered the money to Dr. Bob to help get the school opened; but he would not take the money. I looked forward to the summers when I could get back into the office to work with Dr. Bob. [Mr. Lee was head of the Commerce Department during the school year.] Dr. Bob had the energy of a dozen men and was doing the work of several men; and yet he was so human, always joking with the help. He and I would play dominoes, which was relaxing to both of us. We would forget all our worries and would be oblivious of everything and everybody for awhile.

God blessed us with a good radio ministry that first summer, and we gained several new students that way. We broadcast by remote control over Station WDOD in Chattanooga. Many families in that area, impressed with Dr. Bob's messages, began to contact the school about enrolling their children. My wife's sister—a school teacher—was so impressed with Dr. Bob's radio message and his sincerity one day as she happened to dial WDOD during her lunch hour that she called her mother, dad, and younger sister to come quickly. "This man is preaching exactly what we believe," she said. The result was that they headed for Cleveland to look over this new school that was opening in two weeks, and they made reservations for the younger sister to be enrolled there. The school teacher attended a later summer session.

On July 12, 1967, some friends whose children had been enrolled in Bob Jones College back in the early thirties had lunch in our dining common. They said, "We remember when Dr. Bob first moved his school to Cleveland. We lived in Chattanooga and listened to him over WDOD. We sent our children to his school, and we still feel that there is no other school in all the world like it."

The Opening

Prior to our arrival in their town, the people of Cleveland had worked feverishly in getting the building ready for our move, but there was still much work to be done. Mrs. Jones, Sr., and several others pitched in to help us move furniture, clean rooms, and do other things that were necessary to put everything in readiness. Readying buildings for the fall occupancy became Mrs. Jones' summer occupation for many years.

September 1, 1933, was our formal opening; and excitement was high as old students greeted each other in new quarters. The new students stood back in amazement at the "one family" atmosphere. They were thrilled to have former students welcome them as though they were new children coming into the family. Dr. Bob wrote to Governor Graves of Alabama:

> I am sorry you couldn't be with us. We had a wonderful opening. We have by far the largest enrollment we have ever had and they are still coming. We know that God was with us in moving here.

Approximately three hundred students assembled for the opening service, and we could feel the presence of the Lord as faculty and students sang Dr. Bob's favorite song, "Amazing Grace." It almost lifted the rafters on the building.

State Department of Education

Shortly after his arrival in Tennessee, Dr. Bob consulted with the president of the University of Tennessee. He explained that we wished to cooperate with the University and that we would like for the University to help us make our contribution to the cause of education. It is interesting that in all the fourteen years we were in that state, we never had any trouble with either the University or the Department of Education. Working relations with the University of Tennessee were so congenial that we almost moved our campus to Knoxville a few years later in order to work side by side with this great institution.

Dr. A. F. Harman, Superintendent of Education for the state of Alabama, wrote a letter to the Commissioner of Education in Nashville, Tennessee, praising the work of our school in Florida and explaining the basis on which the Education Departments of Florida and Alabama had granted certificates to our students. He ended this letter with the plea, "Any cooperation the educational leaders of Tennessee can give to Dr. Jones and the Bob Jones College will be appreciated by many thousands of citizens in the state of Alabama."

Dr. B. O. Duggan of the University of Tennessee, and for awhile Commissioner of Education for the state of Tennessee, was of great assistance in helping Dr. Bob set up his educational system in line with that of Tennessee; and when Dr. Doak Campbell came over from Peabody College to check our standards, he found everything in excellent shape.

About three months after our move to Tennessee, Dr. Bob planned an "Educational Week" that stirred wide interest within the state. Dr. Bob was delighted with our progress in Cleveland in so short a time, and before Christmas that year he wrote to Governor Graves, saying:

> You will be glad to know that we are in good shape here. The students are paying by the month, and we have met our obligations for three months

and have paid almost six thousand dollars on equipment, and we have enough money in the bank to take care of the January expenses.

Many Miracles

Many miracles took place in Cleveland. I wish it were possible to mention all of them, but space and time will not permit. You can multiply the ones I mention by a large number.

The depression was still on, and money was very hard to obtain. We could not just stand still—we must go forward. Dr. Bob "hit the road" to raise money. He felt no qualms about being away; his son, Bob, Jr., who was taking over the responsibilities as Acting President of the school, was quite capable in looking after affairs during his father's absence. These men worked harmoniously in building and promoting Bob Jones University. They complemented each other—one majoring in finances and promotion, the other majoring in culture and education, but both majoring in the spiritual.

At the end of the first year, in spite of many difficulties, Dr. Bob had paid for all the new equipment, had built a classroom building, had given the faculty a generous bonus, and was in sound financial condition.

Evangelistic Calls At Home and Abroad

Dr. Bob kept receiving calls to hold meetings at home and in foreign lands. In the fall of 1934, he decided to accept an invitation to Ireland and some other places to which he felt God was calling him. He took with him on this trip some of our preacher boys, whom he left abroad for several months of evangelistic work. (Today there are more than 850 of our students on foreign fields carrying on an uncompromising ministry.)

The trip to Ireland was good for Dr. Bob. He enjoyed every minute of it. He loved the people, and he felt at home with them because his mother's people were from that section. The people would have set up enough meetings to last a year if Dr. Bob had permitted it.

This excerpt from a letter which Dr. Bob wrote from Bangor, Ireland, to Mrs. Bibb Graves will give insight into conditions in Poland at that time:

There is no business, but I just wanted you to know that Mrs. Jones and I are thinking about you and the Governor while we are on this wonderful trip. We were in Berlin several days. Then we were in Poland. I saw more real, unadulterated New Testament Christianity in Poland than I have seen anywhere in the world. People walked for miles to hear the Gospel and then they would stand for four hours in the morning and four hours in the afternoon. We were in the Russian section of Poland. Those Christians in days gone by have had to suffer for Jesus Christ. However, Poland has religious liberty now and these Christians are very happy that they can worship unhindered. From reliable Christian sources I have information that the persecution of the Christians in Russia is unspeakable. As long as I live I shall carry on the wall of my memory a picture of the upturned, eager faces of these people who loved God so much. . . . It was providential, I think, that I was able to make this trip because I was getting on the ragged edge physically. We have had a wonderful rest, and getting away from the routine at home has helped me greatly.

Bob, Jr., admitted that this protracted absence of his father in 1934 was by far the greatest test of his endurance up to that time. But it was wonderful that this son was able and willing to take over so that the father could take the much-needed rest. Dr. Bob said of this trip, "The first time in all my life I really felt rested was when I was on the boat and could do absolutely nothing except rest."

Dr. Bob's pride in his son and the ability he had demonstrated in his absence is evident in a letter which Dr. Bob wrote to Mr. J. S. Mack, McKeesport, Pennsylvania:

My son ran the college successfully in my absence, and it is a great joy to know that we have built an organization which can function without my being here. The Lord has opened many doors and I am leaving Monday for Adrian, Michigan, then on to Detroit, from there to Chicago for a Russian Missionary Conference and then on to Grand Rapids for Mel Trotter's Bible Conference. From there I go to Pontiac, Michigan, for a meeting. I will then return to the school for a few days before heading for Georgia and Florida for a thirty-day tour, speaking two or three times a day.

Dr. Bob was eager to get his school on a firm financial foundation so that he could spend more time in evangelistic work. Billy Sunday had just died, and there were so few of the old-time evangelists left that Dr. Bob felt that he must spend as much time out in the field as possible. The fields were "white unto harvest," and the whole world was opening up to him. They wanted him for meetings in Australia, New Zealand, the Orient, Scotland, and in every part of America. There was a feeling among fundamental Bible-believing Christians that a real evangelistic program might save the country from communism.

During the summer of 1936, Dr. Bob went on a lecture tour of Alabama and Florida. He spoke over many radio stations—Montgomery, Mobile, Dothan, Pensacola, and Panama City—besides the many mass meetings he had in various cities. Dr. Bob told the people that the modern educators' theories were wrong. He gave a lecture on the subject "The Devil in the School." In this lecture he pointed out that men had unconsciously substituted satanic philosophy for Christian philosophy. He described Christian philosophy as the philosophy of self-denial, and satanic philosophy as the "Do-as-you-please" philosophy. He would go on to explain that "the earliest school teachers in America were not all Christians, but most of them accepted the Christian philosophy and taught it. That's what built the great leaders of this nation."

From Panama City, Florida, Dr. Bob went to Philadelphia for a fifteen-day meeting. While there, he had a conference with Mr. J. S. Mack, Head of the G. C. Murphy Stores, USA, who had become interested in Dr. Bob in McKeesport, Pennsylvania, back in 1927 during his city-wide campaign there. In this conference they discussed the future program that Dr. Bob had in mind for his school. Mr. Mack said that he and his wife would give $45,000 toward this project if Dr. Bob would raise another $45,000. Also, in Philadelphia Dr. Bob interested some other friends in putting up money for him to be on the radio station there twice a week for a year.

From Philadelphia Dr. Bob headed for the West Coast, stopping in Memphis, Dallas, Abilene, and El Paso for special lectures. He spent fifteen days in Phoenix, Arizona, and then went to California for another fifteen days, lecturing in fifteen different places. During his stay in California, he opened a permanent radio program for that area.

Upon his return to Cleveland, Dr. Bob met with officials of the local Chamber of Commerce, who formed a committee of directors to underwrite $33,000. He went to Chapel and raised $2,500 from the faculty and student body. Then he appealed to the Board of Trustees, saying:

> I have always avoided making membership on our Board a burden. I feel, however, that this is one time when our Board can render real service.

He had excellent cooperation from everyone: every Board member, every faculty and staff member, and every student contributed something to the project. Dr. Bob knew that it would be much easier to get money from other people if our crowd had done their part. He contacted friends around the country, explaining our needs and the fact that he must raise $45,000 to match the Mack's $45,000 to complete our building program. The letter ended:

> To make it brief, we need $90,000 to complete our building program. When this is done we will be prepared to take care of comfortably the maximum number of students we feel should enroll.

Many times during our school's history—and even today—we receive donations with the stipulation, "you must 'go out' and match it."

Increased Enrollment

With the idea that a small school is best, Dr. Bob at first limited his enrollment to five hundred. In his advertising he stated: "Attendance is strictly limited to five hundred carefully selected students. A large faculty and staff of consecrated and experienced Christians assures individual attention and personal direction for each student." Dr. Bob went up and down the country extolling the advantages of keeping a school small. He had a noted sermon entitled, "The School That Jesus Built." He described Jesus' school as

a small school having just twelve boys. But He knew His subject and He knew His pupils. Jesus' only classroom was a dusty highway, a seashore, or a hillside. His only laboratory was a wedding feast where He changed water to wine. He never said "I think" or "I suppose." What did He teach? He taught the people how to live and how to die. He taught them it was better to die for something than to live for nothing. His school was a success even though it lasted only three years when the Founder was hanged naked on a Cross. His pupils left Him when He talked of dying. One of the twelve double-crossed and betrayed his Lord, selling Him for thirty pieces of silver. Another one denied his Lord.

But God had other plans for Dr. Bob and his school than that it should be of limited enrollment; and Mrs. Jones deserves the credit for calling this fact to Dr. Bob's attention. She reminded her husband that he prayed earnestly that the Lord would send the right students, and she did not think it was right to turn some of them away. These students could not afford to wait around several years to get into his school, she said, and this meant that they would have to go to some school that might not be spiritually sound. Dr. Bob was impressed with the logic and wisdom of her arguments, and he gladly changed the policy and agreed to take more students.

More About Mr. J. S. Mack

Mr. Mack was becoming more and more interested in the school, but good businessman that he was, he wanted to find out certain things before investing "big" money with us. "How is it possible for you to build and run a school and do evangelistic work at the same time?" he asked Dr. Bob. I quote in full Dr. Bob's answer, because it explains the philosophy of the school.

First, practically every college or university is built on some one doctrine or group of doctrines. Bob Jones is different; it is built on the idea that whatever the Bible says is so. The creed of the school contains the simple fundamentals which all orthodox Christians believe. Our school has an evangelistic atmosphere which is not found in any other institution in America. This is due to the fact that as head of Bob Jones College I have had years of training in evangelistic work. The first night we opened our school in Florida, there were forty-two conversions; one of them was a skeptic who now is a pastor. The ministerial students who go out from our school have evangelistic fervor.

He went on to explain:

The five best soul winners in the United States are young men who graduated from our school. I do not mean that any one of these young men is the greatest soul winner, but the five put together are winning more people to Jesus Christ than any other five men in America.

Second, "This one thing I do," in my case, includes not only the center for the training of intelligent, strong, orthodox, Christian leaders, but it is a base for interdenominational, orthodox testimony for America. Our idea is not only to train leaders but it is to sell, in this rationalistic age, evangelical and educational orthodoxy to the masses of people. We wish to slow down the rationalistic and atheistic drift in the educational life of this nation. My evangelistic work gives me an opportunity to sell the college to fathers and mothers over the country who wish to send their children to a good, orthodox school. So one of the greatest opportunities I have to build this college is to do it in connection with my evangelistic program. Five students signed up and will be here next year because of a two-week meeting in Los Angeles. You understand competition in business. We have the same competition in schools. There are fifty-three colleges in the state of Tennessee. There are several thousand in the United States. There is a terrific drive on now to get students. One by one, colleges are being killed off. No college ever died with a growing attendance; they die from a lack of students. It is my desire to so sell this school to the public during my life that it will not be necessary to sell after my death. All they will have to do is keep it sold. As I see it, my evangelistic work affords me the best opportunity for my salesmanship. While I am selling the school, I am preaching the Gospel, I am slowing down other colleges which have modernism in them, I am putting out orthodox propaganda, and I am winning souls to Jesus Christ.

Third, keep in mind that Bob Jones College in Cleveland, Tennessee, while it operates under another charter, is the same Bob Jones College we had in Florida. It is simply transferred here because here we have a better center and a better base for our work.

Fourth, I absolutely agree with you about the necessity of building an organization. Remember, I am not an educator. I am an evangelist. I tell my boys and girls that they can borrow brain, but they can't borrow character. So I borrow the technical educational brain to run this school. Our dean, Miss Eunice Hutto, has no superior in the educational field. She does all the technical educational work. I could not do it. My son, Bob, Jr., who is twenty-five years old, came up through our high school and our college, and he is familiar with every detail. He is in training, and is an unusual executive and a far better college head than I could ever be. He is a marvelous judge of human nature, and has the respect of the entire faculty and the student body. Our business manager, Robert "Lefty" Johnson, is a graduate of our school and has worked in the office since he entered college. He is a clean, solid, substantial, Christian young man. He is here for life as far as we know. I have trained him in every detail. He is stingy and guards every penny, is a good buyer and a good collector. Every key position is held by somebody whom we trained. We are building here an organization that will be stronger, I believe, than any other school in the country. My old students will keep the school filled in case of my death. I cannot think of a single thing that could humanly be done for permanence that has not been done.

Fifth, as far as the details of operation are concerned, the school has reached a point where the load is, to a great extent, off my shoulders. The details, I mean; I am not carrying any of these details. Now, I hope you will not think I am conceited when I say I am an asset to this college in three particulars. First, I have had years of evangelistic experience, and I know how to keep the religious stimulation. Second, I have the enthusiasm. Third, I am an expert propagandist. Now, all three things in which I excel I can carry on with my evangelistic work. My evangelistic work will really increase my efficiency in the three things where I am a success. I can "blow into" this college about one week in three and set it on fire, "pep it up," generate enthusiasm, keep things on a high pitch, and then go out into the world and preach the Gospel and contact the people over the radio and come back home and set the college on fire again. Bear in mind, all the time I am out, I am selling the school, putting out propaganda, lining up students, and making financial contacts. To illustrate, when I was in Los Angeles, a rich Christian Jew heard me speak and tell about the college. He came to the front at the close of the service and said, "The Lord has put it on my heart to put Bob Jones College in my will, and I am going home and do it." Yes, "This one thing I do": I am building a college to train great leaders, and at the same time as a base of evangelistic, orthodox, educational testimony.

Sixth, do not interpret anything I have said above to mean that I do not absolutely agree with you that there is no use putting any money here to build a college that is not going to be permanent. If I could talk to you one hour, I could show you that that is exactly what we are doing. No, Brother Mack, honest, we do not want the amount of money most institutions have. Too much money would be the worst thing that could happen to us. It would probably keep us from praying as much as we ought to pray. It would probably reduce our energy. We are asking the Lord to supply our needs, and this He is going to do. Dr. Roemer, former president of the Association of Colleges, visited our school three times. He is a brilliant educator, and he is a Christian Presbyterian gentleman. He said, "My business is to inspect colleges. I have inspected over three hundred in the United States. There is something in Bob Jones College I have never found anywhere else in the world. I don't know what it is." Nobody can tell what it is. You have to come here to find it.

Seventh, I started into this thing nine years ago. I knew nothing in the world about a college. I had no idea. God has led me step by step. I know what we can do. I know exactly how I can mingle my evangelistic work which I have outlined with the college program and make the evangelistic program the strongest asset we have in building this college permanently. Now, of course, I understand that I am fifty-two years of age, and the type evangelistic work I do will not be the big tabernacle meetings like I had at McKeesport and Pittsburgh. It would be the short meeting of say fifteen days like I had in Los Angeles. I was in Europe two months last year in evangelistic meetings and they missed me because I keep things pepped up, but those were the two happiest and best months the school has ever had.

Eighth, the presidents of most successful colleges spend a great deal of time away. They attend political gatherings and lecture to clubs. The difference between most of them and me is that I am preaching the Gospel to thousands of people and at the same time am selling my school to the public. The details of running the school is not the burden. My burden for nine years, both in Florida and Tennessee, has been the struggle of digging up money. The worst days are over, and I believe a big part of the strain will be taken off me. I am not going to involve this school in debt, and we are going to operate on a cash basis, God helping us.

Dr. Bob never pushed Mr. Mack or anybody else for money. It was Dr. Bob's policy to present God's work to God's people and let God lead them to the right response. Because Mr. Mack was such a good businessman, however, Dr. Bob often sought his advice on business matters. Dr. Bob wrote to Mr. Mack:

First, when I went to see you recently, Mrs. Jones and I prayed that you might give us some sound advice. That was what we were looking for. We knew you were a successful businessman and that God had endowed you with unusual executive gifts and abilities. We wanted your advice; I did not ask you for a gift. While I am an enthusiastic propagandist, I am a Christian and I do not want any money from any source except what God sends.

Second, I recognize the fact that you are a trustee of God's funds. You got your talent from God. Everything comes from Him. You are absolutely right to carefully investigate every detail before you put God's money into any proposition. I wish we had more Christian businessmen like you. Most of the religious businessmen in the United States are putting their money into institutions which have no permanent value to this nation or to the world. They have invested their money in colleges and universities which are putting out propaganda that will undermine the fortunes of these businessmen and at the same time, undermine the foundations of our government. About this I am absolutely sure. The great danger centers of this nation are our colleges and universities.

Keep in mind that these remarks were made as far back as forty years ago. Everything Dr. Bob predicted has come to pass in even greater measure than anyone could have dreamed possible. The communists and socialists said that they must take over the youth of our nation and subvert them from the kindergarten through the universities. They said that they must get their men into the seminaries and work within the framework of religion to turn out preachers to do a job which they themselves could not do. They began to infiltrate our universities, such as Harvard and Yale; and look at our nation today. We are headed for ruin at breakneck speed. That is the reason why Dr. Bob founded Bob Jones College—to train the Christian leadership he felt this nation so greatly needed to combat these errors. Dr. Bob wanted to incorporate in his school all the fundamentals of the faith, for he knew that they were the basic fundamentals that had made this nation great. Thank God for this man of vision and for Bob Jones University which stands today as a monument to his courage, determination, and foresight.

Dr. Bob decided to invite Mrs. Mack to serve on our Board of Trustees. She graciously accepted the invitation and pledged herself to do everything within her power to help and to promote the school. Mr. Mack, knowing that his wife was a very timid woman, thought that the contact with Bob Jones College would do her good. He pledged, "I am really going to put my shoulder to the wheel and help you in a big way."

Mr. Mack helped not only financially but also by passing on to Dr. Bob some of his practical philosophy. He wrote:

Education is a slow process. The easy thing to do is to hire and fire folks. But that doesn't tend to develop an organization. To build an organization, you hire and train folks and the longer they are in their job—if they are good—the better they become at their work.

Mr. Mack understood Dr. Bob's desire to build an organization that would carry on in case something happened to him; and he realized that it was necessary for Dr. Bob to be away a great deal, selling the school's program to the public and raising money to carry on the work. These contacts, he observed, were paying dividends. (In two years we received over $500,000 from people who left our school in their wills because of Dr. Bob's great work in the evangelistic field years before.)

Plans for Expansion

On the train, as he was returning from a meeting in New York in February, 1937, Dr. Bob was taken sick with a bad case of flu; and the Lord put him in bed for a week's rest. Dr. Bob did not lie around idly, however; he kept busy, figuring how to expand the school. First he wanted to build a substantial Student Loan Fund. Then he wanted to build a new dining hall, rebuild our heating facilities, brick veneer the boys' dorm, and put up several other buildings. It would be necessary to borrow money, of course; and Mr. C. W. Harle, president of the Merchants Bank in Cleveland and also a member of the Executive Committee of the Board of Trustees of Bob Jones College, suggested that we try to

"Old Main" in Cleveland, Tennessee

get the money from some New York bank at a low rate of interest. Mr. Mack, fearful of another depression, advised that we float the loan at home and pay the extra interest rate. Big banks might try to foreclose in hard times, he warned. But Dr. Bob always had a desire to keep the school from going into debt, and he wanted to go slow on borrowing any money. The Chamber of Commerce in Cleveland had agreed to put on an annual drive until the indebtedness on the purchase price for Old Centenary College was paid. Dr. Bob said, "I feel that this debt is provided for. I am very desirous of completing the building program that is absolutely necessary and then stopping until we raise enough cash for our next buildings."

We had spent over two hundred thousand dollars on buildings and improvements, and for four years had started school heavily in debt. Every year we had had to "sweat blood," so to speak, to liquidate our indebtedness. This was hard on Dr. Bob's nerves, for it was his responsibility to raise the money. Mr. Mack had given us some stock which we could have sold or used at the bank for collateral. But Mr. Mack asked us not to sell his stock. It would keep going up, he said, and later we would be able to sell at a higher rate, pay off our debts, and still have stock to spare. Meanwhile, we could borrow money at three per cent, continue making four per cent on our stock, and our stock was increasing in value. We could not lose, he said.

Even though Dr. Bob had built an average of at least one building a year, he could not build fast enough to keep pace with the growth of the student body. He found it necessary to set up temporary quarters in the auditorium dressing rooms and in the gymnasium to house some of the boys. This maneuvering took a physical toll on Dr. Bob; so in the fall of 1937, Mr. Mack decided that Dr. Bob should get away more often for a rest. To encourage him in this direction, Mr. Mack presented his friend with a new trailer. "I do trust the little trailer will not disappoint you," he wrote, "but will be all that your enthusiasm and optimism believes it to be, and that 'Darlin' ' will like it equally as well." ("Darlin' " was Dr. Bob's affectionate name for his wife.) Dr. Bob laughed and said that Mrs. Jones did not like trailers and that she knew him well enough to know that he would pull the trailer all over the country. She had traveled with him for thirty years, but she was not about to travel with him in a trailer.

Dr. Bob's "trailer travel" was short lived. He took exactly one trip in it. He had some real problems coming up, and he wanted time to think them through. Hitching the trailer to his car, he headed for his beloved boyhood home place to rest, to think, and to pray. He had not pulled the trailer through very many states, however, until he decided that he had had enough and that he would rather sell the trailer and use the money in the Lord's work. Our good friend and Board member, Mrs. P. B. Mayfield, bought the trailer; and she and her daughter Bess enjoyed it for several years.

At the time of the building of the auditorium, the gymnasium, and the dining hall, Mrs. Mack asked Mrs. Jones to find out how much money we needed. Dr. Bob wrote to Mr. Mack, saying:

> Now Brother Mack, we do not ever want to put pressure on you. If the Lord directs you and you feel you can afford it, I honestly believe that this is the best place on earth to put some money. I believe we can do more with a dollar in the way of accomplishing moral and spiritual results than any other place. I believe the Lord is going to send in the $50,000 we need to finish these buildings.

Mr. Mack replied, saying not to worry, a check would be forthcoming.

By the end of June, 1938, we had paid all we owed with the exception of $25,000 in New York and the amount the Chamber of Commerce had underwritten. Mr. Harle was urging Dr. Bob to start a dormitory immediately to house two hundred boys. Dr. Bob decided to spend an additional $50,000 updating "Old Main"; another $50,000 on a new building, the basement of which we could use for a Science Department, the first floor for boys, and the second for teachers; and another $75,000 to house ninety girls and take care of our Commercial Department. Building conditions for such a project were favorable. Money was scarce, building costs were down, carpenters were not working, and everyone was eager to pitch in to help build cheaply. Banks were eager to lend money, and this afforded us low interest rates. Trusting God, we launched this mammoth building program.

In May, 1939, Dr. Bob and Bob, Jr., put on the pressure to get Mr. Mack to accompany his wife to Commencement at Bob Jones College. Mrs. Mack had been to several of these programs, but Mr. Mack had never been able to arrange his schedule so that he could attend. The "pressure" brought results; Mr. Mack made the long trip to Cleveland, Tennessee.

Mr. Mack was delighted with our setup. He attended our annual Board meeting and was impressed with the dedication of our Board. He thrilled as he heard them vote unanimously to raise $60,000 within twelve months to liquidate certain debts on buildings just completed, to make certain other improvements, and to start rebuilding our depleted cash reserves. Several Board members pledged $1,000 or more, and others pledged smaller amounts. Mr. Mack pledged a substantial sum toward an endowment. Everyone expressed thankfulness to the Lord for His manifold blessings, and many were so overcome with emotion that they had to make several attempts to say what was on their hearts.

In spite of our having built seven buildings in six years, we were able to present a marvelous financial report. Mr. Mack said to Dr. Bob,

I wish to compliment you on your financial statement. You handle your finances in a masterful way. If you, Bob, Jr., and 'Lefty' keep your finances in that shape, you need not lose any sleep at night.

Dr. Bob answered:

It delights me and it is encouraging to have you say our financial statements look good. We have done the best we could, but we feel we owe thanks to God. When I stop to think of the institutions in this country, many of them highly endowed and others with Conferences, Conventions, and Associations back of them, and yet they have not been able to meet their overhead, it just seems too marvelous that this little college is able to keep its head above water and keep on keeping on. Our prospects for the future are brighter than ever.

As a result of this Board meeting, we hired an architect from Chattanooga, Tennessee, and had him re-design the interior of our auditorium. We added some studios, rearranged the seating, laid new aisle carpets, and added a beautiful new colonial front to the building. Mrs. Mack put up several thousand dollars for this project, and since the building would bear her name and would be one of the show places of the campus, we were eager to have it just right. Although there were larger and more expensive buildings in Tennessee, none were better equipped insofar as lighting and staging were concerned.

Mr. Mack studied our crowded conditions and recommended that we "quietly, yet persistently, and without any inside or outside strain or hurry, begin to acquire property adjacent to the school." He committed himself to put up fifty per cent of any money spent for property, and added that if we needed more, he would increase his gifts. This man realized that we meant business and that we were careful in spending the Lord's money. This made him want to help even more.

Our landscaping at this time left much to be desired. Mr. Mack said, "I look at landscaping as the frame of a picture. I have seen good pictures badly marred and their beauty obscured by the cheap, unsightly frame." To put our landscaping into good shape, he sent his landscape engineer to Cleveland with the instruction to work out an extensive plan covering several years.

Another suggestion Mr. Mack made was that I was too conservative in my bookkeeping, and he invited me to his home office in McKeesport to get helpful pointers from his CPA's. He notified the officials of his company to expect me and later to expect Bob, Jr. I was to bring back certain reports which Bob would study before making his trip to McKeesport. Mr. Mack had asked that I bring with me to his home office certain architectural plans that could be studied by his men with the idea of air conditioning our dining common.

Mr. Mack was not well while I was in McKeesport. In a letter to Bob, Jr., he referred to the fact that he had had a long, hard battle, but believed he was gaining ground. He added, "I trust that our friend, 'Lefty' Johnson, will take back some 'white meat' which will be of use to you and your good institution in the days that are ahead."

The "white meat" I brought back enabled me to put in a completely new system of bookkeeping which has served us well throughout many years. I could never express in words my feelings of gratitude to Mr. Mack and his organization for their help. Our school has felt the impact of this man's greatness and generosity.

After his 1939 visit to our school, Mr. Mack sent us eight hundred shares of G. C. Murphy stock as well as increased monthly checks and even added extra checks from time to time. Dr. Bob wrote him, in part:

> Men like . . . and men of that type who have very little spiritual vision can give to non-essentials. God has given you the spiritual apprehension and vision, and He has made you prosperous. You have a good Christian wife. Most men who are prosperous do not have spiritual vision. I have prayed that God would lead you in your giving and in your contacts.

> At the judgment seat of Christ when the returns are in, men who have invested their money in orthodox Christian programs will share in the rewards that will be given out. Brother Mack, when you think of the changing world conditions and feel the uncertainty of everything that is temporal, it is a great joy to be conscious that we are investing here in eternal realities. Your money is here and every time a boy is converted, every time a girl gets a new vision of life, you share in it as much as if you were the president of Bob Jones College.

Dr. Bob, in his usual unselfish way, talked Mr. Mack into helping other good causes of the Lord. He wrote to him in behalf of Winona Lake, Indiana:

> I am very much interested in holding Winona in line as a base of conservative religion. At this time the greatest peril that threatens this nation is the subtle, modernistic education and religious drift. (Such men as . . . are supporting modernists with their money and helping build things that are sooner or later going to undermine his own fortune and the traditions of America.) As you know, the communistic influences are at work in this country. Many of our modernistic preachers have communistic leanings. Winona is a great center of evangelical orthodoxy. Dr. Biederwolf is trying to reorganize it somewhat on the orthodox basis of our college, so it will be permanent in its testimony along orthodox lines. Of course, my experience

in evangelistic work has been rather wide, and I am more or less familiar with the different institutions in our country. Your desire to give conscientiously appeals to me very much.

Mr. Mack agreed to invest money in Winona "provided Bob Jones, Jr., is put on the Board to safeguard things." Bob, Jr., wrote Mr. Mack, thanking him for the faith he had in him and agreeing to serve as Mr. Mack had requested.

Mr. Mack's strength did not return as quickly as he thought it should, and he went to Johns Hopkins for a thorough checkup. It was his prayer that God would heal him completely. At Christmas he wrote that he would send an extra check of $250 each month for a period of three years. Dr. Bob decided to combine this with other gifts which the Lord was sending in through His saints and use them to promote evangelism throughout the country. He organized several groups which he sent out under the auspices of THE GOSPEL FELLOWSHIP ASSOCIATION which he had founded many years before. By this means we were able to distribute Gospel literature into every home in these areas.

For a number of years Dr. Bob had been formulating plans for evangelizing rural districts. He knew what needed to be done; the problem was how to finance it. He was seeking to raise $1,000 a month to carry on the work as he felt it should be done. He said:

> It grieves me when I think of all the thousands and thousands of dollars that have been spent on building ecclesiastical machinery that does not reach as many people as the one man we have in Dothan. . . . The schools are open to him, and he goes into rural districts where no preacher goes.

Mrs. Mack made a monthly pledge to the project. Many evangelical leaders from various parts of the country thanked Dr. Bob for starting the movement, saying that they had been thinking along the same lines.

Dr. Bob was also working on plans for a wider radio ministry. He was worried about the religious life of the nation. It seemed that more and more people were staying away from church, and he decided that it would be a good idea to go directly into their homes with the Gospel. He was on more than seventy new stations and was planning to have more than 150 by early spring. He had recorded several series of fifty-two sermons which he was sending out all over the world—to China, Hawaii, Puerto Rico, Alaska, Australia, and New Zealand. This gave double exposure: the people had the Gospel presented to them in an effective way, and the testimony of God's school was spread to the ends of the earth.

Early in January of 1940, Dr. Bob had to get away for a much-needed rest. Mrs. Jones said that she was going to take him so far away that he could not speak the language of the citizenship and therefore could not spend all his vacation preaching. I say this to point out that this man never took his eye off the goal of winning souls. It was an all-consuming passion with him. Vacations meant little to him if he had an opportunity to proclaim God's message of love and salvation.

By the middle of January, 1940, we had paid for College Arms, our faculty apartment house, and for all the other property we had bought. It seemed that at last we might take things easy for a spell. By May of 1940, however, we realized that we would have to expand further. We needed a girls' dormitory and a library building which would also house our executive offices. Mr. Mack promised to pay up to one half of the total cost. The Board of Trustees accepted Mr. Mack's proposal and thanked him for all that he had done for us through the years. At Commencement, 1940, Bob Jones University conferred on Mr. Mack the honorary degree of Doctor of Philanthropy. In presenting the degree, Dr. Bob said:

> Mr. Mack, many people know something of your philanthropy since it has been so widespread. However, only a few even of your most intimate friends know how generous you have really been in your support of humanitarian and Christian causes in many parts of the world. It so happens that the founder and president of this college is your close friend and knows enough about your generosity to recognize the fact that you are, indeed, most worthy of the honorary degree of Doctor of Philanthropy. I therefore, by the power invested in me by the Board of Trustees, confer upon you this degree and present you with this diploma.

A special news release of this event was sent out all over the country.

In September, 1940, Dr. Bob said to Bob, Jr., and me, "If Mr. Mack is willing to be generous and put up so much of his money he should have a big say so." Dr. Bob repeated this to Mr. Mack on September 26, 1940. On September 27, 1940, Mrs. Mack wired: "Mr. Mack seriously ill at farm. Will advise any change."

I was with Dr. Bob the night he received the message that our good friend and benefactor had gone Home to be with the Lord. It was a blow, for Dr. Bob loved Mr. Mack. The Macks invited Dr. Bob to participate in the funeral service, and this he was glad to do.

I am confident that God brought these two men together at a time when both needed each other. They were cronies from the beginning; and in many ways, they were alike. Both were of Irish descent, both were forceful and dynamic, and both were successful in their fields of service. Mr. Mack had the gift of making money; and realizing that this gift was from the Lord, he wanted to share his money with Dr. Bob who also could have made money but was willing to give all he had to build a Christian college. Had he lived, Mr. Mack would have helped Bob Jones much more, but his life goes on through the things he did for Bob Jones College during its formative years. Our library in Cleveland was called "Mack Memorial Library"; our library in Greenville bears the name "John Sephus Mack Library." In Cleveland our auditorium was named "Margaret Mack"; in Greenville one of the girls' dormitories is called "Margaret Mack."

At Commencement, 1941, a few months after Mr. Mack's death, a statement of appreciation to the Macks was read. I quote an excerpt:

> A deep sense of personal loss was felt by both faculty and students alike at Bob Jones College with the passing of John Sephus Mack on September 27, 1940, for Mr. Mack had proved himself a sincere friend in the true meaning of the word. Loved and admired not alone for his generosity and acts of philanthropy, but for himself — the memory of his fruitful life will never be erased from the minds of those who knew him.
>
> Had Mr. Mack himself been a graduate of the institution, he could not have shown a greater interest and appreciation for the work Bob Jones College is doing in training Christian leaders for all walks of life. The landscaping of the beautiful college campus is only one of the physical reminders of one whose life exhibited those attributes of character which Bob Jones College endeavors to develop in its students who are receiving their training for Christian service within her walls. Mr. Mack not only contributed liberally to the college during his lifetime but he remembered the college in his will generously.

Mrs. Mack continued to help the school, sending monthly checks. She loved our school and always received a blessing when she visited us. When she passed away on December 5, 1944, Dr. Bob was sick and could not participate in her funeral; but he wrote the two sons a long letter, one paragraph of which I quote:

> Your mother's heart was so responsive to everything here at the college. As long as I live I can see her sitting down in the front in chapel when I was talking to the students and tears would be flowing down her face. The more spiritual the emphasis, the greater was her response. Both you and your children have a great heritage. You had a most remarkable father and mother. I trust that in this hour of sorrow you both may be more definitely and completely yielded to God — the God of your father and the God of your mother.

Friends said, "What a tragedy it was for Bob Jones to lose Mr. Mack!" Dr. Bob missed Mr. Mack, and he gratefully remembered all that his friend had done for Bob Jones College. But he realized that in the long run it was for our good that we no longer had Mr. Mack's support on which to depend. God had always supplied our needs, and Dr. Bob knew that He would continue to do so. Mr. Mack was sent our way at a time when we desperately needed his help. He had gone so far as to say, "Construct your buildings, and send me the bill." Now, Dr. Bob said, "We will go back to trusting God and not looking to Mr. Mack." Dr. Bob said to me: "Our school is on a good solid foundation spiritually and physically, and if we keep up the spiritual pressure and keep God first, our school has no worries."

Interesting Campaigns

Even with added responsibilities at the school, Dr. Bob was still able to hold many meetings. He had a wonderful fifteen-day meeting in Portland, Oregon; a big rally in Montgomery, Alabama; a successful campaign in Detroit, Michigan; a wonderful eight-day meeting in Philadelphia in a non-sectarian tabernacle; an eight-day meeting in Roanoke, Virginia; and on to Toronto, Canada.

In Lake Charles, Louisiana, and Abilene, Texas, Dr. Bob had two of the greatest revivals he had had in many years as far as spiritual stimulation of the people was concerned. The power of God really came upon the people. In Abilene, a large number of preachers came from all over that part of the country; and they commented, "This meeting demonstrates that the old Gospel has lost none of its power." Dr. Bob had the feeling that this nation was ready for a revival. He said, "If the preachers would quit trying to build ecclesiastical machinery and big programs and concentrate on the Gospel, the greatest spiritual awakening the nation ever had would come."

An eight-day tent campaign in Dalton, Georgia, was held at a time when labor trouble was brewing and eleven hundred people were out on strike. The big tent seated five thousand, but it was too small to hold the crowd. Dr. Bob said that he had never seen such congestion of cars at a religious service. All the preachers of the town and many from surrounding areas supported the meeting. They felt that the results would outweigh any problems of such an undertaking.

At Martin's Ferry, Ohio, Dr. Bob was pleased to find that many of the leaders of the various churches were converts of a meeting he had held there thirty-one years before. In the earlier meeting there had been more than three thousand conversions.

Radio Station

I mention the following incident to show that Dr. Bob had good cooperation from people and usually got whatever he set out to get.

Instead of continuing to broadcast by remote control over Station WDOD in Chattanooga, as he had been doing, Dr. Bob decided that it would be better to have a station of our own in Cleveland. Governor

Bibb Graves heartily endorsed this move and offered to help lay the groundwork "without charge." Dr. Bob would not accept his offer, however; he insisted on paying the fee. Dr. Bob never took advantage of his friends. He appreciated their interest and never forgot to thank them and be thoughtful of them. Whenever Governor Graves or Dr. Harry A. Ironside visited our school, Dr. Bob always checked to see that they had two pillows, because he knew that they were accustomed to using two pillows.

There was keen interest in our getting a radio station. Someone sold us a lot for the tower; the governors of Tennessee and Georgia, both senators from Tennessee, and many local citizens, including the editor of the local paper who wrote editorials about the project, did all they could to help. We had set aside for this purpose a reserve of $36,000, and Dr. Bob had even made a trip to Washington and had his application approved. But in the final analysis, he decided that it would be better to let someone else build the station and let us have an hour or so a day.

Greater Opportunities

Bob Jones College was becoming known as the greatest base of evangelical testimony in the world. And small wonder, for Dr. Bob was writing for several hundred newspapers; was speaking by recording on 150 radio stations; and had founded the Young People's Fellowship Clubs, which had spread around the world with clubs in China, India, Palestine, and the British Isles.

In an effort to keep things straight in fundamental circles, Dr. Bob spoke at the World's Fundamentals Association Convention in Boston. He stayed so busy that he could not find time to do many of the things that he wanted to do. He said:

> The years are passing so rapidly, and I cannot help but think how wonderful it will be up in Heaven where we will have plenty of time to do so many things we long to do down here. We live so strenuously and have so much on our minds, we can be of little pleasure and comfort to our friends, and it is hard for us to be courteous.

Any motor running full speed continuously will sooner or later need repair. Dr. Bob had suffered a great deal with kidney stones, and he needed a rest; so God put him to bed for a week. There was an infection in his system which kept him feeling physically low. After the removal of several teeth, his body was cleared of the poison; and he began to feel better and to be free of the annoying rheumatic pains.

By the end of the school year, 1942, we had completed several more buildings, including the beautiful new Mack Memorial Library which was by far the prettiest and most expensive building in Cleveland. We had worked hard. We had built in the face of many odds, maneuvering every way in the world to meet the demand. Times had steadily worsened. Pearl Harbor had been bombed on December 7, 1941; and the government was holding up as much building as possible. But the Lord was with us and everyone rallied to our aid.

About two years after Pearl Harbor, some government men came to check our school to see if we would permit them to put military men on our campus. Dr. Bob told them that we were too crowded. The men were surprised to find a school as crowded as ours when many schools were begging for students. Dr. Bob explained to the men that if the government were to put several hundred soldiers on our campus we would cease to be the type of Christian school he wanted us to be, for students who were not under the rules and regulations of the school could break down our standards. Dr. Bob offered to let them take over the whole school, if they needed it; otherwise, we could not do anything to help. The government representatives said that it was not the government's intention to disturb any school that was filled to capacity like ours.

By 1943, there was among the youth of our country a wave of immorality that was getting so bad that J. Edgar Hoover began contacting chiefs of police all over the country, urging them to put on a real drive against the crime that was so prevalent among the young people. Dr. Bob received innumerable letters from parents who thanked God for a school like ours that was training boys and girls in the right way, and that would help our nation increasingly as time went on.

There seemed to be a letting down of bars in many supposedly Christian schools. Even in places like Winona Lake Bible Conference, the situation was changing. Programs did not seem to be on a high plane, spiritually speaking, and some feared that it was getting away from the basic fundamentals that had been laid down by Dr. Biederwolf. Many people expressed their gratitude that Bob Jones, Jr., was on the Board, for they felt that as long as he was there, he would hold things in line.

After Mrs. Jones talked Dr. Jones into changing the policy concerning student enrollment, we grew by leaps and bounds. By 1944, we had gained over a seventy-five per cent increase in enrollment in three years. We had just completed a girls' dormitory that would house two hundred girls, and the War Production Board had given us permission to begin construction on two more buildings that were much needed. One was a new classroom building which was to be named "Alumni Building," and a new dormitory for men known as "Cosmopolitan Hall." As soon as these buildings were completed and conditions would permit, we planned to build a larger auditorium that would seat twenty-five hundred and a beautiful new gymnasium. It was almost impossible to build fast enough to keep up with the needs. We were praying and asking our friends to raise approximately half a million dollars to help with our expansion program. Out of the Mack estate we were able to pay off our bond indebtedness and also to build our reserves considerably.

Building Problems During War Years

Bob Jones never had a problem that God did not give the answer. Money? It was there. Building materials? They were provided. Whatever the need, God always saw that it was fulfilled. I remember that it was necessary to go through the War Production Board for permission to build. Dr. Bob and I went to see a government representative in Chattanooga, Tennessee. This man lacked the vision to see the problem, and he was most uncooperative. He had the attitude that there were enough schools in the country already; since many of them were empty, they could be filled with our overflow. His attitude provoked Dr. Bob; but in as kind a way as possible, Dr. Bob reminded the man that we were living in a free country, that students had a right to select the school of their choice, and that it would be wrong to force them to attend some other type of school where they might not get the Christian training that he wanted to give them. Dr. Bob asked the man which office had the authority over his office. The man answered, "Knoxville." Dr. Bob said, "We will be in Knoxville tomorrow morning."

The next morning as we walked into the outer office in Knoxville, we overheard a conversation between the man in Knoxville and the one in Chattanooga. From the Knoxville man's answers, we could tell that the Chattanooga man was making every effort to hurt our cause. But God was with us and the men in Knoxville—Christian men who knew and valued the wonderful work that Dr. Bob was accomplishing for Tennessee and the nation—were most kind and helpful. They told us that they would like to help us, but their hands were tied. The head of the War Production Board in Washington had issued orders that there could be *no building expansion*; the materials were needed for war and other purposes. Dr. Bob thanked the men and asked which Board was over the Knoxville Board. They answered, "Atlanta." Dr. Bob said, "We will be there in the morning." The men requested that Dr. Bob give them an extra day to get their reports to Atlanta before he appeared there. The Knoxville men assured Dr. Bob that they would not hurt his cause; in fact, they would have given us the permission, if they could have done so! Dr. Bob expressed his appreciation for their attitude, had prayer with the men, and left, promising to wait the extra day before going to Atlanta.

Bright and early two days later, Dr. Bob appeared before the officials of the War Production Board in Atlanta to discuss the problem. He mentioned that Tennessee's Senator Kenneth Douglas McKellar, member of the Appropriations Committee in Washington, was our friend and would appreciate their cooperation. Dr. Bob had arranged for Senator McKellar to wire Atlanta, requesting help for Bob Jones College. Two or three other telegrams came in from influential friends in Washington. This put the men more or less "on the spot." They wanted to help this man of God who was doing so much for the country, and yet they had received definite instructions from Washington saying "NO MORE BUILDINGS." They requested Dr. Bob to leave the meeting so that they could discuss the matter further. He asked to stay since some question might arise that only he could answer. One man made the remark, "We have the power to grant this, or we have the power to refuse it. In view of the type of work Dr. Jones is doing, and the fact that he has these influential friends backing the school and interested in its welfare, I vote that we let him have his buildings." Turning to Dr. Bob, he asked, "When do you intend to start?" Dr. Bob said, "May I use your telephone?" He called me in Cleveland and asked, "When can you start?" I answered, "In five minutes." We had prayed much about this and had had the assurance in our hearts before Dr. Bob left for Atlanta that God would work out this problem; so all that day we had been getting things ready to start. The building was built in record time.

A little later the government changed the law, stating that the only basis on which people could build was to use their own timbers from their own land. The Lord helped us in this, too. Knowing that we were going to need some new building in the near future, He led us to some people who cooperated with us by letting us have certain pieces of timber land.

Bowen Museum

About this time we had a visit from some friends, Mr. and Mrs. Frank Bowen, who wanted to present a museum to some institution of learning. Sixty-two colleges had tried one way or the other to get possession of these valuable antiquities. It is significant, I think, that the Bowens had started accumulating this material the same year that Dr. Bob had founded Bob Jones College in Florida. On a ship headed for the Holy Land, this couple met Bob Jones, Jr., and became very much interested in him and in the school he represented. When they were ready to give this museum to some school, they prayed much, asking God to direct them to the right place. Each time they prayed, Bob Jones College came to their minds; so they decided to visit our school to discuss the matter. We did not push them for this gift, but said, "If God leads you to give it to us, we would, of course, appreciate it." Today this museum is a part of our lovely Art Gallery.

Upon this gift, we needed not only dormitory space but also space in which to display the lovely treasures. There was much excitement about the proposed buildings. The boys pledged several thousand dollars in labor, and the girls voted to raise money to help with these buildings. Dr. Bob headed me to Knoxville again. I will admit that even though I prayed all the way, I went there with fear and trembling. It was an important task; but if we had faced such opposition in Chattanooga, Knoxville, and Atlanta the time before, we would certainly have a hard job getting the permission to build now. But God went ahead and prepared the way; and the men were in a very receptive mood when we arrived.

Fearing that we might run into some difficulties, I had asked Mr. Hibbard Albritton, president of Cleveland Builder's Supply Company and a wonderful friend of our school, to go with me. We had with us all the information we felt we needed; but the men, even though they were friendly and helpful, said that it was impossible for them to process the application until we had filled in certain forms. I whispered a prayer, asking God's guidance. He gave me the answer on the spot. I suggested to the men that they let us have the necessary forms, and we would have them back into their hands before closing time at five o'clock. It was then almost two o'clock. They thought I was joking, but decided to "go along." I remembered that I had a friend in Knoxville, a Robert Johnson, who was president of Highland Products Company. "Let's get there as quickly as possible," I said to Hibbard. When we arrived, I explained our predicament to Bob Johnson and requested the use of both his office and his secretary to help us fill out the government forms. He graciously granted both requests. He had some business that must be handled that afternoon, and he left us with full use of his office.

Hibbard and I got down to business, figuring how many pieces of timber and the various sizes needed for the buildings. We filled in the information, and with the help of the Lord—TO HIM BE THE GLORY!—we were back at the War Production office at five minutes to five. The men laughed and said that they had not believed it could be done. They accepted the application, processed it as quickly as possible, rushed it to Atlanta, and in a matter of days, our buildings were under way.

The devil, in an effort to harass and stop us, brought about some rough tests. We ran out of certain large timbers that were to support the floors. Roy McClure, our faithful building superintendent, who loved the Lord and loved his school, as he called it, notified me that the job would stop within so many days if we could not get this timber. Dr. Bob, Sr.,

Bob, Jr., and I discussed the dilemma, then had a real prayer meeting concerning the problem. Since neither of the Joneses could leave, I went alone in search of the materials, praying every step of the way. The Lord led me in a seemingly strange way. First, I went into the mountains above Ocoee. I spent hours visiting various sawmills, but could find no mill with timber the size we needed. I kept praying that the Lord would lead me to some sawmill that could produce the timbers to meet the demand. About three o'clock that afternoon I was discouraged and hungry (I had not had lunch) and ready to go home in defeat. Something kept saying, *"Man's extremity is God's opportunity."* (This is another of Dr. Bob's famous sayings.) For some strange reason, I felt an urge to pull to the side of the road and cut off the motor, praying and listening. In the distance I heard a sawmill buzzing. Following the sound up the mountain, I found a man who had a yard full of the very timbers we needed, but no amount of persuasion on my part could talk him into letting us have the lumber. He thought that I was some OPA official checking up on him. (I was an OPA official, but I was not on an "OPA" mission that day.) I offered him the OPA prices and offered to haul the lumber at our expense; this was legal and would save him an extra $3.50 per thousand board feet. The man, still apprehensive, skeptical, and scared, told me that he had promised a man all the lumber that would be on the yard the next morning. I thought the man was making up the story, but he held to it. In desperation I said, "Suppose there is no lumber here in the morning?" He laughed and said, "Are you crazy?" I told him again of our desperate need and promised that if he would sell us the lumber we would give him cash and would have it moved that night. He said, "All right then." He still thought that I was joking, but before he could change his mind, I was in the car and headed for town as fast as I could go. I rounded up some friends who owned trucks and usually looked after our hauling needs, and we headed back to Georgia for the lumber. This time I was praising God for answered prayer, for proving again that nothing was impossible with Him. That night by eleven o'clock we had every piece of that lumber headed for Cleveland.

I remember still another time when God worked out a serious problem for us. Roy McClure said that they could work only three more days, then the job would stop unless we could get sixty-three 2 x 10's twenty feet long. It was impossible to stop; the dormitories had to be ready for the students that would soon be returning to school. Again, Dr. Bob, Sr., Bob, Jr., and I met to pray for guidance to work out this acute problem. We decided that I would again visit the sawmills. Unfortunately, none had any big timbers, but each one promised to produce so many big timbers within a specified time.

With their promises and a prayer on my lips I headed for the Conasauga Lumber Company of Georgia, asking to see their manager. I explained our problems to this man; but he told me that under the OPA ruling it was impossible to let us buy the lumber and, besides that, they did not have the right sizes needed. I told him that we could substitute sizes using 3 x 8's instead. I explained that I was familiar with the OPA regulations and that there was no law that said he could not *lend* us this lumber. I had been praying and God had given me the answer. I remembered that Abraham had bargained with God when he wanted to save Lot and his family. "Will you spare Sodom if there are fifty just people?" he asked. Abraham reduced the number to forty, then to thirty, and down to ten. I put this in reverse, asking the man if he would consider lending us the lumber if I promised to get it back within *ten* days. He laughed and said, "I am game; I will do it." I then traded a little by saying, "Give me *twenty* days."

By this time, we were getting on friendly terms—a little chummy. I liked this burly-set fellow and talked to him about the Lord, telling him of God's goodness and how He had always taken care of us, working out problems for us and supplying every need. The man had a wonderful Christian response, and in a few minutes he was agreeing to wait *thirty* days. God was with us, and in exactly thirty days we had delivered every piece from the various sawmills, thus fulfilling our end of the bargain.

Some time before we decided to leave Cleveland, we ran into more housing problems. Things had tightened up considerably during the years that followed Pearl Harbor. Dr. Bob called the proper governmental department, telling them of our crowded conditions and asking if they could give us any help. They suggested that he come or send someone to Atlanta. Dr. Bob could not go; Bob, Jr., was away; so I went. Dr. Bob had taught me not to ask for anything to which we were not entitled; but if we were entitled to it, then I must never stop until we got what we went after. This advice has paid off well many times. The Lord prepared the way again, and we found the government men cordial and cooperative. They told us that they had many trailers at Oak Ridge, Tennessee, that were not in use and that we could have fifty of these trailers if we would move them. We needed no coaxing. The second semester was beginning in less than three weeks, and we had many new students coming with no place to put them. I thanked the men for their cooperation and told them that I would be in Oak Ridge the next morning.

It snowed several inches during the night and everything seemed to go wrong, but the hard trip was worth the effort. The men at Oak Ridge picked out fifty of their best trailers, tagging them "Bob Jones"; and then they helped fill out the necessary papers for the release. I left Oak Ridge rejoicing, thanking the Lord, and promising the men that we would start moving the trailers the next day. Bad weather set in, however, and for days we were sick at heart, thinking that we had bitten off more than we could chew. Later, I was ashamed of my discouragement.

We hired several men who said that they would move the trailers within ten days. You would not believe how many things happened to hinder the work. The men had every type of trouble imaginable—they broke axles, bogged down in the mud, and had to have large tractors to pull them out. To set the trailers on their foundations and install water, sewerage, lights, and heat, we had to crawl in mud. But God was with us and we were ready for the extra students when they arrived for the second semester.

I want to take this opportunity to pay tribute to the men who worked night and day moving the trailers. At the end of the job we asked how they came out on the contract. They said, "Don't ask us." They had "gone in the hole" about two or three hundred dollars because of broken axles, renting tractors, etc. We gave them an extra check for $500. Bob Jones has never tried to take advantage of anyone, and we appreciated "the extra mile" these men had gone to help us.

Church of God Offers to Buy Bob Jones College Property

The government helped us another time by leasing us seven housing units, which we hauled from Tullahoma, Tennessee. Not having campus space available for these buildings, we leased space from the Church of God. Dr. Bob and I went to check the rebuilding of these units, and we stopped by the Church of God Publishing House to pay our respects to the General Overseer and some of his officials. I believe that God arranged this meeting, for while we were there, we were approached as to the possibility of our selling our Cleveland plant to the Church of God. We had outgrown everything we had; their school was at Sevierville, Tennessee, about ninety miles from Cleveland, and they wished to consolidate.

The officials of the Church of God returned Dr. Bob's visit and asked what he had decided to do about selling our school. He replied, "I thought you were joking, gentlemen, but if you are serious, we will call a special meeting of our Board of Trustees and discuss the matter with them."

On April 4, 1946, we had the special meeting of the Board, and we were amazed at the large attendance. This was such an important decision that everyone wanted to be a part of the occasion. Our Board meetings have always ended in a thanksgiving and praise service and this meeting was no exception. All the members thanked God for His leadership step by step in every important decision along the way and for the assurance that He would not let us make a mistake at this point. The decision was, "Unless you can get the proper cooperation to expand here, then we vote unanimously to move the school elsewhere." Local Board members said that although it was hard for them to think of our leaving, they must agree that unless we could get the land to expand, we had no other choice.

I remember so well the remarks of some of the Board members. One outspoken man was Dr. Robert G. Lee of Memphis, Tennessee. Many times in our Board meetings I had seen him rise to his feet and have to sit down without speaking because he was so filled with emotion. At this particular meeting he thanked God for such a Christ-like school as Bob Jones College, and said that he had watched its growth and God's blessings on the expansion program. Because we had expanded as far as it seemed possible in Cleveland, he said, and as much as he hated to see us leave his state, he would have to recommend that we move unless we could get the necessary land upon which to expand further.

Dr. Lee had been a staunch supporter of the school. He had served on the Board, had preached at our Bible Conferences, and so on, and we were surprised and saddened when he resigned from the board after the school moved to Greenville. While he was still on our Board, he was elected to the presidency of the Southern Baptist Convention. But some Baptists told him that he was hurting their cause by being on the Board of Bob Jones University.

There were three pieces of property near the school that we needed if we were to stay in Cleveland. We offered one man two thousand dollars more than he admitted his property was worth; but no matter how many times or how hard we tried to buy, he would not sell—not until the very last, that is, and then he asked more than twice as much as his property was worth. Another piece of property was across from "Victory Hall," one of our dormitories; it was owned by a widow. We hired three appraisers to evaluate it. Two of the men laughed at the third because he went so high on his appraisal; but he said that the owner was a widow and he wanted to give her every benefit of the doubt. The figure he suggested was $28,000. The woman and her sons held out for $56,000. The third piece of land was needed for an athletic field, because the space which we had at that time for athletics was needed for more buildings if we were to remain in Cleveland. This owner refused to negotiate, arguing that we were bluffing just to get his property. Nothing we or anyone else could do or say would budge him. Finally, on the day we were to make the decision whether to stay in Cleveland or to leave, members of the Chamber of Commerce, the mayor of the town, and Dr. W. A. Lusk, local member of our Board of Trustees, called on this man and begged him to sell us eight acres of land. Backed into a corner, the man replied: "All right, if they will pay me $40,000, they can have it." This was several times its value; so the men came back and said that it was hopeless and that they saw no way for us to stay in Cleveland if we intended to expand.

Even if we could get the land we needed, it would still cost us a minimum of $1,500,000 to relieve the crowded conditions. We decided to offer our property to the Church of God for $1,750,000. They counterproposed, offering us $1,500,000. Even though at the time our book value was $2,242,000, we accepted their offer.

As the word spread around the country that Bob Jones was relocating its plant, offers began to pour in. Friends in Boston offered us twelve hundred acres of land. People in Detroit offered us an estate. Kansas City officials offered us a city park. Orlando, Florida, made the best offer in terms of money—a million dollars over a period of time and the land on which to build a beautiful campus. Asheville, North Carolina, made a strong bid and sent a delegation to Cleveland to discuss their proposition. In this delegation was the city manager, Mr. Burdette, and the head of a steel company, Mr. Dave, and others. We seriously considered their proposal and went to look over the site they had offered. Hendersonville, North Carolina, only forty miles from our present site, sent a delegation to extend an invitation to us. Atlanta, Georgia, offered us a beautiful tract of land in Marietta, Georgia. Chattanooga, Tennessee, made a strong bid, which Dr. Bob considered very seriously.

We decided to move to Knoxville, Tennessee. We had perfect working arrangements with the University of Tennessee; they understood what we were trying to do and would have cooperated with us had we moved there. They majored in the sciences and we majored in the fine arts. Dr. Bob and I made several trips to Knoxville and selected a beautiful site on the Kingston Highway, less than two miles from the University of Tennessee. To work out the final details, Dr. Bob and I met the owners of the proposed site in a lawyer's office. We had enough money in our pockets to pay for the land (one man had promised to put up $100,000 if we would stay in Tennessee). During the process of making out the papers, the lady who owned the property said, "I am not sure at this point that I want to part with my property. It is hard to give up land that has been in the family for many years." I said, "I cannot understand this; you knew this was inevitable. I have been up here many times working out the plans." Dr. Bob said, " 'Lefty,' do not coerce. If the Lord is in this, the plans can be worked out satisfactorily; if not, He must have some other plan for us."

The telephone rang. It was Mr. E. Roy Stone, Greenville, South Carolina, calling Dr. Bob. He said that he understood that Bob Jones

College was contemplating a move, and he urged us not to make a decision until Greenville could contact us officially and make a proposal. The Knoxville lawyer made the suggestion that we draw up a ninety-day option on the Knoxville property and that we leave a certain amount on deposit with the understanding that should we not exercise our option, we would forfeit the money. This we were glad to do.

Greenville was persistent. Mr. K. B. Miles, Executive Secretary of the Chamber of Commerce, called us at least twice a day, telling us they had been instructed to get our school at all costs. The Greenville Chamber of Commerce worked out plans for us to come to Greenville and spend the day looking over several sites which they had in mind. They even sent a special plane to Cleveland to bring us to Greenville. Bob, Jr., was on a preaching mission in the North and could not make the trip. He said, "Take Mother in my place. I will approve anything upon which the three of you agree."

We were cordially received by a group of city and Chamber officials, who took us to several places from which to select a site. The one on which we finally built was nothing but hills, valleys, cornfields, and gullies. Mr. Stone told me that the most amazing thing that ever happened was the way this tract of land was obtained. He said:

> I had visited the school. I knew the marvelous type of work you were doing. I knew also that this school would be a wonderful asset to Greenville. I talked with Richard Arrington, President of the Chamber of Commerce and president of Union Bleachery, and he immediately called the president of a manufacturing company in Cleveland, Tennessee, who told him what a wonderful school Bob Jones College was. Mr. Arrington also called a banker, who said, "Bob Jones College is a wonderful school. They have plenty of money in our bank, and we hate to think of their moving from Cleveland." Dick then appointed eight men to act as a Liaison Committee with the instructions to get Bob Jones College at all cost. My son asked, "Where would you locate the school if it decided to come to Greenville?" My answer was, "God will provide a place." That night as I was praying, the answer came through about two a.m. I decided to call, and I caught Dr. Bob and you in Knoxville, closing out a deal to go there.

Mr. Stone talked to Dr. Bob for thirty-five minutes, begging us not to make a decision until Greenville could contact us. Mr. Miles thanked Mr. Stone for pushing this move. Later, Mr. Miles said, "The greatest thing that happened to me was the moving of Bob Jones College to Greenville; it was a real spiritual blessing to me. I had lived in Chattanooga, Tennessee, for a number of years and had watched the growth of Bob Jones College in Cleveland, and I became very much interested in it."

Mr. Stone has often said:

> I can remember the day Dr. Bob, Mrs. Jones, and you arrived by the plane
> we sent over to Cleveland. Dr. Bob said, "Take me to the place God showed
> you." My reply was, "You are the guest of the Chamber of Commerce and
> they will show you several places, but don't worry. I will be along, for I
> am on the committee." I can remember so clearly when Dr. Bob walked
> out on this piece of land and stood by the tree out in front of the spot on
> which the library is built. He looked around, swung his arm, and said to
> you, "Lefty, this is it." Then he turned to me and said, "Mr. Stone, this is
> the land, isn't it?"

That night the Chamber of Commerce officials gave a banquet in our honor and extended an official invitation to us to accept Greenville as our new home. Mr. Arrington presided. He impressed us as a man of integrity with real convictions. He said, "Please, gentlemen, let us not make any promises to Dr. Jones that we cannot fulfill. This is a big decision for them to make. We do not wish to mislead them, but if they will consider coming here, then they can rest assured that we will stand by them and do everything we can to cooperate with them, and will protect them at all times."

This statement impressed our committee; if this were the type of men who were leading Greenville, then we felt that we might consider this move. Mayor Fred McCullough and other city officials, along with all the directors of the Chamber of Commerce, were present when this official invitation was extended. They promised to buy all the land that was within the roads surrounding our present site, approximately 180 acres which they felt could be purchased for $175,000. On May 31, 1946, in the morning and afternoon papers, a full-page advertisement appeared, paid for by the Chamber of Commerce, telling the people of the action taken and asking everyone's cooperation in carrying out their part of the agreement.

Dr. Bob told the men at the banquet that we had made plans to move to Knoxville. He explained that we had received offers from many parts of the country but that we wanted to place our school where God would have it placed. He promised to consider Greenville's proposal and make a decision by the next Thursday morning. He explained that since all the other places had promised us the land, and Orlando had promised the land and a million dollars, he felt that the least Greenville could do would be to buy the land, and they could let him know what they intended to do.

This banquet was held on Monday night, so the men of Greenville had only two working days to get the options and work out the details. By Wednesday night they had options on all the land; and as soon as they thought that they could deliver the goods, the telephone calls and telegrams began to pour in from Greenville to Bob Jones College in Cleveland.

At this point the Greenville Chamber officials authorized four men to get to Cleveland as quickly as possible and put on the pressure to get us to come to Greenville. On this committee were the following: K. B. Miles, Executive Vice-President of the Chamber of Commerce, who later became a member of our Board of Trustees and served us faithfully until his death; E. Roy Stone, Sr., a local realtor and long-time friend of our school—the man who first interested the Chamber of Commerce in inviting us and who was very helpful during the formative days in Greenville; Walter Goldsmith, another realtor who has been our good friend throughout the years; and R. C. McCall, Sr., industrialist from Easley, South Carolina, who served on our Board and supported us for several years. These men traveled all night in a heavy rain to reach Cleveland and urge us to accept Greenville's bid. They brought with them copies of the telegrams that had been sent from Mayor Fred McCullough, mayor-elect Kenneth Cass, and all members of the Board of Directors of the Chamber of Commerce, urging us to come to their city. The committeemen spoke at our chapel meeting, promising us full cooperation if we would accept their offer. Surely no group has ever been more sought after than we were by Greenville.

What a memorable occasion it was when we decided to take Greenville's offer at face value and cast our lot in their midst! It was no small thing for a school to sell out and move; and people from all area newspapers—THE UNITED PRESS, THE ASSOCIATED PRESS, and others—were there for the great decision. We changed our chapel hour to give Cleveland extra time to talk people into letting us have the land we needed. Looking back, I can see God's hand in our move. We could never have grown into the great institution that we are now in such cramped quarters as we had in Cleveland. Surely "God works in mysterious ways His wonders to perform."

On April 25, 1946, THE CLEVELAND BANNER's front page stated, "FINAL JONES COLLEGE DECISION TO BE MADE BY LEADERS TODAY." THE CHATTANOOGA NEWS-FREE PRESS, Friday, April 26, 1946, came out with large headlines, "CLEVELAND LEADER CITES JONES COLLEGE OBSTACLES." I quote this article by Jack Stewart:

Cleveland, Tennessee, April 26—"Almost insurmountable difficulties" in land acquisition was the main barrier in plans to keep Bob Jones College in Cleveland. . . .

In a statement issued after the announcement by Dr. Bob Jones, Sr., that the college will leave Cleveland, H. B. Carter, president of the Cleveland

Chamber of Commerce, said, "Of course Cleveland regrets to lose Dr. Jones and his staff of fine men and women.

"We realize, though, that the Greenville, S. C. proposition is a most attractive one, and the securing of land in Cleveland essential to the college's expansion program seemed beset with almost insurmountable difficulties."

Dr. Bob Jones, commenting on the efforts of the Cleveland Chamber of Commerce, said they did "everything in their power" and "took a great deal of interest" in the college expansion problem.

"I want to thank the Cleveland Chamber of Commerce, and all friends of the college for their efforts, their letters, their telegrams, and their prayers in behalf of the college." Dr. Jones said, "We also want to thank the Church of God for their splendid cooperation. Our decision to leave Cleveland came after a review of the Greenville offer and a thorough discussion of all possibilities of remaining in Cleveland."

Dr. Jones in a telegram to Greenville leaders explained the action of college officials in choosing the South Carolina site:

The decision of the committee was based on these points:

1. Your city is the center of a great population of typical American people, most of whom have a conservative religious background and are also progressive and responsive and have a forward look.

2. You have a satisfactory all-year-round climate.

3. You have adequate transportation facilities for our needs.

4. Your chamber of commerce and other leaders, while recognizing the commercial value of an educational institution to a community, put first emphasis on the cultural and spiritual values which Bob Jones College has to offer.

5. Since our college offers piano, pipe organ, violin, voice, speech and art without additional cost above academic tuition and therefore draws its students from the best families of all the states of the Union, as well as other lands, talented Christian young people who need an outlet for their Christian testimony and for their talents will have an unusual opportunity along this line in your territory.

6. The cooperative community leadership of your city and the interest of this leadership in all the surrounding territory appeal to us very greatly.

7. We like the speed with which your citizens transact business. We especially admire the rapid-fire, constructive methods of the executive vice-president of the Greenville Chamber of Commerce.

8. The definite commitments contained in your telegram of yesterday, which we accept at full face value.

9. We have absolute confidence that Charles Daniels not only can, but will, have the college plant ready for occupancy for the 1947-48 school year.

10. The location of the ideal, attractive site which Greenville is to purchase for our university plant.

11. We know that our type of institution will have an affinity for your community and the community will have an affinity for our type of institution.

12. In the light of the assurance and development of the last few days, we know we can count upon not only the cooperation of the leaders, but also of the rank and file of the people in your section.

This article also contained an appreciation message to Cleveland friends. Dr. Jones thanked Dr. W. A. Lusk, local Board member; H. B. Carter, president of the Cleveland Chamber of Commerce; the editor of THE CLEVELAND BANNER; all the good friends and especially the forty representative business leaders of Cleveland who worked so hard to obtain the land to keep Bob Jones College in Cleveland. Dr. Bob emphasized in his word of thanks that our only reason for leaving Cleveland was the fact that we were unable to expand there. "Though we regret to leave our friends in Cleveland," he said, "we feel that we must move on into a larger opportunity of service. I am glad that this beautiful plant which we have built for our Lord will continue to be owned by Christian people."

CHAPTER 3

Bob Jones University, Greenville, South Carolina

Before Dr. Bob accepted the invitation of the Chamber of Commerce to come to Greenville, he checked with at least three significant educational groups. First, he telephoned the State Superintendent of Education to see how they would react to our proposed move. The superintendent replied: "We know your work. I have a namesake who was graduated from your school. We know the high standards your school maintains, and we will be glad to have you in South Carolina." Next, Dr. Bob wrote to the president of the University of South Carolina, requesting that a committee be sent to Tennessee to check our work and set up our work in South Carolina in line with the undergraduate requirements of USC. "We will pay the expenses of such an investigation," he added. USC's president wrote back, expressing a willingness to work with us in the same way that the University of Tennessee had done. Finally, Dr. Bob asked, "Will Furman University welcome us?" Furman is an old and established school; we did not want them to think that we were coming here to "compete" with them. Furman's reply was favorable. The officials said that we would do them and the town good.

All "check points" having passed muster, the Executive Committee met to designate responsibility as to the building in Greenville and the continued operation in Cleveland. It was decided that Dr. Bob would spend his time raising money, holding meetings, getting new students, and checking on the building progress in Greenville; Bob, Jr., would look after the affairs of the school in Cleveland, hold some meetings, and make periodic trips to Greenville; and I would move to Greenville to supervise construction. I made the move on June 1, 1946.

On May 31, 1946, the Chamber of Commerce had a full page advertisement in both the morning and the afternoon papers, setting forth the conditions under which they were bringing Bob Jones University into their midst. There they promised to raise $175,000 to buy all the land situated within the four-road boundary—approximately 180

Father and Son

acres. The advertisements were signed by all the men who were directors of the Chamber of Commerce at that time.

We had only three months to close options, buy land, and level off the ground; so it took working and planning day and night to be ready to break ground by September 1. Dr. Bob, Sr., Bob and I had many meetings with the construction company officials and architects to outline the type of buildings we needed and the layout of these buildings. We also had numerous meetings with Chamber of Commerce officials with regard to their raising the money to pay for the land for which Bob Jones University had already advanced payments out of its own funds.

In the August 9, 1946, issue of THE PROTESTANT VOICE, the International Newspaper of Religion, there appeared an interesting article entitled "Bob Jones Builds University" and subtitled "Five Colleges

Construct Modern Units for Three Thousand Students and Take New Name." I quote from this article:

> When Bob Jones College moves into its new 3,000 student unit within a year, it will be known as Bob Jones University.
>
> Bob Jones College has been called America's Most Unusual College. The twentieth session will begin September 4, and will have an enrollment which exceeds more than twelve times the enrollment of its initial opening in 1927.
>
> The school has had unequalled growth. During the past twelve years fifteen new buildings have been erected, three of these having been completed during the war to accommodate the rapidly increasing student body which has more than doubled during war years. The growth of Bob Jones College in this respect has been unparalleled even by any of the greatest and oldest universities. This miraculous growth is just one of the reasons why this institution has been called "America's Most Unusual College."
>
> When Dr. Bob Jones, Sr., founder of the College, was asked to what he attributes the unparalleled growth of Bob Jones College, he said, "First, we believe we are emphasizing the things that need to be emphasized; I mean by this evangelical Christianity where thousands of young people can be trained in an atmosphere of culture. They like music, speech, and art. These young people have found it difficult to get these subjects in an atmosphere such as we have in some of the other schools. There is an idea abroad in this country that if you believe in the 'old-time religion,' you have a greasy nose, dirty finger nails, baggy pants, and you must not shine your shoes. Bob Jones College, by its culture, is neutralizing that idea throughout America."
>
> Bob Jones College made every effort possible to take care of the large number of fine, Christian young people who desired to enroll this fall, but its best was not enough to provide accommodations for several thousand who had to be turned away for lack of room. Since further expansion at the present site in Cleveland, Tennessee, is impossible because of the congested down-town section in which the institution is located, the Board of Trustees voted on April 4, 1946, to sell the present plant and to carry on an extensive expansion program at a new location. Construction is now underway. . . . The first Unit will accommodate 3,000 students, is expected to be ready for the opening of the 1947–48 school term. At that time, the name will be changed to Bob Jones University and "America's Most Unusual College" will become "America's Most Unusual University."
>
> Bob Jones College believes in high academic standards and a well-rounded educational program which includes every phase of life—the spiritual, the intellectual, the social, and the physical. Bob Jones College puts primary emphasis upon the spiritual; but it has well-established academic and cultural standards, and its credits are accepted by leading colleges, universities, and graduate schools in all sections of America. The institution consists of five schools: the Academy, the College of Liberal Arts, the Business College, the Graduate School of Religion, and the Graduate School of Fine Arts.
>
> Bob Jones College is not a "preacher's school," but during the 1945–46 session, more than 400 of the young men enrolled in Bob Jones College

were studying for the ministry. This number will be increased at least fifty per cent during the 1946–47 session with approximately 800 young men preparing for the Gospel ministry.

One of the first things the Chamber of Commerce did was to erect a large billboard on the front campus, facing the superhighway. The billboard stated, "Future Home of Bob Jones University, Beginning Fall of 1947." Passersby would shake their heads that it was impossible. The war situation had been such that materials for building were still restricted, and yet this school would dare to set one year for the entire first unit of eighteen buildings! It was a Herculean task, but not for a moment did we doubt that God would see us through. People who thought that it could not be done were thinking in terms of the human and not of the divine. "The things which are impossible with men are possible with God" (Luke 18:27). He made His presence known in countless ways throughout the entire construction period.

Although we broke ground in September as scheduled, it took a long time to level the hills, fill in the gullies, and make other preparations, such as laying foundations and starting the buildings. It was February and March of 1947 before any buildings began to appear out of the ground; and as late as June, 1947, people were still shaking their heads about the deadline. I could hardly blame them; things looked more than a little doubtful. None of the buildings were finished, and some had not even been started.

Building Problems

There are always problems in building, even in putting up one small building. We were in large-scale production—many large buildings at one time and in the face of great odds. It is small wonder that there were so many annoying things that had to be adjusted.

One of the first annoyances was a sort of "run-in" with the construction superintendent. It happened at the time of the building of his field office. As I watched developments, I began to ask a few questions. He heard about it and became irritated. In a defiant manner he said to me, "I understand that you are asking questions about my job." I replied, "Yes, I am very much interested." He said, "I want you to know that not even Charlie Daniels [the owner of the construction company] tells me what to do." I answered, "I am here to represent the owners of this property. Their money will pay for this work. I am very much interested in the way every penny is spent, and with your attitude, I will watch more closely than ever to see that the money is spent wisely." He gave a feeble apology and said that he must have been misinformed and given the wrong impression. There was a certain resentment on his part with regard to my supervision throughout the period of his working

Bird's Eye View of 30 Million Dollar Bob Jones University Campus at Greenville, South Carolina

with us, but he tried to work as closely as possible with me.

This man was a good builder who knew his business. At first he used rather strong language in dealing with the men; but after we spoke to him about it, he chose his words more carefully. He developed keen interest in meeting the deadline, even suggesting that his crew be allowed to work on Sunday. When I explained to him that we could not allow this, he became quite upset and reported me to Bob, Jr., on his next visit to Greenville. This gave Bob the opportunity to testify to the man. Bob told the man that he was sure that God would give us enough good weather to make up for not working on Sunday. Later, the man finally commented on the fact that the Lord seemed to favor us with a long period of good weather. So many miracles kept manifesting themselves that the man's heart began to soften, and by the time the job was completed, he must have had a real experience with the Lord, for later he wrote a nice letter about what it had meant to him to be on this job.

Architect Problems

The architects were "behind" from the very beginning. Having downtown offices, they were never available for quick decisions. I suggested that we needed better coordination. The head architect informed me that if I did not like his work I could get someone else. For ten days we had no architects. Finally, in desperation, Mr. Daniels said that if we would forgive and reinstate the architects, he would build them an office next door to the superintendent's field office so that they might be available day or night as they were needed. I agreed to this, provided an office would be built for me next door to that of the architects.

Many Miracles

The miracles on this job were as real as the changing of the water to wine in Cana of Galilee. God opened doors for us that needed to be opened, and He closed doors that should not have been opened. To Him be the praise for everything.

1. Some of the land which we had selected as our campus site had been subdivided and already sold. 2. That we were able to repossess this land was miraculous. 3. One owner was a soldier in Europe. But distance is no barrier to God; within a matter of a few days all the land was repossessed into one large tract.

In addition to the land problem, there was the problem of getting a building permit. The War Production Board in Washington had issued strict orders that no new buildings could be built that would draw on the nation's building reserves. Dr. Bob and Mr. K. B. Miles, executive vice-president of the Chamber of Commerce, made a trip to Washington to contact men who had the power to help us. Senator Burnette Maybank,

Sr., was most cooperative. To show how the Lord worked, I wish to explain that just one day after the War Production Board had turned down a state university's request for a $2,000,000 building program, Bob Jones University was granted a permit. God had gone before to open a door that seemed impossible to be opened, thus again proving that "man's extremity is God's opportunity."

Although this incident may seem minor, it was major. It is another incident in which God came to our rescue. We had promised the Church of God that if we did not move from Cleveland within one year, we would pay rent on the basis of $1,000 per week. We had to keep in mind, therefore, that any delay could cost us thousands of dollars in rent. One day the steel company notified us that they had found problems in the design of the auditorium balcony. The first design, they feared, might not be strong enough to hold the weight. To redesign this balcony would cost us dearly in money and in time. It had to be done, however, for we could not have a balcony about which there was doubt as to its safety. That we should have to pay twice for the designing of the same building did not seem fair to us. God took care of this also: in the end, the cost was absorbed by someone else.

"Loan" Problems

A certain insurance company had promised to lend us $1,250,000. Just about the time the loan was ready to "come through," the president of the company with whom we were negotiating was killed in an accident. The other officials became concerned about making such a large loan to a school. In a sense, their concern was understandable. This was a critical time in their organization; some schools had failed to live up to their commitments and had forfeited bonds; and these men did not know Dr. Jones as well as their president had known him. Although at the outset the caution of these men seemed to be working against us, actually it was working in our favor. We had spent the several hundred thousand dollars which we had in the bank and the money the Church of God had paid us, and we were to the point of needing "big" money in a hurry. Dr. Bob made a trip to the insurance company and carefully explained to them our predicament. Instead of lending us the $1,250,000 which they were about to cancel, they agreed to increase the loan to $1,900,000. God knew that we would need the extra money, and He worked out the problem in advance. I have often wondered what would have happened had everything gone smoothly and the original loan been approved. It would have ruined us, because we would have been put in the position of having to put a second mortgage on a school that was not built.

With the Lord's help, I am glad to say, we were able to pay off this

The Dining Common at Bob Jones University

loan ten years ahead of schedule. This resulted in the fact that a banker from Wall Street came to my office one day and offered to lend us some money. He said that he had just left the Jefferson Standard Life Insurance Company in Greensboro, North Carolina, where he had been told that of all the loans they had made in the history of their company, the most satisfactory one was to Bob Jones University in Greenville, South Carolina. "If you ever need to borrow any more money," the banker said, "don't stop in Greensboro; come on to New York and let us help you."

Miracle of Doors

No company could promise delivery of doors for our new buildings before the spring of 1948. Having already announced to the world that we were opening school in our new plant in the fall of '47, we had to do something in a hurry. Again, God came to our rescue. He led Bob, Jr., to accept an invitation to preach on the West Coast. In a conversation with some Christian businessmen, Bob happened to mention our dilemma. Would you believe it? These men acquired a sawmill and some lumber, and they had those doors made and delivered to us months ahead of schedule—not in the spring of '48, as others had promised, but in the spring of '47, thus testifying to the contractors and others that God can do the seemingly impossible.

Transformers

I recall another time when the construction officials seemed quite perturbed. They gave as their reason, "We cannot get the transformers we need." We were building a $100,000 electrical system with underground wiring, and the transformers for this type of project were not to be found. (According to reports, they were being sent to Russia on "lend-lease.") When we contacted the manager of Duke Power Company, he said, "I am sorry but we cannot help you. We have had transformers of this type on order since 1945." I took a plane to Westinghouse, praying as I went. The vice-president of Westinghouse was sympathetic but apparently powerless to help us. I told him that I was sure that God would not let us down; He had supplied every need thus far, and He would help Westinghouse to help us by getting the transformers we needed.

When I returned to Greenville, I called Dr. Bob in Cleveland and asked him to write a nice letter to Westinghouse. His letter brought results; two weeks later I was on another plane and headed back to Westinghouse. The officials reported that the small transformers were ready, but they were having trouble getting the large ones. God moved again. A big company out West cancelled an order for the very size we needed. A man at Westinghouse remarked, "Whoever gets these transformers will be getting a miracle." Soon those very transformers were headed to Bob Jones University!

Cooperation of the Steel Company and State Highway Department

The steel company officials did the impossible on several occasions, and I learned to love and respect those men. Many times they rushed deliveries, sometimes getting our orders to us as much as thirty to sixty days ahead of schedule.

Two weeks before our office staff was to move to the new campus, the construction men were bemoaning the fact that they were unable to get permission to complete the sewer line which was to go through the superhighway about a mile from the campus. With prayerful hearts, Mr. K. B. Miles and I left early the next morning for Columbia, South Carolina. God had gone before and prepared the hearts of the officials of the State Highway Department so that within thirty minutes after our arrival we had their signed affidavits permitting the lines to go through.

Few Accidents

It is a miracle that with six hundred men working we had only one serious accident. The trusses in the gymnasium ceiling fell, throwing three men to the floor. Only one man was hurt. It was a miracle that with eighty van loads of furniture being moved from Cleveland, there was only one accident, a minor one. We could not afford to wait until the buildings were completed to have the furniture delivered; we had to rent seven warehouses around town and store the furniture so that it would be ready to be moved to the campus as each building was completed.

Winecoff Hotel

Dr. Bob found it necessary to go to Atlanta to try to solve further difficulties. He stopped at the Winecoff Hotel. Later he called me to take a plane to Atlanta to bring him some information that was needed. It was the day of the embargo, and there were complications regarding the flight I was to take. For three hours I sat on a plane at the Greenville Airport.

When I finally arrived in Atlanta, Dr. Bob and I attended to the business; and suddenly he said to me, "I am going to leave Atlanta and go to Mobile, Alabama, today instead of tomorrow, as planned. You take my room at the Winecoff and remain in Atlanta overnight to check on some other business." He called the Mobile hotel at which he had reservations for the next day, but they could not take him a day early. There was a convention in Mobile, the clerk said, and all the hotels were full. Never

A reproduction of a portrait of Dr. Bob Jones, Sr., presented to the University, by the Class of 1955.

(by Alfred Jonniaux)

one to give up, Dr. Bob called The Battle House, another hotel at which he had stopped many times through the years. The manager gave the same answer: no vacancy. For a moment Dr. Bob "toyed" with the idea of staying in Atlanta: after all, he had a comfortable room at the Winecoff. But he kept feeling a strange burden to leave. Finally, the manager of The Battle House said, "Dr. Bob, come on down. I will find you a room or I will give you my room."

Having settled his own plans, Dr. Bob started working on mine. He suggested that I go to Cleveland, Tennessee, for the weekend. I did not want to go to Cleveland, and I argued with Dr. Bob. I knew that I could call Cleveland and get the information which I needed. Dr. Bob, however, insisted that I must go to Cleveland. "Is there any reason you cannot go to Cleveland?" he asked. I said, "No, Dr. Bob, but I have not come prepared to take that trip. I can stay here tonight, can attend to the business in Atlanta tomorrow, and can get back to Greenville, where I am needed desperately, by tomorrow night." Finally, Dr. Bob agreed that if we could get an appointment with a certain businessman in Atlanta the next morning, I would not go to Cleveland. We investigated the matter and found that the man whom I needed to see had just left for Nashville, Tennessee, and would not be back for several days. That was my cue. I must go to Cleveland.

I was more than a little disappointed at this turn of events. I went back to the hotel and halfheartedly reported to Dr. Bob that I was ready to take the trip which he had suggested. He tried by telephone to make reservations for me, but because of the embargo there were no plane or train reservations available. That meant that I must travel by bus. You can imagine the crowded conditions of buses at that time.

At 5:30 p.m., I checked Dr. Bob out of the hotel and put him in a limousine to go to the airport. Then I walked slowly up the street to the bus station, arriving there just about the time a crowded bus was ready to leave for Knoxville. I was so tired! I had been up since 3:30 that morning and the day had been a busy one. Boarding the bus, I found "standing room only." In a weak moment of discouragement, I sort of "questioned" God a little bit. I said, "Lord, I cannot understand it. I am trying to serve Thee; and yet as tired as I am, I am having to stand on this bus. We have missed connections; everything seems to be going wrong."

At that moment Romans 8:28 flashed into my mind: "And we know that all things work together for good to them that love God, to them who are the called according to His purpose." I loved God and was trying to serve Him; so this would have to be for my good. Perhaps the plane on which I would have returned to Greenville would never have made it, I thought. Whatever the reason for my present plight, I would rest in the promise that it was working for my good. Little did I realize what actually was happening.

The bus missed connections, and I found myself stranded in the little town of Ocoee, ten miles out of Cleveland, in the bitter cold. I made my way to a telephone and called Dr. James D. Edwards, Dean of Administration of Bob Jones College, who drove out to get me. Because of the lateness of the hour, there was little time left for sleep.

At breakfast the next morning, Dr. Bob's secretary came to the table and anxiously inquired about Dr. Bob. I told her that he was in Mobile. She asked me if I were sure he was in Mobile. I said, "Yes," and went on talking. Finally she grabbed my arm, shook me, and asked, "Are you positive he left Atlanta?" I said, "Marjorie, are you crazy? Of course, I'm positive. I put him in the limousine to go to the airport, and I know he left." "You must not know what happened," she said. Then she told me that the Winecoff Hotel, where Dr. Bob had been staying and where I had almost stayed, had burned during the night, leaving 120 people dead. The fire had broken out on the fifth floor; but most of the damage had been done to the sixth floor, the location of Dr. Bob's room. How ashamed I was of my "gripey" attitude! And how humble I felt to know that I had been divinely protected in the face of such danger! I do not mean to imply that God favored Dr. Bob and me above the 120 who died in the fire; I simply mean that the Lord was not through with us—there was something else He wanted us to do. That is a sobering thought.

Dr. Jones' Physical Strength

That a man of Dr. Bob's years and activities could hold up under the terrific strain of those construction days is a miracle. There were many pressures, not the least of which pertained to the financial pressures. The Church of God had been given a certain time for the payment of their money. Once when we had spent practically all our money and were in desperate need of funds, our founder, our president, and I got together to try to figure a way out. The Church of God's payment had not come in the morning mail, as we had hoped it would. During our conference we heard a timid knock at the door. A secretary opened the door and, apologizing for the interruption, said, "I have a letter which I think will interest you." It was a large check from the Church of God!

There has never been a time when funds were completely exhausted and we had no way to turn. Whenever funds seemed dangerously low, something unusual would happen. One time Dr. Bob was almost discouraged and was talking to Bob and me, warning us to be careful. Someone handed him a check for $1,000; and he said, "Boys, this is just another little pat on the back, showing us that the Lord is with us and that He wants us to trust Him and not be discouraged."

Ministerial Students in a Recent Year at Bob Jones University

Dr. Bob laughingly referred to himself as "The Budget Boy." People used to remark, "I wish we had someone in our organization who could raise money like Dr. Bob Jones. No wonder Bob Jones University can grow as it does—Bob Jones is out raising the money." One man said to Dr. Bob, "I don't understand; you have no one in the field raising funds, and yet you have money for whatever purpose it is needed. Who raises the money? How is it done?" Dr. Bob answered, "I mean this reverently: God raises it for us. He lays it upon the hearts of Christians all around the world to send it in."

I believe that Dr. Bob's fund-raising ability was a gift from God as much as any of his other gifts were of divine bestowment. Many of the larger schools are heavily endowed and are able to run successfully because of the backlog of reserves. Dr. Bob realized that because of the emphasis of Bob Jones University we could not and should not depend on big foundations for help, nor could we bank on the help of denominations to help build an independent Christian school. More important, however, he knew that he needed no one except God Almighty. He trusted God to direct His people to rally behind this cause. Dr. Bob was cautious in the way we spent the money that was sent in; he realized that it was from the hand of God. He would say, "Lefty, we must watch the pennies and not let any waste develop in our operating expenses or our building programs. It would be a sin to get careless or take anything for granted and let something happen to God's money." Under his wise tutelage, we learned to "stretch" money, so to speak, and make it go twice as far as would be normally expected. Much of the success of the school stems from this basic principle.

Bob Jones University has had an enviable record of "discounting" all its bills. Dun and Bradstreet wrote us years ago, stating that they had watched the growth of Bob Jones College, had studied its financial setup, and wanted to say that it was on one of the soundest business bases of any school they knew—and they had checked them all. Dr. Bob endured a great deal trying to build his school and keep it going. It has been said that it will kill three men to build a school, and yet Dr. Bob built three schools.

Greenville Failed to Fulfill Its Commitments

Internal problems within the Chamber of Commerce caused unnecessary problems for Bob Jones University. It seemed that one group in the organization was against anything the other group suggested or did. As a result, the officials failed to meet its full obligation to Dr. Bob. Instead of raising the $175,000 that had been promised and had been mentioned in the advertisement of May 31, 1946, they raised only $97,000. This left a balance of $78,000 which they promised to raise later if we would agree to their arrangement. I urged the men to raise the balance at that time; I knew that they could never buy the land that cheap again. Dr. Bob talked to the men and wrote to them. The balance has not been raised to this date! Bob Jones University has had to spend over $500,000 of its own money to purchase the land that could have been bought for $78,000 at the time the arrangements were made.

Thousands of friends around the world were praying for Dr. Bob and his school during the hectic days of construction here in Greenville. On Easter Sunday, 1947, Mr. E. Roy Stone, Dr. Pettingill, and a number of outstanding Christians met at the front corner of the auditorium, which was under construction, for an Easter Sunrise Service. Mr. Stone was impressed that so many older people wanted to be on this hallowed ground for this service. They had a wonderful time in the Lord and thanked Him that He was bringing such a wonderful school into their midst.

I should like to close this part of the South Carolina story with an article by Dr. Bob Shuler, a long-time friend of Dr. Bob and a man who worked closely with the school as a member of the Board of Trustees. The article appeared in THE METHODIST CHALLENGE, September, 1947.

A SENSATIONAL UNIVERSITY

More than a quarter of a century ago I met a man who is one of the most unusual men I have ever known. He was at the time possibly America's greatest evangelist. His converts at altars of penitence and faith numbered into the hundreds of thousands. As a preacher he excelled. Few have ever come the way of the American pulpit who could equal him.

Then suddenly, he veered off into the educational field. He continued to preach but his chief emphasis was in the education of young men and women. Just as the idea of Christian education began to fade out and grow limpid in many denominational schools, he founded an institution that lifted that standard anew. Bob Jones College at Cleveland, Tennessee, became the very embodiment of Christian education. The college almost immediately grew into one of the most sensational educational institutions within the nation.

I use the word "sensational" purposely. Bob Jones College became sensational because of its strict discipline, its Christian emphasis, its loyalty to the fundamentals, its superior scholastic requirements, the unanimous enthusiasm of its student body in relation to the school, and its swift and constant growth in numbers of students and influence across the nation. Bob Jones, the gospel preacher and evangelist of more than a quarter of a century ago, became the center of this great college. His personality was from the first its chief asset.

I watched this school grow from a few hundred students to where hundreds were turned away each year. Last year I spent a week on the campus. From 1940 to 1946, the student body had trebled. The students came from the best homes in America. They were the choice of the land. A public address system connected two chapels, both taxed to capacity at every convocation. The dining hall was filled three times at every meal. Applications poured in from everywhere from young men and women who wanted the advantage of this truly great Christian college. Bob Jones rented every available room within blocks. He built furiously. But finally, he was faced with the fact that the physical requirements for this swiftly advancing college could not be met by the limited acreage upon which the buildings stood. Bob Jones College had outgrown its location.

I was present when the Board of Trustees voted to move. They decided that the hour had come to build a great university. Faced by the fact of phenomenal success in its present location, the Board moved slowly. I doubt if a member present wanted a change. But that Board faced a great necessity. The vote was unanimous.

And now there will open the first of October in Greenville, South Carolina, Bob Jones University, with eighteen new buildings of the first unit complete. With the next five years, there will be added at least eight more buildings. The new campus contains 180 acres. There are no limits to the possibility for expansion. The new setup provides for 2,000 dormitory students and at least 1,000 students from Greenville and nearby towns. The unit now being completed will cost $3,000,000.

But the sensationalism attending Bob Jones University will not be the product of beautiful buildings, lovely landscape and tremendous proportions. It will, in my opinion, almost immediately become America's most unusual university, not because of the thousands of students who will troop in that direction or the excellent academic results that will accrue. This university inherits something invaluable. Bob Jones College handed over to it a spirit that I have never known duplicated, a passion that is superb and a loyalty that many educational institutions would give millions to possess.

I have watched her graduates sign a statement which declared that they would help to destroy their Alma Mater if she ever departed from the faith or lowered the standard. There have been no scandals at Bob Jones College. Her student body has marched as an army. They have stood unitedly for all that is clean and wholesome and true. All this the college passes on to the university. No modernist is on the faculty of Bob Jones University. Again, the college passes on the glorious requirement that every teacher and instructor be a Christian, sound in faith and true in life.

Every class in the new university will be opened with prayer. Every day, the students will meet as a body for worship. And yet there will be no "holier than thou" attitude in this great Christian school. I can say these things because I have known the college. The university is but an expansion, an enlargement. The spirit, the aim, the purpose, the goal of Bob Jones College is to be the spirit, aim, purpose and goal of Bob Jones University.

As Bob Jones University opens next October in Greenville, S. C., 3,000 splendid young Americans will stand and repeat that same creed. The merging of Bob Jones College into Bob Jones University will not disturb the foundations upon which, years ago, Bob Jones, God's man, the preacher of Christ's abundant gospel and eternity's champion of a lifted cross, built in Cleveland, Tennessee, one of the greatest Christian colleges this nation ever saw.

Old things will become new in October. So the Board of Trustees of Bob Jones University unanimously elected Bob Jones, Jr., as its first president. The old lion steps aside for a younger monarch and wisely so. Bob Jones, Jr., is all that his father has been, plus a training and fitting for the peculiar task that God has sent his way. But "Old Bob" will be thrumming the strings and the harmony will not belong wholly to the younger man. God meant it thus.

CHAPTER 4

Dr. Bob's Son and Grandson, Successors

BOB, JR.

The story of Dr. Bob's life would not be complete without at least a brief resumé of the life of his son, for the work of each, although quite distinct, is definitely tied in with the work of the other. These men have worked toward a common goal—that of proclaiming the full counsel of the Word of God and of setting up an institution that would stand without apology for the old-time religion, would train Christian leaders, and would keep "first things first." According to statistics, not all sons of all preachers turn out well. Dr. Bob and Mrs. Jones are to be commended for the contributions their son has made and is making toward making our world a better place in which to live. Dr. John R. Rice wrote many years ago in his paper, THE SWORD OF THE LORD:

> One of the greatest evidences of God's blessing upon the life of Dr. Bob Jones, Sr., is his son, the splendid scholar, the mighty preacher, the strong fundamentalist leader, Dr. Bob Jones, Jr. His character, his tremendous brain, his holy convictions, and the great demand for his services are a joy to everyone who is concerned about the future of America. What blessing could God give a man better than such a son as Dr. Bob Jones, Jr.

It is not my intention to give a detailed account of Bob, Jr's., life. Others, no doubt, will do that later. I merely mention a few isolated incidents—some to amuse and show how human are all people, and others to show how God uses parents to mold a life to His glory and how He gives the wisdom to solve the many problems encountered along the way.

Bob was born in Montgomery, Alabama, on October 19, 1911. Certainly no man was ever more blessed of God or better trained spiritually and culturally to take over the leadership of a school and to be a dominant voice in a corrupt and apostate day than Bob, Jr., has been. The Joneses accepted their son as "an heritage of the Lord" (Psalm

127:3), and they dedicated themselves to bring him up "in the nurture and admonition of the Lord" (Ephesians 6:4).

* * *

As thankful as the parents were, they were not beyond feeling some of the burdens of parenthood. They "sort of hit rock bottom" one night when their "bundle of joy" turned into a "bundle of sadness" and cried hard and long. Finally, in desperation, the father got dressed and went in search of a store where he might buy a pacifier for the baby. Anything for peace, he thought.

At the store, an older man looked at the sleepy-eyed father and asked, "How many children do you have?"

"This is my first," Dr. Bob replied.

"Well, don't worry about it," the older man said. "You will get used to it. I haven't slept a full night in thirty years." What encouragement!

* * *

Bob was a clever lad; he knew how to work things *his way* with his father. On an occasion of a father-son visit before the father was to leave on an extended trip, the son affected a sad look and told his father of his hard life with his mother and grandmother. During prayer the lad "piously" prayed, "Lord, help Mother and Grandmother to be good to me while Dad is away. You know how nervous some women are." Mrs. Jones happened to overhear the conversation and prayer; and after the train had pulled out of the station, she turned to her son and said, "Let me tell you young man — you are going to 'toe the mark.' You can't work *me* as you do your father." Bob's "piety" turned to meekness as he turned to follow this woman who wielded such heavy power over him.

As soon as he was old enough, Bob and his mother often accompanied Dr. Bob on his evangelistic tours. In Indiana, when Bob was about three and a half years old, the Joneses hired a girl to look after him during the evening services. The girl began to sneak the lad off to the movies; and, childlike, Bob told on her. The girl denied it, saying, "We only looked at the pictures outside the theater." But when Bob kept describing what he had seen "on a big screen inside a big house," the parents knew that their son had actually been to the movies. This was most embarrassing to Dr. Bob, for he had been preaching against movies. The little "sitter" had to be relieved of her duties, of course.

* * *

Bob was endowed with a healthy curiosity. This fact has had a large part in bringing him to the position he has today. It takes imagination and curiosity to climb the ladder he has climbed, and it takes imagination and fortitude to stay at the top.

An embarrassing incident that almost occurred during prayer in a certain meeting will point up his curiosity at the age of three. A sweet little woman attended the meetings—a little woman who had a physical infirmity that caused her to walk on her knees. Bob just could not understand anybody's being so small of stature. Finally, his curiosity got the best of him; and he decided that while people had their eyes closed for prayer, he would investigate the situation. But just as he was reaching out his chubby little hands to lift the woman's skirt to see if she had any feet, his alert mother, yielding to an impulse, opened her eyes. Horrified, she quickly reached for his hand and held it for the remainder of the prayer.

As smart as he was, it is a marvel that Bob did not catch on to the fact that he could not outwit his intuitive mother. Perhaps he did, but found it good sport to keep trying.

* * *

At the age of four, Bob surprised his mother by asking, "Mommy, what would we do if Daddy got a 'revorce' from us?"

Another time he shocked her by asking permission to eat breakfast in the kitchen with the cook.

"Why?" she asked.

" 'Cause I'm tired of this Bible reading stuff," he calmly replied.

* * *

In childlike faith at the age of five, Bob accepted the Lord as his personal Saviour. Although everyone expected great things of this precocious child, no one could foresee that by the time he would reach middle age he would have preached around the world many times.

* * *

Preachers' children are not beyond the need for correction. Bob tells of a time when at five he was with his father in a meeting at Winona Lake, Indiana. He was seated at the front of the church and began to misbehave. Dr. Bob quietly left the pulpit, led his son out under a big tree, "dealt" with him, and led him back into the service to the same pew. Bob repeated the misbehavior. The father repeated the punishment. After the second trip out, Bob decided that his father's sermon "You Can't Win" applied to more things than he had thought; and he sat in church, meekly subdued.

Years later Bob used the same method to "put the fear of the Lord" in his own young son who was with him in services at Winona Lake. Dr. Bob had often quoted the song "Pass It On," and I suppose Bob thought that this was as good a lesson as any to pass along.

* * *

Occasionally Bob got into fights. One day a larger boy was getting the best of him, and Bob began to back away. Dr. Bob scolded his son for running from a fight. Bob protested, "But Dad, I wasn't running. I was just retreating."

* * *

Because Dr. Bob had to be away for six weeks or more in some of his campaigns, much of the burden of training Bob was on the mother and grandmother. Mrs. Jones says that Bob was always hard to "get up" in the morning. One morning she made several attempts to get him moving. Finally she sternly called, "Come at once, Bob. Breakfast is getting cold."

Bob slowly made his appearance, and his mother started lecturing him about being on time.

"You will never amount to anything," she scolded, "if you do not learn to get up and get moving." Then she commanded, "Now say your verse of Scripture."

Very "piously" Bob quoted, "A soft answer turneth away wrath: but grievous words stir up anger" (Proverbs 15:1).

His mother replied, "Good understanding giveth favour: but the way of transgressors is hard" (Proverbs 13:15).

Later, the wise mother carefully explained to her son that they must never again quote Scripture to "get at each other."

* * *

Mrs. Jones was strong of discipline. She believed the proverb, "Spare the rod and spoil the child"; and she applied it often, Bob says, and then adds, "for I needed it."

When he was about seven, Bob disobeyed his mother. Instead of accepting the punishment he deserved, Bob argued with his mother and threatened to "run away" if she insisted on punishing him.

Shortly after he left, a severe storm arose; and both mother and grandmother were almost sick with worry about their boy. The grandmother insisted that the mother get into the car and go look for the lad. After a reasonable amount of time had elapsed and the lad had not returned, Mrs. Jones was about to take her mother's advice. A knock was heard at the door, and Mrs. Jones flung open the door. There stood Bob, his nice clothes dirty, his tie twisted around to the back, and—to quote Mrs. Jones—"He looked a mess!"

Quickly regaining her composure, Mrs. Jones asked, "Where have you been?"

"Down on Woodley Road," Bob meekly answered.

"Are you ready to take your punishment?" she asked.

"Yes, Ma'am," he sobbed, "if you will not tell Daddy."

Mrs. Jones was so happy to see her son that she gave him only three light licks, which she felt were necessary because a principle was involved. The grandmother thought that the principle was somewhat obscure; but Mrs. Jones reasoned that if she let her son pull this stunt and get by with it, he would never again respect her authority.

* * *

Bob's grandmother taught him to love art, music, good literature, the Bible, and great hymns. It is not surprising that he often quotes his text from memory: he cut his teeth, so to speak, on the Bible. By the time he was eleven, Bob knew practically every hymn in the old Methodist hymnal. I have been told that his punishment sometimes involved sitting in the corner and learning hymns. However that may be, his grandmother's emphasis on committing these hymns to memory has enabled Bob to follow spiritual trends. He has noted that as spiritual decline has come there has been a definite veering from hymns based on the blood to a new emphasis on cheap, jazzy tunes.

* * *

There was never a time when Bob did not enjoy acting. His mother says that once when he was still very young, he and some young neighbors decided to put on a show. It was in the fall of the year, and the weather was crisp and cold. The young actors, scantily clad, were turning blue from the cold. "Director Bob" yelled, "Keep moving. Jump up and down, and you won't be cold." Mrs. Jones heard the strange orders and looked out to see what was going on. She was horrified and was sure that one child would have pneumonia before morning. Early the next day, under the ruse of asking for a certain recipe, Mrs. Jones called the mother of the little boy she was worried about and inquired about the family. The mother answered, "For some reason, my boy has the sniffles; otherwise we are all right." Mrs. Jones heaved a sigh of relief!

* * *

By the time he was thirteen, Bob was sent to "prep" school to be under the tutelage of Dr. Starke in his military academy in Montgomery. This military training seemed ordered of God, who in His infinite wisdom and perfect foreknowledge, knew that Dr. Bob would be starting a Christian college within a few years, and that in connection with the college there would be a military academy and the need for strict discipline. Bob has never got away from the basic lessons in discipline which he learned from "The Professor" who sought to build the character and stiffen the backbone of his boys.

* * *

In his senior year of high school, Bob transferred to Bob Jones Academy, which his father had founded in conjunction with Bob Jones College in Panama City, Florida. Bob obeyed all rules and regulations in his father's school, for he knew that he could be and would be "shipped" if the offense demanded it.

* * *

Bob was graduated from Bob Jones College before he was twenty, and immediately he became an instructor in history and also the coach of the dramatics club at the college. During the summers he attended the University of Pittsburgh, from which, in 1933, he obtained his master of arts degree. He took advanced work at the Universities of Alabama and Chicago and at Northwestern University. The subject of his thesis in history was "The Vocational Evangelist in America from 1854 to 1915." As he did the research for this work, he was forcefully impressed with the fact that the criticism brought against evangelists by the "new social-gospel crowd," which was just springing up at that time, and by the ungodly was echoed in the resolutions passed by various church councils, synods, conventions, and assemblies in an effort to "control." Having been brought up in sawdust aisles and having studied this field all his life, Bob knew evangelism inside and out; he did not appreciate these criticisms of men of God who earnestly sought to get people to obey the Word.

* * *

As the son of such a famous father, Bob would seem to have had it made for him on the ladder of fame. However, he has always been a man of deep thought, excellent planning, and independence; and he did not wish to rest on the laurels of his famous father. The discerning father observed in his young son certain tendencies that must be brought under control, but he realized that certain qualities of real leadership also were involved. From the beginning, he allowed his son to develop under the hand of the one who had forged his talents and placed them as a chain about his neck. Though no doubt many times the boy was strongly tempted to go afield in some endeavor, the chain of God's will held him in tow.

* * *

Bob displayed strong initiative. Once while Dr. Bob was away from the school, Bob went to work renovating the chapel. This was only the beginning. Since that time, he has made old things look beautiful by tearing out this, by adding that, or by drawing interesting plans for new buildings and new departments.

* * *

On a trip abroad Bob made such a favorable impression on a couple — Mr. and Mrs. Frank Bowen — that years later, when they were looking for a home for their Collection of Biblical Antiquities, they decided to investigate the school of which they had heard the nice young man speak. The result was that Bob Jones College became the recipient of their collection.

* * *

In 1933, at the age of twenty-one, Bob, Jr., was made acting president of Bob Jones College in Cleveland, Tennessee. This shifting of responsibility enabled Dr. Bob to spend more time in meetings.

Mrs. Jones says that before Bob took on the "mantle" of the school, she and her husband took him aside and told him that they did not want him to take on the work to please them. If his heart were not sold on it and if the Lord had not called him to the task, he should not consider it: it would not be good for him, and certainly it would not be to the good of the Cause. They urged Bob to take a short trip and think over and pray about the situation. But Bob declined, saying, "My mind is made up. I am ready and willing to take my place here." You can imagine the joy and thankfulness the Joneses felt toward the Lord for their son's attitude.

* * *

Bob, Jr., had a popular lyceum attraction — "Curtain Calls" — in which he portrayed many characters from Shakespeare. He gave performances at colleges and universities, and at various civic clubs. In Montgomery, Alabama, his program was received with more acclaim than any similar program ever given there.

Bob could have named his price in Hollywood or in any country in Europe. He had attractive Broadway offers. But God had other plans for His servant. More and more the Lord was "pushing" Bob into the ministry, using him over the radio and in many other ways. In October, 1940, in a large city in the Midwest, Bob spoke in one of the churches on Sunday, did some radio work, and then gave his Shakespearean program on Monday and Tuesday. At a breakfast in his honor, he was offered a five-year contract of $100 per day for acting. Later, another group offered $350 a performance, with the promise that he could have as many performances as he cared to have. Bob declined all these offers, saying, "My heart is in the Christian college God called my father to start. I want to help build a great Christian university that will never pussyfoot or compromise. I appreciate your offer, but I will have to refuse."

By 1940, Bob was drawing his lyceum engagements to a close. Dr. Bob wrote to Governor Bibb Graves of Alabama:

I am enclosing a leaflet that will show you the itinerary Bob, Jr., had last summer. He has completed his last lecture-recital tour. He is never going to take any more lyceum engagements. He is now preaching. He goes to the Moody Church in Chicago to supply on April 27th, and will speak in a theatre downtown and over the radio under the auspices of the "Business Men's Evangelistic Club" for a week. Next summer he is going to make a Western tour. You know you told me one time that Bob could make a million dollars in Hollywood and I told you I did not want the million, but I

Dr. Bob Jones, Jr., as General Ewell in "Red Runs the River"

would rather he preach the Gospel than to be the greatest actor in the world. You and Mrs. Graves pray for him.

* * *

One of the outstanding decisions Bob made during these years was to withdraw from the Methodist Church. He saw certain trends in the denomination that were not good. He said, "I am not going to be a party to having my Lord betrayed and slandered by godless preachers or seminary school teachers." When the church to which he belonged in Cleveland, Tennessee, brought in a modernist to speak from their pulpit, Bob told the pastor that he could no longer be a member of that church.

* * *

At the age of twenty-one Bob had an illness which was diagnosed by a leading diagnostician of the South as a "bad case of leukemia. Life expectancy short." The Joneses moved Bob by ambulance to Atlanta, Georgia, to be checked by an outstanding Christian physician. After several tests, the physician was delighted to inform the worried parents that their son did not have leukemia. If the first diagnostician was correct—and we have no reason to suppose that he was not—the great Physician had performed a physical miracle in the son's life, as He had done for the father when he was about the same age.

Before this incident God, on another occasion, had protected this young man and his parents. On their way back to their new home at College Point, Florida, their car went out of control and overturned twice. The parents noticed that Bob's shoe was full of blood, and they became quite alarmed. After a careful examination the doctor reported that the Achilles cord had been cut. This meant that Bob would have a "stiff" foot and ankle for the rest of his life. But God intervened, and everything turned out well.

* * *

Who could properly measure the honors or name the accomplishments of this servant of the Lord? Certainly not I. They are many, and they are varied. I can but sketchily list a few.

In 1935, Asbury College honored him with the honorary degree of Doctor of Literature. Since that time Bob has had many honors from many colleges. He has written numerous songs, poems, books, and at least one outstanding play. WINE OF MORNING, one of his books that was made into a film by our film department, has been the means of winning countless souls to the Lord. He has also made educational and religious films based on Shakespeare's works, has served on numerous Christian boards, has preached around the world, has been on local and national radio and television, and has supported Christian work at home and abroad.

* * *

In 1947, when Bob Jones College was moved from Cleveland, Tennessee, to Greenville, South Carolina, and set up as a University, Dr. Bob insisted that he step down as president of the school and that Bob take over this office. Dr. Bob assumed the strain of the financial responsibilities, calling himself "The Budget Boy," and left it to Bob to tackle the educational and administrative details. Under their leadership the school became world renowned as the "World's Most Unusual University."

Let me digress to say that we at Bob Jones University did not apply the term "World's Most Unusual University" to ourselves. As Bob, Jr., wrote to someone, "The name is the spontaneous reaction of educational leaders, of preachers and laymen, of Christians and non-Christians alike, a tribute to the combination of evangelism, culture, high academic standards and Christian discipline. These things are not found in exactly this same combination anywhere else, and Bob Jones University has proved that blended together in the crucible of a student's character they produce a dynamic life for Christian service."

* * *

In March, 1950, Bob was put to bed for several weeks. This curtailed his activities, but it did not stop his ministry. During this illness he found time to write his Christian novel, WINE OF MORNING. A friend wrote Bob that he was praying that God would raise him up right away. Bob answered, "Don't pray that God will raise me up speedily; pray that I will learn the lesson He has in store for me while I am in bed. I am praying that God will give me the patience to stick it out."

Governor Strom Thurmond of South Carolina was one of Bob's first visitors during this illness, and Bob sent Thurmond one of the first copies of WINE OF MORNING. The governor replied, "This volume will be a valuable addition to my library."

Dr. John R. Rice wrote: "My heart has a genuine bit of praise to God for the improvement in your health, Bob. May God prosper you, both physically and mentally." That prayer, along with the prayers of other friends all around the world, found favor with God; and Bob found joy and peace in the Lord as he wrote the beautiful book that went into a second edition soon after its release.

* * *

Bob, Jr., is as strongly against modernism, liberalism, and compromise as his dad was, and he faithfully and forcefully decries these evils.

One organization from which Bob has had to withdraw support is YOUTH FOR CHRIST, an organization to which formerly he had lent strong support. We sent to YFC's publication an advertisement containing the following statement:

This is the term (ultra-fundamentalists) which modernists, infidels and the disciples of the so-called "New Evangelicalism" apply to those who refuse to compromise on the matter of the Inspiration and the Infallibility of the Word of God.

YOUTH FOR CHRIST rejected the advertisement. Dr. Bob wrote two letters and Bob wrote one to the president of the organization ask-

Portrait of Dr. Bob Jones, Jr., presented to the University by the Class of 1957.

(by Aram Shikler)

ing why the advertisement had been rejected. No reply ever came.

Bob's charge in the advertisement was simply that the New Evangelicals had adopted a term of double-talk invented by modernists and infidels, and that along with modernists and infidels they were using it to

Portrait of Mrs. Bob Jones, Jr.

(by Aram Shikler)

attack men who were contending for the fundamentals of the Faith. "We do not classify the 'New Evangelicals' with modernists and infidels as regards their doctrine," Bob explained, "but they are guilty of the thing we say they are guilty of."

YOUTH FOR CHRIST has also retreated from their former position of urging people to attend a Bible-believing church: they now urge, "Attend the church of your choice." Bob feels that this is a dangerous trend, and he does not feel that he can support such an organization. There are, of course, many other reasons he cannot go along with this group; but we do not have time or space to include them.

* * *

The Jones men became aware that the New Evangelicals and the Neo-Orthodox groups were gaining inroads in mission work around the world. Mission boards which formerly had stood in bold defense of the fundamentals of the Faith, for obedience to the Word of God, and for separation from all that was not in harmony with these things were beginning to compromise with groups that were not adhering to scriptural principles. Many of our graduates and other friends of fundamentalism urged Bob Jones University to start a foreign mission board that would contend for the Faith and stand true to the principles of God's Word. The Executive Committee of THE GOSPEL FELLOW-SHIP ASSOCIATION felt that such an activity could be incorporated in their organization, and their recommendation was unanimously and enthusiastically approved by the Board of Trustees in their annual meeting on May 30, 1961. The new branch of this organization became GOSPEL FELLOWSHIP MISSIONS, which now has missionaries on several foreign fields.

Another significant move which Dr. Bob and Bob, Jr., made was to set in motion THE INSTITUTE OF CHRISTIAN SERVICE. It seemed that there was a great human potential for Christian service that was virtually untapped. There were many people with practical minds who were not interested in, or perhaps qualified for, advanced technical studies. These people, however, were eager to equip themselves to serve the Lord in full-time or part-time Christian occupations. THE IN-STITUTE OF CHRISTIAN SERVICE is not a Bible Institute. It is not designed to meet the standards of a Bible college or of any other type of college. It carries with it no academic credit. It merely gives men and women a basic knowledge of the Word of God and the practical and psychological "know-how" and incentive to win souls and serve Christ effectively. Socially and culturally, students in this department have the same training as our other students; but academically, they have their own faculty and sub-administration and curriculum.

* * *

Dr. Bob was always quick to give his son the credit for all the cultural aspects of the school; but he was happy that his son was just as spiritual and perhaps a harder fighter than he himself was. Dr. Bob used to say to me, "Bob is a better preacher than I am. He has a polished, finished message that I could never preach." Dr. Bob contended that if the evangelistic pressure were ever removed from Bob Jones University, the school would be "gone." He felt no concern with his son at the helm.

Mrs. Jones, Sr., feels that there is a growing similarity between the preaching of her son and that of his father. Bob does not try to copy his father, but all of his associates are aware that unconsciously he is becoming more like him. No son could have sat at the feet of such a dominant personality and not have picked up many of his father's traits.

* * *

In 1950, Bob, Jr., conceived the idea of creating an ART GALLERY OF RELIGIOUS PAINTINGS. It was designed as a project to benefit the students and at the same time be another means of getting out the Gospel. But Bob could not possibly have known what the future held in store concerning this department. It is now one of the major cultural attractions in Southeastern United States and is known to connoisseurs around the world as one of the important American collections. The first gallery, formally opened on Thanksgiving Day, 1951, consisted of some forty paintings and a few pieces of sculpture in two galleries. So rapid was the growth that we had to add room after room, until finally we had to move the collection into a larger building; and now we have some thirty galleries. At a symposium on "Culture and the Visual Arts" that preceded the opening of the new gallery in 1965, a critic from Boston said, "This is a wonderful collection. I do not see how Dr. Bob Jones, Jr., could have done it. He is a combination man—an art critic, art pirate, and a go-getter."

* * *

In February, 1951, Bob, Jr., made a trip overseas. The six weeks abroad seemed to stimulate him further, for upon his return he announced that he would start a new department at the University— UNUSUAL FILMS—to make religious and educational films. The first film produced by this department was one of Dr. Bob's old-time sermons, LIGHT OF THE WORLD. The second was Shakespeare's MACBETH in which Bob, Jr., played the lead. Many films have followed in the wake of these two, and several have won many awards. WINE OF MORNING, filmed version of Bob, Jr's., novel of the same title, won four awards. It has been labeled by many "The most spectacular production in the history of Christian films." It was the official representative of American colleges at the International Congress of Motion Picture and Television Schools held in Paris and Cannes, France, in conjunction with the Cannes Film Festival. Other nations—notably Russia—could hardly believe that such a film could be produced in an independent Christian school in America, and the Russian representative became so engrossed in the story that he forgot to watch for points to criticize afterward.

* * *

Dr. Bob Jones, Jr., Recognized Shakespearean Scholar, Playing Shylock

Bob is modest about his accomplishments, but other men are lavish in their praise of him. Dr. Charles D. Brokenshire—one of the smartest men Princeton University ever graduated, Dr. Robert Dick Wilson's associate for many years, and until his death the Dean of our Graduate School of Religion—told me many times that Bob, Jr., was the only man in Protestantism who could accomplish what needed to be accomplished. Other men have told me that when Protestants have looked for a spokesman, they have found the same recommendation: "Dr. Bob Jones, Jr., president of Bob Jones University, is your man." It is easy to understand why conservative men in Protestantism have turned to Bob for advice and leadership: he is a man of conviction, and he has the courage to take an uncompromising stand.

Bob's advantages, his background in Hebrew History—which he both studied and taught—his foundation in Bible, his speech training and acting ability, and his sound spiritual slant, destined him in some ways to excel his father. Both men have been leaders in the religious and educational world, and both have been fighters, differing only in their approach. Dr. Bob had the rough-and-tumble, bulldog-tenacity, sawdust-aisle approach; Bob has the polished, well-educated approach, with a voice that flows like ripples of water in a clear running mountain stream. Because of his long span of years in the ministry in the heyday of evangelism, Dr. Bob had experiences that few men have had; and his son has been the beneficiary of those experiences. It is small wonder, then, that fundamentalists have leaned on the knowledge and wisdom of both men, and that liberals, seeing in them definite foes, have kept track of their moves.

* * *

In 1958, Bob gave a series of four messages over the American Broadcasting Corporation network. The programs, entitled "The Unity of the Church," were presented in cooperation with the American Council of Christian Churches. In 1963 Bob was asked to join Dr. Noel Smith and Dr. Allan MacRae in a discussion about "Ecumenicity—What Is Wrong With It?" etc. Two of the programs of the latter group were recorded in advance on the campus of Bob Jones University in the studios of WMUU, one of the best-equipped and best-loved radio stations.

* * *

WMUU has already been mentioned above, but let me add that two of the most popular programs on WMUU are "DR. BOB JONES SAYS," an early morning broadcast with an estimated listening audience of 100,000 which continues even after Dr. Bob's death, and "PREXY'S PROGRAM," Bob, Jr's., afternoon program of Bible reading, comments, or interviews.

An efficiency expert, representative of a large consultant management firm with offices in the largest cities in this country and in many foreign lands, called at my office, and I asked, "How are you getting along?" He replied, "I don't know. I thought I did until I heard Dr. Bob

Such a Typical Pose of Dr. Jones!

Jones speak over the radio as I drove into town this morning. His message went straight to my heart. I don't know how many other people heard it, but the message seemed to be directed to me." A certain preacher remarked, "I listen to Dr. Bob's wonderful radio message on Sunday morning, and I go into my own pulpit on fire for the Lord because of the inspiration of this great man of God."

There have been conversions because of Dr. Bob's program, and not a few people have been led to help us financially because of the blessing of his messages. Years ago someone heard him speak over the radio in Buffalo, New York, and was so impressed with his sincerity and convictions that he left the school $50,000. Miss Evelyn Howell, for whom our science building is named, first heard Dr. Bob over the radio in New York City. She left us $165,000. A Greenville lawyer said, "For fourteen years I have never had my radio dialed to anything except Bob Jones' station." In 1963 we purchased a radio station in Atlanta, Georgia. The money which we used to buy this station came from a contact that Dr. Bob had made a half century before in a large campaign in Gloversville, New York. It is impossible to properly evaluate the work of our radio station which the Lord led Bob and his dad to found.

* * *

Exactly one year from the day that Dr. Bob, Sr., had a plaque unveiled in his honor in Alabama (see page 332), the student body of BJU presented a plaque to their beloved President, Bob Jones, Jr., who had reached his fifty-second birthday. The framed scroll, a pledge of confidence and loyalty, was presented in chapel by the president of the student body. It said:

On this occasion of your birthday, we, the student body of 1963–64, wish to state our gratitude for your sincerity and loyalty to the task the Lord has given you.

We are assured that you as president will continue to uphold the principles and philosophies of the school as set forth in the original charter. At this time we want to pledge our confidence in your convictions and abilities and our loyalty to you as administrative head of Bob Jones University.

We appreciate the work you are doing, not only as president of Bob Jones University but also as evangelist, world traveler, connoisseur of the arts, and student of history. Thank you, Dr. Bob, for your friendship and your interest in shaping our lives for "fit vessels of service."

* * *

Divine endowments, such as those bestowed upon Dr. Bob, upon his son, and upon Bob, III, are not so much privileges as they are responsibilities—responsibilities of such magnitude that those who are thus endowed cannot be free of them any hour of the day or night, and responsibilities that carry with them such heavy accountability to the Lord for their fulfillment these men would know better than to treat them lightly or to pervert their use to selfish ambition or gain.

At his retirement Dr. Bob, Sr., left things in excellent condition. Spiritually we were strong; academically and culturally we were soaring; and financially we had a plant worth approximately twenty-eight million dollars, free of debt, with some reserves. Dr. Bob said: "I am not concerned about the future of the school; so as far as the position of the school is concerned, there will be no change whatsoever. I, of course, am still going to do what I can. But as I see it, the future is brighter for Bob Jones University than it has ever been."

* * *

At the end of Dr. Bob, Jr.'s, first year as Chairman of the Board, we had in addition to a "new look" on the campus — larger office space, more adequate dining facilities, and additional housing for faculty — one of the most successful years we had ever had financially. No one was happier, of course, than dear old Dr. Bob who had proved to the world that things could run without him. Indeed, that had been his purpose all the way through — to lay a foundation that would stand, and upon which his successor could build to the glory of God. Bob Jones, Jr., is a living monument to the thoroughness of his father's work for the Lord.

* * *

I have touched only the surface of the accomplishments of this very talented son. I am convinced that many books will be written about him in the years to come. He has already reached the heights in many fields of endeavor, and is known as one of the mightiest exponents of orthodoxy.

He is not only an author, having written many outstanding books but he is also now a playwright, having just premiered his majestic play entitled PROLOGUE — the life of John Hus — on Thanksgiving, 1968. I wish to close this section with the Bob Jones University Hymn which Bob, Jr., wrote many years ago.

Bob Jones University Hymn

Wisdom of God, we would by Thee be taught;
Control our minds, direct our every thought.
Knowledge alone life's problems cannot meet;
We learn to live while sitting at Thy feet.

Light of the world, illumine us we pray,
Our souls are dark, without Thy kindling ray;

Torches unlighted, of all radiance bare,
Touch them to flame, and burn in glory there!

Incarnate Truth, help us Thy truth to learn,
Prone to embrace the falsehood we would spurn;
Groping in error's maze for verity,
Thou art the Truth we need to make us free.

Unfailing love, we are so cold in heart,
To us Thy passion for the lost impart;
Give us Thy vision of the need of men,
All learning will be used in service then.

Giver of life, we would not live to please
Self or the world, nor seek the paths of ease;
Dying Thou bringest life to sons of men;
So may we dying live Thy life again.

Captain of Might, we yield to Thy command,
Armored by faith, Thy Word our sword in hand;
Fierce though the battle, Thine the victory,
Bravely we'll strive and more than conqu'rors be.

Eternal Lord, let heavens pass away,
Earth be removed, no fear our hearts shall sway;
Empires may crumble, dust return to dust;
Secure are they, who in their Saviour trust.

Great King of kings, this campus all is Thine,
Make by Thy presence of this place a shrine;
Thee may we meet within the classroom walls,
Go forth to serve Thee from these hallowed halls.

BOB, III

I should like to go back a few years to the time when Bob Jones, Jr., and Fannie May Holmes were united in marriage. The year was 1938, and the wedding was one of the loveliest of the season. Having been one of the pioneer members of the Student Body and a member of the first graduating class, Fannie May was in a position to know and to fully appreciate the work of Bob Jones College, as it was known at that time.

Fannie May was born into the God-fearing family of Mr. and Mrs. John Edward Holmes of Fort Deposit, Alabama. Dr. Bob said of Brother

Holmes, "Whenever I think of an honorable man with integrity, I think of Mr. J. E. Holmes." One of Fannie May's former school teachers in Alabama told me, "Mr. Holmes was a man of character; he was as 'straight as a die.'" As superintendent of the county schools, Mr. Holmes felt a keen responsibility for the young people. On one occasion when his county could not raise money and planned to vote in liquor "for the revenue," Mr. Holmes personally signed a note for several thousand dollars to keep the evil from their midst. "I do not have the ready cash," Mr. Holmes said to the Council, "but if the only thing we need to protect our young people from this great evil is a sum of money, I will mortgage my farm and raise the money. . . ." Mr. and Mrs. Holmes were ardent admirers of Evangelist Bob Jones, and they supported his work in every way possible. It is not surprising that they sent Fannie May to Dr. Bob's school in Panama City, Florida.

Upon her graduation from Bob Jones College, Fannie May attended graduate school in Greeley, Colorado, where she received an advanced degree in Home Economics. She was invited back to Bob Jones College to be dietitian and head of our home economics department. She has been of tremendous value in both departments.

The Lord blessed Bob and Fannie May with three wonderful children. Captain Jon Edward Jones, the second son, made an excellent record scholastically, and has been outstanding in the service of his country. Following his graduation from Bob Jones University (he was also graduated from Bob Jones Academy) at the age of nineteen, he entered the Law School of the University of Tennessee, where he was graduated second in his class. He served an apprenticeship with a federal judge in Nashville, Tennessee, and with an outstanding law firm in Chattanooga, Tennessee. A captain in the JAG Corps, Jon is stationed at Fort Benning, Georgia, where he teaches. Jon married one of our fine students, Betty York, who is a graduate of our Academy and also of our University.

Joy Estelle Jones, now Mrs. Gerald Jordan, received an M. A. degree in interpretative speech at Bob Jones University. She played important roles in some of our Shakespearean plays and studied one summer at the Shakespeare Institute at the University of Bridgeport (Connecticut). Joy's husband is an alumnus of Bob Jones University and the University of Florida; Joy and "Butch" teach in Columbus, Indiana, Butch's home town.

For obvious reasons, my emphasis is on the first son, Bob, III, who is now Vice-President of Bob Jones University. As Bob, Jr., predicted, God has laid upon the shoulders of this son the burden of the work of the university. Mrs. Jones, Sr., tells this story: "Bob, Jr., had always taken it for granted that his first child would be a boy. I told him he might be surprised, that he might have a daughter. He calmly replied that the

Lord had given him every assurance that his child would be a son to help carry on the great work which God had called his father to start."

When Bob, III, was two years of age, his grandfather wrote to a friend:

We have enjoyed Bobby very much. He is a bright baby, but he has the most determined will of any baby I ever saw. If he gets converted early in life and gets lined up with the Lord, he will do something.

Having been brought up under the influence of Dr. Bob, Sr., and Dr. Bob, Jr., and in the wonderful spiritual and cultural environment of Bob Jones University, this young man has had advantages far beyond those of an average boy. Even as a lad, he traveled to Europe and the Holy Land with his father on some of the Bob Jones Tours.

With Dr. Reveal

Bobby had an unusual opportunity when he was sent, at an early age, to Camp Reveal, a camp which had been founded by Dr. Ernest I. Reveal of the Evansville (Indiana) Rescue Mission. Dr. Reveal was a true man of God, a real prayer warrior, and a long-time friend of Dr. Bob, Sr. Both the Jones men felt that Bob, III, could profit by association with this man whose child-like faith God honored time and again. Let me give an example.

One afternoon Dr. Reveal closed his eyes and prayed, asking God for a station wagon. Afterwards he felt led to write to two people about this need. Both friends answered immediately, enclosing a check for more than enough to cover the cost of a station wagon. Dr. Reveal said to his wife, "It is not my fault that God gave me two when I asked for only one. Both checks came in the same mail, and I can't send either one back. They are from God." A friend asked, "How did you come out?" Dr. Reveal answered, "All right. I knew all the time that God had sent one of those checks for the station wagon and the other for something else; otherwise, He could not have told me to write both letters. I was slow to realize that one check was for the upkeep and expenses of the car."

Bob Jones University conferred upon this saintly man an honorary degree of Doctor of Divinity, and named a men's dormitory for him. Dr. Bob said of Dr. Reveal:

I have met many interesting Christian workers down through the years, but I have never met a man who is more individualistic, unique, interesting, consecrated, and has more practical, down-to-earth common sense than Dr. Reveal. I do not know anybody in the Christian world who is a better diagnostician than Ernest Reveal. He knows what is the matter with people.

He knows that they are sinners, and he is certainly a good doctor. He knows that the blood of Jesus Christ, God's Son, cleanses from sin; and he knows that Jesus Christ can save any sinner. He has been practicing for over twenty-five years converting . . . all sorts of sinners; and they are in good spiritual health because Dr. Reveal told them what was the matter with them and told them how to get well. . . . We have never been more proud to give a degree than . . . this degree of Doctor of Divinity, which we are conferring on . . . Dr. Ernest I. Reveal.

Dr. Reveal first "got his eye on" Bob, III, in 1945 when the lad was only six years of age. Dr. Reveal wrote:

Bobby, III, made his debut and seemed to enjoy his first evangelistic campaign, which his father, Dr. Bob, Jr., was conducting. I introduced Bobby to the congregation. He stood up and gave his name and said he was from Bob Jones College, Cleveland, Tennessee. The crowd was very much impressed and gave Bobby a great ovation.

In the summer of 1955, Bob, III, spent eight weeks at Dr. Reveal's camp. The older man used Bob on the radio every third day, an experience which did a great deal for Bob's training. Dr. Reveal wrote that he found Bob "a serious lad" with "the common touch and a genuine interest in serving the Lord." He said further:

I always have Bob, III, hooked on at the Mercy Seat. At a campfire meeting, eighteen boys and girls stepped out for Christ. He is preaching with power and is a clean-cut young man. As Billy Sunday would say, "He is as clean as a hound's tooth." The Lord has given you something in that boy. He is getting experience here and is seeing the rough side of life. He is going good.

Bob pulled a sermon out of the barrel Sunday night and it was a good one, "The Weeping Saviour." He had some good illustrations in his sermon. He was on the job doing personal work after he preached, and souls were saved. . . .

You can be assured that Bobby will carry on after you and Bob, Jr., pass on, because he will stand and never waver. Day by day the Lord is training and equipping him for the work He has called him to do. Training and using him in his youth will keep him "hot on the griddle." When Granddad and Dad lay their armor down, Bob, III, will take it up so quickly that Gabriel and the angels will be amazed. Let the devil growl and howl, but Bob Jones University will stand. I tell you these things because it shows how the Lord has blessed you with His wonderful promise, "For the promise is unto you, and to your children, and to all that are afar off, even to as many as the Lord our God shall call" (Acts 2:39).

Dr. Reveal, at Bob, III's, suggestion, built a swimming pool at Camp Reveal. When it was time for the dedication, Dr. Reveal wrote Dr. Bob:

When we dedicate the pool we want Bob, III, here with bells on to see his vision come to pass. This will be one of the many things the Lord will reveal to him as time rolls on.

Another letter Dr. Reveal wrote about Bobby was in regard to his preaching ministry with one of our Summer Ensembles:

We were glad to have the Brass Ensemble with us; they had a good service. Just a word in behalf of Bob, III. He brought some real Gospel messages here Saturday night and Sunday. The sunday morning broadcast, 11:00 to 12:00, that reaches Kentucky, Indiana, and Illinois, was wonderful and brought good results. . . . He spoke at the camp in the afternoon and then back at the Mission last night. Some day, and not because he is your son do I say this, he will be the top-notcher graduate of Bob Jones University. . . . He has good common sense, preaches the Word, pulls no punches and knows when he is through. Like his dad and granddad, he will be a great preacher and administrator as President of Bob Jones University. Bobby is no snob, he loves the people, Jesus has given him humility, and his family, especially his dad and mother, have laid a good foundation on the Rock.

Bob, III, was at Camp Reveal on his sixteenth birthday. The Reveals celebrated the occasion with a dinner in Bob's honor. That same summer Dr. Reveal forwarded to the Jones family a letter which a lumberman had written about Bob, III's, preaching. The man had also enclosed a donation for Dr. Reveal's camp and had offered any further assistance he might be able to give.

Bob really had it on the ball in that message. We made four recordings of his messages. All glory is to the Lord, just shows that training and prayer tells and then he was dedicated to the Lord before his birth. He was saved when he was five years old. Just listened to him preach this morning on a recording for the broadcast; his message was good and his illustrations, many of them original. We will just keep praying for him that the Lord will keep His hand upon him. I talked to Bob and prayed that the Lord would make his shoulders broad for the great calling to make known Christ.

A communication of February 16, 1959, from Dr. Reveal stated:

Am writing in behalf of your son who did a job for Jesus here that was extraordinary. He preached to large crowds and there were two alcoholics saved who were well-dressed men. They made a stand for Christ and came back to testify. There was a young soldier saved . . . as well as others. I watched Bob and could see the hand of the Lord on him. He had the punch and God's message but it was different than the other speakers.

Bob, III, appreciated Dr. Reveal's love, prayers, and interest. On October 7, 1966, he said to Mr. Clarence Noelting, chairman of the

Evansville Rescue Mission Board and faithful member of the Board of Trustees of Bob Jones University:

> I often think back on my days at Camp Reveal and the wonderful inspiration Dr. Reveal was to me. I do not know of any man who has been of more encouragement or had a greater impact on my life than he. I revere his memory and would be broken-hearted if the day ever came that the good work he founded and carried on for so many years ceased to major in this business of soul winning. I thank the Lord for men like you who are dedicated to carrying on the work which he established.

It was with reluctance that Bob, III, became a member of the Bob Jones University staff. He debated with himself and prayed much before accepting the offer that was made to him. "But the more I prayed and thought about it," he says, "the more I came to realize that this is my job—to accept my responsibility in helping to perpetuate the ideals and standards which my grandfather had set up when he founded the school."

Bob has served as a member of the speech faculty; Assistant Dean of Men; member of the Cooperating Board; and, since 1961, member of the Regular Board. At the age of twenty-one he was elected by the Board to assist his father and later to be the Vice-President of the school. Dr. Bob was grateful to the Lord for His goodness in calling his grandson to the great work of Bob Jones University, and he was pleased with the strides the boy made. Upon the resignation of his grandfather, Bob, III, was elected to replace him on the Executive Committee of the Board of Trustees.

Like his father, Bob, III, has an interest in the cultural aspect of Bob Jones University. He handles the booking of the Artist Series, and he and his wife, Beneth Peters Jones, a spiritual and capable young woman, have presented their joint graduate recital in other schools and colleges. Bob, III, played minor Shakespearean roles when he was a small child; and at the age of fifteen he played an outstanding role in WINE OF MORNING, the filmed version of his father's novel. His portrayal of one of the thieves who died on the cross when our Lord was crucified was very touching. As Jeb Stuart in RED RUNS THE RIVER, he was humorous as well as entertaining. His characterization of Jon Hus in PROLOGUE, his father's recent play, made us feel that we should go out to serve the Lord in a greater way than ever before. All the parts Bob, III, has played in THE CLASSIC PLAYERS productions have been forceful and noteworthy; however, Bob's main interest, like his father's, is in preaching the Gospel and in training young people to do service for the Lord. By conducting tours to various foreign countries, Bob, III, is able to keep up with trends around the world.

Dr. Monroe Parker, during his presidency of Pillsbury College,

The Three Bob Joneses

Owatonna, Minnesota, invited Bob, III, to speak at Pillsbury. Afterwards, Dr. Parker wrote:

> It was good to have Bob here for our Conference on Evangelism. He did a splendid job. He is a fine young man and I thank God that he is growing as he is and that we can have so much confidence for the future.

On January 23, 1966, we laid to rest one of the best friends Bob Jones University ever had: Mrs. W. D. Neves, Greenville, South Carolina. Mrs. Neves was a wonderful little prayer warrior who kept Bob Jones University constantly before the throne of God. It was her belief that God had His hand on Bob, III, for something special and that she must devote special prayer time in his behalf. When "Miss Bessie" passed away, Bob, III, in the absence of his father, was asked to conduct her funeral. This was not easy, because he had known her from his childhood and had visited in her home many times. I wish that I could quote the entire eulogy which Bob, III, delivered; but for lack of space, I will give only an excerpt:

> I would love to have been at the Pearly Gates when Mrs. Neves walked through them. Down here she had trouble with her sight and hearing; there she can see the glories of Heaven and can hear the beautiful strains of celestial music. All who knew her were aware of her enthusiastic response to things here. We could just hear her exclaim upon entering Heaven, "Ooooh, isn't this wonderful?"

Although Bob, III, is still young in the ministry, he receives far more calls than he is able to accept. Under his ministry souls have been saved, lives have been rededicated, and young businessmen have been led to sell their businesses and go into training for the ministry. Bob is a forceful speaker; to me, his very strong point is the invitation and challenge at the end of his message. There is an irresistible, magnetic quality in his appeals. Surely Dr. Reveal's prayer, "I prayed that the Lord would make his shoulders broad for the great calling to make known Christ," is being answered in a marvelous way.

Let us join our prayers to those of Dr. Reveal, Mrs. Neves, and all the others who pray for this young man. Dr. Bob, Sr., pioneered in this work. It was given to him to lay the groundwork. Bob Jones, Jr., has had to make the transition from helping his father carry the load to carrying the load by himself. Many people had predicted that the school would never be the same when Dr. Bob was gone. Bob, Jr., has proved that it could be the same. He is building on the same foundation that the Lord led his father to lay. Both men have had a difficult place to fill. But it seems to me that Bob, III, has a very difficult, if not the most difficult, place of all; he faces a world that promises greater turmoil than we know today. Surely we can help bear the burden of this work by praying for this young man and for all who assist him in this great work.

PART IV
ECUMENICAL CONFLICT

Part IV
Ecumenical Conflict

CHAPTER 1

The Billy Graham Issue: Yoking Up With Unbelievers

The Billy Graham issue is a spiritual issue. It deals with the compromise evangelism in which God's Bible-believing people are being led to join hands with God's enemies to put over a program that violates clear commands and principles of God's Word. Dr. Bob cited numerous passages with reference to the proper attitude in a situation like this, and he offered $1,000 to anyone who could find Scripture to support a position contrary to that of the fundamentalists. Perhaps his most frequent reference was II John 9–11: "If there come any unto you, and bring not this doctrine, receive him not into your house, neither bid him God speed: For he that biddeth him God speed is partaker of his evil deeds." He would quote John 7:17: "If any man will do his will, he shall know of the doctrine, whether it be of God. . . ." Then he would say:

> That is significant. God never leads His servants down opposing avenues in any doctrinal conflict. God's man is commanded to "speak . . . things which become sound doctrine" (Titus 2:1), "holding fast the faithful word . . . that he may be able by sound doctrine both to exhort and to convince the gain sayers" (Titus 1:9). Why? "For there are many unruly and vain talkers and deceivers . . . Whose mouths must be stopped . . ." (Titus 1:10, 11). "All scripture is given by inspiration of God, and is profitable for doctrine, for reproof, for correction, for instruction in righteousness: That the man of God may be perfect, throughly furnished unto all good works" (II Timothy 3:16). If we want to know and are willing to follow the right way, we have the promise of Him who is faithful that *we shall know.*

Some thought that this issue was *a personality clash between Dr. Bob Jones and Billy Graham.* That is not true. Dr. Bob *loved* Billy Graham, and until Billy started hobnobbing with liberals, Dr. Bob promoted him. It was when Billy adopted unorthodox methods that Dr. Bob took issue with him. To be scriptural himself, Dr. Bob had no alternative. No one will ever know how earnestly Dr. Bob prayed that Billy would see that the liberals, the enemies of God, were not interested in promoting God's Word or Cause but were seeking to control Billy and hold back what good he might do. It seemed that Billy had come under the spell of the wrong crowd, and his warped conceptions were becoming more and more apparent as he accepted invitations to speak in such places as Union Theological Seminary and as he began to mention with favor men who were rank modernists. Dr. Bob said:

> I think that at heart Billy is good, but I am convinced, that what he is doing is "selling our crowd down the river"; and if we do not build up a counter movement similar to the effort we are making in lining up evangelists to stand, the Cause is going to suffer.

In a sense, it would have been easy for Dr. Bob to sit back and keep silent on the issue. In the first place, Billy had said to Dr. Bob,

"Call Me One of Your Boys"

In Los Angeles, California, many years ago, Billy visited Dr. Bob at the hotel where Dr. Bob was staying during a meeting. In substance Billy said:

> Dr. Bob, I did not stay long at Bob Jones College, and I did not make a very good record. However, all I know about evangelism, I learned there. I got my start in Bob Jones College, and I feel that I owe you what I am. Would you call me one of your boys?

Dr. Bob replied:

> I am the last of the old crowd, Billy. My days are about over. You are young. You have a chance to do something for God, *if you stay true to Him.* God is looking for someone to do a job; but I cannot believe you are the one.

Dr. Bob had observed that as a student Billy was a "straddler" and that he took lightly the rules of Bob Jones College. By his own admission over nation-wide television, Billy deliberately disobeyed a rule about checking off campus and going out of town. This indicated a flaw in Billy's character. Would he now hold himself "in tow" with regard to scriptural rules?

Dr. Bob kindly, but candidly, said to Billy, "You were always on both sides of any issue, Billy."

Billy answered, "Dr. Bob, I have changed."

When Dr. Bob returned to the campus, he told his approximately 1200 preacher boys about his conversation with Billy; and he asked them to pray that the young evangelist would stay true to God and live up to his commitments.

Many Team Members Our Graduates

Practically all of Billy's team were trained at Bob Jones College in Cleveland, Tennessee. Cliff Barrows and his wife are graduates of our school, and Cliff was on our Board for many years. When Cliff came to Bob Jones University, he was such a separatist that he would not attend a Southern Baptist church; he would not attend any church but a GARB church. Dr. Bob had a real affection for this couple. When they decided to make their home in Greenville, he gave me instructions to help them in every way possible, and I did. Grady and T. W. Wilson are from our school. Grady was with us only three years, but T. W. stayed four years. T. W. also served on our Cooperating Board. Billy's campaign manager, Willis Haymaker, was associated with Dr. Bob for approximately forty years. Dr. Bob took Willis as a boy and trained him to be his campaign manager. Willis's mother was housemother at Bob Jones College for a number of years, and at least two of Willis's children were educated in our school. Selfishly speaking, therefore, Dr. Bob could have "preened his feathers" in pride that these former boys and girls had stepped out into the limelight. After all, it focused attention on the home base.

Not even for the sake of friendship and fatherly pride, however, would Dr. Bob sit idly by and watch God's orchard being damaged and not do something to hold back the blight. Dr. Bob made up his mind to stand by the lesser lights in the evangelistic field and encourage them not to compromise.

Not a Personal Attack on Billy

Not one time did Dr. Bob impugn Billy's motives. Dr. Bob was dealing with principles; and if those principles reflected on a man, Dr. Bob could not help it. He had the delicate and serious problem of handling hundreds of preacher boys, as well as being an "answering service" to countless numbers who through the years had looked to him for guidance. He was a "top name" in evangelistic circles for more than fifty years, and he had a large "clientele," one might say; this "clientele" kept him bombarded with questions about this major threat to scriptural evangelism. Dr. Bob sought to build moral backbone in these people by emphasizing that "*it is never right to do wrong even to get a chance to preach.*" "If Billy is right in his approach," Dr. Bob argued, "then all the rest of the fundamentalists in evangelistic work throughout the years have been wrong."

Although he spearheaded the counterattack to Billy's compromise and bore the brunt of the opposition that was hurled into the camp of the fundamentalists, Dr. Bob was

Not Alone in the Conflict

Dr. Bob Jones, Jr., Dr. John R. Rice, Dr. Noel Smith, Dr. Robert Ketcham, Dr. Carl McIntire, Dr. Charles Woodbridge, Dr. Bob Shuler, Dr. Archer Weniger, Judge James E. Bennet, and many others became greatly concerned as they watched the devil first get a foot in the door of some organizations and institutions and later slip in and take over. It was hard to believe that it was a deliberate "sellout" on Billy's part, and yet it was harder to conceive of a man of Billy's training being led up a blind alley in such gullible fashion. These veteran evangelists did their best to alert Billy to the dangers toward which he was steering and to safeguard him. They prayed for Billy, they talked with him, and they wrote to him, pleading with him to be careful; but nothing they said or did seemed to curb Billy's unhealthy tendencies. It seemed that, like King Ahab, Billy had sold himself on an evil course. He may not have believed that the way he had chosen was evil; there is always the tendency to "gloss over" things we want to do. Nevertheless, Billy should have been warned that his way was not right, simply by virtue of the men who opposed it. These men had reached the position of "specialists" in the field of evangelism, and it was a serious mistake on Billy's part not to listen to them. Billy threw their counsel to the winds, so to speak, and began to make up more than ever to "the powers that be."

For awhile even some God-fearing preachers joined hands with Billy. Dr. John R. Rice was one of these. When a modernist was allowed to serve on the sponsoring committee in the Atlanta, Georgia, crusade, Dr. Rice took Billy to task about it. Billy answered that on his knees he had asked the Lord's forgiveness for having unwittingly allowed a modernist on his sponsoring committee and had promised God that he would not let it happen again. Later, Billy went so far as to tell Dr. Rice that he would not have as a special guest or as a sponsoring participant in his meetings anybody who was not out-and-out true to the Bible on the great fundamentals. Within a very short time, however, Billy had completely reversed himself; and the pendulum began to swing farther and farther to the left.

Billy seemed to be enamored of publicity, and some of his weaknesses began to manifest themselves. As headlines became bigger and the demands greater, Billy began to soft-pedal his message. Dr. Bob realized more and more that Billy's type of evangelism was weakened by compromise. He felt that the younger evangelist was being "weighed in the balances" and that if he were not careful, he would be "found wanting."

Kindly but firmly, therefore, Dr. Bob warned Billy that the path he was taking would wreck future evangelism.

The farther to the left the pendulum seemed to swing, the more the liberals made overtures to Billy. Whereas they had feared this young man who was making such strides and having such success, they soon saw in him a champion—one who would not hurt them but who would promote their cause in a greater way than they themselves could do. E. Stanley Jones is reported to have made the remark, "At last we have a champion who can bring the fundamentalists and liberals together in a liberal camp." The head of the National Council of Churches said, "Billy is doing a job we cannot do. He is building our [liberal] organization for us." How true! After the New York crusade, Billy left with the sponsoring Protestant Council $67,000, which they used to put field men to work to the end that one year later they had increased from 1,700 churches to over 3,400. Billy doubled the strength of this liberal group.

John Henry Jowett once said: "When a man finds that a certain course of conduct is receiving popular applause, he is led on to further excesses. He is often doubly betrayed by the seductions of the shouting crowd." I believe this happened to Billy. It is in line with Dr. Bob's remarks:

> I personally think that it was at this point the devil took Billy up on a high mountain and showed him the kingdom of this world, and how popular he would be. Whether it was the height that made him dizzy, the excitement of what the world had to offer, or the thought that he could win great numbers to the Lord, I believe that at this point Billy sold out true evangelism; and instead of doing the good he might have done, he set in motion the wheels that would harm generations to come.

Dr. Bob became so exercised about the seriousness of this situation that he lay awake at night praying and meditating. He commented:

> As far as I know, I think Billy loves me and respects me. But he has one serious and dangerous fault for any evangelist. He wants to please everybody, and that cannot be done. The fellow who tries it sooner or later gets into trouble. I wish Billy would listen to me.

The fundamentalists felt deep concern also about Billy's approval of the Revised Standard Version of the Bible. They could not understand Billy's failure to see that he was playing into the hands of the modernists and the denominational bosses and was actually delivering into their hands the evangelistic movement of the day. It was heartbreaking to see that the only crowd Billy was downgrading were the out-and-out Bible believers and that he seemed to favor those who either did not abide in the doctrines of Christ or who soft-pedaled the doctrines in order to please men and get on the bandwagon.

As time went on and things grew worse, Dr. Bob and Dr. Rice agreed that Billy was "gone" and that there was no turning back. They felt that regardless of any plans he might bring forth to modify his method of yoking up with modernists, they would not be able to trust him unless he came all out and confessed that he had been morally and spiritually wrong in running with the modernists. Dr. Bob expressed it this way: "There will have to be both repentance and repudiation — overt and public — on Billy's part before we can ever consider trusting him." The faith of these men that he would do this, however, was weak.

Some people have argued, *"Dr. Bob practiced mass evangelism, and Billy Graham's ministry is mass evangelism. What is the difference?"* Mass evangelism of the day of Billy Sunday and Bob Jones was built on the straight preaching of the Word. Evangelists such as these did not "trim their ways to seek love"; and people flocked to the front on clear-cut calls to salvation, not on this pussy-footing, watered-down Gospel that is being preached today.

Instead of the Bible-centered evangelism that characterized the former day, there is wholesale mass evangelism in our day — a discount type of religion, if you please. I believe in wholesale buying and selling in business. Sometimes I am laughingly referred to as "wholesale Johnson," because in handling the Lord's money in this Christian institution I try to buy as inexpensively and as wisely as I can. However, in spiritual matters, to quote Dr. Bob, we cannot afford to cut the price — indeed, the price is not ours to cut. God has set the standards, and these standards are found in His Word. God does not change; Jesus Christ does not change; the Holy Spirit does not change; and the Word of God does not change. The Word is forever settled in Heaven, and it is magnified above all His name (Psalm 138:2; 119:89). To water it down is to diminish it; to interpret it by man's ideas or to claim that it is set aside by the Holy Spirit is to add to it; and God's Word condemns both practices. Jesus said, "If you love me, keep my commandments." The acid test of our love for God is obedience to His Word.

People have ignorantly asserted that *Billy Graham follows the same procedure as that of Billy Sunday.* Men who have studied evangelism the greater part of their lives and who knew Billy Sunday personally know that that is not true. He openly denounced modernists and modernism, but Billy Graham omits such denunciations from his preaching. Mr. Sunday was an energetic man in the pulpit. On one occasion he ran over to some preachers in a meeting and, pointing his finger at them, said: "I understand that some of you preachers do not believe in Jesus

Christ—that He was born of a virgin. If you do not believe that, you are going to Hell like anyone else."

Little by little Billy Graham backed himself into a corner. He was making such remarks as "God has by-passed fundamentalists." This was a slap at great men like Dr. Bob, Dr. Bob, Jr., Dr. John Rice, Dr. W. B. Riley, Dr. H. A. Ironside, and many other wonderful men of God who were proud to be called "extreme" fundamentalists, "rank" fundamentalists, "fun-*dam*-mentalists," or any other names as long as people knew that they were standing without apology for the authority of the Word of God and for the doctrines of Christ. Billy stated most emphatically, "I will go anywhere under any sponsorship as long as I can preach the message I want to give." That sounds good, but it does not take much listening to him to realize that Billy does not seem to want to give the full counsel of God's Word as advocated by the Apostle Paul and others right down to this day.

Mr. Willis Haymaker, a man who has been my personal friend as well as personal friend of the Joneses, states that he sets up meetings for Billy Graham as he used to set them up for Dr. Bob. This is a gross misapprehension of the facts. To a point there is similarity. However—and this is the important thing—we have in our files correspondence to prove that Dr. Bob instructed Willis *not to allow any modernists on the sponsoring committees.* This admonition is in line with the resolution which Dr. Bob, Dr. Biederwolf, and others drew up years ago at Winona Lake, Indiana.

November 23, 1940—letter from Willis Haymaker to Dr. Bob regarding the Chicago meeting:

> The thing I objected to was in the report of the Findings Committee's report where the committee included, without any qualification, the phrase—"in cooperation with the churches." I suggested we qualify that with the addition of "Where the churches are orthodox and evangelical." The committee, however, felt that there was a difference of opinion on that point and that churches which were not orthodox and evangelical would not cooperate anyway.

December 2, 1941—letter from Dr. Bob to Willis Haymaker:

> If the backing is good and the orthodox preachers will get back of it, I believe I could work it out, so I could start on Sunday, March 15 and close Sunday night, March 29. . . . I would not want to go in with any preacher who does not believe in the virgin birth and the blood.

A point of great concern to the fundamentalists were the headlines over the country which declared that Billy would not attack Romanism,

Judaism, or Protestantism. To announce in advance that no one had anything to worry about was wrong. It is not God's will for any man to go contrary to His Word in order to boost evangelism. God does not work that way.

The fundamentalists could conclude no other reason for Billy's compromise than that his ambition was overpowering his judgment. Billy was smart, and he was orthodox. However, he was *"sacrificing the permanent on the altar of the immediate,"* and that would not work. They felt that Billy had sold himself "a bill of goods," that what he was doing was all right.

Dr. Graham's New York Campaign

The full import of the issue began to manifest itself in its true light when Billy accepted the sponsorship of the wrong crowd in New York. Even though in his heart Billy may have sold himself on the idea that by his methods he could reach more people for the Lord, his way was disastrously wrong. Dr. Bob decided that it was time to begin an *offensive* attack rather than simply to stand by in a *defensive* position. Men of God who agreed on the fundamentals needed to band themselves together and wage an all-out warfare.

Judge James E. Bennet Pleaded with Dr. Graham

Judge James E. Bennet, a great man of God, tried to hold Billy in line with regard to this campaign. He said:

I loved Billy—he called me "Uncle Jim" and I called him "Son." For three days I stayed behind closed doors with Billy trying to show him where he was headed and begging him not to compromise and sell out God's people, but to come to New York under the sponsorship of the fundamental crowd—the Bible-believing people who wanted to promote God's Cause. They had tried so hard to get him. I asked Billy, "What is it you are after? If it is prestige, we will see that you get it. If it is money, you can have it. If it is crowds you want, we can get them for you. We have brought you to Madison Square Garden twice, and each time we have turned away thousands. Please, Billy, for God's sake, do not come under the sponsorship of that modernistic crowd." But Billy would not listen to me.

CHRISTIANITY TODAY, a magazine that many people say was started and backed by Billy Graham—it is reported that he gave $10,000 to help get it started—came out with an editorial aimed at several well-known fundamentalists and evangelists. This article grouped "extreme liberals" with "extreme fundamentalists," saying that both were "throwing up road blocks of criticism, disparagement and contempt," with the result that they are "highlighting unbelief on one hand and divisiveness on the other."

On March 4, 1957, Judge Bennet answered this article. He distinguished between fundamentalists and liberals, and then he said:

> You devote the greatest part of your space to fundamentalists and let liberals off with practically no criticism. Do you consider that fundamentalists are more dangerous to the Cause of Jesus Christ than out-and-out unbelievers who deny His deity?

Dr. Bennet also gave a partial resumé of the issues he had with Billy's setup. Later, Judge Bennet sent Dr. Bob an eleven-page document entitled, "THE BILLY GRAHAM NEW YORK CRUSADE, WHY I CANNOT SUPPORT IT." In this document he referred to the invitation

> in 1951 of a group of fundamental ministers in New York City . . . which asked Billy Graham to come to New York for a campaign. . . . A breakfast was held in one of the hotels with 750 present, and growing out of that a committee of 87 was chosen—66 of them by those at the breakfast, and 21 later by the 66, largely at the selection of Billy Graham. This committee formed an executive committee, upon which Rev. John S. Bonnell was placed. A study of the committee indicated that there were a number of so-called modernists on the committee.

Dr. Bennet stated further:

> Billy Graham had announced that he wanted every Protestant church in this Metropolitan area included, irrespective of its denomination, council, or creed, to enter into the campaign and also that he wanted every participating church to place at least two or up to five of its members on each of the committees, which would control and operate the campaign.

> It was apparent that these liberals would constitute a "mixed multitude." Therefore Jack Wyrtzen called together a group of about ten influential ministers and laymen, and explained to them that this was contrary to all principles upon which he had heretofore worked for the Lord, and he felt personally that he could not enter into such a campaign, although he was a very strong friend of Billy Graham. The other men in the group agreed with Jack and some related unfortunate experiences which they had had in city-wide programs with liberals on committees of management. The result was that the group decided that it would be necessary to have everyone on the committees sign a statement of faith, to show that all were in one accord. . . . Dr. Bonnell is reported to have said that in general he believed in the doctrinal statement, but he did not think his people would want him to sign it, and he resigned from the general committee. Later, Billy Graham is reported to have said that the committee was no longer representative of the churches in the area and he wrote a letter in which he outlined several certain conditions, upon which he would come to the city.

> That the committee unanimously endorse the program of an ecumenical spirit to be exhibited throughout the campaign. I am willing that we go

forward with the present committee, if in all of our actions we shall present an ecumenical spirit of love toward those of all stripes. I have never been, nor will I ever be in favor of a modernist being on the committee or in any way having any working fellowship in this meeting. I am urging you, however, to accept into our fellowship any man who accepts the deity of Christ, and who will rally to my preaching.

We knew then, and we have learned much more since, that the word "ecumenical" is that adopted by the World Council of Churches, and its affiliates, to mean a church or body including all forms of religious belief into one body, and forming one group, which will cover all religions of the world.

. . . Finally, Billy Graham announced that he would not come to New York at that time, under prevailing conditions, claiming (among other things) that the fundamentalists were too badly divided among themselves.

In the summer of 1954 . . . Jack Wyrtzen drew up a petition addressed to Billy Graham asking him if he would come to New York for a campaign to be conducted under the auspices of a group of born-again Christians. This petition was read over the radio by Jack Wyrtzen, and it was reported that it was signed by a large number of people, and was presented to Billy. At practically the same time, the Protestant Council of New York, which is reputed to be liberal and modernistic in its teaching and preaching, and is affiliated with the National Council and World Council of Churches, invited Billy to come to New York, under its auspices. After a long delay, Jack's petition was not accepted, but that of the Protestant Council was accepted. . . .

Dr. Bennet gave lengthy statements about the men on the committee and the results of the meeting. Then he said:

Billy Graham . . . completely reversed the position taken by him in his letter of May 29, 1951, when he said: "I have never been, nor will I ever be in favor of a modernist being on the committee, or any way having any working fellowship in this meeting."

Other Conservative Evaluations

It was hard to evaluate the actions of some of the conservatives; they took the position that for the sake of the unsaved millions they would "go along" with the New York campaign. They soon realized, however, that it would not work and that they had made a serious mistake. Dr. Rice said:

The official position and my own conviction is that the only way to deal with the Billy Graham compromise is that it is a sin, going against the clear command of God in the Bible. It is true that sin does not work out right, but people ought to do right because it is right and not only because they find out sin gets them in trouble. People ought not yoke up with unbelievers, because it is forbidden in the Bible and because modernists get more out of the compromise than fundamentalists do.

Dr. Bob commented:

When the evangelistic house that has been erected in America on a compromising foundation falls (and this house will fall sooner or later), the tools will be left in the hands of the religious liberals, and they will dig up the foundation on which the evangelistic house was built; and the orthodox crowd that goes in with that kind of sponsorship will be left too anemic to lay another evangelistic foundation.

New York "Old Ground" to Dr. Bob

New York was "old ground" to Dr. Bob. He had held one of his great campaigns there when he was a young man, and for seven consecutive summers he was invited back to conduct evangelistic services under a big tent. The New York papers gave splendid cooperation to these meetings; therefore, Dr. Bob knew what he was talking about when he said that if Billy would accept the sponsorship of the fundamentalists, the newspapers would stand by him, people would turn out in great numbers, thousands would be saved, and orthodoxy in New York would be made aggressively evangelistic.

Bob Jones University Requested to Pray About New York Campaign

A paid worker of Billy Graham's team wrote to Dr. Jones, Jr., asking permission to stage a rally in Bob Jones University auditorium. This rally, as we understood it, was to enlist the faculty and student body in prayer and support for the New York crusade. Bob, Jr., answered that he was sorry but that he could not grant the request. For the sake of the record, I quote Bob's letter in full.

COPY

November 7, 1956

Dr. Ralph W. Mitchell
The Billy Graham Evangelistic Association
1620 Harmon Place
Minneapolis, Minnesota

Dear Friend:

Your letter of November 2 is on my desk this morning. You put me in a very embarrassing position indeed. Because of my long-time friendship—indeed warm personal affection—for Billy, I naturally would like to say "yes." Because of my friendship for you, I would like to say, "Come ahead—the platform is open to you." However, Bob Jones University has an official responsibility and a spiritual obligation not only to our students but also to the testimony as a whole.

It is our sincere and heartfelt conviction that what Billy is doing in seeking the sponsorship of the liberals and the modernists, who repudiate the inspiration of the Scripture and the fundamentals of our faith, is contrary to the plain teaching of Scripture and unfair to the brethren who have stood for the Gospel and endured the attack of these above-mentioned liberals and modernists. It is our sincere conviction that in the long run Billy is going to wreck evangelism and leave even orthodox churches, if they co-operate, spineless and emasculated.

As much as we love Billy personally, if he came to Greenville on the same basis as he goes to these other cities, we could not cooperate or in any wise endorse a campaign. Since you are now at the present time visiting Christian colleges in the interest of promoting the New York Crusade, for you to appear here on our platform would carry the implication that we are endorsing that setup. For the sake of our testimony and for the Cause, we have to say, "We are sorry, but we cannot use you."

I am enclosing a copy of this letter for Billy. With kindest personal regards and good wishes.

Sincerely yours,

BOB JONES, JR.

President

Bob and his father said that anyone who felt led to do so *might pray privately* for Dr. Graham but that the University itself could not officially endorse a program which God's Word warns is unscriptural. The University could not change a policy which it had been following for thirty years—that of maintaining a sharp line between fundamentalism and modernism, between belief in the historic Christian faith and denial of that faith. Although there were other schools that refused to support the crusade, no issue was made of the fact. Bob Jones University had to be the issue. The team member who had written to Bob, Jr., sharply criticized his attitude in not allowing the rally; and he read Bob, Jr's., reply to a group of ministers, apparently hoping thereby to reflect upon Bob Jones University and its president and on other fundamentalists who were opposing Billy Graham. The preachers, however, answered, "Thank God, somebody is not going to be swept away and go along with just anything."

Dr. Nelson Bell's Vicious Attack

It was no surprise to Dr. Bob when Dr. Nelson Bell, executive editor of CHRISTIANITY TODAY, leveled a personal and vicious attack against him and against the University. Dr. Bell wrote that he had heard a shocking thing: that Dr. Bob Jones had forbidden anybody on Bob Jones University campus to pray for Billy Graham. "Was this true?" he wondered. (We still hear this false charge.) Dr. Bob wrote to Dr. Bell that it was unthinkable that anybody could control the private prayer life of individuals, whether students or teachers; and he assured Dr. Bell that he personally prayed for Billy every day. He explained that he could not pray for God to bless the organization as it was set up or for the crusade which obviously violated Scripture, but that he could pray for God to bless Billy and to help him get out of his dilemma and do right in the future with regard to yoking up with unbelievers. "The University," Dr. Bob said, in substance, "is already on record to stand for the fundamentals of the faith and to stand against yoking up with modernists. Public services on the University campus are properly the official business of the University; and any kind of service calculated to put the University officially in support of an organization which in itself is wrong would, of course, not be permitted. The University could not officially permit any kind of service which could be construed as an endorsement of any unscriptural combination with widely-known modernists." This letter was kind and factual and could not have been easily misunderstood.

Dr. Bell's answer, on the other hand, was unkind and unchristian. He did everything possible to discredit Dr. Bob and wreck Bob Jones University. He sent out thousands of letters attacking Bob Jones University, Dr. Bob, and Bob, Jr. Our Board of Trustees received copies of Dr. Bell's letters, and they resented his sending them. At the 1957 meeting of the Board, therefore, they went on record as approving Dr. Bob's position against the modernistic sponsorship of the Billy Graham New York campaign. Dr. Bob was right, they said, and they wanted the world to know that he was not standing alone.

Dr. John R. Rice "went to bat" for Dr. Bob and wrote an article in THE SWORD OF THE LORD about "GOD'S BLESSED MAN, DR. BOB JONES – The Man Who Could Not Be Bought Nor Bluffed Nor Scared, Who Avoids the Counsel and Company of the Wicked, Who Delights in and Defends the Bible." Dr. Rice pointed out the depths to which some men will sink to try to prove themselves right when they know there is no scriptural backing for their wrongdoing; and then he reviewed how Dr. Bob got his start, how he suffered for Christ's sake, how God blessed his endeavors, how God led him to build a school to train Christian leadership, and how the school developed into God's last large conservative base of testimony. I quote a paragraph from this lengthy article:

The more immediate reason for calling attention to the character and conviction and the blessing of God upon this great soul winner, Dr. Jones, is the fact that a well-organized, well-financed scheme to ruin his name, to ruin his influence, to ruin Bob Jones University, and to cripple the whole fundamentalist movement, through Dr. Jones, has now largely failed. I write, therefore, to encourage Christians not to be frightened by those who smear and persecute Bible believers. I write to urge fundamentalists, those who still hold to the great fundamentals of the Christian faith and defend them boldly, not to be bluffed or out-talked or soft-talked into denying Christ and the Bible by unholy compromises. And I write that those who appreciate God's great and good man may tell him so and make holy vows that you, too, like him, will stand true to Christ and the Bible, will aggressively defend the historic Christian faith as the Bible commands us to do!

Dr. Bob began to be bombarded with requests to evaluate Billy and his compromised evangelism. He answered:

Naturally, headlines can be made by the World Council, the National Council or the Protestant Council of Churches. I would rather make headlines in Heaven than to make them in this world. I have made headlines. Before I was Billy Graham's age, in New York City, I made them. If Billy would preach one night on the Blood, the New Birth, the Holy Spirit, and Hell, he would not have the large crowds he is now having.

. . . . . .

The meeting was not the success that on the surface it might seem to have been. You cannot judge an evangelistic campaign by the number of people who are saved. Some people are being converted all the time. During seventeen weeks in New York City, the orthodox Christian personal workers will always lead several hundred people to Jesus Christ. An evangelist is not given to sinners any more than a layman. According to Scripture the evangelist, pastor and teacher are given to the building up of Christians. They are to perfect the saints for the work of the ministry. During World War I, Billy Sunday was in New York and had almost a hundred thousand decisions for Jesus Christ. He did not call them "inquirers"; he called them "trail hitters." When they came down the aisle, they came on a definite clear-cut proposition to trust Jesus Christ. I had a campaign in New York soon after Billy Sunday's campaign, and the orthodox Christians in the city were out winning souls to Christ. The Christians were on fire. The saints had been perfected unto the work of the ministry.

If Billy Graham is right in his evangelistic approach, then all of the great evangelists who have lived for fifty years have all been wrong. Remember that I have known personally and have had contact with all the great evangelists for this period of time. I admired these men and have never in my life said one word against any of them. I have preached and taught mass evangelism, and I have trained a large percentage of the evangelists whose names are often seen in the newspapers. I know what I am talking about. I am sure that Billy is sacrificing the cause of evangelism on the altar of a temporary convenience. All of the evangelists who have lived for fifty years have made mistakes. They were human. Some of them may have over-headlined their work. Some of them may have had too big a budget. But not one of them ever made the fatal mistake that Billy Graham is making.

Billy is the only evangelist I have ever known who is doing the type of work that is destroying the foundation upon which the evangelistic house is built. When World War I started, I was at the height of my evangelistic career. I went through World War I conducting great campaigns. Billy Sunday had some of his greatest meetings during World War I. When the war was over, the house of mass evangelism was blown down, *but the foundation was left intact.* Immediately after World War I, some of us started to build the evangelistic house again, and we built it on the same old foundation.

Billy Graham, by working under the type of sponsorship he is working under and by not giving a clear, unequivocal statement against the modernistic conspiracy to take over the religious leadership in this nation, is putting the tools in the hands of the modernists; and when the evangelistic house which he is building is blown down, the tools will be left in the hands of the modernists; and they will completely dig up the foundation. The conservative, Bible-believing pastors and churches that are going into the Billy Graham movement with the modernists will be too anemic to ever lay another foundation. . . . Evangelism is in the greatest peril it has ever been. . . . Only the Lord knows how it hurts me to see the harm that Billy Graham is doing.

Billy Graham is a charming personality. There is nothing personal between us and never has been. I do not say that he is intentionally tearing down the evangelistic house. I think he has probably sold himself on what he is doing, but he is wrong—dead wrong. I would not stand in his shoes and take the responsibility for the consequences of what he is doing for all that this world can give any man.

Let me say that I am familiar with the set up in New York. I have been in touch with that section for many years. I spoke for seven consecutive years under Tent Evangel in New York. It so happened that my last year there, a newspaper man from the South put my meetings in the headlines of the first pages of the New York papers; and we could not seat the crowds. I could hardly get within a block of the tent. New York was even then and is now filled with hungry hearts. I have carefully investigated reports about how the campaign of Billy is set up in New York, and it is a direct violation of Scripture.

Billy Graham needs to stop and think. "*It is not right to do wrong to get a chance to do right.*" It is not right to violate the clear teaching of the Word of God to get a chance to preach the Gospel. God wants all people to have the Gospel more than Billy wants them to have it, but God's Word tells us *how not* to give the Gospel as clearly as it tells us how to give the Gospel.

I am convinced that when you consider the publicity, the way the work is headlined, the crowds that are being drawn, and the money that is being spent, Billy Graham is having possibly the smallest percentage of conversions of any evangelist who has lived for fifty years or any evangelist who is living today and is being sponsored by orthodox, Bible-believing pastors and churches. When the returns come in, we are going to find that some of these "little" men you have never heard of and whose budgets are not heavy and who never make the headlines have led more people to Jesus Christ than Billy Graham is leading.

Billy Graham could have gone to New York under the sponsorship of the conservatives that did all they could to get him, and he could have given a strong evangelistic leadership to the Bible-believing pastors and churches and could have done the greatest job that has ever been done in America. My friends who are on the inside have told me the story of how they did all they could to get him. The liberals did not invite Billy Graham to New York. The conservatives invited him; but Billy's organization, by its pressure, brought the modernists into the picture; and the hearts of some of the dearest friends I have in the New York area are broken. They are not unreasonable men. They are good people. They love the Lord. Some of them were keeping the evangelistic fires burning before Billy Graham was ever born.

A preacher from New York—an old-time, intelligent, orthodox preacher— called long distance, telling Dr. Bob how distressed he was about the meeting. "We are in a terrible fix in New York," he said. "The Protestant Council is in power. We orthodox preachers and laymen who went into the meeting are discredited and the leaders of the Protestant Council have completely taken over New York City. They are going so far as to get all the independent, Christian radio programs off the air."

With all his heart Dr. Bob believed that God was laying at his door the responsibility of spearheading a crusade against this evil trend. To this seasoned evangelist, a man's orthodoxy should be like Caesar's wife's virtue—beyond question! "If there is a question about a man's orthodoxy," he said, "he is either tainted with liberalism, doctrinally ignorant, or an out-right compromiser."

In October, 1957, Dr. Bob had to go to the hospital for an operation. He was a good patient, and proved a real blessing to the doctors and nurses. He often quoted the verse, "And we know that all things work together for good to them that love God, to them who are the called according to his purpose" (Romans 8:28). During his recuperation he had time to study this compromised evangelism from every angle. He said, "When I get my strength back, I am going to focus my attention more and more on soul winning, scripturally organized and scripturally emphasized."

Dr. Bob was in the hospital on his seventy-fourth birthday. Many friends around the country sent letters and flowers. Dr. Rice sent beautiful red roses and a wonderful letter stating:

> On your birthday I want to say again how grateful I am for your steadfastness, your staying true to Christ at any cost, through these years. You have been a great comfort to me, and an encouragement. Better yet, thank God, you have inspired thousands of other ministers to stay true to Christ, whatever the cost. Your ministry goes on in the ministry of thousands of others. You have much reason to be happy and grateful on your birthday.

Billy Graham and some of his group sent Dr. Bob a telegram and some flowers. Dr. Bob felt that in their hearts they knew that they were wrong in the unscriptural and unholy alliances they were making, but he did not have any hope that they would change. He said:

> From all the information I have been able to get, they have set their "course" and they mean to go through with it regardless of how much it might grieve the Holy Spirit or hurt the Cause of Christ.

Other Campaigns

By Billy's own admission, his sponsorship in Glasgow, Scotland, was more liberal than in New York. The campaign in San Francisco was much more open in its modernistic alliances than was the New York campaign. Billy's actions warranted the accusation that he was less and less interested in fundamentalism. He had gone on record that he was not a fundamentalist and that God had "by-passed fundamentalists." It seemed that as far as Billy was concerned, fundamentalists could "go jump in the river."

During the Los Angeles campaign hosts of people were swept off their feet because they did not know the true issues of the day. They had either been blinded and could not see them, or else they deliberately refused to see the dangers. To sell the setup to the Los Angeles people, Billy brought in one of the men who had been active in the New York meeting. However, many of Dr. Bob's boys were on the West coast, and these "boys" knew the issues and were able to give the facts.

A woman who took part in the Los Angeles meeting said to me:

> I am a Christian woman, and I wanted to help in the Billy Graham crusade. I was heartbroken when I saw how the converts were channeled into modernistic churches. I tried to work as a counsellor; but we did not have time to channel the people into the right churches. Then, too, the masses were deceiving. A group of advisors and a counsellor would go forward with each convert—at least two for one. Many came forward because of burdens on their hearts rather than because of any conviction of sin; and this accounts for the very few that really stick. It always seemed like a Hollywood sensational affair. All churches closed on Sunday nights and they would send out buses to swell the crowds. They would sell candy, gum, and cigarettes on Sunday nights in the lobby.

Everywhere Billy held meetings, the answers were the same: "The conservatives were left out and the liberals were **exalted**."

Dr. Bob said:

> The sad part about the thing is that Billy has been led and encouraged by certain men to take the wrong stand, and many of them were of the National Association of Evangelicals. Some who were intellectually proud and

were self-seeking to the point where they would not positively stand for anything where it cost them to do so. There were others who had always been strong in their loyalty to the Scripture, aggressive in its defense, and had zeal for lost souls who had also been blinded and deceived, and their influence was more effective and therefore did more harm. These men will have to share in Billy's disobedience to God's Word.

Dr. Victor Sears commented:

No tool for this day has ever been more molded and sharpened to the cause of Satan to deceive people than Billy Graham. This is true because of the great acceptance of Billy's message and leadership by the multitudes. The philosophy of the day seems to be an unusual emotionalization over Billy. People can say anything about Jesus and get by with it, but they cannot say one word against Billy Graham and get by with it.

At our 1968 Bible Conference, Dr. Ian R. K. Paisley from Ireland said:

This ecumenical movement is sweeping in like a mighty tide, and Billy Graham is doing much to bring it about. Instead of opposing these liberals, Billy plays up to them. Elijah, instead of flirting with the prophets of Baal, cut off their heads. God called His people to come out and be separate; Billy feels that he must bring them together. Moses took reproach rather than the treasures of Egypt. Billy could not take reproach for Christ's sake. If Billy could have asked, "Who is on the Lord's side?" he would have seen that these apostates were not on the Lord's side. Their only motive was to control Billy and his meetings. I would rather be jailed than be in the camp of this apostate group.

Dr. Archer Weniger said:

The ecumenical movement is nothing but the Social Gospel, which is socialism. It is doing more to damn our nation than anything else. They are mutilating the Bible, minimizing sin, humanizing Christ and deifying man. These ecumenical preachers cannot preach, for they have nothing to preach. They go out and get others to do their preaching. They saw in Billy Graham a champion.

Dr. Bob Wells said:

The people flock to hear Billy because he tickles their ears. There is no real meat in Billy's messages, and the latest thing is that Billy claims it is not the job of the evangelists to preach on the blood. It is the job of the pastor to do that, he says. God's Word says, "Without the shedding of blood is no remission." If it is not the evangelist's job to preach the blood, whose job is it? This is just Billy's excuse for not preaching it himself.

Some people, of course, warned Dr. Bob to "go easy" on Billy and his compromised evangelism. They said that it would hurt Bob Jones University. But Dr. Bob had never felt more led of the Lord to oppose anything than to oppose this movement. He told Mrs. Jones that he must take this stand even if it cost him hundreds of students and his closest friends. He had not fought for God's Cause for fifty years without sensing the dangers of any movement that would oppose it. Bob Jones University is God's school, and Dr. Bob knew that the Lord would not let anything hurt His school against His will.

People frequently would ask, in defense of Billy's compromise, *"What about the souls that are being saved?"* On the surface this sounds good. But as one saint of God answered, "Think of the thousands that are being damned while a few are being saved." Dr. Bob made this comparison:

> Suppose I have a beautiful garden, and you are a fruit gatherer, and you tell me that you will gather my fruit. I go away on a trip. You gather the fruit and pile it in the corner. It looks good. But when I go out into my orchard, I find that my trees are ruined. The limbs are broken, there is damaged bark on the trunks, and the roots are damaged and exposed. My trees begin to die, and there is no more fruit. That is the harm that Billy is doing future evangelism.

Finally, *critics began to accuse Dr. Bob of being a jealous old man.* Let us analyze this.

(1) Could a man of Dr. Bob's background of adhering to the fundamentals of the faith have been jealous of someone who handled those fundamentals loosely? Dr. Bob said:

> Billy does not have one thing I want, and I would not trade places with him for all the prestige or money the world has to offer. We are living in bad days when infidels cannot only be heard, but they can get a following. Hell is not going to be hot enough for these men who deny the Word of God. The Bible says it would be far better if a millstone were tied around their necks and they be thrown into the bottomless pit. Instead of condemning these men for their infidelity, Billy insists on being sponsored and promoted by these godless apostates and infidels.

(2) Could Dr. Bob have been jealous of Billy's consorting with men who scorned the fundamentals of the faith and presenting them as God's prophets or warriors of the faith? Dr. Bob said:

> Whereas Paul asked God to curse these folks who perverted the Gospel, Billy praises and promotes them. Billy's compromised evangelism is a far cry from the old reformers like John Wesley who split heads with his straight Gospel preaching.

(3) Could a man as consistent as Dr. Bob have been jealous of a man of changing moods? Several years ago when the first ecumenical meeting convened, Billy expressed the opinion that "it could be the forerunner

of the Antichrist." Later, in San Francisco, Billy put his arms around Bishop James A. Pike, Dr. Eugene Carson Blake, and others, and invoked God's blessing on these men and on the ecumenical movement. He expressed the comment that this second ecumenical meeting could be a "second Pentecost."

At the outset of his ministry Billy courted the favor and support of Dr. Bob, Bob, Jr., Dr. John Rice, Judge Bennet, and other fundamentalists. Later he turned to Dr. Vincent Peale, Dr. Bonnell, Bishop Pike, Bishop Gerald Kennedy, and others of their ilk. Dr. Bob was disheartened at the way Billy changed his opinion of men. Billy began to speak of Dr. E. Stanley Jones—a man who denies the inspiration of Scripture and is the leader among liberals—as his great friend and adviser.

Billy commended the Episcopal Church of California for having such a wonderful spiritual leader as Bishop James A. Pike to head up their work. Later, when Billy's biography was released, this "wonderful friend" was conspicuous in his absence. Why was this? Could it have been because of unfavorable reports of this man whom formerly he had praised? Several other omissions in the biography seemed controlled to project an image of Billy that would disprove some of the things true men of God were saying of him.

God is not the author of confusion. He would not cause a man to have a right opinion today, and a wrong one tomorrow. When a man is changeable, how does one know which opinion to trust? God's men who follow His way always follow a consistent path and their trumpets give a "certain" sound. Billy is having to find out the hard way that the discerning men who had tried to warn him about Pike and such men knew what they were talking about.

(4) Could Dr. Bob, who fought the World Council and the National Council of Churches throughout his ministry, have been jealous of the way Billy was playing up to these groups, speaking before them and promoting them? I answer an unequivocal NO! These groups claim to represent millions of people. They are trying to control institutions and remove fundamentalists from radio stations. Dr. Bob would have had no part in their evil doings.

THE GREENVILLE NEWS, in an article headlined "SECRET ECUMENICAL CONCLAVE ASK CUBA BE RECOGNIZED," March 8, 1968, page 14, stated:

> The General Board of the National Council of Churches meeting in San Diego last month recommended seating Red China in the United Nations. And recognizing Castro's Cuba and accepting the communist government of East Germany.

The Board also called for a change in American foreign policy with the United States giving up "unilateral action" or sovereignty and be subject to international agreement.

One man of God said:

Billy Graham has been taken over by the NCC, doing untold harm to God's Cause. This inclusivist evangelism or ecumenical evangelism, as it has now come to be called, is being used to build the National Council of Churches and to defend it when men arise with their criticisms.

Dr. G. Paul Musselman, executive director of the Department of Evangelism of the National Council, gave this commendation of Billy: "I call Billy the newest and the greatest of the ecumenical voices."

Following Dr. Graham's crusade in Chicago, several leading liberals in that area said, "We are grateful for all that Billy Graham is doing, for wherever he goes he is building the ecumenical movement all over the world."

(5) Dr. Bob surely could not have been jealous of Billy's efforts in foreign lands. Dr. Bob had preached around the world with eternal success. Wherever Billy went, the answer was always the same:

"People now go to any church without suspicion as to false doctrine, and the mingling of so-called evangelicals with the apostates is now without restriction. Nothing we have ever seen has set back the work of the Lord as has the Billy Graham visit."

A missionary in Japan said that for months his group had taught people the difference between fundamentalism and modernism. They had alerted the people to a certain liberal who was doing much harm. "But when we took these converts to the Graham meeting," this missionary said, "there sat Kagawa on the platform, smiling out at the audience. Down the drain, in a few minutes, went all the good we had built up over a long time." Other missionaries in Japan expressed the opinion that the stand which Dr. Bob, Dr. Bob, Jr., Dr. Rice and others had taken in America had brought the matter somewhat to a climax in Japan and that a group of people there had made a very clear agreement that they would not cooperate except with those who agreed to the statement: "I believe in the Bible as the only inspired and infallible Word of God, our only rule of faith and practice."

Clippings sent in from the Glasgow, Scotland, newspaper during the "Tell Scotland" campaign, bemoaned the modernistic setup and stated that those who were "sound in the Word" took a stand against the meeting because of its involvement with modernism. Newspaper clippings from Australia questioned:

If Billy has no intentions of preaching against the sins of Australia and considers America's sins so very bad, why did he bother to go to Australia? Wouldn't he have done much better to stay in America and preach where he is needed?

In London Billy was questioned by a three-man panel on the British Broadcasting Corporation. These men asked why he projected his own image instead of the image of Christ.

(6) Dr. Bob certainly could not have been jealous of Billy's unsuccessful venture into the field of education. Both Dr. Bob and his son were delighted when Dr. W. B. Riley chose Billy to succeed him as president of Northwestern Schools, for at that time Billy was holding true to God's Word. At a Memorial Service for Dr. Riley at the First Baptist Church, Billy is quoted to have said:

I believe in everything that Dr. Riley believes. He constantly warned me in his last months of ever compromising one point as far as the Gospel is concerned or doing that which would dishonor my Lord.

Feeling that with his personality and opportunities Billy could do exploits for God IF HE WOULD STAY TRUE TO HIM, the Joneses brought Billy to one of our Commencements and conferred on him an honorary degree. Dr. Bob commented:

If Billy will just go ahead and preach a positive Gospel, be humble, not strain after headlines, not go too fast making contacts that he should not make, he can be used mightily for God as a headline man for evangelism in this nation. I do not think there is a man on earth who has the opportunity that Billy Graham has to do so much for evangelism or who is in a position to do more harm.

(7) Any one who knew Dr. Bob—even slightly—would know that he could never have been jealous of Billy's sellout to the Catholics. In 1928 Dr. Bob had done all he could to keep Al Smith out of the White House. He felt that our country would not be safe in the hands of a Catholic President. He said, "The Pope's voice is the voice of God to Catholics. The Catholic Church has full power of jurisdiction over all its faithful members, and it has the duty to guide and direct them in action and the right to intervene even in the political field." Billy had said, "I feel much closer to Roman Catholic tradition than to some of the more liberal Protestants." Dr. Bob wondered that Billy could not see the dangers of the Catholic machine.

Billy's sellout to Romanism is apparent in an article from the BLU-PRINT, Vol. XV., No. 38, October 6, 1964. The article was entitled "*Cardinal Cushing Endorses Graham.*" THE WICHITA BEACON, September 15, 1964, the BLU-PRINT said, reported:

> Cardinal Cushing, archbishop of Boston, said Graham's preaching "will surely be of great importance for many Christians in the Boston area. I rejoice with my Protestant brothers and neighbors upon this occasion . . . and although we Catholics do not join them in body, yet in spirit and heart we unite with them in praying God's blessing upon his Christian and Christ-like experience in our community.

Opinions expressed by Catholic leaders are significant. I quote from a letter written by the executive vice-president of Belmont Abbey College, Belmont, North Carolina, dated March 19, 1965:

> Dear Mr. . . . I am the one who, being acquainted with Billy Graham, invited him to speak to the Fathers, the Nuns, students and invited guests, and I am pleased to reply to your inquiries.
>
> Billy Graham gave an inspiring and a theologically sound address that may have been given by Bishop Fulton J. Sheen or any other Catholic preacher. I have followed Billy Graham's career and I must emphasize that he has been more Catholic than otherwise, and I say this not in a partisan manner but as a matter of fact.
>
> Knowing the tremendous influence of Billy Graham among Protestants and now the realization and acknowledgment among Catholics of his devout and sincere appeal to the teachings of Christ which he alone preaches, I would state that he could bring Catholics and Protestants together in a healthy ecumenic spirit.
>
> I was the first Catholic to invite Billy Graham; I know he will speak at three other Catholic universities next month; I believe he will be invited by more Catholic colleges in the future than Protestant colleges.
>
> So I am well pleased, then, to answer your question: Billy Graham is preaching a moral and evangelical theology most acceptable to Catholics.
>
> Very Sincerely yours, /S/ Cuthbert E. Allen, O.S.B.

Then this Catholic institution brought Billy back to Belmont Abbey and gave him an honorary degree.

On Thursday, May 5, 1966, the writer had an interesting conference with an ex-Catholic, who spoke of the dangers of the Catholic machine. He said:

> I have been a good friend of Billy Graham, and have given him a check each year. But when Billy, while in Boston, went to see Cardinal Cushing, I knew something was wrong. A thing like that just did not happen. I knew that Billy had "made a deal" when the Cardinal came out with a statement

that all Catholic children could go hear Billy — that he would never say anything that would hurt them in any way. I told Billy to his face that he had sold out completely and I would never give him another cent — not even a counterfeit dollar.

On page 1 of THE GREENVILLE PIEDMONT, November 19, 1967, it was stated:

"Today," Graham said, "religion is front page news around the world. What is happening in the ecumenical revolution is of interest to people all around the world — to Catholics, Protestants, Jews, and even Buddhists.

"This is the beginning of something so fantastic it could change all of Christendom and will affect you, your children, and their children." He ended up his talk by saying he considered his first talk at a Catholic institution as "a very important part of his ministerial career."

(8) Finally, no uncompromising minister in his right mind would be jealous of a man who leads other men astray. Many people felt that Billy was influencing others. His own alma mater — Wheaton College — seemed to be drifting further afield. Dr. Bob said:

By the great extent of Billy's compromise and his influence he has put a blight on so many different institutions and people, that Youth For Christ is not what it was before Billy came along. We will never know this side of eternity the harm that Billy has done.

Every move seemed to bring closer the ecumenical movement that God's people felt Billy was trying to bring about. Dr. Bob Jones, Jr., said:

You have no more right to join up with the devil's crowd, God's enemies, than you have to join up with a pagan communistic government.

Oh, the tragedy of it all! If only Billy, years ago, had heeded Dr. Bob's admonition:

You have a chance to do something for God, if you will stay true. You can be used mightily for Him. I do not think there is any man on earth who has the opportunity to do as much good or who is in a position to do more harm.

JEALOUS? Dr. Bob was jealous for nothing but God's Word; and when anyone attacked that Word, Dr. Bob had no thought except to fight and die, if need be, in defense of it and the Faith.

Greenville Invasion of 1966

When Billy decided to "invade Greenville," as some people expressed it, many people felt that his motive—in part, at least—was to embarrass Bob Jones University and to discredit an old warrior who had stood the gaff, never faltering in his effort to hold things in line for God. Dr. Bob, Jr., wondered "why Greenville, South Carolina, such a small town, is the only one that Billy is going to in 1966."

On Friday morning, March 4, 1966, at the top of page 38 in THE GREENVILLE NEWS there was a four-column spread in large letters:

BOB JONES SAYS BILLY GRAHAM DOING MORE HARM TO THE CAUSE OF CHRIST THAN ANY LIVING MAN

The article stated:

Dr. Bob Jones, Jr., lashed back at Dr. Billy Graham yesterday in a "non-personal" controversy with Graham over his theology.

In a statement prepared prior to his departure yesterday for New York and a tour to the Holy Land, Dr. Jones replied to Dr. Graham's remarks made at a press conference Wednesday in which Dr. Graham said he really didn't know what had accounted for a split between him and his old alma mater and the Joneses.

"The objection," said Dr. Jones, "is purely on a scriptural basis." He said that in his opinion Dr. Graham "is doing more harm to the cause of Jesus Christ than any other living man."

A spokesman for Dr. Graham said at a late hour last night when asked about the Jones statement: "No comment."

The Jones statement . . . read as follows:

SCRIPTURAL BASIS CITED

"I am addressing this statement to the citizens of Greenville who are interested in the facts and to remind Dr. Graham that the objection of Bob Jones University to the Billy Graham crusade is purely on a scriptural basis. What Dr. Graham is doing is forbidden by the Bible, which we believe is the infallible and authoritative Word of God.

"The Bible commands that false teachers and men who deny the fundamentals of the faith should be accursed; that is, they shall be criticized and condemned. Billy approves them, Billy condones them, Billy recommends them.

"I have in my files a telegram which Billy Graham sent to the people of the First Methodist Church of Shreveport, recommending Bishop Kennedy, approving him when he was coming there for a crusade. Bishop Kennedy denies the virgin birth and the infallibility and authority of the Word of God. He is known religiously as a left-wing, liberal preacher.

"Billy has recommended Bishop Pike. He congratulated the people of California on this 'great spiritual leader.' He has had Bishop Pike pray over his crusade. He appears consistently on the National Council of Churches and the World Council of Churches. Billy calls these men 'great Christian leaders.' He says the World Council of Churches can bring a 'second pentecost.' God's Word says it is preparing the kingdom of Antichrist and the church of Antichrist.

"So we object to Billy and to what Billy is doing on the basis of the Word of God, which forbids it. There is nothing personal about this. It's purely a matter of obeying the Scripture.

SENDING OF CONVERTS: "Billy says he'll send his converts back to anybody—Catholic, Protestant, or Jewish. Well, we believe the Bible teaches separation on these points. We do not think it is right to send a man back to a false teacher or to a Unitarian Church if a man claims to be a Christian. We believe that man ought to be sent where he can be fed in the Word of God, and that is what the Word of God says.

"We've offered a thousand dollars to any man who can quote any Scripture that justifies what Billy Graham is doing in sending his converts back to unbelieving churches and to false teachers and Unitarians.

"Nobody has ever tried to accept the thousand dollars and win the prize. They can't do it because you can't find Scripture that contradicts Scripture, and the Scripture forbids what Dr. Graham is doing.

"So our objection is on the basis of his sponsorship, which is unscriptural, and on his practice of turning his converts back over to unscriptural churches and to false teachers, and recommending such men. I think that Dr. Graham is doing more harm in the cause of Jesus Christ than any living man; that he is leading foolish and untaught Christians, simple people that do not know the Word of God, into disobedience to the Word of God. That is wrong, and it is doubly wicked in that he is doing it under the pretext of being a soul-winning ministry."

At the close of the Greenville meeting, Dr. Bob Jones, Jr., commented:

The loyalty of our faculty was shown when Billy Graham's crusade came to Greenville. I think Dr. Graham came to Greenville to try to break down this opposition that has been a thorn in the flesh to him through the years. Although we love Billy personally, what he is doing is contrary to everything this University stands for as far as separation from apostasy is concerned. Billy knew we would take this stand, but he thought he would lick us. We had such a strong aggressive loyalty on the part of both students and faculty, the crusade did not hurt us.

Although in Greenville Billy seemed to "pad" his messages with more "meat" than usual, his crusade here was a far cry from real revival. This town was not changed, and the same sort of statements that had come out of other meetings were echoed here.

A woman from another city told the writer that she went to hear Dr. Graham "out of curiosity." She said:

I was appalled at what I saw and heard. I turned to a Baptist preacher and asked if he really thought the meeting was of God. He replied, "Do you have any special reason for asking that question?" "No, I really want to know if you think this type of meeting can be of God," she answered. The preacher shook his head and said, "No, it cannot be of God."

Another person said of the meeting:

If I want to go to church, I will go to church. If I want to go to a circus, I will go to a circus. Billy's meeting was nothing more than a show. One of my friends sang and got well paid for it. One of my devout friends went to one meeting and told me she had planned to attend several, but one was enough. I know of eight people who went forward, and each was asked what church he wanted to join rather than his reason for coming forward.

During the Greenville meeting two of the team made statements that were not accurate. First of all, when Billy was asked why Bob Jones University could not support his campaign, he answered, "I do not know." A leading businessman of this area remarked to me: "Isn't it too bad Billy is such a little boy that his father-in-law always has to do his speaking for him? And imagine his saying over television, 'I don't know why Bob Jones University cannot cooperate with my crusade.' Dr. Bob told me ten years ago that he had written Billy a letter repudiating his unholy alliances, including his liberal sponsorship."

Willis Haymaker made the statement that he got his training under Gypsy Smith, when as a matter of fact Dr. Bob had trained him. In the first article that stated that he received his training from Gypsy Smith, Dr. Bob was not even mentioned. Later, when it seemed to their advantage to do so, reference was made to Willis's having been with Dr. Bob.

I asked Mrs. Jones, Sr., about the early days when Willis Haymaker was with Dr. Bob. She answered:

I guess I know more about this than any living person, with the exception of my husband, who may not remember all the details that I do. [Dr. Bob was still living when I had this interview with Mrs. Jones.] Dr. Bob took Willis right after he was out of the Navy, as a lad of about eighteen. At first, my husband used Willis to stoke the furnaces. Willis was a bright young man; and as he grew, Dr. Bob encouraged him and gave him more and more responsibility. Under Dr. Bob's tutelage Willis developed until he became campaign manager, staying with Dr. Bob for approximately forty years. Billy wanted to use Willis because of his training under my husband. Willis was with Gypsy Smith only a short time.

On page 4 of THE GREENVILLE NEWS, Sunday, March 6, 1966, an article appeared from Montreat, North Carolina. "(AP) GRAHAM DEFENDED BY FATHER-IN-LAW." In this article Dr. Bell made an attack on Bob Jones, Jr., for his rebuke of Billy's disobedience to God's Word.

We must go back a few years to see what Dr. Bell is supposed to believe. The quotation below was written by Dr. Bell and appeared in the September 26, 1951, edition of the PRESBYTERIAN JOURNAL. In the first part of the article, Dr. Bell lamented the fact that some of the Presbyterian churches did not have evening services and that the members of these churches were not careful in selecting a good, Bible-believing church. He summed up his feelings in these words:

When erstwhile evangelical groups unite with Unitarians on a basis of equality it shows a loss of Christian conviction which but highlights the spirit of theological inclusiveness which is gradually destroying the influence of the church. How can Christians unite in worship with those who deny the deity of our Lord?

What do I consider the greater importance, a great organization or the content of the Christian faith itself? As desirable as a united Christian witness is—and we think it of the greatest importance—we believe such a witness can only be effective when based on unity of belief.

Dr. Bell also stated:

The primary task of the church is to preach Christ crucified, risen, and coming in triumph. What shall it profit in the church if she neglect this task or dilute the content of the message while helping usher in a world order still in the clutches of the devil?

Dr. Bell thought it "strange that Bob Jones should line up with the extremists against Billy's method of evangelism." I say that it is strange that Dr. Bell's eyes could be so blinded by his loyalty to his son-in-law that after years of speaking out boldly, saying that it was impossible to work with God's enemies, he has changed his mind and approves Billy's flirting with modernists, extreme liberals, and apostates. Things seem to have taken on a "new look": if anyone dares to lift his hand in defense of God's Word against compromised evangelism, he is viciously attacked by Dr. Bell. It is significant that Billy's crowd never picks on anybody but the fundamentalists, except for a few extreme liberals who have also spoken against Billy. They charge that we have conspired with these extreme liberals to hurt Billy.

In the BAPTIST BIBLE TRIBUNE, Friday, April 22, 1966, page 4, there was an article stating that the PRESBYTERIAN JOURNAL is a "one-way-street journal." The editor's note explains that a great deal has been published about the refusal of Bob Jones University to cooperate with the Billy Graham campaign in Greenville, South Carolina.

We give our readers authoritative documents which give the complete story. We give the facts. Our readers may reach their own conclusion on the basis of the facts. Incidentally, these documents show that if you get the facts in so important a matter as this, you will have to get them from some source other than journals of religion like the PRESBYTERIAN JOURNAL.

THE STORY PUBLISHED IN THE PRESBYTERIAN JOURNAL: Dual crusade sessions attended by 287,700. Greenville, S. C. — For the first time in an American campaign, Evangelist Billy Graham preached at dual services during his Southern Piedmont crusade here. Total attendance during the 10 days was 287,700. Decisions for Christ were registered by 7,311 during the services.

Seating was arranged for 21,000 in New Textile Hall, a large exhibit building. Crowds were turned away during the first weekend of the series, and the decision was made to conduct dual services during the last five days. Several near-capacity audiences attended after the new schedule began, and average daily attendance on the last five days was 30,000.

Criticisms of the evangelist were leveled at the beginning of the crusade by Bob Jones, Jr., president of Bob Jones University here. Mr. Graham refused to publicly answer the criticism. But from his home at Montreat, N. C., Dr. L. Nelson Bell, the evangelist's father-in-law, replied to both Dr. Jones and to Dr. Colin Williams, a National Council of Churches official who recently took exception to the Graham style of evangelism.

Dr. Bell said he would reply since Dr. Graham would not do so.

He likened the view of Dr. Jones, who had declared that Mr. Graham "is doing more harm to the cause of Jesus Christ than any other living man," to that of the Pharisees.

The view of Dr. Williams, who said in January that Mr. Graham's "traditional evangelism" is a "danger to the kingdom of God," was likened by Dr. Bell to that of the Sadducees.

According to Dr. Bell's statement, Dr. Williams "does not believe the Gospel which Mr. Graham preaches, nor does he believe in the conversion experience Mr. Graham says is the process by which a man becomes a Christian. Dr. Williams is like the many Sadducees who, rejecting the simple Gospel to be found in the Scriptures, reject those who preach it."

Of the other critic, Dr. Bell said, "Dr. Bob Jones' attack on Mr. Graham is similar to that of the Pharisees. He does not like the company Mr. Graham keeps, nor does he like Christian love being placed above hard orthodoxy. He is typical of the Pharisees of our day — legalists, who forget the greatest of all Christian virtues is love."

Dr. Bell continued: "These men, along with Mr. Graham, stand before God and He alone is the Judge. Furthermore, until Dr. Williams and Dr. Jones have something to show for their brand of Christianity which brings changed lives and new hope, one wonders if they would not be wise to keep quiet."

Dr. Smith quoted correspondence between Rev. G. Aiken Taylor, the PRESBYTERIAN JOURNAL and Dr. Jones, Jr.

BOB JONES' LETTER TO THE Presbyterian Journal

My dear Mr. Taylor: In the interest of fairness, I believe the enclosed letter should be carried in full. However, if your magazine lacks this sense of fair play, I am instructing you to carry the enclosed letter—preceded by this letter—as a paid advertisement in your next issue and authorize you to bill me for the same.

THE LETTER ADDRESSED TO THE Presbyterian Journal

My dear Mr. Taylor: Someone has sent me the clipping from page 5 of the March 23 issue of Presbyterian Journal in which it is stated, "Criticisms of the evangelist were leveled at the beginning of the crusade by Bob Jones, Jr., president of Bob Jones University here." This is followed by a considerable amount of space dealing with Dr. L. Nelson Bell's hysterical and illogical personal attack upon me.

It is most significant, however, that the Presbyterian Journal fails to set forth the basis for my objection to Dr. Graham's ministry and my "criticism" of it. I think in the interest of fairness you should carry in full the radio talk which I made in answer to Dr. Graham's false assertion that he did not know why Bob Jones University objected to his ministry.

[Dr. Jones' letter quoted the article which appears on page 297. For the sake of space, I shall omit it here.]

The Presbyterian Journal wrote in reply:

Dear Mr. Jones: I have your communication, just received, and hasten to reply.

I do not believe that anything constructive will be served, or the Lord's cause advanced by any prolongation of the matter covered by your letter. Consequently, I do not believe that we will want to use it in the Journal.

With best wishes in the Lord's service. . . .

"KNOWING ECCLESIASTICISM, BOB JONES IS NOT SURPRISED," Dr. Noel Smith wrote, as he quoted the next communication from Dr. Jones, Jr., to Rev. G. Aiken Taylor.

My dear Mr. Taylor: Your letter of March 30 is completely in character and just exactly the sort of thing I expected you to write. A man who is afraid to take a firm scriptural stand while at the same time talking about orthodoxy and pretending to defend it is, of course, not a logical thinker and would not be expected to have any sense of fair play and common decency.

I would like to inquire when any "constructive cause" was ever served by the Presbyterian Journal and whether you feel that the article to which we object served any "constructive purpose."

I was brought up to believe that any editor who published an attack upon a man and refused him the opportunity to answer it was a contemptible rascal and a lily-livered coward.

I find it very difficult to get away from my upbringing.

Dr. Carl McIntire in THE CHRISTIAN BEACON, March 17, 1966, also defended Dr. Jones, Jr., and Bob Jones University in its stand against Compromised Evangelism. The article follows:

BOB JONES, JR., CALLED "PHARISEE" IN GRAHAM DISPUTE

The press stories concerning Bob Jones, Jr., and Evangelist Billy Graham have brought again to public attention the serious issues that are raised by Evangelist Billy Graham's campaigns and compromises. Bob Jones, Jr., is right; Billy Graham is wrong on these questions of the demands of Scripture.

. . . . It is significant that Billy Graham does not answer directly. His father-in-law, Dr. L. Nelson Bell, takes the part. Dr. Graham has tried to evade these issues for many years by simply remaining silent, refusing to talk, thinking that in some way this would protect him in his inclusivist program. His compromise is with the clear commands of Scripture in regard to our fellowship and the work of the Lord. Also, Dr. Nelson Bell does not deal specifically with the questions raised by Dr. Bob Jones, Jr. He does not discuss Billy Graham's policy of turning converts back into the apostasy and into the National Council of the Churches of Christ in the U.S.A. and even into the Roman Catholic Church. He does not discuss Dr. Graham's policy of including top leaders of the National Council of Churches and well-known modernists on his platform and his sponsoring committees. Obviously they cannot be discussed directly and on their merits because this is true.

What then is the reply that Dr. Bell makes? It is an attack upon Dr. Jones, Jr., and what Dr. Bell represents as Dr. Jones' position—that of the Pharisees. It is an old strategy of debate, when you cannot answer an opponent's arguments or meet the charges which he makes, to try to discredit him by name-calling or other tactics.

Dr. Bell's reply is significant. First, he takes issue with a secretary on evangelism of the National Council of Churches whom he equates with the Sadducees who deny that Christ is the Son of God and attribute the Lord's miracles to Satan. All this does is to emphasize that the National Council of Churches is unworthy of the support of God-fearing people and should embarrass Dr. Graham for having their leaders on his platform and as members of his sponsoring committees. Yet, this, of course, justifies Dr. Jones in his statement. But the blasphemy of the "God-is-dead" theologians and the Bishop Pike repudiation of the Trinity and the virgin birth of Christ are so blatant today that even Dr. Graham finds himself embarrassed. It is this embarrassment which is getting worse and worse while Dr. Graham continues to carry on his inclusivist ecumenical evangelism. This, of course, admits the validity of Dr. Jones' criticism.

CHRISTIANITY TODAY, March 18, 1966, reports that Evangelist Billy Graham has accepted an invitation to be a luncheon speaker at the next General

Assembly of the National Council of Churches to be held in Miami, Fla., Dec. 5 to 9, 1966. CHRISTIANITY TODAY reported, "This will be the first time the nation's most widely known and respected churchman has been an NCC program participant."

Thus it would appear that Graham is going to have more fellowship with the Sadducees!

In regard to Dr. Jones himself—he turns out to be a Pharisee! Let us analyze specifically this accusation.

1. The Pharisee objected to Jesus Christ keeping company with publicans and sinners, not with the Sadducees. In fact, Jesus Christ did not keep company with the Sadducees at all. He denounced them, rebuked them. But Billy Graham does keep company with the modern Sadducees and has them on his sponsoring committees. Thus the Pharisees' criticism of Christ is here misapplied.

2. Dr. Bell touches the heart of the issue when he criticizes Jones thus, "nor does he like Christian love being placed above hard orthodoxy," and at this point Dr. Bell himself is in great difficulty and in real error. "Hard orthodoxy," so far as Dr. Jones is concerned, is just plain Christianity, the Gospel which cannot be compromised. It is the "hard orthodoxy" of Dr. Jones which generates and produces love; you cannot separate love from it. Paul did not have the love of Christ which constrained him until first he had the Christ who died on the cross and was raised from the dead. So, Dr. Bell again is confused and he alleges Dr. Jones "is typical of the Pharisees of our day—legalists, who forget the greatest of all Christian virtues is love." Thus love is used in this instance as a weapon to soften men's obedience to Christ and their commitment to the trust of the Gospel. At this point Dr. Bell himself is over on the side of the liberals who are constantly attacking the fundamentalists for being too rigid and lacking love. But the Gospel does not bend and no one was more rigid than our Saviour when He said, "I am the way, the truth, and the life; no man cometh unto the Father, but by me."

Yet, in these matters Dr. Jones is not a Pharisee; he occupies the position of Jesus Christ which led Christ to denounce and repudiate the Pharisees. The application of the phrase, the Pharisee, therefore, to Dr. Jones is inappropriate and false.

Moreover, at this point we are face to face with the realities of Billy Graham's "ecumenical evangelism" in which he also welcomes the Pharisees into his sponsorship. His policy of going into a community and asking the support of all the groups includes the support of both the Pharisees and the Sadducees. If Billy Graham will include the Pharisees, how then can his spokesman, Dr. Bell, write in this manner? Would Jones be any less a Pharisee if he joined in the Graham campaigns?

Dr. Bell continues: "As is usually true with the Pharisees, Dr. Jones resorted to only half truths in his attack on Mr. Graham." No, what Dr. Jones said about Dr. Graham and his sponsorship and his placing of his converts is not a half-truth. It is a basic part of Graham's whole strategy of evangelizing. Dr. Jones told the truth.

What then is the half truth here referred to? Dr. Bell proceeds to defend

Dr. Graham from the reference to Bishop Pike. Dr. Jones quoted the story that referred to Bishop Pike of California, a leader of the National Council of Churches and the World Council of Churches. At this point Dr. Bell has many WCC leaders he needs to defend. We would like very much to see his defense of Billy Graham's association with the Archbishop of Canterbury who thinks some present-day atheists are going to be in Heaven.

Now it is argued, "Neither Mr. Graham nor the local committee knew at that time that Bishop Pike was later to renounce much of the Christian faith." But Bishop Pike had renounced his Christian faith long before. The NEW YORK TIMES, February 22, 1954, carried the headline, "Dean Pike Calls Peace With God Heaven, Just As Not Being Right With Lord Is Hell." The NEW YORK TIMES, Monday, March 23, 1959, gave a four-column head to a story on "Christ in Jeans," a modern version of the crucifixion and resurrection presented by Bishop Pike's radio program. There was hardly any resurrection to it.

Pike's modernism has been his chief trademark.

Moreover, in 1960, when the National Council of Churches met in San Francisco and Dr. Eugene Carson Blake spoke in Bishop Pike's pulpit and announced his church union program, that very afternoon Evangelist Billy Graham also stood in the same pulpit along with Bishop Pike and was featured in a service related to the National Council of Churches.

What we like about this aspect of Dr. Bell's reply is that he is definitely yielding to the concepts of Scripture which are clear that God's people ought not to be in fellowship with such unbelievers as Bishop Pike. It is this position in Scripture that Dr. Jones stands upon and is seeking to honor in what he has said about Billy Graham. Here again Dr. Bell is retreating in his reply to a position which actually does vindicate Dr. Bob Jones, and does not help Graham.

We congratulate Dr. Jones for raising these issues again and in drawing from Dr. Bell a statement which enables Christian people everywhere to see that all the zeal of Graham and his many World Council companions cannot justify or fill up the measure of his disobedience. The operation of his campaigns, the confusion which is produced, and the thousands of people who are misled concerning the great issues of the Gospel and the program of the great apostasy are indeed aiding in developing the one-world church! Graham's contribution to the production of this Babylon of the last days is indeed great. God's commands are, "Wherefore come out from among them . . . and touch not the unclean thing." Graham's inclusivism is filled with all manner and degrees of devices of "touching." His Gospel trumpet knows not the call of separation from apostasy, the National Council of Churches, and the World Council of Churches.

Under the headline, "DR. BILLY GRAHAM . . ." in THE SWORD OF THE LORD, Friday, May 6, 1966, Dr. John R. Rice had this to say:

Early in March Dr. Billy Graham had a campaign in Greenville, S. C., in the new Textile Hall. That stirs memories for this editor, since some six-teen or eighteen years ago I had a city-wide campaign in the old Textile

Hall in Greenville, with great blessing and many saved. Of course, the difference is that my campaign was sponsored by Bible-believing churches only. No modernist was invited to sponsor the meeting or help control it or to sit on the platform and lead in prayer, and the wicked unbelief of those who deny the virgin birth, the inspiration of the Bible, the deity of Christ, was openly denounced from the pulpit. So, of course, in all my campaigns and in all the campaigns of . . . old-time evangelists including Billy Sunday, R. A. Torrey, Dr. Bob Jones, Sr., etc.

In the Billy Graham campaign, modernists were invited, were on the committee, and the out-and-out fundamental churches in the area were not even invited to participate. . . .

. . . . We are glad for anybody to be invited to hear the Gospel. We are not glad for infidels to be called Christians. We are not glad for new converts to be turned over to Catholics and false cults and to infidel churches which are openly on record as enemies of the Bible and denying the deity, the virgin birth, bodily resurrection, and the blood atonement of Christ. We want all to hear the Gospel, but we do not want any infidel to be patted on the back and called "brother" and put in charge to help control and sponsor a revival campaign, or to run a local church, or to preach in a pulpit, or to teach in a Christian school, or in any otherwise to be counted as a Christian when he is not.

Since the Billy Graham organization, publicly, on the radio and on television and in the daily press, attacked Bob Jones University, accusing them of hypocrisy and of being "Pharisees," and since Dr. Graham publicly said he did not know why Dr. Bob Jones and the University would not cooperate and since paid propagandists of Dr. Graham have misled the people and slandered the University, it seems wise here to give news reports of the campaign and call attention to the fundamental stand of Bible believers against yoking up with infidels.

Dr. Graham claims to be a Bible believer, and we trust he is. He ought not to yoke up with those who are against the Bible, even though it gets him bigger crowds and more financial support. We think he does not get as many people saved as he would get saved by obeying the Bible and being true to the whole Gospel and the command of Jesus to "Beware of false prophets" (Matthew 7:15), and the command to "earnestly contend for the faith" (Jude 3), and the command to have no "fellowship with the unfruitful works of darkness, but rather reprove them" (Ephesians 5:11). We are not against revivals when we say what the Bible so clearly commands, that we are not to take unsaved people, even infidels, into our churches or pulpits as Christians, are not to be yoked up with enemies of the Bible, deniers of Christ.

Note carefully, good Bible-believing Christians say it is wrong to turn God's work over to unsaved unbelievers or have them sponsor and control churches or revivals.

Dr. Rice quotes an article from Time magazine, "DR. GRAHAM'S GREENVILLE CAMPAIGN," with the subheading "Boycotting Billy." Point by point he exposes the errors in this article and shows that the

Billy Graham team dodges the true issue. The last paragraph summarizes it:

> The true issue was that the campaign was sponsored and controlled by those who do not believe the Bible, do not believe in the virgin birth of Christ, His bodily resurrection, His blood atonement, and the Bible-believing, fundamental Christians were—some of them—intentionally left out of the campaign, not even invited to attend and others were played down to get the support of modernists and denominational leaders, Catholics and cults. Dr. Graham and his paid workers made no issue of all the other churches which cooperated in the campaign that are separated and do not have Negro members. Why should they pretend that desegregation was an issue with the University? It was never mentioned in connection with the Billy Graham campaign by the University. It was mentioned by the Billy Graham workers, evidently with the intention of avoiding the issue of being true to the Bible, having only born-again Christians who believe the Bible to sponsor and run the campaign.

With regard to Billy's cooperation with the Catholics, Dr. Rice wrote:

> Interestingly enough, Billy Graham's claim that his compromise is effective in winning men to Christ is not true. In fact, Earl Heffner, writing in THE CHARLOTTE OBSERVER of Dr. Graham's sermon at the Benedictine Belmont Abbey College under the headline, BILLY WINS CATHOLICS TO BILLY, said: "Baptist evangelist Billy Graham may not have won any Catholic converts to Protestantism Monday night, but he won a number of them to Billy Graham."

> If Dr. Graham does not agree with Catholics "in the joining of One Church," why does he by his presence and his words endorse the efforts of the World Council of Churches, which apostate organization has plainly declared that its purpose is the building of a One-World Church including Catholics and Protestants?

> Dr. Graham has put himself in the position where he cannot warn anyone against infidel churches, Seventh-Day Adventist churches, cultist groups, and other unscriptural religious organizations teaching what the Bible calls "damnable heresies," because the pastors of those churches are on Graham's sponsoring committee.

T. W. Wilson and Dr. Bob's Funeral

I do not feel that this section would be complete without some mention of an incident that occurred in connection with Dr. Bob's funeral. The Billy Graham team, as well as individual members of the team, sent flowers. Our radio station received an ASSOCIATED PRESS release which stated that the team would be represented at the funeral by T. W. Wilson. No one had consulted us about this matter; and in view of former relations between T. W. and Dr. Bob, it seemed insensitive and callous.

As a background to this incident, let us go back a few years to a conversation in the Dining Common of Bob Jones University. T. W. dropped by for a visit, and I took him to my table at lunch. My wife and I were somewhat surprised during the meal to hear T. W. speak disparagingly of Billy Graham. T. W. impugned Billy's motive for being in "big-time" evangelism. He laughingly told us that in Florida a girl had spurned Billy, telling him that he would "never amount to anything." Billy decided to show that girl whether or not he would ever amount to anything, T. W. said, and to make her sorry that she had turned him down. There were other points in which he questioned Billy's motives and practices, and he said that he did not feel that he could be connected with the organization. Soon after this, however, T. W. was connected with it and enthusiastic in Billy's favor. He took Dr. Bob, Sr., to task in a strong letter for his attitude toward Billy's ministry. How unkind and unscriptural—rebuking an elder who had invested time, money, training, prayer, and concern in T. W. and in other Graham team members! Certainly Dr. Bob did not deserve that letter.

Of all the Graham team, I suppose T. W. had been perhaps, Dr. Bob's favorite. I wish I had time to go back to Cleveland days and tell of Dr. Bob's interest in T. W., and not only Dr. Bob's but also Mrs. Jones' interest and concern. If I were T. W. Wilson, I would not want his last letter to Dr. Bob on my conscience; it would grieve me the rest of my days. But when a man stills his conscience with regard to going against God in an unholy alliance in evangelism, it is not surprising that he could dull his conscience with regard to his treatment of God's man.

Bob, Jr., realizing the far-reaching effects of such a letter on T. W., wrote and urged T. W. to apologize to Dr. Bob. "The letter will be a hindrance to you after my father is gone," Bob told T. W. But T. W. never replied to Bob's letter, and he never wrote an apology to Dr. Bob.

In view of this situation, Bob, Jr., when he heard from WMUU that T. W. would represent the team at Dr. Bob's funeral, felt constrained to send T. W. a long telegram that he was not welcome at Dr. Bob's funeral. Dr. Bob, Jr., was right in his attitude. In the first place, I do not see how or why T. W. could or should be at the last rites for a man he had addressed in such an unkind manner. I quote Bob's telegram. Parenthetically, it should be pointed out that the Graham organization appointed T. W. Wilson to be their representative at Dr. Bob's funeral knowing full well that he was *persona non grata* as far as the Jones' family was concerned. Here is the telegram:

Dr. T. W. Wilson
Montreat, North Carolina
January 16, 1968

See from the papers that you are representing the Graham organization
at the funeral. In view of the vicious letter you wrote my father some years
ago, a man who had done everything for you, the family prefers that you
not attend the funeral. Your presence here would be sheer hypocrisy, and
we have no wish to be a party to providing a cloak of respectability to a man
who stabbed his benefactor in the back. If someone else from the Graham
organization chooses to come, that is up to him; but you are not welcome at
my father's funeral as a representative of the Graham organization or as a
private individual. When my father's heart had been broken by your wicked
and unkind letter, I wrote you without his knowledge and urged you for
the sake of your own conscience to apologize while he was still living. We
do not want you coming to stand with pious pretense over his casket now. —

Bob Jones, Jr.

When I think of the "pious" and "loving" men who condemn and
oppose the stand of such uncompromising servants of the Lord as Dr.
Bob Jones, Dr. John R. Rice, and others, I feel a holy distaste. Men who
talk love from their lips but whose hearts prompt them to act unkindly —
many times in sort of an undercover — may look good on the surface
and in the eyes of non-discerning men; but to Bible-believing, Bible-
obeying people, they have about them an odor of compromise and
hypocrisy which is offensive to spiritual people and must be a stench in
the nostrils of Almighty God.

No Formal Ending

That there is no formal ending to this chapter is deliberate. I feel
that this leaven of compromised evangelism will continue to work. We
cannot stop the apostasy, it is true. Nevertheless, God has called us to
"earnestly contend for the faith" and to separate ourselves from that
which opposes His Word, His Son, and His Cause; and even though Dr.
Bob has gone to be with the Lord, he "being dead, yet speaketh" through
the written words he has left and through the multiplied thousands he
has influenced to take their stand on the right side of the issue. Almost
any man with the "right backing" can "*sell*" himself; it is our desire to
"sell" the Lord Jesus Christ to lost men and women and "sell" Christians
on taking a proper stand, whatever the issue may be.

CHAPTER 2

Short-Term Conferences

In Dr. Bob's early evangelistic campaigns he had been accustomed to large campaigns of six weeks or longer, but as conditions worsened around the country he conceived the idea of short-term conferences. In this way he could get to more places and could acquaint more preachers with the true conditions, strengthen them in the faith, and instruct them in effective means of conducting evangelistic services.

These short-term meetings in turn led to the establishment of the one-day conferences for which Dr. Bob and Dr. John R. Rice became so noted. The association between Dr. Bob and Dr. Rice dates back to 1937 when Dr. Rice—at that time pastor of the Fundamental Baptist Tabernacle in Dallas, Texas—and a group of fundamental, premillennial pastors in the area banded together to bring in some faithful Bible teachers, pastors, and evangelists for special Sunday afternoon services. Dr. Bob was one of the speakers they invited. I believe that God brought Dr. Bob and Brother John together to do a job that needed to be done in the field of evangelism. With their warm evangelistic hearts and their uncompromising stand, they could do much to sound the alarm and alert other God-fearing preachers to the dangers that threatened evangelism.

In 1942 Dr. Rice visited Bob Jones College in Cleveland, Tennessee, and was delighted with the spirit he found there. Dr. Rice's slant on spiritual matters impressed Dr. Bob very much, and he said to Dr. Rice: "There is so much let-up and compromise in our land today, it is refreshing to know that there are still a few men like you left who will not trim the sails." Later Dr. Bob commented, "I think that Dr. Rice and I are more thoroughly agreed on all 'principle' matters than any other men in the world. I depend on him more, believe in him more strongly, and would risk him further than any other preacher in the world, for he would stand by a friend and die for his Lord."

Dr. Bob, as he traveled about, became increasingly concerned as he observed the development in various organizations. His concern was well founded. Radical preachers and educators, in a subtle and secret way, were seeking to overthrow the established religious, social, and political standards of our nation. Ecclesiastical bosses seemed to be taking the churches further afield. They were advocating "big programs" and neglecting to preach the Gospel as Christ intended it to be preached. Many preachers were promoting organic union among various religious bodies around the world, and many religious liberals in the National Council of Churches were taking dominant places of leadership with great authority in most of the ecclesiastical organizations. Some of these men had communistic leanings, and these radicals were promoting all types of strife, such as the race problem. To combat these trends, Dr. Bob felt an urge to spearhead a counter-movement. He wrote to Dr. Rice:

> Confidentially, I have in mind an evangelistic preaching crusade for America. I have discussed this idea with the National Association of Evangelicals (NAE); and if they do not use this plan, I would like for you to use it intelligently, and I am willing to help you as far as I can.

The plan "caught on" with the younger evangelist, and he expressed the opinion that the NAE should sponsor the crusade and have Dr. Bob at the helm. To be a success, Dr. Rice said, it must have at its head a man of real leadership who loved souls and who knew mass evangelism. Who could fill this position better than Dr. Bob?

In July of 1945, THE SWORD OF THE LORD sponsored a big Conference on Evangelism at Winona Lake, Indiana. The plan was to bring in outstanding evangelists who were faithful to God's Word and effective in the ministry, to teach pastors and other evangelists how to conduct evangelistic services, give effective invitations, advertise meetings, and organize and promote both single-church and union campaigns. The good response led Dr. Bob to suggest that this type of conference be promoted in large centers in several sections of the country. More permanent good could be accomplished in this way in one year, he thought, than could be accomplished in five years of regular meetings.

As one might expect, the devil did not take this effort lightly; and opposition set in. Dr. Bob received a copy of a letter which the NAE had circulated in an effort to tie to their organization the evangelists who were "on the borderline." Dr. Bob commented, "This letter revealed how far down the line this organization had gone." A noted preacher went to Japan and made a strong attack on the American Council and the International Council of Christian Churches—spiritually sound organizations—saying that the men connected with these councils were under the delusion of Satan, were against evangelism, and were a fifth column in the ranks.

Dr. Rice did not appreciate the attitude manifested in this accusation, and he felt led to resign from the Committee on International Relations of NAE. Dr. Bob and Bob, Jr., had already quietly removed the University and THE GOSPEL FELLOWSHIP ASSOCIATION from membership in the NAE. The UNITED EVANGELICAL ACTION published a list of schools that were supposed to be orthodox in creed and in practice, but some of the most modernistic schools in the country were on the list. Because of these trends, and others, Dr. Bob and his son decided that Bob Jones University could render better service by not belonging to any organization as such, but by cooperating with those efforts which did not conflict with their uncompromising convictions.

There was a certain book published which had dirty digs about "self-promoting evangelists grabbing for reputation and money." The teachings of this book influenced many preachers during their seminary training. Some were led so far astray that they decided not to plead with men to be saved, and many ceased giving invitations. Dr. Rice took an aggressive stand against the book, which stated, in effect, that "a revival is abnormal rather than normal and in no way should become a habit, much less a sanctioned method of work." Dr. Rice wrote to Dr. Bob:

> Fighting this book and the harm it is creating, win or lose, I know I am right and that God is with me. I do not shrink too much, I trust, from the reproach of Christ. What I am doing I am doing not for myself but for all evangelism and evangelists and I believe that, by God's help, we can change the color of Christian thought for a whole generation by being faithful.

Dr. Bob expressed the opinion that Dr. Rice was in a position to work out this problem in such a way as to influence mass evangelism to the good and at the same time strengthen his own position in the field of mass evangelism. "We are in the same boat together," he said to Dr. Rice, "and I will take the bullets with you." Dr. Bob wrote an article for THE SWORD OF THE LORD which helped to settle the controversy.

In recognition of Dr. Rice's editorial work and the many books he had written — many of which had been translated into several foreign languages — and the stand he was taking, the Board of Trustees of Bob Jones University, at the suggestion of Dr. Bob, voted to confer on Dr. Rice the honorary degree of Doctor of Literature. We have been proud to have this man of God as an honorary alumnus of our school.

Although many times it seemed as if Dr. Bob and Brother John were standing alone, there were many encouraging signs; and Dr. Bob felt that the conservatives were gaining ground. He said, "I feel confident that we are going to have a real spiritual movement in America that will be put on by God Almighty. It will not make big headlines, but the loyal people of God will stand true."

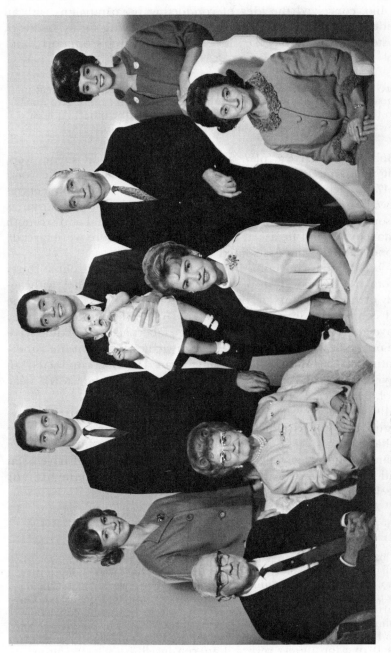

THE JONES FAMILY
Front, left to right: Dr. & Mrs. Bob Jones, Mrs. Bob Jones, III, and Mrs. Bob Jones, Jr. Back, left to right: Mrs. Jon Jones, Mr. Jon Jones, Dr. Bob Jones, III and daughter, Dr. Bob Jones, Jr., and Joy Jones (now Mrs. Gerald Jordan).

The National Laymen's Evangelistic Association local chapter in Lima, Ohio, conceived the idea of conducting big campaigns with an independent setup in each town, the leadership being in the hands of local pastors and churches. Dr. Rice sought Dr. Bob's opinion about the plan.

> You are the oldest and wisest evangelist, and I shall listen with great interest to anything you have to say on the subject. If you cannot give much time to the matter, still I want you in it some way or the other. At least, I would want your 'okay', your wisdom, and your fellowship.

Dr. Bob sanctioned the plan and offered many good suggestions, including the names of some men he felt would be effective in the work.

In 1947 this group planned a state-wide campaign of union meetings in the two Carolinas and Virginia, with THE SWORD OF THE LORD as co-sponsor. Dr. Rice felt that Dr. Bob and Bob, Jr., would add strength to the movement, and he asked their cooperation. There were already twenty-one leading evangelists lined up.

Dr. Bob accepted a meeting in Spartanburg, South Carolina, thirty miles from the new location of his school. Twelve churches with aggressively orthodox pastors participated, and there were as many as one hundred conversions in one night. Later, Dr. Bob remarked, "If they could have got a big tent or had built a large tabernacle, they could have had one of the best revivals ever held in any community on the American continent." In March of the same year, Dr. Bob conducted an eight-day meeting in Asheville, North Carolina, another town near his school. Scores came forward each night.

In 1949 in Presque Isle, Maine, a town of ten thousand people, several neighboring towns joined hands to have a meeting. There were no less than fifty conversions any night, and on most nights there were more than two hundred saved. People remarked, "It would have been a revolutionary movement if the meeting could have continued two or three weeks longer."

Of one meeting in Canada, Dr. Bob wrote:

> In the "balmy" days of evangelism down South I have never seen more old-time religion or more wonderful results. In the old days they thought they could not have an altar call until the meeting had run a week. Up in Canada the meeting broke on the third night, and large numbers were saved. On the fourth night, which was Sunday, the people had old-time conviction. Hard sinners were converted and a great number of prominent people came to the Lord. It is my feeling that the whole Dominion of Canada is ready and ripe for a great revival. I am convinced that if the right man could go there and carry on a conservative, straight-forward preaching

program, who would be tactful and would know how to go along with God, he could lead that whole country into a great revival.

Dr. Bob returned to Ottawa in June of that year for a fifteen-day campaign, and it thrilled his soul to find that the chairman of the sponsoring committee was *one of his converts of twenty-five years before* in Pittsburgh, Pennsylvania.

It would take volumes to give the background of Dr. Bob's withdrawing his support from such organizations as The National Association of Evangelicals, Campus Crusade, TEAM, World Vision, Youth for Christ, and others. Many Bob Jones University graduates were active in these groups. Dr. Bob and Dr. Rice helped to formulate the doctrinal statement of Youth for Christ. Incorporated in YFC's doctrinal statement was the phrase, "Bible-believing church" to be applied wherever reference was made to cooperation with local churches. Soon, however, it was reported that the leaders of YFC were announcing, without qualification, "We stand back of the churches. We work with the churches. Go to the church *of your choice* tomorrow." Dr. Bob felt that this was a dangerous thing to say. Certainly it was not a consistent attitude, and he wrote YFC's president that Bob Jones University could not longer support this organization that claimed to believe one thing and yet used its influence against the very thing that it claimed to believe.

Dr. Rice could have sold out to denominational leaders and their program and could have been popular with them. He could have more than doubled subscribers to his weekly paper. However, he would not sell out. He was willing to make any sacrifice necessary for the sake of Christ. He said to Dr. Bob, "God helping me, I will keep pouring on the teaching concerning modernism and separation, honesty in evangelism, correct reports or none, humility and brotherliness among evangelists." Dr. Bob and Dr. Rice agreed that if they could keep the heat on, more evangelists would turn to strong preaching against sin and would seek to maintain separation from those things that were against God's Cause.

Dr. Bob wanted Dr. Rice to be the leader in their work together. He wrote to Dr. Rice:

> I am convinced that the sort of thing you are doing in promoting evangelism is the sort of thing that should be done all over the United States. . . . This country has been waiting a long time for some man like you, who has grit and determination and consuming passion to promote evangelism. God can use you in a wonderful way if you will just go down the road and keep on insisting that what this country needs is evangelism and that is right, John. That is the way God is moving right now. I am for you, and I will help you, John, all I can in promotional work. I think you are the one to lead and should always be kept in the light. You have the contact through your

paper, and you have vision. I am praying that the Lord will lead you more and more to focus your paper on the one theme of evangelism. . . .

By this time, THE SWORD OF THE LORD had surpassed the best-known fundamental Christian magazines in subscriptions. There were at least a hundred thousand subscribers, including subscribers in eighty foreign countries. Forty thousand preachers and missionaries were receiving the paper, and many who had preached for years were being made aware of the seriousness of conditions around the country. Dr. Bob suggested that THE SWORD OF THE LORD be required reading for Bob Jones University preacher boys and that the boys be required to outline the sermons in each issue of the paper. The impact of this periodical on our young preachers has followed them into all parts of the world.

In the ecclesiastical setup the trend seemed to veer from the spiritual to autocratic control in leadership. In some denominations there were a few individual preachers who were all right, but many pastors were becoming so entangled in the "machine" that their effectiveness was limited. The only hope that Dr. Bob could see was for independent churches and preachers to rise up and stem the tide. He realized that it would take not only much grace but also logical thinking and a strong backbone in order to stand the test. The younger generation had not been educated under the old system that developed character, and if he and Dr. Rice were going to make a contribution to the saving of evangelism, they must do something and do it quickly. Dr. Bob prayed much over the situation and decided that the time was ripe for them to get together and work out a consistent plan. Never in his life had he felt a stronger leading of the Lord. He had no thought of directing these men; he planned simply to get them to agree on certain principles and policies, and then furnish a list of these men to all evangelical churches. The following statement was prayerfully signed by participating evangelists.

I believe that God has called me to be an evangelist; and I am, by God's grace, determined to be true to my calling.

First: I pledge myself that I will not accept a church meeting on the invitation of any pastor that I know does not stand for the inspiration of the Bible, the virgin birth, the incarnation, the vicarious and substitutional blood atonement, and the bodily resurrection of the Lord Jesus Christ.

Second: I will not accept an invitation from any group of pastors if I know there is one in the group that does not believe in the fundamentals outlined in the preceding paragraph. I will, however, be glad to conduct an evangelistic campaign under the sponsorship of the other pastors who do accept the doctrinal position stated.

Third: I further pledge myself not to personally support financially or encourage anyone else to support any program of any church which I know is contrary to the Gospel which I believe and preach.

Fourth: I am ready, if my schedule can be satisfactorily arranged, to enter any door that the Lord opens where there is an opportunity to cooperate with faithful, orthodox pastors in helping to build up the saints and win the lost to the Lord Jesus Christ.

Dr. Rice approved the fellowship of evangelists which Dr. Bob suggested, and he prayed earnestly that the Lord would lead in the matter. He said:

I will be glad to sign the statement that you have written, and any other Christian should be glad to sign it, too. In my opinion it sums up clearly the Bible statement about the unequal yoke.

Out of thousands of letters that were mailed, only two letters of resentment or disapproval came back. One enthusiastic pastor wrote:

It took courage to say what you did in view of the almost overpowering effect of the campaign under mixed sponsorship, but you are right that the sponsorship of modernists will eventually prove fatal to biblical evangelism; that the rank and file of the evangelists will find it extremely difficult to keep on and that ecclesiasticism is the peril that chokes out the very life of evangelism.

This encouraged Dr. Bob to say to Dr. Rice:

I tell you, Brother John, if we work shoulder to shoulder and keep our heads clear and our hearts warm in this matter, the Lord is going to do something. I never have had such confidence about anything with which I have been connected.

There were approximately one thousand Bob Jones University preacher boys who gladly pledged their support of this move. They presented to Dr. Bob a book that contained the following statement signed by all the boys:

Having clearly understood the positive position of Bob Jones University, its founder, Dr. Bob Jones, Sr., and its president, Dr. Bob Jones, Jr., concerning the principles of orthodoxy and evangelism, we, the undersigned of the Ministerial Association of Bob Jones University, hereby solemnly pledge to uphold, cherish, and defend the tenents of the faith as set forth in our University policies and creed; to stand uncompromisingly against any form of modernism, and that we refuse to support any program which is sympathetic to or actually affiliated with modernism.

Dr. Bob suggested to Dr. Rice that he should set up one-day evangelistic conferences all over America. There would be a morning service, a luncheon for Christian workers and preachers, an afternoon service, and a big rally in the evening. The idea was to stimulate Christians to accept their responsibility in helping to win souls to Jesus Christ.

Dr. Bob had but one motive, and that was to save evangelism. After much prayer, he decided that it would be good strategy to call a meeting in Chicago and discuss plans with interested evangelists for putting into the field someone to visit pastors of orthodox churches and acquaint them with the perilous trends and help them to work out a plan to combat the danger. A large number attended the meeting and the response was good. The evangelists gladly signed a pledge not to preach the Gospel under the sponsorship of modernists or disbelievers.

The Resolutions Committee was made up of a well-balanced group of educators, preachers, evangelists, and businessmen — outstanding Christian fundamental leaders such as Dr. Bob Jones, Jr., Dr. John R. Rice, Dr. Robert T. Ketcham, Judge James E. Bennet, Dr. Dan Graham, Dr. Jack Hyles, Dr. Tom Malone, Dr. Ernest Pickering, Dr. Jack Murray, Dr. Horace F. Dean, Dr. W. O. H. Garman, Dr. Linton C. Johnson, Dr. Allan MacRae, Dr. Monroe Parker, Dr. Beauchamp Vick, Dr. James A. Franklin, Dr. Oliver B. Green, Dr. Henry Grube, Dr. Ford Porter, Dr. Lee Roberson, Dr. William H. Lee Spratt, Dr. W. B. Bedford, and Dr. Archer Weniger. Dr. Bob felt that Dr. Rice, because of his editorship of a widely-circulated paper and his being in great demand as an evangelist, should head the Resolutions Committee. There had never been a movement in America like this, and Dr. Bob was praying that through this effort a revival would break out and true evangelism would be saved. Every day brought into sharper focus the fact that they were on the right track.

This proposed Chicago meeting brought to mind another meeting that had been held there years before. At the earlier meeting certain enemies of God had set about to mold evangelism and to take over. Dr. Bob publicly denounced the move saying:

Fellows, this will never work. God never made two of us alike. I may do it one way. You may do it another. We certainly cannot do it alike; and if we try, the devil will swallow once and get us all. I oppose this idea, and will kill it if it is brought up.

Dr. Bob did kill the move, and he stemmed the tide at least for awhile.

Dr. Bob wanted his Chicago meeting to put fire into his younger colleagues, to inspire them to lay great stress on the essentials of the faith, and to put them on guard against holding meetings under the sponsorship of any man or group that did not hold true to the essentials. The results were better than many people dreamed possible.

On the day after Christmas, 1958, a large number of outstanding conservatives poured into "the windy city" to attend this unique conference. Dr. Bob was the first speaker, and his topic was "Problems of Evangelism Today." He opened the meeting with an inspirational devotion in which he gave a little history of evangelism in America. He pointed out that to a great extent evangelism in the past had been destroyed by mistakes of the evangelists and that the best way to avoid their pitfalls was to keep evangelism on the basis of *principle* and not try to have an *organic tying together* of everybody. He outlined some plans and afterwards moderated a discussion on "Organization of City-Wide Campaigns with Orthodox Sponsorship." Dr. Bob and Dr. Rice answered questions and led in a general discussion. Dr. Archer Weniger spoke on "The Aftermath of Ecumenical Evangelism." Dr. Rice discussed "What Bible-Believers Lose to Gain Modernistic Sponsorship in Revivals," giving particular details concerning the New York and San Francisco Crusades. Dr. Bob Jones, Jr., spoke on "The Four Groups in Protestantism Today." He had made a thorough study of the evangelistic situation on a number of foreign fields, and he had relevant material that many of the preachers had not had the opportunity to gain for themselves.

Dr. Bob suggested making THE SWORD OF THE LORD the official organ of the evangelistic group, and then he warned the men to be careful.

> If the devil does not trap us into making one mistake or trap us into softening up somewhere, I believe that God is going to do something through THE SWORD OF THE LORD and through Bob Jones University contacts; and by working together we can, under God, put over this movement in a way to accomplish a great deal for the Lord.

Dr. Bob said to Dr. Rice:

> Wouldn't it be wonderful, Brother John, if the revival should come in a strange, unexpected way through God's little men? Wouldn't it be marvelous if in this day God would just vindicate these faithful saints?

Then he told the men:

> The Bible is as clear on the question of bad company, of wrong associations, of spiritual compromise as on the message or as on the fundamental doctrines which are accepted by all Bible-believing, orthodox Christians. It is not right for an evangelist or any other Christian worker to disobey the clear teaching of the Scripture by working under the sponsorship of men who

do not accept the fundamental doctrines of the Christian faith and to
declare that he is doing this because it gives him an opportunity to obey
God to preach the Gospel. It is not right to disobey God in order to obey
God.

Big Headlines

The fact that a group of evangelists, pastor-evangelists, and Christian
educators from all over America would meet in Chicago the day after
Christmas caught the eye of the press; and big headlines in THE CHICAGO
SUN-TIMES, Saturday, December 27, 1958, page 12, stated:

FUNDAMENTALIST EVANGELISTS REJECT
ANY SPONSORSHIP BY MODERNISTS

A national group of evangelists Friday denounced compromise "in evangelistic campaigns or any other form of Christian work" with persons who
do not believe in the divine inspiration of the Bible.

The evangelists declared that "America needs an old-time Bible revival"
and pledged to preach whenever and wherever they can except under the
sponsorship of "modernists" and those who deny the "essentials of the
Christian faith."

Purpose of the meeting at the Hamilton Hotel was to rally "old-time Bible-
believing Christians around fundamentals to which all Bible-believing
faiths can subscribe," said evangelist Dr. Bob Jones, Founder of Bob Jones
University, Greenville, South Carolina.

Dr. Jones said more than 150 prominent evangelists in a resolution have
pledged not to accept invitations to preach for sponsors who do not believe
in what he termed orthodox Christian fundamentals.

He described those fundamentals as the absolute authority of the Bible; the
virgin birth and deity of Christ; His vicarious atoning death and bodily
resurrection; and His second coming.

A spokesman explained that the move was an attempt to resolve a controversy between evangelists who accept any sponsorship with modernists and
the Jones adherents.

Dr. Jones said the resolution is not aimed at any individual. But he noted
that big meetings and mass campaigns "are resulting in the fewest converts — 'declarations for Christ' — in the history of evangelism."

Chairman of the resolutions committee was Dr. John R. Rice of Wheaton,
Illinois. . . .

THE COLUMBIA STATE, South Carolina's largest newspaper, included
in an article a list of the names of the one hundred and fifty preachers
who attended the conference. THE GREENVILLE NEWS gave full coverage
to the Resolutions which the pastors, evangelists, and educators present
adopted and signed.

The resolutions dealt with the pastors' and evangelists' reaffirmation of their loyalty to the fundamental truths of God's Word; their renewed dedication and determination to promote God's Cause at home and abroad; their willingness to suffer, if necessary, as did the prophets of old; and their withholding of their support in gifts, influence, or labor

The Bob Joneses at 50th Wedding Anniversary of Dr. and Mrs. Bob Jones, Sr.

from any religious institution, man, or program which denies, contradicts or perverts any of the essentials of the faith, such as the authority of the Bible, the virgin birth, the vicarious blood atonement, the bodily resurrection, and the second coming of our Lord.

Dr. Bob was willing to spend his own money in putting over this program, and he meant to do all he could in following up the Chicago meeting. He sent thirty thousand letters to conservative ministers all over the country, telling about these one hundred and fifty evangelists who had gone on record that they would uncompromisingly preach the full counsel of the Word and stand true regardless of consequences. Then he went to work in a big way, setting up the one-day conferences around the nation. Dr. Bob felt that by getting right down to business they could accomplish as much good in these one-day concentrated efforts as they could normally accomplish in a three-day conference. He said, "I believe that God is giving us a real opportunity, and I want to take every advantage to do a real job for Him."

Dr. Bob was pleased with the response of his preacher boys around the world. He had not realized how many key positions these boys were holding, and he was thankful to the Lord for their opportunities and for their willingness and boldness to stand.

Even at the age of seventy-five, Dr. Bob embarked on a nation-wide crusade to arouse Protestant ministers to a defense of the fundamentals of the faith; and everywhere he went newspaper representatives sought an interview with him. I quote Mr. Claude Keathley, religious news editor of THE BIRMINGHAM NEWS, who interviewed him with regard to one of the strong issues of our day—segregation.

MORE HARM THAN GOOD—NEITHER RACE WANTS MIXING, SAYS PASTOR

As the big civil rights guns begin to boom in the United States Senate today, one of the nation's best known old-time evangelists expressed concern that integration of the races would do more harm to Christian colored and Christian white people than it would do good.

"I am sure that Christian colored people, as well as Christian white people, feel the same about it as I do," the old, vigorous minister and educator declared. "I still believe the Bible," says Dr. Jones, "and believe the Bible still makes some things very clear."

Elaborating on this view on integration of the races in the South, Dr. Jones said that the Bible makes it clear that there are three classes of people, the Jews, the Gentiles and the church of God. When people say that segregation is unchristian they are slandering God, because God is the author of segregation of the races. . . .

In this regard let me say that the colored people never had a better friend than Dr. Bob. Being from the "deep South," he had a love for them and an understanding of their problems. He worked with them when he was a boy on the farm. He preached to them while he was still in knee pants. He knew that basically these people were religious and that there was no sweeter relationship anywhere in the world than the relationship of the good white people and the colored people of the South before the agitators began to come in and do harm.

When the integration problem broke, Dr. Bob went on the air and warned the colored people to be careful, to keep their religion and be sensible, and not to let the agitators force sit-in demonstrations and other disturbances. He reminded them of the great preaching they had heard before the Civil War. There had been nothing like it since the apostolic days, he said. He spoke of the great work the colored preachers had done in the South, and he told the people that God had made the races as they are and that it was He who had separated them.

Many Negro leaders had requested Dr. Bob to build them a school; and he would have done it, had he felt the Lord's leading. All through the years he had helped the colored people in every way possible. Marion D. Bennet appreciated Dr. Bob's efforts on his behalf and he wrote Dr. Bob the following:

I would like to take this opportunity to express my heartfelt thanks to you for what you and Bob Jones University have meant to me. You may not remember me. I am the colored boy who worked at Bob Jones University and came to know Christ while under the employment of the school. I received a call to the ministry and later gave my testimony on your radio station WMUU. I came to see you and you gave me some wonderful books. You also suggested several schools that I might attend. You wrote to the draft board and got me deferred from the armed services so that I could continue my training and prepare for a career in the ministry. This took place in the early 1950's.

I want you to know your help was not in vain. In 1957, I graduated from Morris Brown College and in 1960 from Gammon Theological Seminary, Atlanta, Georgia. After serving churches in Anderson, S. C. and York, S.C., I became the minister of Zion Methodist Church, Las Vegas, Nevada in 1960. God has really blessed my ministry here in this "sin city." Many have come to know Christ through my work. We have just completed a new church edifice to the glory of God.

Again, I want to thank you, Dr. Jones. I do trust that some day we can have a school like Bob Jones University for Negro men and women.

Dr. Bob's work in his last active effort in the cause of evangelism made headlines in Rochester, New York. The writer stated:

BOB JONES INSPIRING AUDIENCES AFTER 61 YEARS

At fifteen Bob Jones stood under a "brush arbor" of tree limbs in Alabama and started to preach. So effective was his message that fifty-five of the people present organized a church and made Jones their leader.

Last night, some sixty-one years and many more evangelism meetings later, this same man was still inspiring his audience.

A veteran of many crusades and former president of the 1,100 member Association of Evangelists in Winona Lake, Ind., when Billy Sunday was a member, Dr. Jones described himself as a "religious conservative," that is, a man who believes in everything the Bible says.

This does not begin to "scratch the surface" of the joint efforts of Dr. Bob and Dr. Rice; but it will at least give some idea of their slant on the religious situation of our day and their boldness in fighting the good fight, earnestly contending for the faith. Dr. Bob and Brother John were close associates for many years, and I am sure that no friend at Dr. Bob's funeral felt the situation more keenly than Dr. Rice. We deeply appreciated the presence of this good friend on this occasion.

PART V
THE LAST DAYS

Part V
The Last Days

CHAPTER 1

Honors

Dr. Bob received many personal honors and many honors in behalf of Bob Jones University. At the age of twenty-one he was urged by friends to run for Congress. These friends believed that Dr. Bob's spiritual slant, practical philosophy, winning personality, and political acumen equipped him to provide leadership that this country greatly needed. No doubt the political pressures of his friends tempted Dr. Bob, for he always had a sort of weakness for politics. But as strong as was the pressure and as worthy as the cause may have been, this young man kept his eye on the *main* goal: one hundred per cent, twenty-four hours a day, so to speak, an ambassador for Christ in evangelism and later in education. He lived by the idea that "*for God's man, all ground is holy ground and every bush a burning bush. Wherever God puts a man is the most sacred spot in the world for that man.*" The Lord knows that we need spiritual men in office and He calls some men into politics; but this did not seem to be His will for Dr. Bob, and Dr. Bob turned it down.

Even at this youthful age Dr. Bob was having some of the most successful evangelistic campaigns of his career. About him was a sort of spiritual aura that drew men to the One he represented. His eyes seemed to penetrate the very souls of those who sat in his presence, and even over the radio his voice seemed to have a magnetic appeal. By the time he was forty-two, Dr. Bob had won a million souls to the Lord. But this was only the beginning: God was to lead this servant to higher heights that would reach unnumbered souls around the world through the students whom he would train in Bob Jones University.

Early in its history the school which Dr. Bob founded became America's largest independent, fundamental, Christian institution; and its high standards have been evidenced in many ways. For seventeen consecutive years the scores of our students on the *National Teachers' Examination* have been much higher than the national average. On the *Graduate Record Examination* our seniors have scored well above the national average and have been admitted to leading graduate schools in America and abroad. Business majors taking the *American Institute of Certified Public Accountants Examination* and the *Advanced Business Tests* have ranked Bob Jones University at the top. In Art and Music and in Shakespearean and Opera Productions there has been wide acclaim. THE MUSIC JOURNAL, November, 1963, paid tribute to Bob Jones University in an article that ended with these words:

> Congratulations to Bob Jones University for outstanding work in music and the arts. Though it has outgrown the small college category, it is still within the concept of an institution doing more than its share in the advancement of music in America.

Students and faculty of our speech department have won recognition and honors in national and area contests and have been featured artists in the concert series of other schools and colleges. Our radio stations — WMUU, AM and FM in Greenville, and WAVO, AM and FM in Atlanta — have a tremendous ministry in spreading the Gospel and in giving to the public programs of educational and cultural emphases. "DR. BOB JONES SAYS (Dr. Bob, Sr's., taped messages), PREXY'S PROGRAM by Dr. Bob Jones, Jr., HYMN HISTORY, and MIRACLES are "aired" in many parts of the world. UNUSUAL FILMS also is known around the world and our films have led countless souls to salvation. Our religious art treasures, valued in the millions, are displayed in our Art Museum of thirty galleries, which has won the acclaim, "The finest Art Gallery and collection in America." Pictures from this collection are in demand "on loan" for special exhibition by noted galleries around the world.

Yes, Bob Jones University's growth has been phenomenal. Its value is well over thirty million dollars; and to even the most casual visitor, there is a certain something on this campus that sets this school apart from all others. People sense here "a spirit and an atmosphere" that they do not sense anywhere else. As Dr. Bob was always quick to say, "To God be the glory, the praise, and the honor for everything!"

Of Dr. Bob's personal honors, I can include but a few. The first I should like to mention is

The Unveiling of a Plaque in His Honor Near His Old Home Place

Although much credit for initiating this honor belongs to Dr. Charles Bishop, the pastor of Calvary Baptist Church, Bainbridge, Georgia, I believe that the idea originated in Heaven. I sincerely believe that God Himself laid it upon Charlie's heart to promote this high honor to a worthy workman in God's vineyard. An alumnus of Bob Jones University, Charlie was one of the preacher boys whom Dr. Bob had taught "how to *load* the 'Gospel gun' and also how to '*shoot*' it."

When Charlie was in Dothan, Alabama, to conduct a funeral, the idea came to him that a marker honoring Dr. Bob should be erected in this locale. Immediately Charlie contacted Senators, Congressmen, bankers, Alabama state officials, and businessmen and women to see how the idea would be received. In response, letters poured in by the hundreds, many including donations to help defray the expenses of such an undertaking.

Having felt the pulse of the people, Charlie contacted Bob, Jr., who, of course, was delighted that these friends wanted to extend this high honor to his father during his father's lifetime. The Board of Trustees, the administration, the faculty and students, the Alumni Association, and many friends of the University expressed gratitude to Charlie for instigating the move. Mr. and Mrs. B. W. Connell of Dothan gladly donated the land for the Marker.

Dr. Bob was touched by this gesture of love and honor on the part of his boys and girls and friends. He was especially pleased that the site chosen was near Clark's Cemetery, where the bodies of many of his family rest. He wrote to Charlie:

> I think the plan you have for Brannon Stand is very wonderful and kind. I hope when we have the program that if it is the Lord's will, my mother and daddy can look over the battlements of Glory at us. . . . I know I haven't very much longer to live, at the best; and I certainly would want to be at Brannon Stand when this memorial is unveiled.

> Most of my old friends are dead and gone; but I think of two or three who would want to be at the program. I want to have Mrs. Jones, Bob, Jr., and Bob, III, and their wives with me.

October 18, 1962, was the day of the celebration. THE DOTHAN EAGLE, Thursday, September 13, 1962, published a nice picture of Dr. Bob, Sr., and stated:

> In a field at Brannon Stand, where the Rev. Bob Jones, Sr., spent his youth as a farm boy, alumni and friends of Bob Jones University will unveil a marker October 18 to honor the school's founder and namesake.

> Dr. Jones, who once gathered young friends in a wooded area and preached to them, founded the school in 1927, at Lynn Haven, Florida, with $25,000 in savings and contributions.

> The Dothan Chamber of Commerce is cooperating with the University's Alumni Association in erecting the bronze plaque to mark the birthplace of the Veteran evangelist and educator.

> The marker will be located about four miles west of Dothan near U. S. Highway 84 West.

> South Carolina's Sen. Strom Thurmond, who has accepted an invitation to

attend the dedication, has called the Greenville school "one of the outstanding universities of the nation."

Alabama Gov. John Patterson, replying to an invitation to attend the October 18 ceremony, wrote that Dr. Jones is "one of Alabama's most famous native sons," whose evangelistic work is known throughout the world. The Governor is happy that Dr. Bob is going to be honored and wants to have a part in that program.

I wish it were possible to quote all the wonderful letters that Charlie received about the project. Many of them came from political leaders in Washington and throughout the nation. However, I must limit myself to these brief excerpts from a few of the communications.

Congressman George Grant of Alabama:

> Please let me congratulate you upon such a worthy suggestion. Count me in on anything that you do and I will do everything possible to aid.

Senator Strom Thurmond of South Carolina wrote that he would be glad to attend the celebration and that we could count on his support.

Mrs. Bibb Graves, widow of a former governor of Alabama:

> I read with keen interest your plans for placing a marker at the birth site of Dr. Bob Jones. It will be a fitting tribute to a man whose extraordinary abilities, winning personality, unbounding energy, and Christian dedication have established this great University, and who, himself, has brought so many thousands of young people to a true and working faith in an all-wise loving Father and a desire to walk in the footsteps of His Son, our Holy Redeemer.

Dr. John R. Rice, Board member of the University, evangelist and editor of THE SWORD OF THE LORD:

> I think it proper to class Dr. Jones in that great galaxy of stars who will shine forever, along with Moody, Spurgeon, Billy Sunday, W. B. Riley, and R. A. Torrey. For spiritual wisdom, for a holy integrity of character, for his impact as one of the mightiest soul winners in the last half century, I feel that Dr. Jones has no superior. I rejoice that a memorial will remind thousands of Dr. Bob, Sr., as God's gift to all of us and to America.

Dr. Harry McCormick Lintz, evangelist and Board member of BJU:

> I consider Dr. Bob Jones, Sr., the outstanding evangelist, philosopher, preacher and teacher and Christian educator of his generation. There never has been and never will be another Dr. Bob. When God made him, He threw the molds away. He ought to go down not only in church history

but American history as one of the greatest brains and hearts that has ever been given to a nation.

Most touching was a letter from an Air Force officer whom Dr. Bob had befriended many years before. I quote most of this letter.

While on an Air Force trip to Myrtle Beach, S. C., I noticed an article in the Charleston newspaper. This article stated that you were to be honored at an affair that would be in Dale County, Alabama. The article further stated that a plaque would be unveiled in your honor and that friends from all over the United States would be assembled for the dedication.

The purpose for my writing will undoubtedly come as a surprise to you. Early in 1941, I was enroute via rail from Baton Rouge, La., to Fort Dix, N. J. I was to join the first American Air Force unit. At that time I was a young lieutenant. . . . I had left my family suddenly and I presume that I very much carried a puzzled look on my face while riding the railway to my ultimate destination. You must have noticed me for as you came down the passenger coach you greeted me, sat down, and struck up a conversation.

I would like to bring out the fact that the good part of that day in which we rode in the railway car gave me needed additional faith and courage—all of which was supplied by you. All the personal contacts that I know you have made in your years of travel and association with people would certainly at least tend to your not remembering this particular instance. However, I felt that I would like to take this opportunity to let you know that I had never forgotten.

I send this on with best wishes and the assurance that had I been near Dothan, Alabama, I would have been standing with that group which recognized you on the specified day I refer to.

Mr. Ed Driggers, managing editor of THE DOTHAN EAGLE:

Incidentally I have been among the millions who admire and love Dr. Jones. I grew up in this county, on the farm, and have picked cotton on the very farm where he was reared near Brannon Stand. As a boy I remember looking upon the old Jones home with genuine reverence, so to speak, because I knew it was where the already famous Bob Jones once lived.

The DOTHAN EAGLE published advance stories of the unveiling and also sent complete coverage of the event to THE ASSOCIATED PRESS and THE UNITED PRESS. THE MONTGOMERY ADVERTISER sent a representative to the ceremony. Dothan radio and television stations gave good coverage. The highway patrol and the sheriff's department cooperated commendably in handling the traffic problem.

Mr. Dee Clark, in whose home Dr. Bob had stayed when he was a boy in school, had been requested to participate on the program; but his daughter—Lena Clark Horn—sent his regrets:

The Jones Family At Birthplace of Dr. Bob Jones, Sr. At left: Dr. and Mrs. Bob Jones, Sr. At right: Dr. Bob Jones, Jr., in center, with sons Jon (right) and Bob III (left). Before him is Mrs. Jones and daughter Joy.

My father plans to attend the dedication at Brannon Stand. . . . He loves Dr. Bob and appreciates being asked but doesn't feel up to taking part on the program.

Dr. Allen Smith, Dr. Bob's boyhood chum, said, in part:

I count it a great honor just to have my name on any program that has the name of Bob Jones on it. There is not another preacher in the world that I love as I do Bob. Each day I thank God for him and for what he has done, is doing, and will do till Jesus comes for the honor and glory of our Lord.

Dr. Bob took great delight in greeting friends and relatives at the ceremony, and he regretted that he could not stay over for a visit with them. He had speaking engagements elsewhere, which necessitated his leaving Dothan by plane immediately after the ceremony. There was not even time for him to attend the special luncheon hosted by Bob, Jr., for more than one hundred guests who could stay the extra hour or so.

On October 19, 1962, the day after the Unveiling, THE MONTGOMERY ADVERTISER had a three-column spread, including a picture of the plaque and its wording:

NEAR THIS SPOT WAS THE BOYHOOD HOME OF

REV. BOB JONES D.D., LL. D.

INTERNATIONALLY KNOWN EVANGELIST AND FOUNDER

AND FIRST PRESIDENT OF BOB JONES UNIVERSITY,

THE ELEVENTH CHILD OF W. ALEXANDER AND GEORGIA

CREEL JONES. HE WAS THREE MONTHS OLD WHEN THE

FAMILY MOVED TO BRANNON STAND IN 1884, WHERE HE

LIVED UNTIL HIS FATHER'S DEATH IN 1900. FOUR

YEARS AFTER HIS CONVERSION AT THE AGE OF ELEVEN,

BOB JONES HELD HIS FIRST REVIVAL UNDER A BRUSH

ARBOR TWO MILES FROM HERE.

Alabama's Governor John Patterson sent photographs and motion pictures of the occasion to Dr. Bob and expressed delight "that a memorial marker has been placed at Brannon Stand marking the location of Dr. Jones' childhood home."

The Marker is a blessing to thousands who pass that way, and many go out of their way to visit this hallowed spot. A sister-in-law wrote Dr. Bob:

> I was so happy to see each of you at the unveiling ceremony. I feel this was a high personal recognition to you for all these years of unselfish devotion to God and your fellowman. Several of the old friends who were unable to attend the ceremony have driven over to see the plaque, and there is a well-beaten path to the Marker. When we arrived several people were standing around. We stayed for a while and several groups stopped. The people lingered and talked, and when we asked the neighbors who lived there about people stopping they said it went on day after day.

Dr. Fred Garland wrote:

I pulled my car over to the side of the road and slipped over and read the Marker that stood there on the highway. I bowed my head, and with my hat in my hand, I prayed, "Dear Lord, I would not be jealous, nor would I want to be perhaps ungrateful. I would not want to ask for all; but if it be possible, let just part of the mantle of Dr. Bob Jones, Sr., fall on me. Let me have just a little bit of his integrity, his honesty, his desire to do God's will. Let his goal be my goal, for Jesus' sake." I shall never forget that moment.

Dr. Charles Bishop wrote in the fall of 1968:

The other day I had an occasion to go to Dothan, Alabama. While there, I wanted to take another look at the Bob Jones Marker in Brannon Stand. I had not seen the Marker since they had placed it in the median of the new four-lane highway. As I looked at the Marker, many thoughts ran across my mind. I glanced out into the open field and could imagine some of the things that had transpired in the life of Dr. Bob.

After a few minutes, I went up to one of the little stores nearby and began to talk to some of the people who had gathered there. I asked them if they had any recollection of some of the ministries of Dr. Bob. Each man had a story to tell; in my mind these two were outstanding.

One man told of a time when Dr. Bob returned to Brannon Stand and went out into a cotton field near his homeplace, where some colored people were picking cotton. Dr. Bob watched a while, and then he started to preach to the men. Before long, several of the workers were kneeling in the field and had accepted Christ as their Saviour.

Upon another occasion, Dr. Bob's car became stuck in the mud, and a man came along with a tractor and pulled him out. The man started to leave, but Dr. Jones waved him down, thanked him, and pulled out his Testament and started to witness to him. "And," the man continued, "right there in the rain Dr. Bob Jones talked to that man about Christ. The man was on his tractor and Dr. Bob Jones was standing on the ground. Finally, the man turned off the motor of his tractor, bowed his head, and let Jesus come into his heart. Dr. Jones told the man he appreciated his pulling him out of the mud but that he appreciated more being able to talk to him about Christ.

Eightieth Birthday

No student body has ever loved and respected its Founder more than the students of Bob Jones University have. For a number of years they have celebrated Dr. Bob's birthday as Founder's Day. Because his eightieth birthday brought special recognition, I shall elaborate on that Founder's Day.

Telegrams, letters, and birthday cards poured in from all over the world. One of the most appreciated telegrams was from the Mayor and City Council of Cleveland, Tennessee, where our school was located for fourteen years. The telegram read:

We, City Commission and Mayor of Cleveland, Tennessee, extend heartiest congratulations on your obtaining your eightieth birthday tomorrow. We love you very much and miss you greatly.

W. F. Fillauer, Mayor
B. H. Fair
C. S. Kelly
George R. Taylor, Commissioners

Another telegram that meant much to Dr. Bob was from Mrs. R. L. McKenzie, Panama City, Florida, of whom I have already spoken. Among other things, Mrs. McKenzie said:

Only eternity will show the complete impact of your efforts for Christ on our city and nation through the lives of its young people.

The president of Piedmont College in Winston-Salem, North Carolina, wired:

Your many friends throughout America and the world take occasion on this your eightieth birthday to praise the Lord for you. You have been used of the Lord to bless millions. Few men in this generation have done so much for so many. Piedmont College, faculty, and students greet you.

Senator Strom Thurmond wrote:

Your wise dedicated leadership has been of immense value not only to Bob Jones University but to our nation. We need more people in this country today with your sound views and philosophy. Liberalism seems to be spreading over the country, but if we had more Bob Jones Universities, this would not be the case.

It is a pity that the faculties of so many of our colleges are liberal. . . . Keep up your good work and be assured that the people who believe in genuine Americanism appreciate the fine work that you are doing and the great service that Bob Jones University is rendering our country.

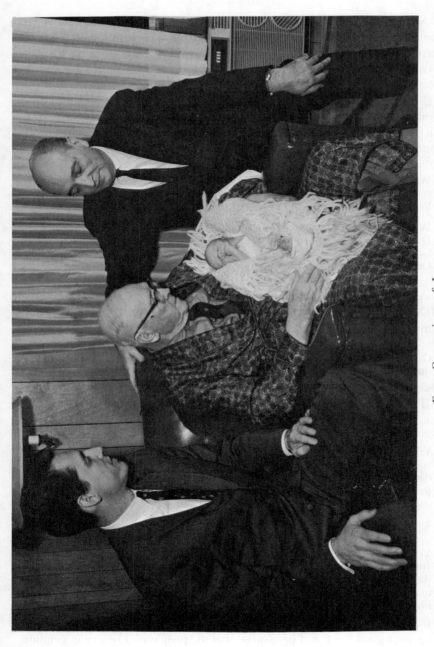

Four Generations of Joneses

Many editors wrote tributes to Dr. Bob, but I cannot take time and space to mention them. Instead, I shall quote excerpts from some of the speakers at the special chapel service that day. The theme of the program was "God's Chisel."

The president of the Student Body:

We, the student body, faculty, staff, and friends observe a man great, not merely because of what he has accomplished but great because of what Dr. Bob's Lord has accomplished through him. The Lord Jesus Christ has taken Dr. Bob's heart, his hands, his eyes, his backbone, his voice, and yes, even his feet, much as an artist would take a slab of marble and his hammer and a few cutting tools, and has created a mighty tribute to Himself. During the early and impressionable years of Dr. Bob's childhood, God used his parents to help in the forming of a tool that would influence many to serve a living Saviour. It was as if God Himself were speaking through Dr. Bob's own mother when she would say: "You're going away now, son. Be a good boy." To this task to be a good boy, Dr. Bob has been faithful in carrying it out, "being confident of this very thing, that He which hath begun a good work in you will perform it until the day of Jesus Christ." Today, thousands upon thousands are serving Christ because Dr. Bob, Sr., was faithful to the injunctions of God. Therefore, in tribute to the influence and impact that your life has had in the hands of God, we proudly dedicate to you this program.

Mrs. Jones, Sr.:

When my husband was just a little boy, God's light shone into his heart, and that heart was changed and it has always been changed. Not only a light was put in his heart but a fire was kindled that nothing has ever been able to put out. I think it has shown brighter and brighter through the years. I think God has meant more to him, his Saviour has been sweeter and dearer every step of the way; and I feel I am in a position to say that if anyone ever has truly loved God, my husband has.

Representative of foreign students:

Being the son of a sculptor, I would like to use this illustration. As the chisel is in the hands of the sculptor, so are you in the hands of God. But there is one outstanding characteristic in this comparison. Whatever form this chisel has or whatever stone it cuts, in the hands of the sculptor it will produce the most beautiful art and reflect the most uplifted thought of the artist. So through you, Dr. Bob, many lives have been molded to specifications. You have been an inspiration as a preacher by keeping this platform hot. You have been an example as a husband, a godly father, and a loving grandparent. You, through this school, have showed us not in the first place how to make a living but how to live for Jesus Christ. In behalf of the foreign students, I can say that your influence has stretched far beyond America's borders.

The president of the Senior Class in Bob Jones Academy:

In a day when young people have ideals to whom they look, we in the Academy look to you, Dr. Bob, for our example. We see in you the principles needed in our Christian lives, such as looking to God, relying on Him and giving Him all the glory.

The president of the Ministerial Class:

We shall always be indebted to this great man of God, who through the years has molded an example of courage to contend, stability to stand, and pertinacity to persevere. With his high standard of conduct in service for the Lord, Dr. Bob has molded an example which will always command respect, not only in the ranks of Christendom but also in every facet of life.

Dr. Edward Panosian, speaking for the faculty and staff of Bob Jones University:

In thinking how the faculty and staff of Bob Jones University could best honor you today, Dr. Bob, and underline again our genuine appreciation for your consistent devotion to God's Word and His will, we were reminded of one thing you have stated often that you would like someday to do: "Someday I would like to take a few months and get on a boat and take a trip around the world."

As a visible symbol of our love and loyalty, and with grateful recognition of our debt to one whom God has so signally honored, the Bob Jones University faculty and staff have the privilege today of presenting you that complete trip around the world.

It is our hope that this will be for you a unique opportunity to fill the role of missionary statesman—to see and survey the fields on which the feet of many from this place have trod through the years, to visit and encourage those missionaries, and to bring word to us of their labors.

On this your attainment of fourscore years, Dr. Bob, we present you the tickets for your trip, as we say, "Bon Voyage, and God bless your journey!"

Around the World

Dr. Bob had preached around the world many times. In *1952*, for instance, he decided to revisit the various mission fields of the world— Italy, Palestine, Pakistan, India, the Philippines and Hawaiian Islands, Japan, Korea, and Formosa—to see if the approach were in line with true scriptural principles. The greatest hindrances to the spread of the Gospel, he found, were the *ecclesiastical* approach and the *academic* approach. In every land there were well-educated and well-trained men, many of whom, though they were orthodox, were looking at the entire missionary program through ecclesiastical glasses. The only ones who seemed to be looking through Gospel glasses were the independents.

Seeing Dr. & Mrs. Bob Jones Off for Their Trip Around the World

In Formosa Dr. Bob presented Generalissimo Chiang Kai-Shek with an honorary degree. Bob Shelton, one of our boys who serves as a missionary there, wrote an interesting report of this visit:

> I was just one of hundreds of people waiting at Taipei's International Airport for the arrival of Dr. Bob Jones, Sr.
>
> Generalissimo Chiang Kai-Shek was represented by several highranking officers. The Madame had sent a delegation of ladies to present Dr. Jones with armloads of beautiful flowers. The rest of the crowd was made up of American missionaries and curious Chinese who wanted a glimpse of the man who was to present the leader of Free China with an Honorary Doctor's Degree from a Christian school in South Carolina, U. S. A.
>
> Dr. Bob asked me to meet him at the airport, but that was a request I could not carry out. There must be a law some place that states that before you can meet someone you must get close to him. The best I could do was to get in my car and follow the long procession to the Liberty House, a special place for Free China's honored guests.
>
> After a little Chinese red tape, I was permitted to see Dr. Jones. . . . His first statement was, "Boy! Am I glad to see you. I don't know how much more of this fuss I can take." He took quite a bit more and just for the record's sake, I believe about the time he left he was beginning to enjoy it.
>
> The next morning, Dr. Bob, Dr. Leland Wong and I were taken to the mountain home of the Generalissimo. The reception was warm and genuine. There were thirty or forty informal minutes of drinking tea and enjoying the hospitality of Free China's great leader.
>
> Then came the moment for which we had all waited. Following a brief ceremony, and a few words from Dr. Bob, the Honorary Degree was presented to the Generalissimo. It was all very impressive, but the words that followed impressed me most, for the Generalissimo turned to Dr. Bob and said, in Mandarin, something like this:
>
> > Dr. Jones, I appreciate this great honor. I have received honorary degrees from many colleges around the world, but this one means more than all the others for it comes from a school that is training young men to preach the Gospel of Jesus Christ.
>
> With these words ringing in our ears we left the home of Generalissimo Chiang Kai-Shek.
>
> As we made our way down the winding road to Taipei my thoughts were of two great men who had just been honored—one for his heroic leadership of a great nation; the other for founding a school that was dedicated to training young men to preach the Gospel of our wonderful Lord Jesus Christ.

In *1959*, at the age of seventy-six, Dr. Bob embarked on another world-wide preaching mission. The HONOLULU STAR-BULLETIN on Tuesday, November 10, 1959, reported in large headlines, " 'THAT OLD

TIME RELIGION' IS NEEDED TODAY, EVANGELIST JONES SAYS." The article, written by Harriet Gee, said, in part:

> What this country needs today is old-time, hell-fire-and-damnation preaching. "This," 76-year-old evangelist Bob Jones believes, would "stop kids from going to jail and slow down divorces."
>
> Dr. Jones, one of the country's few remaining old-time evangelists, left yesterday for the Far East on a world-wide preaching mission.
>
> He said today's evangelists are different from those in his day, and these included men like Billy Sunday and R. A. Torrey. . . . Those preachers preached straight. They did not mince words. They preached against sin, had conviction, and when they held meetings in towns or cities, the meetings made history. Today, there are mostly big-city campaigns which are made up of glamour—Hollywood glamour.

From Honolulu, Dr. Bob headed for the Orient. Dr. Gerry Johnson, one of our alumni missionaries in Japan, reported:

> The meetings were unusually blessed of God as Dr. Bob preached with a great anointing of the Holy Spirit. He preached to Japanese pastors and missionaries, and Dr. Bob was used by God to powerfully impress everyone to stand loyal to the Word of God and not to compromise.
>
> Dr. Bob had to preach in all these services through an interpreter. It was a miracle of God that he could stand up under such a heavy strain and schedule, but how we all praise God for sending Dr. Bob to Japan and giving us such a wonderful "shot in the arm" to stand uncompromising, faithful, and true till Jesus comes.
>
> Dr. Bob spoke to the Bob Jones University Alumni missionaries in Japan, urging them to be faithful and draw the line in this age of compromise. After Dr. Bob's message it was decided by the Japan alumni to draw up a statement emphasizing that they stand where Bob Jones University has always stood, and the missionaries in Japan will not compromise with modernism.

The resolutions were signed by thirty alumni in that area.

The trip which I wish to emphasize in this section entitled "Honors" is the one that Dr. Bob made in January and February of 1964 given to him by the faculty and staff in honor of his eightieth birthday. We knew that Dr. Bob would not take the time or "waste the money" for a mere pleasure trip; he would rather the money be used for missions. But the faculty and staff knew that the best help he could give our more than eight hundred and fifty missionaries on over ninety different fields was the "spiritual shot in the arm" that only he could give; and they sold him on the idea of representing them on the mission field. Because it would not be wise for him to travel alone at his age and because they wanted to honor Mrs. Jones, also, they invited her to accompany him.

Dr. Bob was always quick to accept money for Bob Jones University. He had the attitude that this was God's school, and he prayed daily that the Lord would lay it upon the hearts of friends and alumni to send the money we needed to carry on this great work. He found it hard, however, to accept anything for himself. This round-the-world trip bothered him so much that for weeks he kept asking me, "Lefty, how can we get this money back to them without hurting their feelings? I appreciate what they want to do, but they may do without something they need just to give Mrs. Jones and me this trip. You work it out—give them a special bonus or something. I feel terrible about this."

One day when Dr. Bob and I were having lunch with two vice-presidents of South Carolina National Bank chain and a businessman who is a member of our Board of Trustees, Dr. Bob started to talk about the trip. He said:

> I have lived threescore and ten plus ten, and God has been good to me in letting me live so long. My time is limited. I know that, and I hate to take so much time out for this world trip that our wonderful faculty and staff are giving us. I do not want to sightsee, but if I can do any good on the mission fields, I am willing to try. It will be a great strain, physically, but I will enjoy the fellowship with the missionaries. All my life I have been under a great strain carrying such a heavy load. All I want to do is rest. I would like to get on the boat in San Francisco and not get off until I get back to New York. There is no activity on the boat; I would have nothing to do except rest and prop up my feet and say my prayers. It reminds me of a little rhyme,
>
> > *I wish I were a little rock, Sitting on a hill,*
> > *Doing nothing all day long, Just sitting still.*
> > *I wouldn't eat, I wouldn't sleep, I wouldn't even wash;*
> > *I'd just sit and rest myself a thousand years b'gosh.*
>
> One reason I am glad I can go around the world is that while I am visiting our missionaries on the various fields I can at last have some fellowship with my wife. Just think—I will be on the water for two weeks with nothing to do except to rest my tired feet and talk to Mrs. Jones.

Dr. Bob was always happy to be with his beloved Mary Gaston.

I shall never forget the visit I had with Dr. Bob on the day before their departure. He talked about the goodness of God, and quoted, "Surely goodness and mercy have followed me all the days of my life." Then he commented:

> That is true in our lives, isn't it? God has been so good to us. He knows that we have tried to do what is right. Even our enemies know that we have stood true, and they respect us for it. I have been an awful driver. I know that I have been hard to get along with, and at times have been a little disagreeable. I have many weaknesses and faults. But we have always stood for

God and His Cause, and He knows we would never compromise principle. I can never forget how He has protected our school. It fits better into God's program than any other school in the country, because we have an individualistic school, and this is God's individual age.

He cited three schools that are Christian but were built with a particular slant: one was known as the anti-monkey school, another the second-blessing school, and the third was built around the mind, the hands, and the feet. Dr. Bob continued:

Our school was built on God's Word and a sane, middle-of-the-road approach; and God has blessed our efforts in His behalf. All our folks have a sane, practical outlook on life. They love the Lord and want to serve Him. When I get to Heaven, I want to eavesdrop a little and keep up with what goes on down here. But I am not worried about the school anymore. I know that it is established right and that our people will keep it right.

I thank the Lord for Bob, Jr., and for my grandchildren. Most high-pressure men have had trouble with their children. No one will ever know how much I worried about Bob's acting. I thought Hollywood would get him. It was a real strain until God, in His infinite goodness and mercy, worked it out. How thankful I am to God for the way everything has come about.

Bob, Jr., and his son meticulously planned every detail of the long journey for Dr. Bob and Mrs. Jones, thus relieving them of much of the strain of travel. Date of departure from Greenville was set for January 1, 1964.

Early in the morning on the appointed day, in spite of heavy snow and ice on the roads, more than 150 executives, faculty, and staff went to the airport to see their beloved founder and his wife board the plane for their world trip. It was still dark when the entourage for the airport started, but just as Dr. and Mrs. Jones were boarding the plane, the sun came up in all its splendor and beauty. Mrs. Jones looked lovely in her brown coat and hat, and she looked warm in spite of the twenty-six degree weather. I do not know which were the more excited—the ones departing or those who watched them leave. Television cameras and "still" cameras clicked until the plane disappeared. By that time our hands and feet were like blocks of ice. We soon thawed out, however, as we enjoyed a warm breakfast at the air terminal.

The Joneses visited fourteen different countries, including Japan, Hong Kong, Thailand, India, Iran, Syria, Lebanon, Jordan, Israel, Cyprus, Italy, Austria, Denmark, and France.

Our boys and girls on the mission field could see that even though Dr. Bob was much older than when they were in school, he had not lost his power with God or his touch with people.

Little did Dr. Bob realize as he looked upon the Mount of Olives, the

Garden of Gethsemane, the Golden Gate, and the Temple area in Jerusalem, that soon the school he had founded would own a beautiful tract of land there. The way the Lord worked out everything in a few hours for us to obtain this beautiful, priceless land across the valley from the Temple area was a miracle.

One day after Dr. Bob's return, he and I were having lunch with three local friends and Dr. Bob started talking about prophecy. He said: "The Jew has been a 'sea of nations' all through the years. The miracle of miracles is that they have not been digested. God preserved them and gave them a mark." Dr. Bob mentioned a former visit to Palestine of several years before and how at that time it was so barren and dirty. A newspaperman with whom he talked on that visit was writing a story of the Mediterranean and the Holy Land. Dr. Bob told the reporter something of the history of the land — how God had punished the disobedience of His chosen people by driving them out of the land into captivity, how He was going to bring them back, and how the land of Palestine had been promised to Abraham and his seed and had been given to the twelve tribes of Israel through Isaac and Jacob for an everlasting covenant. The reporter asked, "Do you think the Jews are fools enough to leave New York, Chicago, San Francisco, Los Angeles, Miami, and other places of the world to come back to this God-forsaken country?" Dr. Bob said, "This is God's land of promise. It is a land of purpose. The Jew will gladly come back, and some day this land will be flowing with 'milk and honey' and will blossom as a rose."

On his last trip to Palestine Dr. Bob found it one of the cleanest and most peaceful places on earth, blossoming like a rose. "It will not be long, however," he commented, "before this peace is going to be interrupted and there is going to be a war that the world will long remember."

In a letter to Dee Clark, Dr. Bob commented of his trip:

This was the most strenuous trip I ever had, but God gave me strength and brought me back safely. As I came in on the plane, after traveling over thirty thousand miles, I looked down on Greenville and the beautiful Bob Jones University plant with its wonderful group of buildings, and a strange thing happened to me! I had a picture of my boyhood home in Southeast Alabama and Tabernacle Church and your home when you were a boy; and all the scenes came back to me. I got to thinking about the goodness of God, how He preserved me through the years, and about this trip and the souls I had seen saved on the tour, and the wonderful young people that we have sent out to the foreign mission fields. The memories came to me to remind me of God's wonderful goodness. He has been good to spare my life to see so many of my dreams come true and to give me an opportunity to serve.

You know, Dee, the older I get, the more real I am sure Heaven must be. I think of your father and mother and the other old friends, and I think of the days I spent there in your home when I went to school. God was training me then for the ministry I have had through the years.

Dee, the Lord has led Bob Jones University up to this day. All the training we have ever had and all the experiences we had have come to us to equip us for this time.

Christian Hall of Fame

The last outstanding honor I shall mention is one that came to Dr. Bob on Easter Sunday, 1966, when he was chosen as the only living person to be represented in the Christian Hall of Fame in Canton, Ohio. The portraits of sixty-six Christian leaders were hung in the Canton Baptist Temple's Hall of Christian Fame.

The idea for this Christian Hall of Fame came to Dr. Harold Henniger in November, 1964, as he lay in the hospital recovering from a heart attack. Dr. Henniger said of this experience:

After reading the eleventh chapter of Hebrews, I heard a radio announcement referring to the Professional Football Hall of Fame which is located in our city. The idea came to me that we should put "God's Heroes" on display in our church: the men who through the centuries have stood for the faith once and for all delivered to the saints.

The Christian Hall of Fame is designed to trace the progress of biblical Christianity from the closing of the New Testament canon down through the centuries to the present time. Among these men are early church fathers, reformers, missionaries, pastors, scholars, and evangelists. Though differing in background, education, method and field of ministry, these men had one thing in common: an unswerving devotion to the Lord Jesus Christ and a complete dedication to His Word.

The main purpose of the Christian Hall of Fame is inspirational, not merely educational. It is our prayer that as a result of viewing the likeness of these men and reading a brief history of their lives and service to our Lord, which appears beneath each portrait, many will be inspired to carry the blood-stained banner of the Cross around the world as missionaries. Also that men will be called into the ministry to preach the unsearchable riches of Christ, and that all will be led to a life dedicated to the honor of Him who loved us and washed us from our sins in His own blood, even our Lord Jesus Christ, to Him be the glory.

It is interesting that three of the four artists commissioned to do the the oil paintings were alumni or teachers of Bob Jones University. The portraits are of early church fathers such as Tertullian, Polycarp, and Ignatius; reformers such as Martin Luther, John Calvin, John Knox and Ulrich Zwingli; missionaries such as Patrick, the Irish Catholic saint, and explorer David Livingstone; preachers such as John Wesley, Charles Haddon Spurgeon, Harry A. Ironside, and George W. Truett;

and evangelists such as Dwight L. Moody, Billy Sunday, Gypsy Smith, and Dr. Bob Jones, Sr.

Dr. Noel Smith, Editor of the BAPTIST BIBLE TRIBUNE of Springfield, Missouri, described this event in his paper:

> THE ASSOCIATED PRESS carried the story. The greatest of the Ohio dailies carried long stories and many pictures. NEWSWEEK magazine carried the story. T. V. stations sent reporters and cameras to the church and radio stations gave the opening detailed coverage.
>
> The portraits are uniformly 2 feet wide and 3 feet in length hanging in the Temple Corridor 20 feet wide, 260 feet long. Under each portrait is a 100–125 word biographical sketch. There is a great and restrained dignity in the faces looking down on you from those quiet and chaste walls. They represent a great variety of abilities, intellect, temperament, tastes and culture. But in every case they are completely dedicated to the God and Christ and Holy Spirit of the Bible, and for all of them the Bible was God-breathed.

CHAPTER 2

Dr. Bob's Resignation

On April 3, 1964, Dr. Bob sent to the Executive Committee of the Board of Trustees of Bob Jones University the following communication:

> I feel that the responsibilities incumbent on the Chairman of the Board of Trustees and on the members of the Executive Committee are heavier than I feel able at eighty years of age to continue to bear, and I would appreciate being relieved of these responsibilities.
>
> I will be glad, of course, to serve on the Cooperating Board. As the founder of Bob Jones University, I am certainly as interested in the welfare of the University as anybody could be. I have watched God's blessings on it for more than a third of a century. The institution has been blessed in a financial way and is in fine shape academically and spiritually. It is wielding an influence around the world and is looked upon as possibly the strongest fighting base of uncompromising, scriptural orthodoxy left in America. It is respected for its efficiency as well as for its testimony. On this recent trip which I made around the world, I observed that even those who do not take the spiritual position that Bob Jones University takes, nevertheless highly respect the institution; and I know that as long as the Lord tarries, God is going to continue to bless and use Bob Jones University.
>
> I am in no wise disassociating myself from the University and I shall continue to bear all the burdens I can bear and cooperate in any way possible; but I do feel that the time has come for me to serve on the Cooperating Board rather than carry the heavy responsibilities of the Executive Committee and the Chairmanship of the Board.
>
> I appreciate all you men as well as all the other members of the Board who have served with me and who are carrying on the responsibilities.

It saddened us to accept his resignation, but everyone knew that as keenly sensitive to the leading of the Holy Spirit as Dr. Bob had been through the years, this must be of the Lord. Besides, it would afford an opporunity for Dr. Bob to prove to skeptics who had questioned the school's welfare in the event of his stepping aside that things could continue to run smoothly for the Lord.

Father and Son

Dr. Bob received from Senators, Congressmen, Governors, bankers, professional men, newspaper writers, businessmen, and from his boys and girls all over the world letters of thanksgiving and commendation for the great good he had done for mankind in general.

Senator Strom Thurmond wrote to Dr. Bob about his retirement:

> I can think of no person living today who has promoted the right kind of education to a higher degree than you. I can think of no person today who has stood for higher principle and lofty ideals in our churches and colleges and schools than you. I just wanted you to know that I am among your many admirers who feel that you are topnotch in every way and deserve the highest commendation that can be given to a citizen for service to mankind and the preservation of the American form of government and freedom throughout the world.
>
> It is fortunate that you have an able son and an able grandson to carry on the grand tradition which you have set for them.

Dr. Bob replied to Senator Thurmond:

> The greatest peril that is facing our nation today is the spirit of compromise. I thank God that you are a man who stands for your convictions. This nation is suffering from a bankruptcy of character. Many of our church members have no stamina. I have been preaching since I was thirteen years old, and I am now over eighty; so I have been in this business sixty-seven years, and I am the last of the old-time evangelists. When I was a boy, the philosophy of education in America was in line with the philosophy of the Bible. . . . I cannot tell you how proud I am of you. I thank God that you have Christian faith and that you have backbone. If there is ever anything on earth we can do for you down here or anywhere else, do not hesitate to command us.

Dr. Noel Smith, noted editor and author, summed up the feeling of many when he said from the Bob Jones University platform:

> I have no ulterior motive in saying to you—and I say it as sincerely as I have ever said anything in my life, and I know what I am talking about— sitting here behind me is one of the most extraordinary men the Christian idea of this country has ever produced. There is not any other man I know—with the possible exception of Dwight L. Moody—whose works can be compared with Dr. Bob's. I'll say to you what I said to Mrs. Smith the other day:
>
> If I knew that I could go through eighty years—more than eighty years— of stress and storm and come to the end of it—or of them—with the sweetness of spirit, the genuine humility, the personal love for the person of Christ, the spiritual concern for the souls of men, and the practical concern with no cynicism that characterizes Dr. Bob Jones, Sr., I would count myself one of the most fortunate men ever to be born in this world.

I want to say that God knows that I never felt anything more deeply in my life. This work here, this University with all of its influence throughout the whole world, is one of the finest things and one of the most inspiring effects in the history of these times.

One of Dr. Bob's last official acts was to recommend that we expand. He came before the Executive Committee and said:

Last night as I was praying the Lord seemed to lay upon my heart the burden that we should expand, getting ready for the great influx of students. For sometime I have been thinking about some new buildings and certain improvements, and I would like to recommend that you get these buildings underway as soon as possible.

At the end of the first year of Dr. Bob's retirement, under the able leadership of Dr. Bob Jones, Jr., we were able to present to the Board one of the best reports spiritually, financially, and academically in the school's history. A four-million-dollar building program had changed the complexion of the whole campus, and Dr. Bob had proved to the world that the school could and would run successfully without him.

CHAPTER 3

Prophet Called Home

For the most part I shall rely upon a few excerpts from editorials to describe the event of January 16, 1968, and the few days following. Dr. Bob had been in our hospital for two years; so the news of his death, though it saddened us, came as no real surprise. He had been losing ground steadily. Finally the doctor warned, "It is a matter of days."

Those who attended Dr. Bob during his last illness were blessed by the association. One night an attendant heard him preaching in his sleep. Placing a chair beside the bed, he sat and listened to Dr. Bob preach for an hour without ever repeating. Mrs. Jones says that her husband's last words before sinking into a semi-coma were, "Mary Gaston, get my shoes; I must go to preach." Dr. Bob never fully realized that his preaching days were over. He had been valiant for the Lord for so long that he felt that his Sword was always in his hand and ready to be wielded.

When news of Dr. Bob's Homegoing was released, THE ASSOCIATED PRESS, THE UNITED PRESS INTERNATIONAL, and other news media quickly spread the news around the world. The three major networks—ABC, NBC, and CBS—broadcast the news several times. It was televised on the Huntley-Brinkley Report as well as on ABC; Lowell Thomas paid glowing tribute to Dr. Bob, saying that he had known him personally; and Paul Harvey News announced and commented on the death. Telephone calls, telegrams, and letters by the thousands began to pour in from all parts of the world—from Generalissimo Chiang Kai-Shek; from several governors, senators, and congressmen, from heads of institutions of higher learning; from mission boards; from professional and business men and women; from alumni and former faculty members; and from a host of other friends. A special answering service had to be set up in the office of the University to take care of the influx of condolences.

In an editorial captioned "Rugged Fundamentalist," this statement caught my eye:

Dr. Bob Jones had his foes as well as his friends, his distractors as well as his devotees, but none among them can deny that even at the age of 84, when he met his Maker face-to-face on Tuesday he stood four square as a man of conviction — not compromising.

An editorial in the GREENVILLE NEWS-PIEDMONT lauded Dr. Bob's consistency. I quote excerpts from this significant article:

There was one preeminent attribute of Dr. Bob Jones of the many good ones he had that never failed to impress those who came to know him. He was utterly and completely consistent. He was consistent in his beliefs, his principles, his thoughts, his way of life and his relations with the world.

His consistency was based on the Bible, and whenever he was challenged in any area he fell back on the Bible to support his convictions.

Extensive national reporting of his death indicates a prestige which may not have been fully recognized in Greenville because of close association.

He was, however, a notable personality who drew attention to Bob Jones University and Greenville as he travelled the world to continue preaching to the last his conservative brand of evangelism.

There is no doubt he was controversial and intended to be. The World's Most Unusual University would not exist if he had not been so. What to others seemed controversy, though, was a way of life for Dr. Bob. To our knowledge he never retreated from a position and was willing to defend his opinion against all critics.

His adamant outlook on life was anathema to many liberals, particularly those adrift in a rapidly changing world often disillusioned with historical ethics.

. . . His is a tough philosophy to follow.

Another local editorial depicted Dr. Bob as a "Warrior of the Faith" and cited as "hallmarks of his evangelistic career" his "indomitable and uncompromising" manner in "the defense and extension of his beliefs and in his efforts to achieve his firm purpose." I quote from this article:

On the day that Dr. Bob Jones, Sr., simply fell asleep after eighty-four years and a period of declining health, one who had worked with him and loved him most if not all his adult life summed it up: "There must have been great rejoicing in Heaven this morning when that old warrior arrived at the gate."

We are sure that sentence, spontaneous and affectionate, fully sums up the feelings of Dr. Jones' countless friends and admirers, the thousands who had heard him preach and the many more who knew him only by personal reputation and that of the University he founded and gave his name.

The atmosphere on the campus is not so much one of mourning as of remembering the extraordinary man as a powerful personality and of tribute to his long and fruitful career.

We were struck by the phrase "Old Warrior," used by his longtime associate. In many ways it characterized Dr. Jones' evangelical ministry which spans almost exactly the biblically allotted threescore and ten years.

He didn't stop preaching until a short time ago and as a preacher he was indeed a warrior. "Dr. Bob" was a man of unshakeable fundamentalist beliefs, a born conservative and a fighter by nature. . . .

Those two words applied to his relations with friend and foe alike and such a man always has his foes. . . .

They are reflected too in the fact that his son and grandson are following closely in his footsteps even while progressing each in his own right the individuality which is a part of the Bob Jones legacy.

It would be presumptuous for anyone to attempt to evaluate the life and career of this strong man. For as long as Bob Jones University stands, as long as there is a Jones of his lineage engaged in evangelism, so long will that career extend.

As one man commented, "Practically every paper in the country paid respect to this great warrior with front-page articles." TIME, January 26, 1968, paid tribute, and the CHARLOTTE OBSERVER stated in large headlines, "HE BLISTERED SATAN AND LIBERALS."

Several pages in the CONGRESSIONAL RECORD were devoted to Dr. Bob and to some of the editorials that were written about him. Senator Strom Thurmond attended the funeral services and later introduced in the Senate a resolution paying tribute to his good friend:

Mr. President, my association with Dr. Jones and the school he founded has been inspiring and rewarding. I now pay well-deserved tribute to him; he was a man of character and a man of God. I ask unanimous consent that the tribute by Dr. Jones, Jr., and a number of editorials and articles about Dr. Bob Jones, Sr., appear in the CONGRESSIONAL RECORD at the conclusion of my remarks.

The South Carolina General Assembly paid tribute to Dr. Bob:

A resolution of sympathy to the family of Dr. Bob Jones, Sr., founder of Bob Jones University who died Tuesday was adopted by the General Assembly.

The resolution pays tribute to Dr. Jones who was a world famous evangelist and founded the University now located in Greenville.

The University, the resolution said, has added immensely to the educational, cultural and religious growth of this state and nation.

The citizens of the State of South Carolina are deeply indebted to Dr. Jones for his godly example and for many personal contributions to the development and welfare of the State.

Interment of the beloved body of Dr. Bob Jones, Sr., on the island in the Reflecting Basin before Rodeheaver Auditorium on Bob Jones University campus following the funeral service in chapel on January 17, 1968.

No one will ever know how I felt the day of Dr. Bob's funeral. I loved him as a son loves his father. As I sat in the rear of the Chapel, praying and meditating, waiting to have the doors officially opened for the viewing of the body as it lay in state, I was impressed with the fact that above the casket was a large eighteen-foot picture of the "Ascension" of our Lord. It thrilled my soul to realize that Dr. Bob was now with our Lord in Glory and that he would know no further suffering.

Dr. John R. Rice said of the funeral in THE SWORD OF THE LORD:

Rodeheaver Auditorium was jammed for the funeral at three o'clock. Distinguished men and women from all over the nation were there. The funeral service was magnificent, fitting, spiritually satisfying. . . .

I felt that surely the inspired words of the Apostle Paul as he awaited his martyrdom, would fit Dr. Bob: "For I am now ready to be offered, and the time of my departure is at hand. I have fought a good fight, I have finished my course, I have kept the faith: Henceforth there is laid up for me a crown of righteousness, which the Lord, the righteous judge, shall give me at that day: and not to me only, but unto all them also that love his appearing" (II Timothy 4:6–8).

. . . What a childlike faith Dr. Bob had! He simply depended on the Lord for leading day by day. And the Spirit led him, whether in leaving the Winecoff Hotel in Atlanta by special leading a day early and thus escaping the disastrous fire that killed so many, or in fitting his message to the particular needs which God revealed in preachers and Christian workers who heard him.

He has left us a great heritage. To me he has left a mighty impact of encouragement and example and challenge. And who knows but that the noble and gifted son, Dr. Bob Jones, Jr., may be the greatest heritage he has left to us all.

. . . He lingered for a year or two, more or less incapacitated with illness. Why? Probably that the rest of us might some way become comforted and reconciled to his Homegoing. Now there is no tragedy, but triumph. Perhaps partly so that all of us could see before his going how wonderfully Dr. Bob Jones, Jr., and Dr. Bob Jones, III, will carry on the traditions and councils and convictions of their father and grandfather in the school he founded and in defense of the faith.

Good-night, Dr. Bob! We will see you in the morning!

I also quote from a lengthy editorial by Dr. Noel Smith in the BAPTIST BIBLE TRIBUNE:

Dr. Jones was never an amateur, a novice, not even in his "boy-preacher" days. He was a boy who wanted to tell people about Jesus and see them saved. He steadily grew in grace and knowledge, in experience and maturity. He studied and he worked. I never cease to marvel at the solid substance of his evangelistic sermons and the clean, penetrating, heart-warming and appealing language in which they are clothed.

Dr. Bob Jones, Sr. was a good man. He was criticized chiefly because he refused to be the kind of preacher and educator that his cowardly times demanded that he be.

I look forward to renewing fellowship with him in that world where, as Carlyle said, the "hail-stones and fireshowers never beat, and where the heaviest laden wayfarer at length lays down his load."

"DR. BOB JONES ENTERS THE PALACE"—an editorial by Dr. G. Archer Weniger, Los Angeles, California—closed with a statement of encouragement as to the future of this school:

Dr. Bob Jones, Jr. has taken this occasion to make a solid pledge to God, the alumni, and friends of the University that this institution shall continue in the very same solid biblical principles which were laid down by the founder.

Because of the many requests I have had for extra copies of "A TRIB-UTE AND A PLEDGE," Dr. Bob, Jr.'s, eulogy which was read at the funeral by Dr. Edward Panosian is here quoted in full.

* * *

A Tribute and a Pledge

By Dr. Bob Jones, Jr.

This should not be a day for weeping. This is a time for rejoicing. This should not be a moment of sorrow. This is an hour for gladness. A fight has been fought, a race has been won, a crown is laid up. Nevertheless, such is our human weakness that a son cannot today trust himself to speak and must therefore ask another to read the words which come from his heart.

It should not be thought strange that a son has written a father's eulogy. Aside from my mother, I am sure I knew my father better than anyone else. Others have seen him in the vigor of his great evangelistic campaigns; but I have known him in the quiet of the home as well. Others have listened to the sound advice of his chapel talks; but I have known, too, his chastening love and fatherly counsel in the private and quiet hours of my youth.

Faithful associates have borne with him the burden of the ministry of Bob Jones University and shared with him the fulfillment of his vision; but I saw the birth of the vision and knew not only the reality of his achievement, but also the burden upon my father's heart to which the University owes its existence.

Yet the language shall be limping, the picture unfinished, the story badly outlined. Only the pages of God's Heaven can reveal the measure of his life; only a recording angel report it fully.

Some say that it is only human to be inconsistent; but my father, who was of all men most human in his sympathies and understanding of man's weakness, was the most consistent man I ever knew. In private as in public he never turned for a moment aside from the principles by which his actions were shaped or departed in his own living from the convictions which fired his public statements and molded the lives of other thousands who sat under his ministry.

He was sure that he was right because he drew his convictions from the well of God's Word and rested his principles upon the sure foundation of the Infallible Truth that is forever settled in Heaven. Because he would not sacrifice what he knew to be Truth for the pleasing of men, because he would not yield to the pressures of changing opinions or soften to accommodate to the softness of compromise with apostasy and sin, his enemies—and he had many, as all God's true servants have since the days of the Old Testament prophets—called him "bitter" and "unloving" and "stubborn."

Stubborn he was on matters of principle—thank God—but never on lesser things like method and means. Bitter and unloving he never was; and such was his nature that he could not be.

"Disloyalty," he often said, was "an unpardonable sin" where he was concerned. Loyalty to the cause he demanded in those who associated themselves with Bob Jones University; but I have seen my father when betrayed by one he trusted—one who in fact owed him more than could ever be repaid—moved not by bitterness but deep grief, try to understand a heart which many men would despise; and try to account for the actions which deserved to be condemned. I have seen him, exhausted by lack of sleep and racked with physical pain, spend hours in loving effort to help a man who he knew was no friend.

He was not a patient man—either with himself or others—but he was a long-suffering man. How often have I heard him say, in deliberate disregard for grammar, "You can't do nothing for a fool"; and yet how often have I seen him try. His greatest weakness was his trustfulness. My mother and I have often said to him, "You take people at their face value too readily." Because he was so open and honest in his own heart and his own actions, he could not bring himself to believe—until he was faced with the proof—that others might not be all they pretended to be. He preferred to believe the good rather than the bad. He preferred to suffer the disappointment of being betrayed by one unworthy of his trust rather than to risk thinking a good man bad.

At every other point Bob Jones had amazing gifts of perception. From the pulpit and in private conversations he might irritate his hearers with the truth about themselves; but so keen was his mind and so dynamic his personality he could never bore them. How often have I heard a student say, "I'd rather hear Dr. Bob preach the same sermon half a dozen times than listen to most men preach a new one." And no man who sat for a while under his ministry was ever able to escape completely thereafter from the impact of his words and the impression of his personality. Even those former students who have, for denominational approval or selfish gain or for lack of character, "sold God out" and betrayed the Lord that bought them—even they are still, years after, quoting his sayings (without acknowledging their source, of course) and preaching his sermons (mangled and emascultated and without the force of their author's conviction and that anointing of God which rested upon the man from whom they took them).

He had a way with words. He could paint pictures with language which were more moving than those a fine artist brought to canvas with his brush—yet never did his language soar higher than the thought. He delighted the ear to touch the heart. His homely philosophy is preserved bit by bit—like flies in amber—in the hearts of his "boys and girls" in the pithy sayings that have given direction to many a life.

"Good men are always reasonable men," he was wont to say; and I have found that he was right in that as in so many other things. And my father was himself the finest proof of it. He never expected perfection of others, but sought it in his own undertakings and was always himself most conscious of his own short-comings. He had a gift for recognizing hidden talents and unrealized possibili-ties in the lives of young people; and many of you present today are spending yourselves in the Lord's service because of that sure sense of my father's that saw and awakened in you gifts you never dreamed you had.

What an unusual combination he was: at once deeply spiritual and intensely practical. Possessed of the gift of "the discerning of spirits," he could also dis-cern a good business deal; and the financial stability of Bob Jones University gives the lie to the old adage that "good preachers are always poor businessmen."

Character and integrity were the qualities he most admired. "You can borrow brain," he used to tell us, "but you cannot borrow character." He said to me, "A man of bad character is better than a man with no character at all. Get him con-verted and he'll be a strong Christian; but a spineless man is no good to God or the devil."

Quick to recognize greatness in others, he never, I am sure, recognized the greatness in himself. As deep as was his faith, he used to rebuke himself for lack of it and declare, "I have never had the measure of faith God gives to some men." Then he would add, "But I have found if you act as if you had faith you'll find things come out as well as if you had it; and that develops faith." He worked as if everything depended upon him and trusted as if all depended upon God. His faith was like a child's; his efforts those of an army.

He understood weakness and could sympathize with it; but he never could be for very long patient with it—especially in a Christian. And yet he found it difficult to be stern with a penitent student who had repented the same failure a dozen times before. Looking back, I can see now what an effort it cost him to punish me when I was a child; but his strong character demanded the effort, and he made himself make it.

How he loved children! How, indeed, he loved people. So great was his interest in them that he took on their burdens and shared the secrets his sympathetic understanding led them to pour out to him when they would not open their hearts to anyone else.

My father responded intensely to beauty; but he preferred the colors of God's sunset to the colors in a painting of a sunset. He loved the old hymns. It was, I am sure however, the words to which his heart answered and not the notes, for he could never carry a tune; but "When the Lord comes," he would tell us, "I'll dip my tongue in the melody of the sky."

A man of deep sentiment, he loved to dwell on the memories of his boyhood and of his godly parents; and no man ever had deeper affection for his family than he had for us.

He loved the souls of men and spent his life striving to bring the lost to Christ. Even in these last months, old and forgetful in other things, he never forgot to inquire about the salvation of a visitor he did not remember or recognize. Nor did the ravages of time touch or mar his power in prayer.

But above all, he loved Jesus! "If there were one drop of blood in my veins that did not flow in love for Christ, I'd ask a surgeon to open that vein and let it out." This was the testimony of the evangelist who had met his Saviour at the age of eleven under the dim lamps of a country church in southeast Alabama and who grew up to take the light of the Gospel around the globe and to build the world's largest Christian educational institution.

Almost every boy looks at his father and sees in him a great man. How few men at fifty-six can look upon the venerable face of a dead parent and realize their boyhood opinion confirmed a hundredfold. What a heritage he has left his son! His was a life of many talents, well invested, yielding for his Lord a return abundant. I would I might stand before God with his record or receive the reward for his faithfulness.

His is a fight well fought, a course well run, a faith well kept, a crown well won!

Having spoken as my father's son, it is time now for me to speak as his successor. The tired warrior rests, but the battle rages. The strife-scarred hero takes his repose, but the war continues. The great man is gone, but the work remains. The founder is departed, but the institution stands.

We will not betray the dead. We cannot avoid the challenge. We shall not flee the task. We would not escape the opportunity he has bequeathed to us. Here in the sight of his God and ours—standing beside this casket—we dedicate ourselves, our lives and talents afresh to the continuation of the ministry of the Gospel and the purpose for which he founded the institution which is at once his greatest achievement and his finest monument.

If it is the Lord's will, Bob Jones University shall continue to grow in its physical equipment and its scope, its outreach and its influence. But it shall stand unchanged and unchanging in its purpose and its philosophy. As long as it please God and the Board of Trustees that we shall be entrusted with the administrative responsibility of this university, Bob, III, and I shall continue unyielding in our warfare against Anti-Christ and shall undertake to assure that Bob Jones University shall remain a lighthouse of God's Truth amid the lengthening shadows of a great apostasy. We shall, in the words of our charter:

> conduct an institution of learning for the general education of youth in the essentials of culture and in the arts and sciences, giving special emphasis to the Christian religion and the ethics revealed in the Holy Scriptures, combating all atheistic, agnostic, pagan and so-called scientific adulterations of the Gospel, unqualifiedly affirming and teaching the inspiration of the Bible (both Old and New Testaments); the creation of man by the direct act of God; the incarnation and virgin birth of our Lord and Saviour Jesus Christ; His identification as the Son of God; His vicarious atonement for the sins of mankind by the shedding of His blood on the Cross; the resurrection of His body from the tomb; His power to save men from sin; the new birth through the regeneration by the Holy Spirit; and the gift of eternal life by the grace of God.

Our students shall be continually reminded of their obligation to reach all men with the Gospel and of their privilege of being soul winners. The banner our founder raised here for the Lord Jesus Christ shall never be lowered. These colors we will never dip. The trumpet shall not cease to sound from these battlements nor shall that trumpet sound be muted or uncertain. God's holy, infallible, and living Word shall continue to be the Sword of our warfare and the Light of our path. We shall not depart from Its precepts, cease from Its proclamation, or grow weary in Its defence.

This is, I say, not a moment for weeping. This is a day of challenge. This is not a time for sorrow. This is an hour of dedication! I call upon all the members of the University family — trustees, faculty, students — young and old — upon the far-scattered alumni, upon the former students who are faithful to the institution that gave them their training and touched their eyes to see the vision of a needy world — upon you all I call — surrender your hearts afresh to the Christ whom our founder loved and served for more than seventy years.

Nothing is worthwhile that is not done for eternity. The brick of these buildings may go back to clay; but the living stones laid in the Temple of God through the founder's preaching are there forever. Let us build upon the foundation of God that standeth sure. Our founder was surely sent of God to meet a great need in his day. But the God of Elijah is the God of Elisha as well. The mantle has been dropped. We take it up in humility of heart and with reverent hands.

We thank God for the faithful friends who support this institution and who pray for this ministry. To them I say we need now, more than ever, the weight of your intercession behind us, the upholding hands of your petitions before the throne of God. Cease not day and night to pray for us. The weapons of our warfare are not carnal but spiritual.

To any present on this occasion or who hear this service broadcast or read these words in print and who have never put their trust in Christ, I say this: the same One who could take over the heart of a little country boy and make his life one of blessing to untold thousands can save you and bring you from death to life eternal. Nothing ever rejoiced my father's heart so much as seeing a man or woman come into the saving knowledge of Jesus Christ. May this be the moment when you shall receive Him as your Saviour.

To those of you saved under my father's preaching or living in the service of Jesus Christ because of his influence, and to all of you who rejoice with them in the blessed hope of Christ's glorious appearing, I would leave this final reminder and this assurance: God knows the future. Our times are in His hands and we are His. To Christ be the glory! His Kingdom is forever.

* * *

At the conclusion of this impressive eulogy, more than 5,000 friends, including many out-of-town dignitaries, followed the Jones family from the Rodeheaver Auditorium to the burial site — a beautiful little island in a fountain of cascading pools just across the street from the auditorium. It is significant that overlooking this little island is the Bridge of Nations, so-named because of the world-wide outreach of Bob Jones University; there the flags of twenty-five nations fly in the breeze. From this bridge we can view the resting place of the body of THE BUILDER OF BRIDGES.

The pains of death are past,
Labor and sorrow cease,
And, life's long warfare closed at last,
His soul is found in peace.
Soldier of Christ, Well done!
Praise be thy new employ;
And while eternal ages run,
Rest in thy Saviour's joy.

(James Montgomery in WELL DONE)